Urban Problems in Sociological Perspective

Second Edition

Thomas R. Shannon
Radford University

Nancy Kleniewski
State University of New York
College at Geneseo

William M. Cross
Illinois College

WAVELAND

PRESS, INC.

Prospect Heights, Illinois

For information about this book, write or call:

Waveland Press, Inc.
P.). Box 400
Prospect Heights, Illinois 60070
(708) 634-0081

Copyright © 1991 by Thomas R. Shannon, Nancy Kleniewski, and William M. Cross
Copyright © 1983 by Thomas R. Shannon

ISBN 0-88133-584-3

Printed in the United States of America

7 6 5 4 3

Preface

This book grew out of the authors' experiences teaching urban sociology and using the first edition of *Urban Problems in Sociological Perspective* in our own classes. We have tried to use those experiences to craft not only an updated book but also a very substantially modified one, while retaining the strengths of the first edition.

This version retains the basic orientation of the first edition. We have not assumed extensive background in sociological theory or terminology—thus, we have provided simple and straightforward explanations of both theories and terms. Nor have we assumed that students have much prior knowledge of urban history, or even contemporary urban conditions. This book is intended to provide a relatively brief introductory overview of urban history in the United States, some of the central issues of urban sociology, and contemporary urban trends and problems. Throughout, we have striven for simplicity and clarity.

We have also tried to maintain the theoretical and evaluative balance of the first edition. Where there are major contending theoretical positions or significant disagreements about how to interpret urban conditions or policies, we have tried to provide a fair exposition of the contending viewpoints. Students are entitled to hear both sides of an argument. On the other hand, we have also attempted to make clear our own interpretations of these controversial issues. Such an approach meets the often competing requirements of pedagogical balance and intellectual honesty. We invite both instructors and students to disagree with our interpretations and participate with us in the debates that enliven the study of urban conditions.

This edition also retains the applied, policy-oriented focus of the first edition. We have examined public policy as both a cause and solution to urban problems. Where possible, in this edition, we have included more consideration of specific examples of attempts to deal with urban problems. We believe that it is both appropriate and useful at the undergraduate level of instruction to acquaint students with the notion that the analytical tools of sociology can be applied to think about public issues in a systematic fashion.

There also are significant differences from the previous edition. After nearly a decade, urban conditions have changed substantially, and we have struggled to address those changes. For example, the pattern of regional growth and decline has proven to be much more complex than it appeared at the end of the 1970s. As a consequence, Chapter 2 is essentially a new chapter. Similarly, the problems of the housing disadvantaged have become more severe and more visible, and we have provided more extensive treatment of that issue. Sociological theory has also not stood still. For instance, this edition has substantially increased its treatment of the political-economy approach in urban sociology and introduces the new theories of urban politics which appeared in the 1980s. While the book retains its primary focus on the United States, we have added an entirely new chapter which systematically compares and contrasts urban conditions in the United States with those in other countries. Introduction of this comparative dimension provides students with a more balanced view of conditions in their own society.

Acknowledgments

Previous adopters of this book provided the impetus to do a new edition. They told us what they liked, and did not, in the first edition. They also made it very clear that it was time to revise. Neil Rowe, of Waveland Press, provided the practical encouragement to attempt the revision. Each of the co-authors enjoyed the support services of their respective institutions, which made possible doing the revision in a reasonable amount of time. Special thanks go to Sally Harrington and Carolyn Sutphin for much typing, to Bill Davis for graphics, to Mike Liljegren for computer assistance, and to Leonard Beeghley for comments on Chapter 4. Of course, our students provided the real support for our efforts. Their concern and interest in the issues of this book made the effort worthwhile.

Thomas R. Shannon
Nancy Kleniewski
William M. Cross

Contents

1

Origins of the Urban Crisis

Outline of Topics

To understand the problems of contemporary urban areas requires that we first review the historical origins of urban America. To a very significant degree, the present dilemmas urban areas face can be traced to the past. Current problems are an outgrowth of long-term economic, technological, social, demographic, and political trends. Hence, in this chapter we will trace the development of urban areas in the United States during the 19th and 20th centuries up through the first generation following World War II. In Chapter 2, we will look at the trends of the last two decades, which have had an immediate impact on the most recent problems faced by our urban areas and may play a major role in shaping the nature of urban problems in the future.

The Preindustrial City in America

At the time of the American Revolution, colonial North America consisted of a thinly settled strip along the Eastern seaboard. Most of the population was engaged in agricultural pursuits and lived in rural areas, either in isolated homesteads or small hamlets. Only about 7 percent of the population lived in communities which could even remotely be considered "urban," and most of those communities consisted of only a few hundred residents (McKelvey, 1973:24). A decade and a half later, the first official census in 1790 counted only 24 "urban places" which contained 2,500 or more people, and the largest cities were Philadelphia (44,096), New York (33,131), Boston (18,320), Charleston, South Carolina (16,359), and Baltimore (13,503) (McKelvey, 1973:24).

Despite the small percentage of the population living in those five largest cities, they played a dominant role in colonial society. Economically, their primary role was that of commercial and financial centers (Palen, 1987:63). They were the major ports for the export of raw materials and agricultural products from the countryside (the primary products of the economy at the time). They also served as distribution centers for critical imported manufactured goods and luxury items not produced domestically. They were not, however, major centers for the manufacture of finished goods. While these cities contained numerous craftsmen who produced some specialized items for use in the city and surrounding countryside, production of finished goods remained a very secondary activity in these cities. On the other hand, these cities played a central role in the political system. They were centers of the legal system, government administration (in some colonies), and the politically active upper social strata. This was less true in the South, where the plantation aristocracy dominated political life. (Palen, 1987:64).

In the first few decades after 1790, cities in the United States remained primarily commercial centers (Peterson, 1961:28). Indeed, much early manufacturing was located in relatively small towns — such as the textile mill communities in Massachusetts (Pred, 1971:383). However, the rate of urban growth was extremely high. (An exception was in the 1810-20 period because of the disruptions caused by the War of 1812.) By 1860, nine cities had passed the 100,000 mark in population. All of these were port cities or were located near ports. New York was clearly the dominant city: its great harbor and good transportation connections with agricultural areas in the interior (first by canal and then by railroad) were advantages no other city could match. In 1860 (if you count then-independent Brooklyn), New York was the first city in this country to reach a population of one million. New York was the nation's financial center and handled more than one-third of the country's exports and fully two-thirds of its imports (Palen, 1987:67).

Not all regions shared equally in this urban growth. In 1860, one-third of all the residents in the Northeast lived in cities and towns. In contrast, only about one in ten residents of the South lived in urban areas. The slave-based system of agriculture was oriented toward the export of agricultural products and bound the region to a continued reliance on an agricultural economy. Slave labor discouraged labor-saving technological innovations and discouraged the creation of an urban working class. This was in part due to an active fear of the consequences of concentrating the slave population in cities. Low average income (despite the wealth of the planter class), a small middle class, and the political domination of the rural aristocracy also discouraged urbanization (Wallace, 1980:38). This pattern of slow urbanization in the South was to continue well into the 20th century.

The Rise of the Industrial City

The last half of the 19th century saw the transformation of American cities in the North and Northeast into a new kind of city: the industrial city. This new kind of city was the creation of a fundamentally different kind of technology and system for organizing production: factory-based industrial production.

At the roots of this new system were certain basic technological innovations. Improved agricultural techniques and the introduction of agricultural machinery meant that each farmer could now produce much more than before. This, in turn, meant that farmers could produce much more than their families could consume. Farmers could sell this "surplus" production and use the cash to buy consumer goods and machinery. For society as a whole, this development had two important results. First, there was a growing market for finished manufactured goods. Second, there now were more workers available in the economy to engage in nonagricultural production (the farmers' surplus was available to feed them). These nonagricultural workers, in turn, could be employed to operate the new steam-powered factories to produce more finished goods.

The rapid development of industrial machinery and the application of steam power to production increased the output of each worker immensely. This decreased the cost (relative to people's incomes) of the goods produced. The availability of cheaper manufactured goods stimulated consumption, increased the standard of living, and set off a period of rapid long-term economic growth. Manufacturing grew rapidly as a result.

Steam power for railroads, river boats, and ships meant that raw materials could be moved relatively inexpensively to central factories. Goods produced in one place could be shipped long distances economically. Thus, a single large manufacturer could produce goods for a national or international market.

In short, this "Industrial Revolution" created a system of large-scale factory production. These factories required the concentration of large numbers of workers in one place. In turn, until the early 20th century, these large factories tended to cluster together in just a few cities.[1] The industrial city was born.

Reasons For Industrial Concentration

Why did the factories cluster together in cities? A number of factors favored the cities as places to locate industry.

For one thing, reliance on steam power encouraged industrial concentration. Steam is produced most efficiently in large boilers and cannot be piped long distances. Factory and power supply needed to be close together, and it often made sense for several factories to share a common steam plant. Steam was produced from coal, and the only efficient ways to move coal were by railroad, ship, or barge. Hence, factories had to be located along rail lines or rivers, or near port areas.

Limited transportation technology meant that workers had to live close to where they worked. Only the more affluent could afford to travel by train or carriage every day. Even after the introduction of the electric trolley in the latter part of the century, regular commuting by working-class people was expensive and avoided when possible. As late as the turn of the century, the average commuting distance for workers in New York City was only two blocks (Palen, 1987:71). This created pressures to build working-class housing within walking distance of the factory district. Very quickly, densely packed multiple-story tenement buildings sprang up around the industrial districts. Once a large number of workers were concentrated in a particular city and industrial district, additional industry was attracted, anxious to take advantage of the existing pool of readily accessible (and already experienced) industrial workers.

Movement of bulky raw materials and finished goods also required clustering immediately around railroad switching facilities and dock areas. Once goods left the railroad car, they became very difficult and expensive to move: street transportation was by horse-drawn wagon and handcart.

Moreover, as the early sociologist Charles Horton Cooley pointed out, industry was usually attracted to certain points along the transportation system. These points he called *breaks in transportation*. These are places where goods must be moved from one vehicle to another (lake boat to train, train to train, train to ship, etc.). This entails labor costs. It is cheaper to process goods at transportation breaks because one has to pay the labor costs whether or not anything is done to the raw materials or merchandise. Storage facilities are often required at such transportation breaks, and other facilities such as banks and brokerage houses must be present since ownership often changes hands at these points. This further enhances the attractiveness of building factories at these breaks (Cooley, 1930:17-119). Thus, the city of Chicago grew into a major industrial center partly because it was where the railroad lines came together from the Northwest (lumber and cattle), Midwest (agricultural products), and Southwest (cattle, grain, and coal from central Illinois). At the same time, lumber, grain, and iron ore and other minerals came down the lake by boat. Chicago became home for the production of steel, agricultural machinery, wholesale merchandising, food processing ("hog butcher for the world"), and that great mail-order house for rural America, Sears Roebuck.

To some extent, success and growth tended to bring further success and growth to the already large cities. Larger cities provided a place to locate a factory where there was an easily accessible, very large market. In addition, the existing large cities had the advantages of already having an *infrastructure* of services such as water supplies, warehouses, switching facilities, docks, raw materials suppliers, municipal services, and skilled repairmen. It was cheaper to use these already existing services than to try to create them from scratch at a different location (Wallace, 1980:44). Corporate offices, in an era of slow communications and transportation, needed both to be near their factories and to be adjacent to other corporate headquarters and to such services as financial institutions, legal offices, and courts (Palen, 1987:73). Finally, some areas were better able to capitalize on their local advantages because of the organization and skill of their business and political leaders. These "growth entrepreneurs" mobilized local resources and governmental connections to provide incentives to business for location in their cities (Molotch, 1988). For example, there was competition between Eastern cities to get state subsidies for canal building in the 1830s and 1840s.

Consequences of Concentration

These centralizing forces meant that a large proportion of all industry located in cities and that a few cities grew very large. The last half of the 19th century was a period in which much of the urban population came to be concentrated in a few large urban areas.

Within these urban areas, most of the population lived inside the city limits of one municipal government. This was because urban growth in the 19th century was characterized by the process of annexation. In most states, cities had the right to incorporate surrounding areas (including other independent towns) into the city as it spread out from the center. For instance, in 1854, Philadelphia swallowed 28 cities, towns, and boroughs in a single year (Kotler, 1969). This process was enhanced later in the century by the introduction of the horse-drawn cart and then, at the end of the century, the electric streetcar. Streetcars expanded the potential space of the city and made possible the outward expansion of the city. Growth proceeded outward along the streetcar lines and allowed convenient commuting as far as 12 miles from the downtown areas. Where streetcar lines crossed, these "breaks" in the transportation system encouraged the creation of small, neighborhood business districts. Gradually, the space between the streetcar lines filled in (Hawley, 1971:92).

A convenient (if somewhat arbitrary) date to designate as the zenith of the industrial city is 1920. In that year, the census found 51 percent of the population living in cities and towns. In a statistical sense, U. S. society had become a predominately urban society. Moreover, despite

Table 1.1   **Percent Population Urban, Urban Population Size, and Total Population Size, United States, 1790-1987 (Selected Years)**

Year	Percent Urban	Urban Population (in millions)	Total Population (in millions)
1790	5	.2	4
1840	11	2	17
1890	35	22	63
1920	51	55	107
1940	57	75	133
1960	70	126	181
1980	75	167	226
1987	77	187	243

SOURCE: U.S. Bureau of the Census

the fact the movement of industry to suburban areas had already begun (see Table 1.1), central cities still clearly dominated the urban landscape. There were three cities with more than a million in population and nine with between half a million and a million (U.S. Bureau of the Census, 1973).

What was the industrial city like? There was an extremely compact and crowded downtown district. The attraction of this downtown area was simple. It was centrally located, and transit lines radiated out from it like spokes on a wheel. This made it the single most accessible point in the city. Offices clustered together to make possible easy communication by means of messenger and face-to-face contact. Office workers could commute in on the transit lines. Stores and places of entertainment catering to a mass market could be reached by the most people with the least inconvenience by locating in the downtown district. Intercity transportation was by train, and massive passenger terminals were usually located near the edge of the business district. The fact that once downtown, people had to walk required that the downtown be very compact. All this meant that competition for space in the downtown district was intense and the price of land very high. In 1930, street frontage on Wall Street sold for $100,000 a foot. That meant that downtown location was practical only for business enterprises, and only for those businesses which had the greatest need for accessibility to large numbers of customers or workers. Banks, hotels, department stores, luxury shops, corporate headquarters, legal firms, other business professionals, and the like crowded together within easy walking distance of one another. The premium on space and the need to be close meant that the invention of the elevator and steel girder building quickly led to taller and taller "skyscrapers." These buildings allowed jamming very large numbers of people together with rapid access to one another by elevator.

Factories, warehouses, and residential housing—activities which required large amounts of space—could not afford to locate in the central downtowns. Rather, they located, depending on their transportation needs and ability to pay, in different parts of the city. Each part of the city tended to specialize in a particular type of land use.

Adjacent to the downtown was usually a district of railroad switching yards, warehouses, factories, and slums. The factories needed to be close to the railroads, warehouse facilities, and each other. Workers in these facilities needed to be close to their work, and they could not pay much for either transportation or housing. The result was densely packed working-class housing districts mixed in with and adjacent to the factory district. Multiple-story tenements housed huge numbers of people under conditions of appalling squalor and crowding. Families of six to eight people crowded into one, two, or three rooms, often with no plumbing facilities (or with the bathroom down the hall and shared by several families). There were dangerous, poorly vented coal stoves for heat, few or no windows for light and ventilation, and inadequate fire escapes. The danger of fire, desperate cold in the winter and suffocating heat in the summer, ghastly sanitation and hygiene problems, and disease were part of the shared experience for many in the urban lower classes at the beginning of this century. At the end of the 19th century in New York, urban reformers of the day considered it a major victory to require that newly built tenements at least have windows facing into air shafts for ventilation and outside, metal fire escapes. Overall densities of these areas were higher than at any other point in our urban history. In Chicago, in 1894, one district on the West Side was three times more crowded than the most crowded portions of Tokyo or Calcutta. In some neighborhoods, density reached 900 people per acre (Mayer and Wade, 1969:256).

As one moved beyond the working-class districts, the quality of the residential areas improved. However, limited transportation still required that people be fairly close to their places of work: streetcars were very slow. Competition for land close to the center meant that land costs were high. Hence, by modern suburban standards, the housing was still densely packed. Apartment buildings, row houses, and two-family houses were the order of the day for most of the better-off, skilled workers and average middle-class families of the period. In this regard, it should be remembered that the average purchasing power of even these more affluent workers was much lower than it is today. Hence, what a middle-class standard of living implied for such things as housing and basic comforts was much different than now.

Those neighborhoods of large Victorian clapboard houses and tree-lined streets which seem to be the popular image of the urban past were really preserves for a small portion of the population: the affluent upper middle classes composed of successful professionals, independent successful businessmen, and the new class of corporate managers. Even in these areas, the premium on land in the city often meant relatively large houses crowded together on small lots.

By 1920, in many cities, the affluent upper middle classes and the upper classes had also begun settling in suburban towns outside the city limits. Many of these communities had started out as independent rural towns in which wealthy people in the 19th century had built summer homes. Gradually these summer residences were converted into year-round homes. Early commuting to the city was made possible by the availability of rail passenger service. Later, the streetcar lines were extended beyond the city limits to create "inter-urban" trolley systems which actually ran cross-country between cities. (At one time, it was possible to travel between New York and Boston by streetcar.) These streetcar systems further spurred suburban growth. By 1920, most large cities had suburban "bedroom" communities from which people commuted to the central business district. By and large, these were fairly prestigious enclaves of affluent residents, such as Evanston, just north of Chicago (Wilson and Schulz, 1978:1190-191; Jackson, 1985:113-115, 120-122, 256; Warner, 1962:20-29, 43-45).

The early 20th century also saw another movement which was an indication of the future directions of urban development. Industries began locating (still on rail lines, of course) outside the city in industrial "satellite" towns. Up until 1900, industrial employment had increased most rapidly in the central cities. But between 1899 and 1909, industrial employment in cities grew by about 40 percent, while in areas surrounding the cities such employment increased by 98 percent (Gordon, 1977:74). Thus, for example, the newly-formed giant of the steel industry, United States Steel, built a whole industrial city outside of Chicago and named it after the chairman of the board of directors, Judge Gary (creating Gary, Indiana).

A very significant fact about this development of affluent suburban communities and industrial satellites in the early 20th century was that it did not, as it had in the past, lead to annexation by the central cities. The great wave of annexation in the 19th century crested with the consolidation of the city of Brooklyn into New York in 1898. The pace of annexation abruptly slowed in the early 20th century. Of the twenty largest cities, thirteen had stopped expanding by 1910 (Gordon, 1977:77). Partly this was the result of ethnic and class hostilities. The

"WASPs" (white, Anglo-Saxon Protestants) of the suburbs feared and disliked what they saw as the corrupt, lower-class, immigrant-dominated political "machines" which had come to power in the central cities (Banfield and Wilson, 1966:37-44). The new suburbanites also did not want to pay taxes for services which went to the lower classes, and wanted to control the quality and type of services in their neighborhoods (such as schools). Large corporations had fled the central cities partly to escape taxes, the lower-class dominated city government, and the unions. They also wanted to locate in communities in which they had more political control. Hence, they also resisted annexation (Gluck and Meister, 1979:133). Rural-dominated legislatures, also fearing the political power of the growing cities, were understandably sympathetic to the fears of these groups and quickly created legal barriers to annexation (Gluck and Meister, 1979:133). But these trends seemed only distant dark clouds on the horizon in 1920. For all their poverty, coal-polluted air, political corruption, and squalid slums, the great industrial cities early in this century were vibrant economic, cultural, and social centers of an optimistic and rapidly growing new industrial society. They were massive symbols of one of the most fundamental social and economic transformations in human history. Not surprisingly, they quickly became the focus of scholars from a new academic discipline, itself an outgrowth and response to this transformation: sociology.

The Human Ecology of the Industrial City

One of the major concerns of the early urban sociologists was to search for uniformities in the patterns of physical development in these new industrial cities. Underlying this search was the assumption that the physical structure of the new cities reflected certain basic social and economic structures and processes in industrial societies. This perspective for studying cities came to be known as the human-ecology approach in sociology. This approach asked two key questions about cities: (1) do cities all tend to develop some common general physical form, and (2) what accounts for this common form?

Concentric-Zone Theory

The most famous theory to develop out of the human-ecology approach was the one developed at the University of Chicago in the 1920s by

Ernest Burgess and Robert Park (Burgess, 1924:88-97). Their basic concern was to develop a generalized model of how, as cities grow, land-use patterns change. Their model was based on several general principles which they saw governing the process of urban growth.

Invasion and Succession

Burgess and Park were looking at cities in which urban growth had been very rapid. Hence, they saw a pattern of rapid outward expansion, as cities spread out from their original centers to accommodate more people and economic activities. This outward growth from a common center meant that land that was originally used for one purpose frequently was converted to other purposes as the city expanded. Thus, for example, residential areas which had originally clustered around the small commercial areas of a city would be torn down to accommodate factories and rail yards. Later, downtown expansion would replace the warehouses and factories with stores and office buildings. Since growth was outward, the general process was one in which activities in the center would expand outward into adjacent areas which, in turn, would expand outward into areas next to them. This was labeled the process of invasion and succession. Inner areas (such as the downtown) were constantly expanding and invading the areas further out, replacing one land use with another.

Competition and Segregation

Burgess and Park noted that cities tended to consist of a set of homogeneous land-use areas. Factories would cluster together in one area, middle-class homes in another, and slums in another. This, they argued, was because different areas of the city had different degrees of attractiveness. Most critical in determining attractiveness was accessibility. Generally, this meant that locations in the center of the city were the most attractive. Each kind of land use competed with other kinds to obtain the most attractive location. This drove up the value of the land in the center. Only those activities which could use the land very intensively and pay its high cost could locate in the center. As one moved away from the center, the value of land declined and less intensive kinds of land-use activities could afford to locate there (e.g., factories and housing). Thus, each land use tended to find the location it could afford, and those activities which could not afford a central location had to place themselves further out. The result was areas of homogeneous land use Burgess and Park called *natural areas* because they were the result of the "natural" processes of free-market competition, rather than the result of zoning or government planning. Because each land-use area tended to attract people of certain occupations and classes, they also tended to be homogeneous in terms of their demographic characteristics.

Structural Results: Concentric Zones

The resulting general pattern of land use, claimed Burgess and Park, was a set of *concentric zones* of homogeneous land-use areas. In their most general formulation, they suggested five such zones. (See Figure 1.1.)

Zone 1 was the *central business district* (CBD). This zone was where large mass-merchandise stores, luxury shops, theaters, hotels, banks, central offices, and professional services centered. Surrounding the outside edge of the zone were warehouses, wholesale markets, and railroad stations.

Zone 2 was called the *zone in transition*. It contained railroad yards, the old main factory district, and the most decayed and densely packed lower-class, slum housing. Burgess and Park called it the zone in transition because, at the time they were writing, central business districts were rapidly expanding into ("invading") this zone. Slums could afford to be located so close to the center because, even if the rents were low, the high density meant that the actual income produced from each building was high. Also, the area attracted land speculators who bought property there in anticipation that future CBD expansion would make it more valuable in the future.

Figure 1.1 **The Concentric Zone Theory**

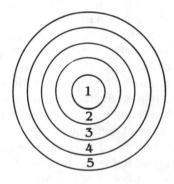

Key
1 = Central Business District
2 = Wholesale Light Manufacturing
3 = Low Class Residential
4 = Medium Class Residential
5 = Commuters' Zone

SOURCE: Chauncey D. Harris and Edward L. Ullman, "The Nature of Cities," *The Annals of the American Association of Political and Social Science*, 242 (November 1945), pp. 7-17, Adapted.

Zone 3 was called the *zone of workingmen's homes*. This was where the more affluent working-class families lived. At least in Chicago, this area consisted mostly of smaller apartment buildings and two-family houses.

Zone 4 was the *zone of better residences*. Essentially a middle-class residential area, it consisted (in Chicago in the 1920s) of simple single-family homes combined with modest-sized, good quality apartment buildings, and some residential hotels. The latter type of structure suggested the beginnings of invasion from Zone 3.

Zone 5 was designated the *commuter zone*. These included the early suburbs we discussed previously and functioned as residential "dormitories" for upper middle-class and upper-class workers, most of whom commuted by transit (and even by car in the 1920s) to the CBD.

Evaluation

How accurate a picture of the industrial city was the Burgess and Park theory? A number of criticisms have been leveled at the theory. We need only note them here. Certainly, the picture painted of the city was oversimplified and overgeneralized. Real cities of the time only crudely approximated the kind of structure Burgess and Park hypothesized. Land use was never as regular and homogeneous as the theory suggested. Moreover, the theory never did apply to all cities everywhere. At best, it applied to large, North American cities, with significant concentrations of industry, which were built mostly after 1860 and before 1920. Thus, the less industrialized cities of the South in 1920, cities like Los Angeles (which grew later), European cities, and cities like New York and Boston (with special topography and economic functions) fit the concentric pattern very poorly or not at all. However, in a crude way, Burgess and Park captured some general tendencies of a type of city which housed a large portion of the North American urban population at the time (Schnore, 1972; Smith, 1970:423-453; Haggerty, 1971:1084-1093). Decayed and surrounded by suburban sprawls, these monuments to early industrialization continue to dot the urban landscape.

Sector Theory

Given its crudity, it is not surprising the Burgess-Park formulation provoked not only criticism but attempts to modify it or refute it by proposing alternative models.

One such attempt was the modification suggested in the late 1930s by Homer Hoyt (Hoyt, 1939). Based on the study of rental costs in different areas of 142 cities, Hoyt rejected the notion that "natural areas" always tended to form continuous rings around the center. Hoyt discovered what he felt was a much different pattern from that of concentric rings. He concluded that "high-rent" areas were more likely to form pie-shaped sectors which extended out from the CBD. These areas, according to Hoyt, tended to extend out along existing transportation routes and favored areas away from industrial districts with such scenic attractions as high ground or shorelines with good views. In general, they tended to be protected from other land uses by barriers or buffers of medium-rent housing. Hoyt also pointed out that industrial districts tended to be arranged along transportation lines or in dock districts, rather than forming concentric zones. (See Figure 1.2.)

Figure 1.2 **The Sector Theory**

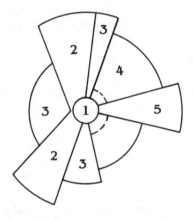

Key

1 = Central Business District
2 = Wholesale Light Manufacturing
3 = Low Class Residential
4 = Medium Class Residential
5 = High Class Residential

SOURCE: Chauncey D. Harris and Edward L. Ullman, "The Nature of Cities," *The Annals of the American Association of Political and Social Science*, 242 (November 1945), pp. 7-17, Adapted.

Hoyt's theory really is not a full theory, but rather a set of descriptive generalizations drawn from empirical observations. Nor (as the figure indicates) is it a total rejection of either the processes or the patterns suggested by Burgess and Park.

Multiple-Nuclei Theory

A much more ambitious attempt to develop a completely different theory came in the 1940s when the geographers C. D. Harris and

E. L. Ullman suggested the *multiple-nuclei* theory (Harris and Ullman, 1945:7-17). They rejected the notion that cities had just one center from which they simply expanded outward. Rather, they believed that cities had several different centers (nuclei). Each center specialized in a different activity—such as finance, government, wholesaling, or warehousing. These different centers may have sprung up at about the same time, or they may have originally started in some common center and later separated from that center. Thus, for example, manufacturing originally started near the downtown in Chicago. However, it eventually scattered to subcenters, such as the concentration of the steel industry in the southeast of the city. (See Figure 1.3.)

Harris and Ullman were skeptical about the possibility that one general model of city structure could do justice to the tremendous diversity found in actual city structures. They felt that different historical influences in each city's development tended to give it its own unique physical structure. However, they felt that four factors influenced the development of homogeneous land-use areas:

(1) Certain activities require specialized facilities and cluster together to share these facilities. Thus, retail stores will tend to locate together near transportation facilities.

Figure 1.3 **The Multiple-Nuclei Theory**

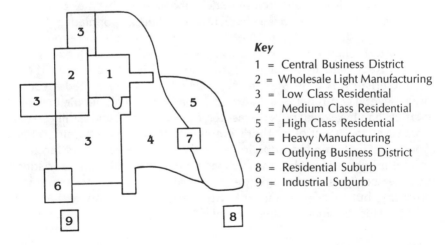

Key

1 = Central Business District
2 = Wholesale Light Manufacturing
3 = Low Class Residential
4 = Medium Class Residential
5 = High Class Residential
6 = Heavy Manufacturing
7 = Outlying Business District
8 = Residential Suburb
9 = Industrial Suburb

SOURCE: Chauncey D. Harris and Edward L. Ullman, "The Nature of Cities," *The Annals of the American Association of Political and Social Science*, 242 (November 1945), pp. 7-17, Adapted.

(2) Similar activities will tend to group together because they benefit from being close to one another. For example, a new car dealership will often locate near existing dealers, since people looking for cars already come there.

(3) Certain dissimilar activities may be harmed by being close to one another. Obviously, heavy industry and expensive housing will not be close together because the land is too expensive for the industry, and industry will make the area less attractive for high-status residential use.

(4) Certain activities, such as warehouses, must avoid downtown locations because land costs are too high, and there is no economic advantage to location in the CBD.

Multiple-nuclei theory does not logically exclude the possibility that some cities may develop patterns that approximate concentric zones at some point in their development. Thus, it is not really a total rejection of Burgess and Park's description of cities like Chicago in the 1920s. It does have the advantage of applying more generally to all cities of the period (e.g., New York) and correcting the excessive emphasis on the CBD in concentric zone theory.

Social Area Analysis

Social area analysis is an attempt to describe land use in cities by means of concentrating on the social characteristics of urban population. Social rank, family status and housing, and race and ethnicity were the traits considered. Shevsky and Bell (Shevsky and Bell, 1955:18) examined census tract data in order to learn how census tracts shared these characteristics. A high percent having them was designated a social area. Several combinations emerged. In San Francisco, people in some districts had low social rank (measured by social class) and family status (measured by extent of mother's employment), but high ethnic status. These residents tended to be lower class, and also had large families in multiple housing, along with clear ethnic or racial characteristics. In other sections of the city, people were low on family status and ethnicity, but high in social rank. Shevsky and Bell emphasized that urban residents regarded these social characteristics as very important.

Factorial Ecology

Factorial ecology put computers to use in the analysis of urban social characteristics. All characteristics were analyzed, not only the three looked at in social area analysis. All traits were compared, to see which ones were related. Those found to be associated were then used to describe a city's land use patterns. The original choice in social area analysis of social rank, family status, and race or ethnicity were given substantial support. Berry and Rees (Berry and Rees, 1969:445-491) emphasized that all earlier land use theories (concentric zone, sector, and multiple nuclei) were partially correct, and that factorial ecology brought them together under one umbrella. Census data patterns, as sorted out by computer, suggested that family status was best described by the concentric zone model; social rank by sector theory; and race and ethnicity by multiple-nuclei theory (Berry and Rees, 1969:445-491).

Cities in Transition: 1920-1945

Viewed from the perspective of the late 20th century, the industrial city was a transitory phenomenon. The very kinds of forces which rapidly created it, just as quickly replaced it with new urban forms. In the 1920s, the direction of the change urban areas were to undergo was already apparent.

Early industrialization had been a force for concentrating large numbers of people in relatively compact, very densely settled cities. As industrial society matured, the process began to be reversed. Most of this century has been characterized by the growing decentralization of urban areas and accompanying decreases in density.

By the 1920s that process was in full swing. While the old industrial cities were still the predominant urban form and the place where most metropolitan residents still lived, rapid outmovement of population and industry was underway. For the first time in the 1920s, suburban population growth outstripped the central cities (Wallace, 1980:79).

As the suburbs grew in the 1920s, the nature of the suburbs began to change. For one thing, they were no longer located solely on the commuter railroad and streetcar lines. The number of cars in the United States increased from nine million in 1920 to twenty-six million in 1930 (Wilson and Schulz, 1978:191). This greater flexibility in the transportation system allowed the development of suburban housing away from transit lines and farther out from the city limits. (However, suburban development was still hampered by the slow expansion of the paved highway system outside the cities, and this remained a barrier to suburban development for the next few decades.)

The 1920s also saw the further "democratization" of the suburbs.

More and more average middle-class people could afford to live in the suburbs. For middle-class people at least, the 1920s were a period of prosperity. The cheap, mass-produced car was within their financial reach. (A Model T cost less than a thousand dollars.) The 1920s also saw the appearance of the first housing subdivisions, providing modest single-family houses at affordable prices.

The result was a brief suburban building boom in the last half of the decade. In the absence of building codes and zoning requirements, suburban real-estate speculators and contractors hurriedly mapped out subdivisions and developed commercial strips along the highways. This created the first suburban "sprawl" of scattered, haphazard land use. It finally also led to the first large suburban shopping center (Country Club Plaza in Kansas City).

The Great Depression of the 1930s brought an abrupt end to this suburban boom. Purchasing power fell abruptly, and with industrial production drastically reduced, expansion of industrial plants outside the cities virtually ceased. Real-estate speculators went bankrupt, and the new housing market collapsed. For the first half of the decade, American cities were in a state of virtual suspended animation (despite the completion of a few spectacular projects such as Rockefeller Center and the Golden Gate Bridge). The modest and uneven economic recovery towards the end of the decade did little to change the picture immediately. Some small-scale suburban construction resumed. A few of the early urban expressways were opened (such as the West Side Highway in New York), and extensive planning to create more was underway. Even modest recovery in urban and suburban growth was cut short by World War II. The war-time economy boomed, but shortages of building materials and labor prevented any construction not directly related to war production (Wilson and Schulz, 1978:191-192).

At the Crossroads: The Industrial City in 1945

At the end of the war in 1945, the effect of fifteen years of economic stagnation followed by war meant that the great industrial cities and their modest surrounding suburbs had changed little from 1930. Central cities were still the dominant places of residence and employment. Central business districts were still the major centers for commercial, retail, professional, and office activities. But beneath the appearance of stability, pent-up forces for long-term change and a host of accumulating central-city problems had set the stage for another period of rapid change in American urban areas (Hawley, 1950).

Both the residential areas and the factories in the industrial districts of the large industrial cities were getting old. The problem was compounded by the fifteen years in which little new housing had been built, and old factories had not been replaced or modernized. As a result, there was a tremendous need to repair, modernize, or replace the physical structures of the cities.

The growing reliance on the automobile and the failure to build highways at a rate to accommodate the increasing traffic in the previous decades meant that urban streets and highways were congested, slow-moving, and often in bad repair. Cities were being strangled by the automobile. The fact that public transit had been allowed to decay (see Chapter 5) added further to the transportation problem. Gasoline rationing during the war had led to a temporary resurgence in transit use, but with the end of rationing, urban residents abandoned the aging and inadequate transit systems in droves in favor of the more convenient transportation which the car (despite congestion) seemed to offer.

In most cities, most of the large tracts of open land were gone. Both in industrial districts and residential areas, the remaining open land was in relatively small parcels and very expensive. Construction of housing, for example, was mostly limited to the construction of single homes on widely scattered open lots or the construction of higher-density housing (e.g., apartments) on land cleared of lower-density, older housing (an expensive proposition).

The current crisis in our cities tends to obscure the fact that the cities in the past were also centers of severe social and economic problems which made major portions of these cities unattractive places to live and work. For example, according to the 1950 census, one-fifth of "low-income"[2] urban residents renting housing lacked complete plumbing facilities, and an equal proportion lived in overcrowded housing (deLeeuw et al., 1976:122). Thus, poverty, slums, high crime rates, and spreading urban decay affected many urban neighborhoods. Ethnic group hostility, not just between blacks and whites, but between the various white ethnic groups, was considered a serious urban problem. In short, cities were plagued by major social problems and, just as importantly, were seen as places where those problems were concentrated.

The period immediately after 1945 was characterized by a severe housing shortage. Little new housing had been constructed in the previous fifteen years. At the same time, marriages, which had been postponed by war and the Depression, occurred at a rapid rate as veterans returned home. The large group of babies who had been born during the 1920s (when the birth rate was fairly high) were reaching the age of marriage. These young families began to have children at a very rapid rate (the "baby boom"). The result was that there was a tremendous increase in the number of growing young families in need of housing. The existing stock of housing in the cities did not even begin to meet their needs.

Suburbanization and the Rise of Megalopolis: 1945-1970

These problems combined with rapid economic growth and a continuation of the process of economic decentralization which had begun earlier. The result was a process of massive, rapid suburbanization of population and economic activity after 1945. As a consequence, by 1970, the basic nature of our urban areas had been transformed. Along with this transformation came the conditions which underlie the contemporary "urban crisis."

The Process of Suburbanization

As we have seen, suburbanization prior to 1945 had consisted of industrial satellite communities and middle- and upper-class residential communities from which workers commuted to the central city. The initial wave of suburbanization after 1945 was a continuation of this pattern. The open fields around the cities were quickly being filled with subdivisions of single-family homes to provide housing for young, increasingly affluent and mostly middle-class, office workers.

However, it quickly became apparent that this suburbanization was different from the past. For one thing, it was on a much vaster scale than before. Forty million people in the United States were living in metropolitan areas outside of central cities in 1950. By 1960 that figure reached sixty million, and by 1970 it had reached seventy-six million. Instead of the suburbs being a fringe of settlements around a central city, central cities rapidly became islands in a sea of suburbs. For the country as a whole, central cities grew slowly, and many cities began to actually decline in population size. By 1970, more metropolitan residents lived in the suburbs than lived in central cities. Thus, after 1945, urban growth was essentially suburban growth. (See Table 1.2.)

The size of this suburban growth also reflected another trend: suburban residents gradually became a much more diverse group in terms of socioeconomic background. Instead of just being middle- and upper-class enclaves, the suburbs also became home for a substantial

Table 1.2 **Population by Residence: United States, 1970 to 1986**

	Population (millions)			Percent Change		Percent
Residence	1970	1980	1986-87	1970-80	1980-86	1986
MSA's*	155.9	172.5	187.1	10.6	7.2	77
Central Cities	72.2	72.8	76.3	0.9	4.7	32
Outside Central Cities	83.7	99.6	108.6	19.0	8.9	45
Nonmetropolitan Areas	47.3	54.1	56.3	15.1	4.1	23
U.S. Population	203.4	226.5	243.4	11.4	7.4	100.0

*Metropolitan Statistical Area

SOURCE: *Patterns of Metropolitan Area and County Population Growth:* 1980-87. Current Population Reports, Population Estimates and Projections, Series P-25, no. 1039, pp. 14, 18, 19, 103, 117.

portion of the (white) working class and even lower class. Popular stereotypes to the contrary, the "typical" suburbanite was no longer always a middle-class office worker or professional (Palen, 1987:183). He or she was, however, almost exclusively white (an issue to which we will return in a later chapter).

The changing class composition of the suburbs was reflected in another change in the nature of the suburbs: mass produced housing. Early suburbs, even when they contained subdivisions constructed by the same building contractor, consisted of mostly custom-built housing which was constructed one house at a time "on order" for a particular family. After 1945, it became more and more common to build large numbers of fairly standardized units (hundreds at a time) and then sell them. These mass-produced subdivisions helped open up the suburbs to a wider range of income groups.

The new suburbanites were also more dependent on their cars than those in the past. Suburbs were now much less likely to be tied to mass-transit lines. In part, this reflected another, even more significant, change. Fewer and fewer suburban residents were commuters to the CBD of the central city (Palen, 1987:184). This was the result of the massive movement of employment to the suburbs and the wider range of workers residing in the suburbs.

This brings us to a fundamental point to be made about post-1945 suburbanization. Suburbanization of residence was only one part of the process. Equally significant was the suburbanization of most (but not all) kinds of economic activities. An increasing portion of industrial employment moved to the suburbs during this period, resuming a trend interrupted by the Depression. Retail activities in the CBD's of the central cities grew little after 1945. Instead, most of the very substantial growth in retail activity occurred at the scattered suburban shopping centers and malls which sprang up to serve the growing suburban population. Similarly, services and service professionals followed their customers to the suburbs. The result was that the whole focus of economic activity and employment growth moved to the suburbs. Hence, by 1970, the average suburban resident worked (and, of course, shopped) in the suburbs as well. Census figures show that by 1970, a full 72 percent of the suburban residents in the fifteen largest metropolitan areas were also employed in the suburbs (Palen, 1987:184).

The resulting pattern of urban settlement was, by 1970, quite different from that which existed in 1945. Urban areas were no longer dominated by a compact central city, but by low-density "suburban sprawls" covering large areas. The basic pattern of land use was a "multiple-nuclei" of specialized land uses similar to that suggested by Harris and Ullman. In part because of the independent zoning power of suburban governments and the desire of suburban residents to live in homogeneous communities, each suburb tended to specialize in a particular land use. Thus, some suburbs specialized in middle-class residential use. Others were primarily upper-middle or upper class. Still others combined working-class housing districts with industrial parks and strips of commercial development along major highways. In other words, the basic pattern was a great diversity of land uses across the metropolitan area, but homogeneity of land use within each particular community. Moreover, most research suggests that each suburb tended to maintain considerable continuity over time in terms of the social status of its residents relative to other suburbs. This tendency, called *suburban persistence*, meant, for example, that a suburb which started out middle-class residential tended to maintain its basic character for decades. Some recent research, however, suggests that such persistence may not be universal in all metropolitan areas—especially rapidly growing ones. Other researchers have detected a gradual evolution of suburban status rankings when they employ different measurements than earlier researchers. Certainly, over the very long term, an aging housing stock will create conditions favorable to urban decay and status declines even in relatively affluent suburbs (Farley, 1964:38-47; Guest, 1978:251-264; Logan and Schneider, 1981:175-186; Stahura, 1979:937-947). (See Chapter 10.)

Suburbs came to cover vast land areas surrounding the cities not just because of the large number of people who moved into them, but also because of low-density land-use patterns. Single-family residential areas with each house on a substantial lot meant much lower residential densities than in the central cities. Low-rise shopping malls, single-story factories, and low-rise office complexes, all surrounded by massive parking lots, further reduced density. Finally, suburban development was characterized by what is called *leapfrogging*. Rather than always locating housing and economic activities on the open land closest to the central city, suburban developers frequently jumped over this closer-in, often more expensive, land and located in the relatively more open areas further out. The result was a substantial amount of land left undeveloped between existing built-up areas. Hence, suburban development consumed very large areas of land to accommodate people and activities once accommodated in much more compact and dense central cities. The resulting urban areas were massive in their territorial scope.

This scattered, spread-out pattern of land use was also one in which there was no one single center of industrial, retail, commercial, or office activities. Some workers and (fewer) shoppers in the suburbs continued to head downtown to the old CBD. However, the majority of suburban residents by 1970 were headed to a multitude of specialized subcenters scattered throughout the metropolitan area, and they frequently were traveling very long distances to do so. As we will see (in Chapter 6), this pattern of *multiple destinations* has important implications for urban transportation.

Thus, the popular stereotype of the suburbs as a homogeneous sea of middle-class "bedroom communities" had less and less validity after 1945. The suburbs had a diverse mix of working class, middle-class, and upper-class residential areas and substantial, but scattered concentrations of industrial commercial activities. The suburbs had matured from mere "bedrooms" of central cities to complex systems of residence, work, shopping, and entertainment. In other words, to a very large degree, the suburbs had become the new form of urban development in the United States.

Muller (Muller, 1981:162-167) notes the emergence of important multi-use centers in suburbia which encompass virtually all the facilities found formerly only in the downtown areas of central cities. These areas are in effect suburban mini-cities, and are built around large regional shopping malls. Conveniently adjacent are a large number of such diverse activities as manufacturing plants, warehouses, hotels and motels, apartments, restaurants, and cultural and religious centers. A number of these suburban centers have become very specialized, providing such services as year-round convention centers. The development of such mini-cities has resulted in a number of increasingly complex traffic problems. One such example is *gridlock*, the clogging of roads and highways that is getting increasingly worse in suburban areas.

As the suburbs spread outward from the central cities, something else happened. In those areas where the existing central cities were close together, their suburbs eventually grew into each other. This process of metropolitan areas linking up to one another to create large areas of continuous metropolitan land use is known as *conurbanization*. Huge urban strips of low-density suburban sprawl linked nearby central cities together to create "supermetropolitan areas". The most spectacular example of this phenomenon was on the Eastern seaboard. With some gaps, a massive metropolitan strip was created linking urban areas between Boston and Washington, D.C. Sometimes nicknamed "Boswash" or the "Eastern Metropolitan Strip," geographer Jean Gottman (Gottman, 1964) christened this new form of urban development *megalopolis* ("supermetropolis"). Based on the trends of the 1950s, many demographers and geographers expected (or feared) that the eventual consequences might be the creation of even larger systems of linked urban sprawls. They would form continuous urban environments covering thousands of square miles. (Imagine driving all day and never being out of sight of subdivisions, shopping centers, and the "golden arches" of McDonald's.)

The Causes of Suburbanization

What set off this massive suburbanization? The causes are complex and interrelated. However, for present purposes it is possible to distinguish between two general groups of factors: (1) factors contributing to the suburbanization of residence and (2) factors contributing to the suburbanization of industry. Obviously, in reality, these factors were closely related and mutually reinforcing.

Suburbanization of Residence

As we have seen, suburbanization began in the context of rapid family formation, continuing urbanization of the population, and the baby boom. At the same time, there was an extreme shortage of housing in the cities. Obviously, people had to be provided new housing of some kind, somewhere. What is not so obvious is why the particular housing pattern of suburban, low-density, single-family housing emerged in the United States. Other urban societies also grew after 1945, but the pattern of urban growth was not identical to that of the United States. In other words, the question is not why did American urban areas grow, but why suburbs? Suburbs developed the way they did in the United

States not because of the workings of some inevitable, universal natural laws, but because of the convergence of certain particular factors which favored one form of urban development instead of another.

Government housing policy was one such factor. There was some government construction of new housing for the urban poor (See Chapter 5). But the basic thrust of government housing policy was to subsidize construction of private housing for the middle class and the more affluent sections of the working class. This is known as the *trickle-down* approach to housing policy. The basic idea is to encourage the creation of new housing for the more affluent. As these groups move into new housing, they abandon their older neighborhoods. These older neighborhoods then become available and affordable to less affluent working-class people. In turn, as these working-class neighborhoods become older and newer neighborhoods open up to working-class people, they become progressively less attractive and even less affluent people move in. Finally, physical deterioration sets in, and the neighborhood becomes a lower-class slum. In this way, each neighborhood houses successively lower-class individuals over time. Housing gradually "trickles down" to the poor (Downs, 1973).

Thus, after World War II, the federal government tried to create more housing for everybody primarily by subsidizing the more affluent sections of the population. Put these people into new housing, the thinking went, and the less affluent could "inherit" the housing that the more affluent abandoned. The basic mechanism for this policy was the FHA (Federal Housing Administration) and VA (Veterans' Administration) mortgage-loan guarantee programs. Through these programs, people could obtain private mortgage loans with very low down payments, low interest rates, and long pay-back periods. Financial institutions were willing to make these loans because there was very little risk to them. If the person failed to pay the mortgage, the federal government would repay the loan.

This program represented a massive effort to subsidize primarily suburban housing. This was because of the fact, first of all, that eligibility requirements for the program meant that a family had to at least be affluent working class to qualify for a loan guarantee. In addition, the program was oriented toward encouraging the purchase of single-family dwellings. Given land availability and the need for new housing, such housing had to be constructed in suburban areas. Various FHA and VA restrictions also made it easier to get loans on new housing, rather than old housing in the cities. In fact, there is evidence that internal procedures at FHA essentially excluded a large portion of central cities from participation in the loan guarantee program (Larsen and Nikkel, 1979:241-246).

The other critical role government played in suburbanization was in the area of transportation policy. Federal subsidy of the urban expressway system (and failure to assist mass transit in the cities) encouraged car use and made suburban commuting convenient. At the same time, car ownership became almost universal. The result was that most workers could afford to be much more flexible about where they lived and how far they could travel to get to work. (See Chapter 6.)

The economics of housing construction also favored suburban development. The loan guarantee program created a huge potential market of home buyers. Hence, contractors could build large numbers of houses "on speculation" with the assurance that there would be buyers for the completed homes. Standardized mass production of identical houses cut construction costs. Large tracts of land in outlying areas could be obtained at low cost per house lot. Building code restrictions were often less stringent outside of the city. This cut costs even further. Overall, then, builders could offer "more house for less money" in the suburbs and, thereby, attract buyers more readily.

The two decades following World War II were also a time of steadily rising average purchasing power. After deducting the effects of a modest rate of inflation, the average family doubled its real buying power during that period. Housing costs increased more slowly than average income (deLeeuw et al., 1976:136). This, combined with government loan programs, increased the percentage of the population that could afford to buy a new home.

There also was an undeniably strong public preference for suburban residence. Partly this preference can be seen as a continuation of the North American cultural tradition that tends to idolize small-town life and view cities as immoral, impersonal, lonely places. (We will return to this issue of traditional "anti-urban bias" in Chapter 3.) In addition, many observers in the 1950s felt that the move to the suburbs reflected, in part, the status appeal of the suburbs (Whyte, 1956). Most people at the time perceived the suburbs as middle- and upper-class preserves. Hence, to move to the suburbs could be seen as a means of asserting one's middle-class status. It symbolized having "made it" in society. This was especially true for the children of working-class parents for whom moving to the suburbs could be seen as proof positive of successful upward mobility and an achievement of the "American dream." (For the generation that has grown up in the suburbs and that tends to either take suburban life for granted or be critical of it, such a view of the suburbs may seem somewhat curious. But for many of the people who made the move to the suburbs in the 1950s, with their memories of fifteen years of economic depression and war, that "little house in the suburbs" represented real personal achievement.)

Two decades of sociological research on why people preferred the suburbs, however, point to another factor which overshadows the rest. Studies of suburbanites during the period reveal a strong concern for a lifestyle which emphasized nuclear family relationships, joint family activities around the home, and rearing children. Most suburbanites also displayed what sociologists call a strong "local" orientation: the primary focus of concern was on things immediately related to family life such as neighborhood quality, schools, and local community problems (Fava, 1975:10-24; Bell, 1958). This general orientation toward life has come to be known as *familism*. And, familism appears to have reached something of a peak in the 1950s and early 1960s. (Remember this was also the time of the "baby boom.") Thus, the choice of suburban residence during the period can be seen partially as a result of this familism. As late as the early 1960s, studies of why people moved to the suburbs indicated that, for most people, the move represented an attempt to provide for family needs, especially those of children (Wilson and Schulz, 1978:200). The suburbs were perceived as a "good place to raise the children."

Most popular accounts of the movement to the suburbs have emphasized another, essentially negative, motivation for moving to the suburbs. This motivation is usually summed up in the term "white flight". In this view, middle- and working-class whites moved to the suburbs to flee the growing problems of the central cities: urban decay, high taxes, poor schools and city services, high crime rates, and very importantly, the growing black population in the central cities. However, this popular view turns out to have exaggerated the extent to which suburbanization represented a "flight" from the problems of the central cities. Most of the available evidence suggests that white flight was a relatively minor factor in suburbanization — though it played some role which probably varied from city to city, time to time, and family to family. Rather, it appears that the positive attractions of the suburbs and the simple fact that the suburbs were where the newer, affordable housing was to be found were of primary importance in the growth of the suburbs after 1945 (Marshall, 1979:975-994).

Finally, as a simple practical matter, suburban residence became more attractive because, increasingly, that was where the jobs were. We now need to turn to the issue of why that became true.

Suburbanization of Industry

As we have seen, suburbanization of industry really began earlier in the century. The process was interrupted in the 1930s, but resumed at a rapid pace after 1945. A number of factors were involved.

Changing energy technology substantially increased flexibility in the choice of plant locations. Instead of relying on coal-fired plants, increasingly, industry turned to oil, natural gas, and electricity. Hence, industrial plants no longer needed to be located near rail lines or docks.

By the 1950s, major changes were also taking place in terms of the kind of industrial activity which dominated the economy. Most earlier industrial growth had emphasized the production of heavy manufactured goods (e.g., steel, machinery, automobiles). These industrial plants required bulky raw materials, and the resulting products were often large and heavy. Railroads were the preferred and generally necessary method to move these raw materials and finished products. Post-1945 industrial development began to move in the direction of lighter "high technology" products such as electronic equipment. These could just as easily or more easily be moved by truck. Again, this freed industry from railroad dependence.

Industry could take advantage of truck transportation because trucks were becoming larger and faster, and truck fuel was cheap. Also, the highway system (including the Interstate System in the 1960s), both within and between urban areas, steadily improved as the result of a massive government highway-building program.

Industry also increasingly needed large tracts of land on which to build factories. Single-story factories were more efficient than the old multiple-story factories in the central cities. Employees were more likely to commute to work by car and needed a place to park. Little open land was available in the old city industrial districts, and what was available was expensive. It was also likely to be heavily taxed by city government. Suburban locations, in contrast, offered ample, relatively cheap, and lightly taxed land on which to locate.

With almost universal car ownership, factories also no longer needed to locate near working-class residential districts or on mass transit lines. Industry could count on workers being able to commute longer distances by automobile.

In addition, industry wanted to escape the power of highly unionized workers who were demanding higher wages and restrictions on the authority of management. In many cities, this union power was augmented by the fact that the unions had become politically powerful in city government. The suburbs offered a much more congenial environment from the point of view of the companies. Workers, even when they belonged to a union, tended to live in more dispersed locations and were, consequently, less likely to be active in union activities. The new union locals in the suburbs were more likely to be composed of younger workers who lacked the militant union traditions of the older workers in the old plants in the city. Politically, the power of the unions in the suburbs was also much less (Gordon, 1977:76-79).

As residential suburbanization continued, location in the suburbs was also more attractive because that was where the workers, especially the more skilled white workers, lived. And to some extent, like white families, industry began to move to the suburbs in the 1960s to avoid what they saw as the problems of the deteriorating, increasingly black, central cities.

The Decline of the Old Central Cities

The opposite side of the coin of suburban growth was stagnation and decline of the large central cities — especially those in the Northeast and North Central regions. The problems of decline were intensified by the simultaneous influx of the rural poor. By the late 1960s, this combination of trends had produced the conditions which are a major concern of this book: a set of severe economic, social, and political problems in the central cities.

Economic Decline of the Central Cities

As we have seen, even prior to the 1920s, central cities were growing more slowly economically than the surrounding suburban areas. Following World War II, that slower rate of growth began changing into a pattern of stagnation, and by the late 1960s, absolute declines were being recorded in overall economic activity in many of the major central cities in the North. (We will talk about the South in the next chapter.) However, the overall decline was an uneven one. Some kinds of activities declined much more than others. For simplicity, the present discussion will be limited to three general areas of economic activity: industrial, retail, and administrative activities.

Industrial Activity

The most dramatic aspect of central-city decline was in the area of industrial activity and employment. In 1920 about nine out of every ten industrial workers in metropolitan areas were employed in central cities. By the late 1960s, only about six out of ten were employed there (Fremon, 1970:11). In the large Northern industrial cities, these changes generally translated into absolute declines in manufacturing employment (Hughes, 1974: 5).

Moreover, the type of industrial employment lost and the type retained made the trend even more ominous. Industries which stayed in the central city were often stagnant or declining, remaining for the simple reason that they did not need to expand. Even when a factory in a more dynamic industry stayed, the plant was likely to be old and inefficient. Hence, its long-term prospects for continued operation were poor. The new, rapidly growing high technology industries which had the best economic prospects tended to choose suburban locations. Industry which required skilled workers was more likely to leave. This tendency is reflected, for example, in the fact that statistics which compare average wages of workers leaving central cities, and workers remaining or entering, reveal a consistent tendency for central city workers to be less well paid (Gorham and Glazer, 1976:20).

In short, central city industry became more and more characterized by old, inefficient factories, employing less skilled, less well-paid workers, in the more "marginal," stagnant, or declining industries. By the 1960s, it was clear that central cities were rapidly losing their dominant position as industrial centers. Further industrial decline appeared likely.

Retail Activity

Overall, the percentage of the total sales in metropolitan areas accounted for by CBD stores steadily declined. In some cities, this meant absolute declines in retail sales volume and the closing of major retail stores. In other cities, it meant that the CBD simply failed to grow, and all retail sales growth occurred in the suburbs. In all metropolitan areas, it meant that the CBD was no longer the dominant center of retail activity. Hardest hit were the mass merchandising stores catering to middle-income customers and dependent on high sales volume (e.g., department stores, furniture stores). Smaller stores and stores serving the needs of the lower class were more likely to survive because of the high percentage of these people residing in cities. Luxury shops were also more likely to survive because of the continued presence of well paid office workers in the CBD (Palen, 1987:250-252).

Administrative Activity

The one relatively bright spot in the central city economy was the continued importance of the CBD as a location of administrative offices for both government and private industry. While there was some significant suburbanization of office activities by the late 1960s, in general, finance, management, and control activities were much less likely to decentralize to suburban locations. Top executives frequently felt the need for face-to-face contact with executives of other businesses. Professional services were more available and convenient in the CBD. Access to government offices and officials was often important in business administration. Hence, there was a continued tendency for most bank headquarters, major law firms, advertising agencies, and corporate headquarters to stay downtown. Office operations which were more self-contained (e.g., insurance companies), however, often did move to the suburbs (Palen, 1987: 252-53).

This helped some cities more than others. Such cities as New York, Chicago, San Francisco, and Atlanta were major centers for corporate administration. These cities experienced major expansions in office-building construction in the 1960s. Other cities, whose economic base was more dependent on industry and downtown retail activity, were much less fortunate.

Influx of the Rural Poor

Just as the central cities began to experience economic stagnation and decline, they experienced a major in-movement of new residents. These new residents were primarily poor, unskilled migrants from rural areas of the South. Most of them were black, but a significant minority came from rural Appalachia. The total number of people involved was quite impressive. Between 1950 and 1970, the total black population in central cities grew from 6.6 million to 13.1 million. Or, put another way, in 1910, nine out of ten blacks lived in the South, and 73 percent were rural residents. By 1980, only about half the black population lived in the South. Blacks are more concentrated both in large cities and metropolitan areas than are Caucasians. More than half of all blacks in the United States live in central cities, and about 20 percent live in suburban areas (Palen, 1987:222). Appalachian movement was less: Southern Appalachia lost about 3 million residents from migration between 1940 and 1970 (Brown, 1972:130-144).

For rural Southern blacks, this movement to Northern central cities was a continuation of a trend begun around 1910 but interrupted by the Depression. The single most important reason for the movement was that employment opportunities in Southern agriculture steadily declined during most of this century. Mechanization of production and the changing nature of agriculture in the South were eliminating the need for agricultural laborers and sharecroppers and making survival of the small, independent black farmer more and more difficult. The Southern urban economy was unable to absorb all of these surplus workers because of the extremely late industrialization of the South. Rapid urban industrial growth only began in the 1940s, and it was not until the 1970s that this growth finally could provide employment for all the available workers. The end result was that the only places the displaced rural poor could go was to the Northern cities. There, the majority could at least survive by working as unskilled laborers in industry and service occupations. And there was at least some hope for eventual economic advance. In this respect, blacks resembled the European immigrants who had come before them to American cities. (Immigration was severely restricted after 1920.) The difference was that blacks came at a time when the period of economic growth in the cities was coming to an end. And, of course, blacks faced special social barriers which were much more difficult to overcome than the social barriers faced by the immigrants. (We will explore the nature of these special barriers in Chapter 4.)

Appalachian migration was also partially a response to the increasing difficulty of surviving on small, subsistence farms. However, the big push to the cities really came with the rapid decline of employment in the coal industry after World War II and the absence of significant industrial growth in the region until the 1960s (Brown, 1972:130-144).

The Industrial City in Crisis

The result of these changes is that by 1970, instead of simply talking about "urban problems," more and more observers began raising the alarm in regard to an "urban crisis." At the root of their concerns were certain basic trends in the old industrial central cities in the North.

Most of the larger central cities in the North were experiencing declines in population size. They declined despite the influx of the rural poor because of the rapid suburbanization of younger, white middle- and working-class families. Economic decline had reached the point where the absolute number of job opportunities in a large majority of large central cities was decreasing. Moreover, the best-paid and most highly skilled kinds of jobs were increasingly being moved to the suburbs. In short, there were fewer jobs and poorer jobs available in the central cities. Continued industrial decline was making the situation progressively worse.

The result of these trends was that central-city populations were composed of increasing proportions of the poor, the black, and the elderly. Low-wage workers and the very poor stayed behind in the cities while the more affluent left for the suburbs. These poor were joined by additional poor people from the rural South. Young families left the cities while the elderly (especially the poor elderly) stayed. Whites left for the suburbs, while a growing black population remained concentrated almost exclusively in the cities.

In turn, these trends were much of the basis for a number of specific problems which we will examine in later chapters: neighborhood deterioration, government financial difficulties, racial hostilities and discrimination, increasing transportation costs, deteriorating conditions in schools, rising crime, and much, much more. We will explore the connection between these problems as we proceed. For now, we need merely to note that central cities had become enmeshed in a complex web of serious problems. Underlying these problems, as we have seen in this chapter, were deep-seated, long-term changes in technology, the economy, and the basic spatial organization of urban life which made these problems extremely difficult to treat. America's northern cities were "in crisis."

Evaluation

In this chapter, we have traced the development of urban areas in the United States from their beginnings, pointing out that contemporary urban conditions are the outgrowth of a very long historical process. The lesson should be clear: urban problems are not isolated events which spring out of nowhere. They have their origins in a complex chain of events growing out of the very forces which have shaped the basic nature of our society. In a very real sense, the same technological forces and methods of social and economic organization which brought prosperity, national power, and the "Big Mac" helped create slums and urban decay. Just how they did so will be explored in more detail in later chapters.

Main Points

1. Cities in colonial America were small and housed a small percentage of the population. They served primarily as commercial and political centers rather than centers of production.
2. Rapid urbanization in the 19th century was the outgrowth of industrializa-tion. Industrialization resulted in the concentration of workers and factories in cities because of the reliance on steam power, rail transportation, the need for workers to live very near the factories, the effect of breaks in transportation, and the need for factories to be near large urban markets and to use urban services.
3. Industrial cities were large (because of annexation), geographically compact, and very densely populated. There tended to be one large central business district which dominated retail activity and housed central offices, recreational and cultural activities, and government offices. Compact industrial districts were surrounded by large, very crowded, and squalid working class slums. Even middle-class residential areas were relatively

dense and close to the central business district. By the 1920s, residential suburbs for the more affluent and industrial satellite cities had developed.

4. The "human-ecology" approach to studying cities tried to develop a theory about the nature of the physical structure of the industrial city and the causes of that structure. Three main theories were developed: concentric-zone, sector, and multiple-nuclei theory.

5. Rapid suburbanization in the 1920s gave way to a fifteen-year period of relative stagnation in urban areas caused by the Depression and World War II.

6. By 1945, North American urban areas were facing a number of severe problems: physical aging, transportation and congestion problems, high land costs and lack of land to build on, concentrated social and economic problems, and a housing shortage.

7. Between 1945 and 1970, urban areas in the North experienced a period of explosive suburbanization. The suburbs were transformed from residential enclaves for the affluent to sprawling, low-density urban areas which contained a wide range of different land uses: industrial, commercial, and residential. By 1970, most suburban residents also worked in the suburbs. The suburbs were the focus of most economic growth during the period. Conurbanization created massive urban sprawls connecting metropolitan areas together into a type of urban system called a "megalopolis."

8. Residential suburbanization was the result of a number of factors: government housing policy, government transportation policy, car ownership, the economics of housing construction, rising purchasing power, and public preference for suburban residence.

9. Suburbanization of industry was the result of: changing energy technology, changes in industrial production, changes in transportation technology, the need for large tracts of land for factories, the desire to avoid city taxes, the attempt to escape the strong worker unions in the cities, the desire to avoid city problems, and need for a skilled work force.

10. The result was the economic stagnation and then decline of the central cities. At the same time, the large central cities of the North experienced a large influx of the rural poor, mostly from the South.

11. The net impact of these changes was the creation, by 1970, of an "urban crisis" in the central cities. They were experiencing population and job losses and contained increasing numbers of the poor, blacks, and the elderly. In turn, these changes were the basis for a number of other serious social and economic problems which will be the topic of concern in later chapters.

Key Terms

Annexation   The process by which cities have added surrounding areas to their legal jurisdiction. The condition under which it occurs is governed by state law.

Central Business District or CBD   The central retail shopping area and dominant commercial district of a city.

Competition and Segregation   Basic ecological processes in concentric-zone theory by which economic activities compete for the most attractive locations in a city and end up segregated in different areas of the city based on their need and ability to afford different locations.

Concentric-Zone Theory   The ecological theory set forth by Park and Burgess which suggests that the basic pattern of land use in cities resembles concentric circles of homogeneous land-use areas.

Conurbanization   The process by which metropolitan areas grow outward until they merge with other metropolitan areas.

Factorial Ecology   The application of computer technology to the analysis of the social characteristics of an urban population.

Familism   The cultural orientation associated with post-1945 suburban life which emphasizes the importance of family life and child rearing.

Human Ecology   The study of community structure through the analysis of the spatial and temporal distribution of persons and groups, and the factors associated with changes in these distributive patterns.

Invasion and Succession   The process in concentric-zone theory by which land-use in one zone is gradually replaced by that of the next innermost zone as a city grows.

Leapfrogging   The process by which, in suburban areas after 1945, new residential and commercial activities tended to jump over existing partially built-up suburban areas to locate further away from the central city. The result was that open areas were often left between various built-up areas in the suburbs.

Megalopolis   The structure of urban land use which results from large-scale conurbanization; a "supermetropolis."

Metropolitan Area   A contiguous territorial unit economically and socially integrated around a large city or metropolis.

Multiple-Nuclei Theory   The theory of human ecology which claims that cities develop a number of specialized centers rather than growing out from a central downtown, and that urban land-use, while homogeneous, is affected by a number of factors unique to each urban area.

Sector Theory   The theory of human ecology which claims that urban land use resembles pie-shaped sectors of homogeneous land use areas.

Social Area Analysis   The description of urban land use in terms of the social characteristics of the population.

Suburban Persistence   The tendency of suburban communities to maintain their original pattern of land use over long periods of time.

Suggested Reading

Glaab, Charles and Theodore Brown. 1967. *A History of Urban America*. New York: Macmillan. A discussion of North American urban growth prior to 1920.

Gordon, David. 1977. "Class Struggle and the Stages of American Urban Development." *In The Rise of the Sunbelt Cities*, edited D. Perry and A. Watkins. Beverly Hills, CA: Sage Publications. A brief analysis of the development of cities in different regions of the U.S.A. from a neo-Marxian perspective. The first part of the article relates to the discussion in this chapter.

Harris, Chauncey D. and Edward L. Ullman. 1945. "The Nature of Cities." *Annals of the American Academy of Political and Social Science* 242:7-17. The classic summary of the early theories of human ecology.

McKelvey, Blake. 1968. *The Emergence of Metropolitan America 1915-1966*. New Brunswick, NJ: Rutgers University. A major review of the development of North American urban areas in the first two-thirds of this century.

Muller, Peter O. 1981. *Contemporary Suburban America*. Englewood Cliffs, NJ: Prentice-Hall. A clear and thorough summary of the details and nature of suburban development.

Thernstrom, Stephan and Richard Sennet, editors. 1969. *Nineteenth-Century Cities: Essays in the New Urban History*. New Haven, CT: Yale University Press. A collection of essays which attempts to dispel many myths about life and conditions in early North American cities.

Endnotes

[1] Not all factories did so locate, however. Some industries located in small communities. The result was the creation of "mill towns" or "company towns" dominated by a single large factory. The state of Ohio, for instance, is still dotted with small and medium-sized factory towns.

[2] These were families with less than $3,000 a year income in 1950. Given income levels in that year, people in this group were not just the poor, they included a large number of working class people.

2

Recent Urban Trends

Outline of Topics

T he 1970s was a period in which those who studied urban trends became increasingly aware of a number of new urban problems and developments. Some of these "new" developments were not really new at all. They represented the results of long-term trends whose effects finally could not be ignored any longer. Others represented a further intensification of problems recognized earlier. Some were, in fact, new developments. Whatever their origin, these trends changed our view of the nature of the urban crisis.

In the 1960s, the focus of concern was on the decay of central cities and the increase in suburban sprawl. Overall, however, urban areas were seen as basically "healthy." Economic growth, the baby boom, and continued migration to metropolitan areas had created massive, generally affluent, metropolitan areas. The one flaw in this apparent success story was the alarming rate at which central cities were decaying. Some analysts argued, however, that if only some of the affluence of the suburbs could be diverted to deal with central city problems, the worst aspects of the urban crisis could be managed.

By the mid-1970s, it was clear that this view of the urban crisis was much too simple. Major economic, technological, political, and social forces were reshaping the American urban landscape. Not only central cities and suburbs but whole regions of the country were affected by the changes taking place. Social scientists were forced to broaden their perspective, examining patterns of growth and decline not only within metropolitan areas but also among regions of the country.

Patterns of Regional Growth and Decline

Certain parts of the country have been growing rapidly—in fact, booming—while other parts have been stagnating or even experiencing declines in population. These patterns of population growth and decline have not been uniform within entire regions. A region's subunits, like states for example, did not necessarily all grow at the same rate. Nevertheless, they have tended to break down roughly on a regional basis. Defining regions as Northeast, South, Midwest (each of these containing smaller subregions), Mountain, and Pacific, it is possible to identify distinctive patterns of growth in each region. In addition, these patterns can and have changed dramatically from one time period to another. (See figure 2.1.)

Figure 2.1 **Regions of the United States**

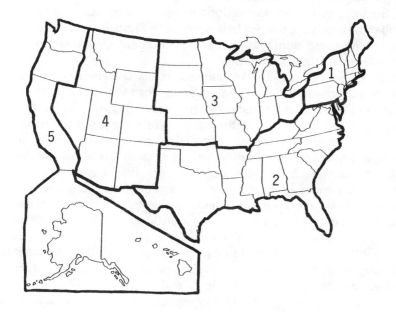

1. Northeast
   New England, Mid Atlantic
2. South
   South Atlantic, South Central
3. Midwest
   Great Lakes, Plains
4. Mountain
5. Pacific

The 1970s: The Sunbelt vs. the Frostbelt

The news about population changes in the United States during the 1970s was dominated by one major fact: massive growth of the Sunbelt. This area, stretching from the Southwest to the Southeast, is anchored roughly by Phoenix in the west and Atlanta in the east. While the growth of this area had begun well before 1970, it became more dramatic during the decade as growth of other areas slowed.

The other rapidly growing area of the country during the 1970s was the Mountain states, those which lie between the West Coast states and the plains. The Mountain states actually had a faster growth *rate* than the Sunbelt, since the populations living in them were substantially smaller than those in the Sunbelt states. The Sunbelt states, then, grew more in absolute numbers, while the Mountain states added larger percentages of their population.

Both the Sunbelt and the Mountain states shared certain characteristic growth patterns that differentiated them from the other parts of the country. The chief difference was that their growth was much less centralized than growth in other areas. While the large metropolitan areas such as Atlanta, Denver, and Dallas grew, even in their central cities, an enormous proportion of the growth occurred outside of metropolitan areas. Some was *exurban* growth, that is, existing suburban growth that happened to cross over the border of the metropolitan area and into an adjacent county. Much of the growth, however, was in smaller metropolitan areas and, most strikingly, in nonmetropolitan areas (small towns and rural areas) far from cities. These types of communities, which had been experiencing population declines for decades, were responsible for the remarkably dispersed nature of Sunbelt and Mountain growth (Berry and Dahlman, 1978).

Some analysts noted that a new type of urban system was developing from this dispersed growth pattern. They called it the *metropolitan regional system*. Such a system is unlike the traditional metropolitan area with a large central city surrounded by suburbs that depend on the center for employment, entertainment, and commercial activity. Rather, the pattern consists of a large geographical area containing a number of separate small cities and towns, still linked together by their common economic activities. Typical of this type of system is the Piedmont area of North Carolina, where several small cities, Greensboro, Winston-Salem, and High Point are interdependent with each other and with numerous other small but growing communities (Leven, 1979).

While the Sunbelt and Mountain states were growing rapidly, the northern states were not. Throughout the 1970s, the northern states (with the exception of northern New England) grew very slowly, or in a few cases, actually lost population. In contrast with the Sunbelt, these states were quickly dubbed "the Frostbelt." However, their slow or negligible growth rates were not attributable solely to their cooler climates. (Nor, as we shall see, was the majority of Sunbelt growth due to the sunny climate!)

The Frostbelt states of the Northeast and Midwest consisted of two kinds of areas: the highly industrialized sections bordering the Atlantic Ocean and Great Lakes and the rural agricultural sections from the plains to central Ohio. In previous times, the industrial areas' cities had acted as "urban magnets," growing steadily from internal population growth, migration from rural areas, and foreign immigration. During the 1970s, few migrants entered the region, and declining birth rates added to the stagnation of population growth.

It is important to note, however, that like the Sunbelt, the Frostbelt experienced uneven growth internally. While some areas were shrinking rapidly, others were keeping a steady state, and still other areas were growing. Although these very different small-scale patterns added up to a larger pattern of slow growth for the Frostbelt as a whole, it would be wrong to conclude that no northern areas were growing in population.

The 1980s: The Coasts vs. the Heartland

In the early 1980s, the patterns of regional growth and decline were similar to those of the 1970s. Gradually, however, a new pattern began to emerge that was expected to modify (but not completely eliminate) the Sunbelt-Frostbelt dichotomy. Examining Figure 2.2, we can see that all of the very high growth states (those with more than a 15 percent increase in population) between 1980 and 1987 were either Sunbelt or Mountain states (with the exceptions of California and Alaska). In addition, more than half of the states experiencing moderate growth (population increases of between 5 and 15 percent) were also from those regions. The states with the smallest population increases were heavily concentrated in the Frostbelt.

During the decade of the 1980s, however, population growth patterns — and especially migration patterns — began to change. By 1987, the Sunbelt-Frostbelt or basically north-south differences in regional growth were no longer the most significant comparison points. Rather, a more complex pattern emerged. For the year beginning March, 1987 and ending March, 1988, for example, the fastest growing areas of the country were on the Atlantic and Pacific coasts. Of the 17 fastest growing states, 13 had an ocean coastline![1] On the other hand, while only six of these rapidly growing states could be considered Sunbelt or Mountain states, six were Frostbelt states, and the remaining five were neither. This means that population growth was no longer as heavily concentrated in the south. In fact, four of the seven states that *lost* population between 1987 and 1988 were Sunbelt or Mountain states (*Population Today*, 1989).

Thus, as we write this in the summer of 1990, it appears that overall Sunbelt growth has slowed and the new, rapidly growing areas are the East and West coasts. This pattern becomes especially clear if we look

Figure 2.2 **Percent Change in Population, by States, 1980-1987**

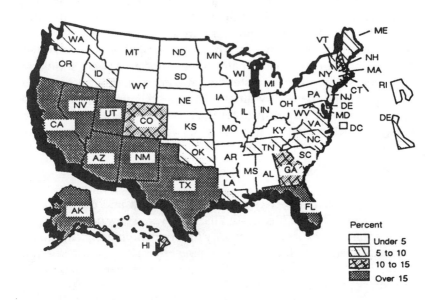

SOURCE: U.S. Bureau of the Census, *Statistical Abstract of the U.S., 1989.*

at migration rates: where are people moving? The recent evidence shows that, again for 1987-88, the two coasts are clearly the preferred destinations.[2] We must quickly add, however, that there is no reason to assume that this trend will continue into the future. For one thing, changing conditions may very rapidly change the direction of population flows. For another, population changes (growth and decline) are the end result of a number of components, each one of them contributing to the final population total.

Components of Population Shifts

According to demographers (sociologists who specialize in studying populations), population changes are made up of three components: migration, natural increase, and immigration.

Migration includes both those people moving into an area (say, a state or region) and those moving out. *Net migration*, or the overall impact of these moves on the population total, is obtained by subtracting the

number of people moving out of an area from the number moving into
the area. (If more people move out than move in, the state or region
will have negative net migration, or out-migration.) The changing
population balance among regions is partly a product of the changing
balance between in- and out-migration. In 1984-85, for example, the
South as a whole experienced very little population increase from
migration, yet it was the number one destination for movers from all
other areas of the country. The reason that the net migration for the
South was very low, despite a huge influx of newcomers, was that the
South had the largest number of out-migrants as well (*Number News*,
2/88:1).

The second component of population change, natural increase, is the
excess of births over deaths. Many factors, such as socioeconomic
conditions and age of the population, influence both the birth rate and
death rate. During the late 1980s, rates of natural increase were
significantly higher in eight states than in the rest of the country; six
of these states were in the Southwest or the West. Ten states had rates
of natural increase that were significantly lower than average; seven of
them were "heartland" states. So regional variation in natural increase
currently favors the Sunbelt area (*Population Today*, Sept. 1989).

Immigrants from outside of the United States also add to population
growth. During the 1970s about 600,000 immigrants per year were
legally admitted to the country (U.S. Bureau of the Census 1989:9).
Since about 160,000 or so leave each year, the net figure for legal
immigration is currently over 400,000 per year (*Number News*, 8/88:1).
Immigrants do not settle in equal numbers throughout the country.
When they arrive, they normally have a particular location already in
mind. These tend to be highly concentrated geographically. In 1987,
fully one-quarter of all legal immigrants stated that they intended to
settle in California, and another quarter said they were bound for either
New York, New Jersey, or Pennsylvania. Thus, better than half of all
legal immigrants were planning to go to only four states (U.S. Bureau
of the Census 1989a: Table 12). In Chapter 4 we will discuss in more
detail the kinds of communities formed by immigrants from various
countries.

In addition to the legal immigrants, the population is also increased
by illegal immigrants. Obviously, we do not have reliable figures on
illegal immigration, but it is estimated to be between 100,000 and
300,000 people per year. This is a net figure, including not only the
many people who enter the country but also those who leave, voluntarily
or involuntarily, each year. Further estimates tell us that approximately
70 percent of those living here illegally are Spanish-speaking and about
55 percent are Mexican citizens. Although we have little data on the

regional distribution of illegal immigrants, they appear to be concentrated most heavily in the South and West (Espenshade, 1990; *Numbers News* 8/88:1).

Undocumented immigrants totaled 4 million to 5 million by the mid-1980s, when Congress passed the Immigration Reform and Control Act. This legislation was intended to "legalize" those immigrants currently living illegally in the United States while simultaneously making it more difficult for others like them to enter the country. Although it is too early to assess the results of this legislation, immigration experts point out that as long as economic conditions are significantly better in this country than in neighboring countries, we should expect to see illegal immigration continue (Espenshade, 1990).

Taking all of these factors (migration, natural increase, and immigration) into account, we can more easily understand why population shifts are difficult to predict. One factor often offsets another, and all of the factors may change over time. In spite of the shifts we have seen in the late 1980s from Sunbelt growth to coastal growth, the momentum from Sunbelt growth in the 1970s is expected to persist well into the 1990s. *If* current trends continue (always a big question), population growth in the 1990s will be strong in both the Sunbelt and coastal areas, but weak in the Northern and central "heartland" areas (*Population Today* 9/89:6).

Explanations of Population Shifts

What accounts for these regional shifts and changing patterns of urban development? The obvious answer, at least for most of this growth, is that the pattern of economic growth and development in the United States has been changing. The potential significance of this change cannot be overstated. It means that urban problems must be seen in the context of more widely-based regional growth and decline. It also means that it becomes necessary to distinguish between the urban problems of different areas of the country. Simply put, some urban problems are specific to declining areas and others to growing areas. Another consequence is that we cannot understand the nature of contemporary urban problems without understanding what has been causing these regional shifts and what current trends may mean for the future.

Unfortunately, the reasons behind the regional shifts are complex and still not entirely understood. A number of explanations, some of them contradictory, have been advanced. We will begin by looking at some of the individual factors which may have had some influence on regional development. Later in the chapter we will examine more general theories of regional development that try to go beyond single factor explanations.

Changing Structure of the Economy

The economy of the United States, like all capitalist economies, is constantly changing. Throughout our history, these economic changes have often had major consequences for regional growth and decline. In the 19th century, for example, the rural, agricultural-based South lost its economic and political dominance as the North gained economic power through large-scale industrialization. Population grew in the Northern industrial regions and stagnated in the South.

The changes in regional population we have seen over the past two decades have been the result of economic trends that have been going on at least since the late 1940s. One of these is a shift in the kinds of products and services being produced in the United States. Manufacturing employment has declined overall, and within the manufacturing sector, certain kinds of products have replaced others. The largest employment declines have been in the so-called "heavy" industries such as the production of steel and autos, as well as certain labor-intensive industries such as producing clothing and shoes. Growth areas of the economy have included "high-tech" manufacturing (e.g., computer components) and the service sector (e.g., health care, accounting, banking, and hotels). In addition to these long-term trends, there are shorter cycles of economic change in certain industries; for example, energy production, in which growth speeds up and slows down rather abruptly as conditions in the world market change.

How have these economic changes affected regional growth and decline? The key fact to note is that many of these industries are concentrated in certain geographic locations.

Thus, in the 1970s, massive declines in steel and auto industry employment were not distributed evenly around the country. Rather, they disproportionately affected the areas around the Great Lakes and Ohio Valley, the country's "industrial heartland." Manufacturing growth during the same period, however, was located disproportionately in the southern and western states, as newer industries were established. For example, the growth of the semiconductor industry in California's "Silicon Valley" helped to drive growth in this area. By the 1980s, however, high-tech manufacturing (and such related industries as research and development) were spreading out — not evenly throughout the country, but leapfrogging the continent to the Boston area. The so-called "Route 128" complex of computer-related companies linked by Boston's circumferential highway of the same name provided one anchor for New England's growth spurt in the 1980s.

Growth patterns in the 1970s and 1980s were also dramatically affected by changes in the energy industry. When the Middle-Eastern oil producing nations formed a cartel (OPEC) in the early 1970s, oil prices soared on the world market. This price rise spurred investment in energy exploration in the United States, again disproportionately located in the Sunbelt and Mountain states (e.g., Texas, Oklahoma, Nevada, Colorado) as well as Alaska. The extremely rapid growth of these areas, however, was a temporary phenomenon. By the early 1980s, once energy prices had fallen, investors withdrew from the industry, employment opportunities dwindled, and the energy producing areas began to lose population. The exodus from these areas is one factor that fed the slowdown of Sunbelt growth in the 1980s (Browne, 1989).

Changes in the organization of agriculture have also spurred regional growth and decline. Century-long trends toward larger and larger farming operations have intensified during the past 20 years, resulting in the emergence of "agribusinesses," huge corporations controlling all aspects of food production. Growth of agribusiness was one of the economic "pillars" on which the Sunbelt growth of the 1970s rested (Sale, 1976). During the 1980s, changing economic conditions speeded up the growth of agribusiness and also hastened the bankruptcy of many smaller family farms. This shakeup in agriculture has had a regional impact since the growing agribusiness-dominated areas are mostly in the Southwest and West, while the declining family farm areas tend to be in the Midwest.

A final type of economic change, one that is increasing in importance, is the trend toward the globalization of the economy. No longer are economic conditions in different industries affected solely by events taking place in our own country. More and more, our economy is linked to those of other nations. One important manifestation of this trend is the emergence of multinational corporations. These companies operate in several nations, with many subsidiaries producing different products and often "trading" with each other. A multinational may have its headquarters in New York or London, its manufacturing plants in Mexico or Singapore, and its bookkeeping services in the Caribbean. Globalization of the economy has affected the regional growth patterns of the U.S. because some areas have become tightly integrated into international trade, banking, and manufacturing operations while others have not. California, for example, has become part of the "Pacific Basin," trading with the expanding Asian nations. The Miami area is a major center for commerce and banking for Central and South America. Texas is the site of many "border-straddling" manufacturing operations, where corporations pair U.S. and Mexican plants to gain the advantages of both technical expertise and cheap labor. New York City has become one of the premier banking and finance centers of the new global economy. These areas have attracted investment, created jobs, and drawn new residents based on their changing roles in the national and international economy.

When areas grow and decline due to these changes in economic structure, the effects are fundamentally different from growth and decline due to the normal ups and downs of the business cycle (booms and recessions). Rather than cycles of expansion and contraction of the same industries within a region, we are seeing a pattern of *restructuring*, in which one set of industries is replaced by another. Restructuring has more long-term consequences for regional growth and decline than do the short-term changes of the business cycle.

Federal Expenditure Patterns

The federal government has played a significant role in economic growth because federal expenditures have had different effects on different parts of the country. The Sunbelt and Mountain states benefited in several different ways during the 1970s.

The Sunbelt received a very large share of the "pork-barrel" public works projects undertaken by the federal government. This was a reflection both of the traditionally depressed economic conditions in the region, which the federal government sought to correct, and the special political influence of the Sunbelt states in Congress. The seniority system in Congress (especially before some recent reforms) meant that Senators and Representatives with the longest service were appointed to the most powerful Congressional committees and had the most say in where public works projects were undertaken. A very high proportion of these high seniority members of Congress came from the South. The result was an influx of federal dollars for such things as power dams, harbor improvements, and river transportation systems. This helped to solve a major disadvantage of the South: it had a poor "infrastructure" (e.g., port facilities) which made it difficult and expensive for industry to locate there (Sale, 1975).

Military expenditures also played a significant role in the growth of these areas. The development of a relatively large, permanent military establishment in the United States in the last few decades also meant the creation of a significant, permanent armaments sector in the economy. For a number of reasons, again including Congressional influence, a disproportionate amount of the military-related industry located in the Sunbelt and Mountain states. This included some very rapidly growing industries related to the aerospace industry, such as electronics. Thus, even the self-proclaimed "Free Enterprise City" of Houston owed a good deal of its growth to government spending (Feagin, 1988).

During the 1980s, however, military spending favored different regions of the United States. As the Reagan administration greatly increased the amount of military spending, it also changed the nature of that spending, significantly increasing the proportion going to high-tech weapons systems such as the Strategic Defense Initiative. Rather than benefiting the established (heavily southern) military bases and naval shipyards, these weapons contracts tended to go to a handful of defense-oriented technology companies: Lockheed, General Dynamics, Boeing, Grumman, and a few others. Military contracts also provided large amounts of money to the new computer-based research and design companies in California and New England. Although defense spending in the South did not cease, military money was more widely distributed around the country in the 1980s than in the 1970s. In a few areas, it was sufficiently concentrated to produce mini-booms like the "New England Miracle" of the 1980s (Browne, 1989).

Southern Advantages

In addition to patterns of economic change and government spending which had somewhat different impacts on regional growth in the 1970s than they had in the 1980s, there are several factors that helped attract investment to the South during both decades. We might call these the "long-term Southern advantages."

A low wage rate is one such advantage. The Sunbelt (and to a lesser extent Mountain) states have traditionally had lower wages than the Northeast or Midwest states. In the past, this had little effect on the location of industry, since Northern areas had other advantages (such as skilled workers and good infrastructure) that offset labor costs. Increasingly, however, employers (especially in manufacturing) are attempting to reduce labor costs. Thus, they may shut down a Northern plant and reopen it in the South (the "runaway plant" phenomenon) or simply choose not to locate new plants in the North.

A related advantage for businesses locating in the South has been low rates of unionization of workers, compared to those in the Northern industrial areas. To employers, unionization in the North meant not only higher wages but also less ability to control the workplace as they wished. In the South and West, however, unions were weak, not only because of a lack of an industrial tradition, but also because of a more conservative political climate. Most Southern and Western states have long had "right-to-work" laws that make union organizing more difficult and reduce the effectiveness of the unions once they are formed. Some Southern states have courted businesses by advertising that businesses could avoid unions by locating in their area (Goodman, 1981).

Tax policies have also helped to spur growth in the South. There has been a persistent pattern of higher-than-average state and local taxes and expenditures in the Midwest, Pacific, and Northeast regions, while, in the Sunbelt and certain Mountain states, taxes and expenditures have been lower than average. Indeed, Northern central cities have the highest rates of taxation in the country (Peterson, 1976). Overall, state and local governments in the Midwest, Pacific, and Northeast provide more services, employ more workers, and pay their workers more. Some of these areas also have slower growing or declining tax bases from which to raise revenue (Bahl, 1984). Whatever their causes, the consequences of these differences are clear: lower taxes have made the Sunbelt attractive both to businesses and individuals.

These "Southern advantages" tend to help the South attract investment and therefore population, all other things being equal.[3] Theorists debate how long-lasting these advantages will be, as we shall see later in this chapter.

Consequences of Regional Change

The same changes that produced so much variation in the growth and decline of regions also had an impact on both the size and the nature of communities within those regions.

Central Cities

One consequence of these changes was that the larger central cities lost one set of functions and gained another. By the early 1970s, it was clear that central cities were no longer going to be the location of the country's industrial activities. It was not clear, however, what would take the place of the departing manufacturing companies. During the 1970s, most of the nation's central cities lost population as residents migrated to suburbs and nonmetropolitan areas. These former "urban magnets" could no longer attract or hold population without the economic base of manufacturing that had given their residents a reason to locate there. Even in the growing Sunbelt area, the central cities were losing population or growing very slowly.

In the late 1970s and 1980s, the impacts of the economic changes we have discussed began to be felt very strongly in U.S. cities, and the implications of the changes have varied from city to city. A handful of the largest cities, those most closely linked to the international networks of the global economy, have become "world cities," centers for trade and finance and home to many multinational corporate headquarters. New York, Los Angeles, Miami, and San Francisco are usually considered in this category. Several other large cities, while not of world city status, have established themselves as economic centers for specific regions. Atlanta, Boston, Chicago, Denver, and Houston fill this role. Their economies revolve around the same functions as the world cities, namely, banking and finance, trade and commerce, and business services such as law, accounting, advertising, and real estate development (Sassen-Koob, 1984).

The changing nature of the economy of these central cities has caused profound changes in other aspects of urban life. The cities' occupational structures, for example, which formerly would have contained large proportions of skilled and unskilled manufacturing workers are now dominated by service sector workers. Many of them are highly-paid service workers such as attorneys, managers, and stockbrokers. A much larger number are clerical workers or relatively low-paid service workers such as janitors, health aides, and security guards.

With the growth of the downtown white-collar work force in many cities, there has been an increase in *gentrification*. This is the movement of the "gentry," or professional workers, into neighborhoods formerly dominated by poor or working-class households. Gentrification began in the 1970s and intensified in the 1980s, as urban workers found alternatives to suburban living in brownstones, condominiums, shingled Victorians, or former manufacturing lofts. (See, for example, Zukin, 1982.) While most urban workers continued to look for housing in the suburbs, the white-collar labor force was so large that even a minority could produce a distinct trend such as gentrification. Gentrification was hailed as an "urban renaissance" by many city officials eager to have large numbers of white, middle-class residents living in properties that were appreciating in value (and tax assessment). At the same time, gentrification has been criticized for pushing out, or displacing, working-class residents (LeGates and Hartman, 1986).

Changes in the urban economy have also prompted major changes in land use in these service-dominated cities. Downtown business districts have expanded into areas that formerly housed factories, small businesses, and homes. In some cases, the older buildings are being demolished and replaced with new structures, but in many areas, the factories and warehouses are being refurbished as offices and shops to meet the space needs of the growing service sector. In Chicago, the growing downtown has threatened some areas of small manufacturing businesses because their proprietors cannot afford the high rents that service sector businesses can pay. Small manufacturing firms have tried to prevent this industrial displacement by enlisting the city's help in protecting certain areas as "manufacturing zones."

What of the former industrial cities that have not become major world or regional centers? Most of these have continued to decline in population. Detroit is one of the more extreme examples, having dropped in population from 1.5 million in 1970 to 1.2 million in 1980 to just about a million in 1990 (*Population Today*, 1/90). Like several other "de-industrializing" cities, Detroit has tried to model itself on the world cities, providing new space for services, offices, tourism, and recreation. City officials have also attempted to retain a certain number of manufacturing jobs in the auto industry, and of course, the United States automakers are still headquartered in Detroit. But through the 1980s, at least, there continue to be "two Detroits," a declining central city surrounded by flourishing suburbs (Darden et al., 1987; Hill, 1984).

Suburbs

Despite the trend toward gentrification in certain cities, the largest flows of population throughout the 1980s continued toward the suburbs. Although metropolitan areas are still growing, the suburbs have been growing twice as fast as the cities during the 1980s. As a result, more Americans now live in suburbs than in central cities (*Number News*, 9/89:3).

In some parts of the country (Southern California and Florida's east coast are good examples), suburbs have begun to merge physically (although not legally/politically) with each other and with small nearby cities. The low-density "sprawl" and "leapfrogging" characteristic of suburban development undergoing rapid growth sometimes makes it difficult to distinguish the boundaries between municipalities. It also makes it less likely that suburban residents will travel to the central city for employment, shopping, and recreation. One area that has become in many ways a "suburb independent of the city" is Long Island.

Formerly dominated by commuter suburbs and farms, it is rapidly industrializing. And its two counties, Nassau and Suffolk, by themselves (without New York City) rank among the top ten metropolitan areas in population (*Numbers News*, 10/88:1).

Towns and Rural Areas

During the 1970s, the nonmetropolitan areas of the country (those towns and rural areas outside of metropolitan areas) grew very rapidly. In fact, their growth surpassed that of the metros by about a third: 1.3 percent per year as compared to 1.0 percent for metros. The most rapid growth occurred in the Mountain and Pacific states, but the South and New England also saw substantial population growth in small communities (U.S. Bureau of the Census, 1989a:28). To a certain extent, this growth was based on prosperity in the primary or extractive industries of agriculture, energy exploration (drilling and mining), logging, and so on. But a good deal of the growth was probably exurban in nature, caused by population spillover from the increasingly built-up suburbs.

The 1980s brought a major slowdown in the growth of nonmetropolitan areas. While metros continued to grow at about the same pace in the 1980s as in the 1970s, nonmetro growth rates were cut in half (U.S. Bureau of the Census, 1989a:28).

Not all small communities were affected in the same way by this growth slowdown. Those that experienced the most severe losses of population were those towns of the Midwest whose economies were based on surrounding small farms. As farms became increasingly susceptible to economic difficulties during the 1980s (chiefly because of high debts and falling land prices), many small farms were sold to larger landholders. In some farming communities, so many farmers went bankrupt that the merchants of the towns were forced into bankruptcy as well, basically shutting down the towns. In other rural areas, however, towns remained prosperous, especially where some industry existed. Thus, residents had a mix of farming and manufacturing available to support themselves.

Consequences for Individuals' Incomes

As economic activity shifts spatially from one region to another, and as population grows or declines, the amount of income available to individuals changes. Economists measure income *per capita*; that is, the total income of an area (state or region) divided by the entire population of the area. In 1988, the per capita income for the entire

United States was $16,444. The Northeastern and Western states' averages were substantially above that figure, while those of the Midwestern, Southern, and Mountain states were lower. New England had the highest per capita income, at $3,569 over the average, while the Mountain states had the lowest, at $2,162 below the national average (*Numbers News*, 7/89:3).

The per capita income figures for 1988 were especially significant because they revealed a reversal of two established trends in income distribution. The first is that the gap between the wealthiest and poorest areas, which had been narrowing steadily since 1969, widened in 1988. The second is that for the first time in 60 years, the South was not in last place. That "honor" belonged to the Mountain states, which had a per capita income $49 below the Southeast and $83 below the Southwest. Whether these trends toward regional income distribution are merely temporary or whether they reflect a new direction for the future remains to be seen (*Numbers News*, 7/89:3).

Theories of Regional Growth and Decline

How do we interpret these regional economic shifts? Does it mean that the Northern urban areas are "dying"? Will regional urban growth equalize in the future? Was the Sunbelt and Mountain state boom just a temporary event, or does it represent a more fundamental change?

These are important issues because they will influence how we interpret the specific problems that both the growing and declining urban areas face. If, for example, the great urban sprawls of the North are in for a period of sustained economic decline, then such problems as physical decay and unemployment are likely to get much worse or require very drastic measures to control.

In fact, there are no certain answers to the question of the actual meaning of these regional shifts. That uncertainty is increased by our inability to predict a highly uncertain economic future. At present, there are several ways to view these trends which seem plausible and which suggest different possible futures for urban areas in the different regions.

Convergence

One possibility is that the Sunbelt and Mountain states have just been "catching up" with the older urbanized regions of the country. According to this convergence theory, Northern urban areas are not dying. Rather, there has just been a temporary shift of urban and economic growth to Southern and Western regions. These areas presently offer cost advantages to industries which make them attractive places to locate. However, according to this view, those advantages will not last. As the new areas mature, they will become more and more like the older urban areas. Labor costs, standard of living, and the degree of unionization will increase. The physical structures (e.g., housing, factories, highways, and sewer systems) in these areas will age and require more maintenance and replacement, as they presently do in the North. As levels of education and income rise, people will expect more services from government. Urban decay will set in and repeat the pattern of decay which occurred in the North. Urban crime will become more serious. In response, government will have to do more and spend more. Tax levels will increase to resemble those in Northern urban areas. Once these new regions are no longer viewed as underdeveloped areas, the pattern of federal expenditures will shift away from them to provide assistance to declining areas in the North.

Over the long term, this view suggests, the urban areas of all regions will *converge* (become more similar). All areas will be roughly similar in terms of their attractiveness to industry. The growth rates of the Southern and Western urban areas will slow, and those of the North will increase. What will emerge is a pattern of balanced growth across all regions of the country. Hence, the patterns of the 1960s and 1970s should be viewed as temporary trends and do not signify that the older urban areas will face steady decline at the expense of other regions of the country (Watkins and Perry, 1977).

Uneven Development

In contrast with the previous theory, several analysts have proposed that, rather than long-term convergence of regions, what we can probably expect is continued uneven development of regions. While many theorists have written on this topic, we have chosen two examples to explain related but somewhat different views of the uneven development process.

In their book about the Sunbelt, Alfred Watkins and David Perry (1977) contend that regions grow or decline for long periods of time because they have certain features that attract specific kinds of economic activities. These features give them long-term advantages over other regions. During each period, these advantaged areas are able to increase their advantages and attractiveness. At the same time, less advantaged areas face continued obstacles to economic growth. In relative terms, "the rich get richer, and the poor get poorer."

Watkins and Perry argue that these periods of regional advantage correspond to different phases in the development of the economy. Thus, during the period in which heavy industry and manufacturing were the dynamic forces in the American economy, the North Central and Northeast were the favored regions. During this time, these regions were able to create a number of *development barriers* which had two results. First, they operated to prevent other regions from developing the economic activities in which the advantaged areas specialized. The other regions remained underdeveloped in terms of the sorts of industry prevalent in the North Central and Northeast regions. Thus, the Sunbelt and Mountain states failed to develop much in the way of heavy industry and mass production facilities. Second, these barriers caused the advantaged areas to specialize more and more in what they did well. In the Midwest, for example, a complex, interlocking set of industries and production plants came into being all related to and dependent upon the production of automobiles. In that sense, the successful regions became "locked into" certain types of economic activity (Watkins and Perry, 1977).

However, the economy did not stay the same. In the last few decades, the economy entered a new phase in which a new group of dynamic industries appeared in such areas as military production, electronics, services, and leisure-oriented mass consumption. Watkins and Perry argue that the older industrial areas failed to develop in these new directions because they were trapped by the very barriers which protected their former advantages: the nature of their urban physical structures, transportation systems, labor force characteristics, and the like. Hence, it was the Sunbelt and Mountain states which were able to take advantage of the new economic opportunities. They were not yet committed to and specialized in the older activities and were in a position to be flexible and innovative (Watkins and Perry, 1977).

From this point of view, Sunbelt and Mountain state development cannot be viewed as a process which will result in the long-term economic convergence of regions. Rather this development is a reflection of a new phase in the economy, one whose activity is highly concentrated in the Sunbelt and Mountain regions. While acknowledging that some of the growth in the new areas was the result of runaway, low-wage plants from the old industrial areas, Watkins and Perry consider the primary source of their growth to be the emergence of new industries. Hence, rather than becoming just like the Northern industrial areas, the new regions are developing in new directions and specializing in a different set of economic activities. Like the older industrial areas before them, they are in a position to create a set of developmental barriers which will assure that they continue to enjoy their initial advantages. The older industrial areas will, as a result, continue to stagnate, as long as the economy remains in this phase of development (Watkins and Perry, 1977).

Neil Smith (1984), while agreeing with Watkins and Perry on the prospects for continued uneven growth and development of regions, does not necessarily hold to their view that regional economic advantages are such long-term phenomena. Rather, he views growth and decline as a "see-saw" pattern of investment and disinvestment based on the nature of investment and profit within capitalist, market economies.

Smith argues that, as economic conditions continually change, new opportunities for investment become more profitable. As changes occur, investors not only channel their money into new investments but they also destroy, abandon, or "write off" their old investments, those which are no longer as profitable as the new investments. To Smith, the destruction of the "old" investment is an integral part of the investment process, since it prepares the way for new, more profitable investment to follow (Smith, 1984).

Like Watkins and Perry, Smith sees these investment patterns as occurring in cycles and as being concentrated in certain geographical areas. He agrees that investment flows into certain regions based on whether the conditions in each region are beneficial for the industries that happen to be growing in that period. Unlike Watkins and Perry, however, Smith does not see relatively long-term advantages accruing to one area over another. He stresses the change and variability of the investment process, noting that development of an area changes the very conditions that made it profitable in the first place. Land prices, for example, may be very low in an area in which no one wants to invest. If investors are attracted by the low cost of land, their investment, the companies they build, and the improvements they make help raise the price of the land to the point where it is no longer viable for investment. Eventually, before it will attract new investment again, the land prices (and the value of the buildings on the land) will have to be reduced (Smith, 1984).

Thus, the up-and-down movement of geographic areas, the see-saw pattern of investment, is a necessary part of the investment process, according to Smith. This occurs not only between regions (such as Sunbelt and Frostbelt) but also within regions (such as growing suburbs and a declining central city within a single metropolitan area). Smith uses the same theory to explain gentrification by noting that normally only those areas that have been sufficiently run down (had their value destroyed) attract the new investment money necessary for gentrification (Smith, 1984).

Evaluation

Overall, the theories of uneven development seem to explain patterns of regional growth and decline better than the convergence theory. Convergence theorists look at long periods of time (e.g., 50 years or more) and large geographic areas (e.g., the entire South) and identify an overall trend. This makes it appear as if the direction of the trend is linear (unchanging) and that the region is homogeneous. By examining shorter periods of time and smaller geographic areas, however, we find more and more variation and complexity, as noted by the theorists of uneven development. The process of investment and disinvestment thus does not appear to be smooth or linear, but proceeds jerkily by fits and starts, through many cycles.

From the point of view of a single location, these economic cycles produce a see-saw of investment and disinvestment, growth and decline, as Smith (1984) has suggested. From an overall point of view, taking a snapshot of the nation at any one time, they produce a *mosaic* (Walker, 1978) of growing and declining areas: growing and declining regions, growing and declining metropolitan areas within a region, growing and declining communities within a single metropolitan area, and even growing and declining neighborhoods within a single city. Combining these two viewpoints, some observers have suggested the metaphor of a "moving mosaic" to describe most accurately the process of regional growth and decline.

Two examples help underline the importance of the changeable nature of economic conditions: Santa Clara County in California and New England.

Santa Clara County, now famous as "Silicon Valley," was a rural agricultural area in the 1950s. The area became attractive to the small firms characteristic of the newly-established semiconductor industry because of its rural setting, cheap prices, and close proximity to major research universities. Once the semiconductor industry's growth took off, however, wages, taxes, and land prices became far more expensive. In addition, Santa Clara County became highly urbanized, polluted, and congested. It thus lost its advantages both as a place to live and as a place to do business, at least for certain kinds of companies. It is somewhat ironic that small, new firms can no longer afford to locate there (and thus are causing the dispersal of the semiconductor industry to new areas). Rather, large, mature firms with their headquarters already in Silicon Valley can afford to remain, even as they expand outside of the area. Thus, the conditions that laid the groundwork for the initial growth of the semiconductor industry in that region no longer hold (Saxenian, 1983).

New England, which experienced an economic growth period in the 1980s, went through a period of severe recession and deindustrialization in the 1960s and 1970s. The two periods may be closely related, according to Harrison (1984). When New England was a highly industrialized region, it had a highly skilled, highly unionized, and well-paid labor force. Because of the long periods of unemployment that accompanied the gradual shutdown of the most highly unionized industries, the nature of the labor force slowly changed. By the end of the 1970s, workers tended to be younger, with less union affiliation, and less selective about working conditions. A higher proportion were women and minorities who had no history of industrial work but fit into the growing service sector. This "new" work force was an attractive advantage to employers thinking of locating in the region and helped draw industry, contributing to the growth of the 1980s (Harrison, 1984). When the boom began, it drove up prices of both labor and real estate, "overheating" the regional economy. Sudden downturns in manufacturing growth and construction in the mid-1980s, coupled with reduced defense spending, threw the region into severe recession once again (Moscovitch, 1990).

The experiences of both Santa Clara County and New England tend to make the observer skeptical of any permanent economic advantage to either area.

The Debate Over Growth

How important is population growth for an area? How much growth is enough? What should government do about encouraging or regulating growth? These questions are increasingly being asked not only by academic researchers but by public officials and residents in both growing and declining areas.

There is a certain logic within our economic system that says that economic growth is good—in fact, necessary. As a consequence (or sometimes a cause) of economic growth, population growth must therefore also be good. In fact, Logan and Molotch (1987) argue that cities in the United States were established precisely to promote economic growth. In their words, cities are "growth machines," generators of profits on investments. Typically, groups of business leaders, political officials, and media representatives (all of whom stand to benefit from growth in the area) promote growth. These groups publicize the benefits of growth (such as more jobs and increased tax revenues) while downplaying the negative effects of growth (such as pollution, increased need for public services, and so on). In Logan and Molotch's terms, these pro-growth groups remove the "value" aspect of growth—i.e., they make growth seem natural—by avoiding questions about who really benefits from economic growth or what problems it generates (Logan and Molotch, 1987).

Houston in the 1970s provides a textbook example of the problems that rapid, uncontrolled growth can produce. Houston was the fastest growing major city in the U.S. during the 1970s: the city added a thousand new residents every week. Unlike most Northern cities, Houston was able to "capture" this new growth by annexing its suburbs as fast as they grew. Consequently, the city government was able to maintain its tax base and keep taxes low. Yet, despite its booming economy, the problems began to accumulate. The highway system was overwhelmed by the increasing population. Rush-hour commuting times doubled between 1975 and 1980 as the expressway system got steadily more congested. The small, antiquated bus system was able to provide only minimal service to a small fraction of the total commuters. Built in a marshy area, with little control over land development practices, the city experienced increasingly severe problems with annual flooding. City services were stretched to the breaking point as the city annexed more population. Houston's understaffed, poorly trained police force was unable to cope with the increased demand for police protection, as the crime rate soared (*Newsweek*, 1/14/80; Feagin, 1988). The pro-growth forces in Houston, however, were able to circumvent attempts to control or manage growth. Indeed, the local "highly individualistic" business leaders joined to fight the tax increases necessary to provide even the most minimal levels of public services (Feagin, 1988).

In the 1980s, while Houston's population leveled off, Southern California experienced the growth problems that Houston had had during the previous decade: legendary traffic congestion, increased smog, overbuilding, strains on the sewer systems, and crowded schools. These problems have generated a political movement of "slow growth" advocates who are attempting to limit future development through legislation. The slow growth proposals calling for land use controls and developer-financed schools and sewers have been placed on the ballot in many Southern California locations. According to observers, local growth controls became the hottest political issue in California in the late 1980s (Salholz, 1988). As rapid uncontrolled growth spreads to other parts of the country, we will undoubtedly see more demands for increased governmental regulation and control on investors.

And what of the declining areas? Here the debate ranges not around whether growth is good or bad but around how it can be increased. Should government be involved? At what level? And what actions should it take? These are all questions about economic development policy.

There is currently no overall federal policy to aid declining areas. In response to the Frostbelt declines of the 1970s, a Presidential Commission suggested, bluntly, that rather than aiding declining areas, the government should simply help unemployed workers move to where the jobs were (President's Commission, 1981).

States and localities, however, are understandably reluctant to follow that suggestion and have put into operation a number of policies designed to stimulate growth. Many of these include incentives to businesses such as low-interest loans, free or subsidized land, and tax abatements (reductions on local or state taxes for a certain length of time). As states and cities compete to attract businesses, they tend to use the same incentives. One negative consequence of this competition is that businesses now expect these expensive incentives from local governments and play them off against each other to try to increase the amounts (Goodman, 1981).

Another direction that has been proposed for localities desiring increased investment and growth has been the *Enterprise Zone* policy. Based on the assumption that government regulation was a deterrent to business, economists within the Reagan administration suggested that certain areas be identified as Enterprise Zones and exempted from government regulations. The original proposal, which would have done away with minimum wage, environmental protection, and workers' health and safety regulations, proved too extreme to be viable. A modified version of Enterprise Zones, however, became law in at least half of the states during the 1980s. While retaining most government regulations, the revised Enterprise Zone legislation relieves businesses of a substantial proportion of their state and local taxes for a specified period of time. While these programs have had some success in attracting investors to targeted (often inner-city) areas, the actual number of jobs generated by this investment has often been quite modest, especially when compared to the price paid by the cities and states in tax losses (Bendick and Rasmussen, 1986).

Instead of spending money to attract investment (or sometimes in tandem with it), many local and state governments try to create what they call a "good business climate." These areas strive to be known as pro-business by implementing certain policies beneficial to business: low taxes, few regulations, and so on. In addition, a good business climate also often includes anti-union legislation, low social spending (for example on health and welfare programs) and an attempt to keep wages down. From the point of view of the work force, a good business climate is a bad labor climate, one in which workers have fewer rights and protections (Harrison, 1984).

Policy debates for both the growing and declining areas can be reduced to a central issue: the role of government in regulating the economy. On one side stand those who say that uncontrolled investment produces much human suffering, dislocation, and destruction. On the other side are those who say that capitalist economies function best without regulation and produce more good than bad. This is not a debate that can be solved decisively with data and scientific analysis, for it is ultimately also a question of ideology and of self-interest. One's position on these issues is almost certainly influenced by whether one is receiving the profits or the pain that result from regional economic growth and decline.

Main Points

1. During the 1970s, the Sunbelt and Mountain states experienced growth rates that were significantly higher than those of the rest of the country.
2. In the mid-1980s, Sunbelt growth slowed, and the growth rates of the East and West Coast states accelerated. Growth in the "heartland" or central states, both Northern and Southern, remained slow.
3. Because of the complex nature of population changes, caused by natural increase, migration, and immigration, it is difficult to predict exactly where growth will be concentrated in the 1990s.
4. Regional variation in growth rates is closely linked to variations in regional economic conditions. Industries of a certain type tend to be spatially concentrated; thus, their rapid growth or decline has a concentrated geographical impact.
5. Government spending has also had an impact on regional growth and decline. As political and federal spending priorities have changed, some states have benefited while others have been hurt.
6. Growth, decline, or change in the economy of a region affects the cities in that region. Many cities have lost their manufacturing functions; some have gained new economic roles as "world cities" while others have simply continued to decline in population and employment.
7. Two main theories have been developed to explain regional shifts. Convergence theory holds that, over the long run, the different regions will become more similar to each other. Uneven development theorists argue that growth and decline run in cycles, with decline being a necessary condition for future growth.
8. An important political and social issue currently being debated is the government's role in promoting and/or controlling growth.

Key Terms

Convergence Theory   The notion that the economic attractiveness of the various regions of the country will tend to equalize over time and that relative rates of economic growth will equalize as a result.

Exurban   Areas adjacent to but outside of the "official" metropolitan area of a large city in which economic activities and residents are tied to the metropolitan area.

Gentrification   The influx of upper-income residents into formerly lower-income neighborhoods.

Globalization of the Economy   The trend for businesses in different countries to become increasingly interdependent.

Heartland   The section of the United States that encompasses the Midwest and South Central states.

Net Migration   The total change in population in an area after the number of people who moved out is subtracted from the number who moved in.

Sunbelt   The group of states in the southern part of the country from Arizona in the West to the Carolinas in the East.

Theory of Uneven Development   The notion that different areas have different growth trajectories and that these are not linear, but result in periods of decline as well as periods of growth.

Suggested Reading

Bluestone, Barry and Bennett Harrison. 1982. *The Deindustrialization of America*. New York: Basic Books. An overview of the impact of industrial changes on regions of the United States and a discussion of policy choices.

Feagin, Joe. 1988. *Free Enterprise City: Houston in Political and Economic Perspective*. New Brunswick: Rutgers University. A case study of the rise of Houston as a major city, showing how both "free enterprise" and government actions contributed to its growth.

Endnotes

[1] According to *Population Today* (17, 9, 1989) the fastest growing states in 1987-1988 were Arizona, California, Delaware, Florida, Georgia, Hawaii, Maine, Maryland, Minnesota, Nevada, New Hampshire, North Carolina, Oregon, South Carolina, Virginia, Vermont, and Washington. Those with population losses were Alaska, Louisiana, Montana, North Dakota, Oklahoma, West Virginia, and Wyoming.

[2] *Population Today* (17, 9, 1989) shows that the states with the highest net migration in 1987-1988 were Arizona, California, Delaware, Florida, Georgia, Maine, Maryland, Minnesota, Nevada, New Hampshire, North Carolina, Oregon, South Carolina, Virginia, Vermont, and Washington. All other states had either very low net migration or out-migration.

[3] It is important to note that while the low wages, anti-union policies, and low taxes of the South are "advantages" from the point of view of businesses that locate there, they can be disadvantages for the working people of the region.

3

The Nature of Urban Life
The Myth of the City

Outline of Topics

I n the two previous chapters, we examined the factors that have shaped basic conditions in urban areas. We now turn to the central focus of this book: the specific problems faced by this urban society.

We are going to start with what is perhaps the most challenging and most important issue of all. Our concern in this chapter is with the general social, cultural, and social psychological consequences of urbanization. Underlying this concern with the consequences of urbanization is recognition of a fundamental fact about urbanization — the industrialization and urbanization process of the last few centuries represents one of the great transformations in history. Only a few other periods of human social development rank with industrialization and urbanization in terms of their effect on society and individuals. What happened, in the short span of several generations, is that the basic nature of society changed. A new kind of society emerged.

The question is: what sort of new society has emerged? What kind of basic social organization and culture has developed? How does it differ from the past? How have the lives of individuals changed as a result? Do these changes represent a problem or threat to individuals or society?

The attempt to answer these questions represents one of the major intellectual themes of the last two centuries. Few areas of intellectual effort have been untouched by the attempt to provide answers. Indeed, sociology can fairly be said to have developed partly in response to the concern with these issues in the 19th century. Almost all the major "founding fathers" of modern sociology addressed these issues in their work.

The result of all this intellectual effort has been the creation of a large body of literature on the nature of urban life. Yet the complexity of the issues involved has meant that no definitive, universally accepted answers have emerged. Rather, as more research is done, the answers appear to be even more complex and elusive than the early writers appreciated. Hence, our discussion here must be both incomplete and inconclusive: an introduction to the issues rather than a summary of accepted conclusions. But that often is the case with really important issues.

The Classical View of the Consequences of Urbanization

Despite tremendous differences in terminology and intellectual approach, it is possible to identify certain themes and conclusions in most earlier sociological theories of the consequences of urbanization.

For want of a better term, we will call this the *classical view*. To lump all these theorists together in one unified approach is, of course, to do real violence to the diversity and richness of these theories. However, it is the only possible way to present a brief summary of early thinking about the consequences of urbanization.

Understanding the classical view is important for several reasons. For one thing, this approach dominated sociological thinking about urban society until fairly recently. In addition, most more recent work represents a reaction to and criticism of the classical approach. You really cannot understand this work unless you understand the approach being criticized. Finally, most sociologists still accept some elements of the classical view (with strong qualifications). As a result, many issues raised by the classical approach remain active sources of concern and research in urban sociology.

The group of theorists included in the classical approach reads like a veritable *Who's Who* in sociological theory. One of the most famous of the early pioneers of the classical approach was Ferdinand Tönnies. Tönnies described the shift to urban society as a shift from *Gemeinschaft* (a community based on kinship ties) to *Gesellschaft* [a society based on common practical interests (Tönnies, 1957)]. One of the major figures of French sociology, Emile Durkheim, suggested a distinction between small communities held together by ties of "mechanical solidarity" and modern urban societies held together by ties of "organic solidarity." The former were ties based on shared ideas and common experiences. The latter were ties based on mutual dependence between people engaged in specialized tasks (Durkheim, 1947). At about the same time, the German sociologist Max Weber had suggested that the transition of urban society was a transition from "traditional" society to "rational" society (Bendix, 1960). An early social psychologist, Georg Simmel, suggested that urban life fundamentally affected the psychology of individuals (Wolff, 1950:409-424).

The themes suggested by these early European sociologists were picked up by the "Chicago School" of urban sociologists at the University of Chicago in the 1920s and 1930s. Most important in this group was a sociologist who was to shape sociological thinking about urban life for more than two decades, Louis Wirth. His (1938) summary article, "Urbanism As a Way of Life," represents the single most important statement of the classical view in sociology in the United States (Wirth, 1938:1-24). Soon afterward, anthropologist Robert Redfield further amplified the classical view's distinction between urban societies and previous societies by suggesting two general types of society: "folk" and "urban" (Redfield, 1947:293-308). More recently, "structural functionalist" theorists (who dominated sociological theory in the 1950s and 1960s) such as Talcott Parsons (Parsons, 1969) and Neil Smelser (Smelser, 1967) incorporated many elements of the classical view into their analyses of industrialization and modernization.

At the heart of the basic perspective on urbanization shared by these theorists was the feeling that industrialization and urbanization were extraordinarily disruptive forces. They saw the emergence of urban society as a process in which a stable society of rural communities was shattered by the requirements of industrial production and the conditions of urban life. The basic characteristics of society—the nature of its social organization and culture—were transformed. At the level of individual social life, this was seen as causing major changes in the nature of people's social relationships. In turn, these changes were seen as creating major problems for individuals and society: social disorganization, psychological stress, anomie, and alienation. Figure 3.1 summarizes this basic model. We now turn to an examination of each of its elements.

Changes in Social Organization

Scale of Social Units

At the most basic level, classical theorists saw the transition from rural to urban society as a change in the size of the organizations and communities in which individuals participate. Rural society was characterized as one in which the individual's most important social ties were with small-scale social units: family, kin, and village. Most people lived out their lives within the confines of a small community of a few hundred people in which everybody knew everybody else. The basic unit of economic production was the family and kin group. Contact and involvement with what larger units existed (e.g., national government, centralized religious organizations) was limited, infrequent, and viewed with suspicion.

In contrast, the classical theorists pointed to the dominance of large-scale social units in modern urban society. People live in "communities" of thousands or millions of people, most of whom they do not know personally. They are aware of and their lives are constantly affected by events in the larger society. Most activities are carried out by very large, often society-wide, organizations: massive corporations and government agencies. Very importantly, people work in large organizations away from home and kin, rather than in small, kin-based work groups.

Social Complexity

Classical theorists characterized rural society as relatively simple in terms of its social organization. A major source of this simplicity was

Figure 3.1 **Basic Model of the Classical View of Urbanization**

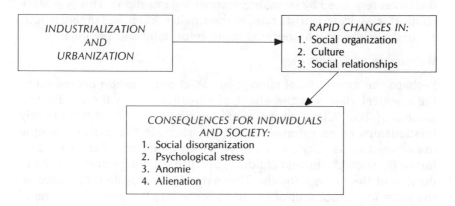

the nature of the division of labor (the division of tasks into separate work roles). Rural society was seen as having a simple division of labor. The basic tasks in rural society were such things as food production, handicraft manufacturing, and family service activities. Every family did most of these things themselves. There was only limited specialization of activities between families. Most people were engaged in agriculture, with only a few people in specialized trades or occupations. The specialization of roles which did exist consisted primarily of specialization within the kinship group based on age, sex, and family relationship.

On the other hand, urban society was characterized by classical theorists as one in which each member engages in some highly specialized task. The engineer designs, the assembly-line worker screws on door handles, and the sales representative sells the finished product. Hence, most activities involve the cooperation of large numbers of specialists who depend on each other. This is called a *complex division of labor*.

Bureaucratization

Beginning with Max Weber, a major theme of the classical view was that urban society is also a bureaucratic society. Very simply, large and complex organizations require a way to coordinate the activities of their members so that everyone in the organization does what is needed, when it is needed. Bureaucracy arose, according to the classical view, as a means to assure the coordination of the activities of members of large organizations. Centralized authority, formal rules and procedures, objective standards of evaluation, and the like make coordination of large numbers of specialists possible.

It also means that people work in, have services provided by, and have their lives regulated by large, impersonal organizations. This is in stark contrast, classical theorists said, to the smaller, kin-based organizations of rural society which operated more informally and personally.

Weakening of Kinship Ties

Perhaps the most critical change in social organization according to the classical view was the effect of urbanization on the family and kinship system. Classical theorists described traditional rural family relationships as an extended kinship system. In this system, people maintained close social ties not just with members of their nuclear family (husband, wife, and children) but also with large numbers of kin outside of the nuclear family. This extended kin system operated as the most important unit of social cooperation, the primary means of "social control" (the maintenance of conformity), and the central source of material and emotional security. Above all else, it was the basic unit of economic production. Kinship relationships were the basis of economic cooperation. In return for this cooperation, the family took care of most of the basic needs of its members: the care and training of children, assistance in times of sickness or need, recreational activities, care of the elderly, physical protection, work opportunities, all basic material needs, emotional support, and intimacy. Because family members were so dependent on their family relationships, the family had tremendous power over its members. Most aspects of an individual's life were regulated by obligations to kin. In a sense, one could not function or survive outside the web of one's kinship relationships. Hence, the individual's desires were subordinate to those of his or her kin. This control over family members was reflected in well-defined rules regulating behavior between kin, and there was a system of authority within the family in which the elder males made decisions binding on the rest of the family members. Thus, according to classical theorists, the family was the central institution of society and regulated most of the important aspects of community life.

All this changed, claimed these theorists, with industrialization and urbanization. The extended kinship system was shattered. It lost its function as a system of economic cooperation. People went to work as individuals in places away from their homes and kin. Government took over most of the responsibility for the education, protection, and basic security of individuals. As a result, the family lost its power over individuals: they were no longer dependent upon their extended family for most of their practical material needs. The move to the city also separated people geographically from their kin. Most of what was left of family relationships was concentrated in the nuclear family. Children still had to be cared for and socialized. In the absence of the assistance of extended kin, this burden fell more heavily on the nuclear family — especially the mother. Lacking the emotional support of extended kin and in the face of what classical theorists felt was the impersonality of urban life, nuclear family members were also much more dependent than before on each other for emotional intimacy. Intense emotional ties between parents and children, and an emphasis on romantic love between spouses, replaced the more pragmatic ties which bound family members together in the past. Freedom from economic dependence on the family, weak kin ties, weakening traditional morals, and the increased emotional intensity in family relationships made the isolated nuclear family of the city much less stable than the rural extended family. The nuclear family was an "emotional pressure cooker" based on the unstable ties of romantic love. Divorce, family conflict, and general family instability were the result, said classical theorists.

Cultural Changes

Secularization and Rationality

The classical view of rural communities before industrialization was one in which the community was stabilized by a strongly held set of cultural beliefs and values. They characterized this culture as one which emphasized the sacred and traditional. By an emphasis on the "sacred," they meant that rules of behavior and methods of doing things were justified and explained by reference to religious beliefs. The reasons for death, when to plant corn, the nature of the obligations between parents and children, and most other aspects of social life were based on religious conceptions of morality and the nature of reality. Moreover, it was seen as a stable belief system which was all the more influential because of its stability. Cultural beliefs and ways of life changed slowly and were revered partly because of this. The stable belief system provided people with a sense of continuity. Tradition represented security: change represented a threat.

Industrialization and urbanization brought in their wake (or, according to Weber, were partly caused by) a shift in cultural orientation. The cultural emphasis shifted to secular rationality. Religious explanations and justifications were replaced by those based on science, empirical observation, logic, and systematic calculation. Beliefs were no longer accepted simply because they were divinely inspired or had "always" been believed true. Rather, they were accepted because they could be "proved" to be true by reason and observation.

Accompanying this change was a growing instability in belief systems.

Today's truth could become tomorrow's falsehood—and it frequently did, as rapid advances occurred in science and technology. Traditional beliefs and the values supported by those beliefs were called into question. Instead of enjoying the continuity and security provided by tradition, individuals had to learn to adjust to a cultural world in constant change, where nothing was certain.

Heterogeneity and Organic Solidarity

According to most classical theorists, traditional rural communities were characterized by a high level of agreement among their members in terms of their cultural values and beliefs. Most people believed the same things, shared the same values, and perceived the world in the same way. This cultural homogeneity was a result of shared experiences, limited exposure to the "outside world," the religious basis of most cultural beliefs and values, and the strong hold of tradition. To disagree with the dominant beliefs and values of the community was to call into question something ordained by God, confirmed by everything people in the community had experienced, and sanctified by long tradition. Conformity was easy to monitor because the community was small: everyone knew everyone else's business. Hence, there were powerful pressures for the maintenance of cultural conformity and little tolerance for nonconformity. In turn, cultural homogeneity was a major source of community unity and prevented deviant behavior. In the terms used by Durkheim, cultural homogeneity maintained community solidarity (identification with and commitment to the community). Durkheim called this kind of community unit *mechanical solidarity*.

Durkheim, and the theorists who followed him, contrasted the high level of cultural agreement in the traditional community to the relative disunity of urban society. In the classical view, the tremendous diversity of urban society in terms of social classes, ethnic groups, religions, occupations, and the like assures that the cultural beliefs and values of urban society will display heterogeneity: great diversity and the lack of general consensus. As a result, argued Durkheim, cultural agreement is not as effective as a source of unity and a means of maintaining conformity. What holds society together then? Durkheim argued that the complex division of labor makes everyone dependent on everyone else for the things they need. People have to exchange or trade the things they make or do for the other things they need produced by others. The baker provides the butcher with bread in return for meat. In this sense, the "glue" that holds society together is the division of labor. What people agree on in urban society are not specific beliefs and values (they have to tolerate disagreement) but rules which regulate the process of exchange. Durkheim called this kind of community unity *organic solidarity*.

Changes in Social Relationships

Impersonality

In the classical view of the small community, social relationships were portrayed as close, emotional, intense, and personal. Everyone knew everyone else, and people interacted with each other based on this very complete knowledge of one another. In short, the majority of relationships were "primary" relationships based on long-term friendship and kinship ties.

In the classical view, this state of affairs in the small community contrasts sharply with the nature of most social relationships in urban society. According to classical theorists, it is simply impossible to spend the time to get to know most other people very well: the urban dweller interacts with too many different people. Consequently, people have to deal with one another based on their particular roles in the social situation (e.g., customer and clerk) following the general social rules deemed appropriate for that situation. There can be little concern about the personal characteristics of these role occupants. All people in a particular role are treated the same. Interaction is superficial, unemotional, and follows a set pattern. People are cold and calculating in their relationships: they interact with one another in order to achieve some specific goal. In short, urban social relationships are supposedly mostly impersonal and occur within the context of "secondary" groups, such as large organizations or small "task groups."

Segmental Social Relationships

Classical theorists portrayed rural community life as a "seamless web" in which the same individuals interacted with one another in different social contexts. The people who worked together were related by kinship, engaged in leisure time activities together, lived in the same community, and participated in its affairs. These were "total" social relationships. This made for intense personal relationships in which people got to know most aspects of each other's personalities. It also made it very difficult to hide deviant behavior since each person knew so much about all the others. And it created a "sense of community."

In contrast, urban dwellers were portrayed as having "segmental" social relationships. Each person interacts with a different set of people in each social situation. The people you work with are not the same people who live in your neighborhood or with whom you spend your leisure time. This contributes to the superficiality and impersonality of urban social relationships and weakens the sense of common identity among urban dwellers. Thus, the urban social world was viewed by classical theorists as a set of compartments in which most of the people in one compartment (social situation) do not have any contact with people in the other compartments. Social life is "fragmented."

Consequences for Individuals and Society

Classical theorists considered these changes in social organization, culture, and social relationships important because of the consequences they had for individuals and society. Classical theorists argued that the sort of society which had emerged was fundamentally and dangerously flawed. In their view, the problem of urban society was the nature of the society itself and what it did to the people living in cities.

The classical theorists, of course, did not deny that there were some positive consequences of urbanization. They acknowledged that the weakening of kin ties, the cultural diversity, the spirit of rational inquiry, and the quest for innovation created a climate of freedom and tolerance. Individuals were much freer to decide what to believe, what occupations to pursue, how to spend their leisure time, and what style of life to adopt. This freedom, they conceded, was augmented by improved material conditions for most people and greater opportunity for upward social mobility.

The problem, in the eyes of the classical theorists, was that these gains had been purchased at a high price. They argued that the rural community had provided people with a stable, well-organized social environment. Life was predictable and the rules of behavior clear. People knew what their social obligations were. There was a stable set of values and beliefs by which to set one's life goals and be evaluated by others. Close personal ties with others provided emotional security and a sense of identity and personal worth.

In contrast, the classical theorists argued, urban society was a disorganized and unstable social environment. The consequences for individuals were psychological stress, anomie, and alienation. The consequence for society was social disorganization.

Social Disorganization

The fundamental problem with urban society in the classical view was that the very conditions which brought freedom to the individual had "atomized" and "disorganized" society.

The close primary ties provided by the extended kinship system had decayed. This meant that the emotional support, intimacy, and security which these ties had provided were lacking in most of the social relationships experienced by urban dwellers. In their place, classical theorists saw only social relationships which were transitory, calculating, and impersonal. The nuclear family was also seen as being isolated from the support of extended kin in times of trouble or need. In addition, weakening of kin ties was viewed as having weakened a formerly important system of social control. Individuals no longer had to worry about conforming to the expectations of their kin.

These changes in kinship relationships were viewed as a problem because the new ways of performing the activities formerly performed by the extended family were considered to be only partially successful. The nuclear family tried to provide the missing emotional closeness. The result, said classical theorists, was to make family relationships too intense and increase family instability. Government agencies tried to provide economic and social assistance to families and individuals in trouble. However, many needs remained unmet. A bureaucratic system of criminal justice attempted to replace the informal social control of the family and community with formal social controls composed of laws, courts, and prisons. Still, urban communities were beset by a high crime rate. In short, the decline of the family had left a social vacuum which urban society had yet to fill adequately.

Cultural heterogeneity was also seen as a force creating social disorganization. Rapidly changing and frequently conflicting values resulted in the loss of clear, consistent guidelines for behavior. Individuals were no longer certain what constituted acceptable behavior or appropriate life goals.

Further, classical theorists claimed that the individual no longer participated in a web of social relationships which they saw as constituting a "community." The pattern of assisting one's neighbors, informal community decisionmaking, joint recreational activities, and the intimate knowledge of and concern for one's neighbors which supposedly characterized the small rural community was considered lacking in urban neighborhoods. In the classical view, the members of each nuclear family tried to care for themselves and were relatively unconcerned about the families living around them. People did not "get involved," and they "minded their own business." This further weakened social control and meant that families needing assistance either had to rely on themselves or turn to the government for help.

Psychological Stress

In the classical view, the psychological consequences of this sort of urban social environment were primarily negative. For instance, Georg Simmel in his famous article, "Metropolis and Mental Life," (Wolff, 1950) argued that the constantly changing social environment, the tremendous diversity of social experiences, and the large number of superficial, transitory social relationships in urban society caused nervous "overstimulation." As a defense against this overstimulation, Simmel believed that urban dwellers learned to be emotionally cold and calculating in their relationships with others. They avoided overstimulation, in addition, by simply learning not to respond to a large number of stimuli in the environment.

A more contemporary formulation similar to Simmel's analysis has been suggested by Stanley Milgram (Milgram, 1970:1461-68). Milgram contended if people tried to become emotionally involved with all those with whom they had contact, the emotional demands of so many relationships would be more than they could handle. The result would be "emotional overload." As a strategy to avoid overload, Milgram argued that people develop interpersonal techniques which limit the amount of time and emotional involvement they devote to most social relationships. At the extreme, this may involve completely ignoring others, even when they are in distress and need assistance.

Perhaps the most extreme version of this view of urban life is that associated with the work of John B. Calhoun on the effect of high density living (Calhoun, 1960:139-148). Studying the behavior of overcrowded rat populations, Calhoun observed that the rats developed symptoms of extreme pathological behavior as population density increased. (Crowded rats tended, for example, to neglect their young, practice cannibalism, or become totally passive.) A number of subsequent observers have suggested that areas of very high densities in cities (e.g., slums) have the same kind of pathological effects on human beings (Hartley, 1972:76).

Anomie

Emile Durkheim coined the term *anomie* (Durkheim, 1951) to refer to another psychological state which classical theorists also believed to be associated with urban social conditions. Anomie is a feeling of "normlessness." As a result of social disorganization and the cultural changes discussed in this section, the individual feels that there are no clear rules (norms) and values by which to evaluate his or her behavior. This uncertainty in regard to what constitutes socially and morally approved behavior creates feelings of anxiety and depression.

Alienation

Frequently referred to in conjunction with anomie, alienation was also viewed by classical theorists as a common response to urban life. The term has been defined in a number of different ways by various writers. For our purposes, a relatively simple definition will suffice to convey the general nature of the concept. Very simply, alienation refers to feelings of: (1) powerlessness, (2) meaninglessness, and (3) social isolation. Individuals have the feeling that they have no control over their lives or a particular social environment (such as work). Power is seen to be in the hands of distant or even unknown people and impersonal forces. Work and other daily activities are seen as meaningless routines with no clear purpose or ultimate justification to make them worthwhile. The person feels cut off from the people around her or him. Others are seen as uncaring or untrustworthy.

Alienation of various types was seen as an outgrowth of a number of conditions in urban society. For some theorists, the key problem was the bureaucratic nature of urban society. Most workers work in large, impersonal bureaucratic organizations in which power is centralized in the hands of distant managers. Work is controlled by rigid rules and frequently involves boring, routine tasks. Similarly, most other activities are bureaucratically controlled: education, public safety, government, etc. Relationships, both in these organizations and in the city's neighborhoods, are superficial and impersonal. Other theorists argued that rationality, materialism, science, and technology create feelings of spiritual emptiness and meaninglessness. Still others blamed weak family ties for an increase in feelings of social isolation.

Behavioral Responses

The end result of social disorganization, psychological stress, anomie, and alienation is, according to classical theory, a severe problem for individuals who, in turn, create problems for society. The stressed, anomic, and alienated urbanite is likely to display any number of pathological responses: chronic depression, increased likelihood of committing suicide, increased risk of mental illness, cynicism and distrust in personal relationships, apathy and withdrawal from community and political affairs, alcoholism and drug addiction, aggression, criminality, and so on. The end result is that urban society is beset by a number of severe social problems: crime, other forms of deviant behavior, mental illness, broken families, low social participation, and political apathy.

Classical Theory: A Summary

Thus, classical theory, with its emphasis on the disruptive and disorganizing effects of the process of urbanization, paints a primarily negative picture of urban life. These theorists conceded that urbanization was accompanied by improved material conditions, greater intellectual rationality, and more freedom. But they saw these benefits from urbanization and industrialization as having been counterbalanced by costs to individuals and society. And they looked at the rural past almost with nostalgia: rural life, for all its poverty and ignorance, was portrayed as a stable, emotionally close community of strong family ties in which people had a sense of social place, continuity, personal importance, and meaning to their lives. Table 3.1 summarizes what has just been discussed.

Table 3.1

The Differences Between Rural and Urban Society According to Classical Theories

RURAL SOCIETY	URBAN SOCIETY
Social Organization:	
Small Social Units	Large Social Units
Simple Social Organization	Complex Social Organization
Kin-Based Informal Organization	Bureaucratic Organizatons
Strong Extended Kinship System	Weak, Unstable Nuclear Family
Culture:	
Sacred and Traditional	Secular and Rational
Homogeneity and Mechanical Solidarity	Heterogeneity and Organic Solidarity
Social Relationships:	
Personal, Emotionally-Based ("primary ties")	Impersonal ("secondary ties")
Total	Segmental
Consequences for Individuals and Society:	
Society Well-Organized	Social Disorganization
Psychological Security	Psychological Stress
Little Anomie	High Anomie
Little Alienation	High Alienation

The Classical View Reconsidered

The classical view shaped sociological thinking about urban society during the first half of the 20th century. Part of its persistence was due, no doubt, to the fact that it was consistent with popular perceptions of urban life. (More about that in a moment.) Yet, even at the height of its theoretical popularity, there were nagging doubts about the accuracy of the classical view's description of urban life. As more and more research evidence accumulated, those doubts developed into systematic criticisms of the classical view.

The basic thrust of most of these criticisms is not that the classical view was totally wrong. Many (but not all) of the changes in social organization and culture described by classical theories appear to be rough approximations of the actual changes which occurred, at least in Western societies. Rather, the heart of the criticism of classical theory revolves around the feeling that: (1) the picture of urban (and rural) life presented is incomplete, and (2) the classical view exaggerates the negative consequences of urban life.

These conclusions are based on a number of specific criticisms of the classical view, which we will briefly examine.

The Myth of the Idyllic Rural Past and the Anti-Urban Bias

Classical theory was based on a comparison between rural and urban society. In making that comparison, the classical theorists painted what we now realize to be an unrealistically rosy picture of life in the small, rural community. The result is that urban society looked bad in comparison. In fact, the classical view ignored or de-emphasized many of the problems of the rural community as well as presenting what we now know to be an idealized view of rural family life and rural social relationships.

In idealizing rural society, sociologists like Louis Wirth were really continuing in a cultural and intellectual tradition which has deep and enduring roots in American society. It is a tradition which stretches from Thomas Jefferson to contemporary television commercials. The most common label given this tradition is the *anti-urban bias*.

North Americans have traditionally felt a deep distrust of cities. Cities were seen as cold, impersonal places in which loneliness, crime, and immorality ran rampant. In contrast, the small community was seen as the repository of all virtues: honesty, strong family ties, neighborliness, hard work, and thrift (White and White, 1962). Even now, with three-fourths of the population living in urban areas, most people in this country think that small communities are better places to live and raise families (Perrin, 1978).

In fact, these beliefs are based on a biased, nostalgic view of rural life. Rural society had its problems too.

Living Conditions

Living conditions in pre-industrial communities were extremely harsh by modern standards. Most of the population worked at often brutally hard manual tasks and obtained a level of living which barely met their basic needs. The risk of fatal disease (especially for young children) was very high, and average life expectancy was low. The stereotype of the spacious white farmhouse neglects the large proportion of the rural population which lived in cabins, shacks, and even sod houses. By modern standards, a large percentage of the population lived under conditions of moderate to severe poverty.

Exploitation and Conflict

The idealized view of rural life has tended to emphasize the degree of harmony and cooperation in the rural community. But there was also a darker side to rural life. Rural life also had its share of "blood feuds," lynchings, slave abuse, and witch trials. The common image of the independent prosperous family farm neglects the large portion of the rural population in the United States who were exploited as bare subsistence tenant farmers, sharecroppers, migrant laborers, and just plain slaves. Even the farmer who owned his own land often lived in almost perpetual debt to town merchants and bankers. (The problem of indebtedness was a recurrent source of rural discontent during the 19th century in the United States.)

The Myth of the Rural Family

Perhaps no myth has died harder (even among sociologists) than the myth of the rural extended family system. The rural family system in North America (and Europe) was never as effective, stable, or close-knit as classical theorists seemed to believe. All the evidence is not in yet: this has been an area of especially active research in the last decade, and considerable debate continues between scholars studying the history of the family. However, enough evidence is in to question the description of the family presented by classical theorists.

For instance, the proportion of "broken" families was almost as high in the 19th century as it is now. The rate of *marital dissolution* (loss of one spouse from the family) has stayed almost constant for a century. In the 19th century, the usual cause was the death of one spouse (Davis, 1975). (Now, the primary cause is divorce, but the result is the same.) Hence, children were almost as likely as now to grow up with one of their original parents absent for part of their childhood.

There is also considerable doubt about the actual strength of extended kin ties in the past. Many nuclear families were geographically separated from their kin as a result of the process of westward settlement. Even when they were not, the extent of closeness and cooperation between kin was probably not as great as the classical theorists thought. Indeed, it is highly questionable that the majority of families could actually be characterized as extended kinship systems. Some have suggested that a better term for what existed is the *modified extended family*. In this view, the basic unit of cooperation and emotional commitment was the nuclear family. However, that family also maintained significant, but less close, contacts with other kin (Gist and Fava, 1974:380). Other observers have argued the family system was basically a nuclear one, with the extent of contact with extended kin highly variable (Shorter, 1975).

Nor should we forget the status and treatment of women and children in the past. This was certainly one of the less attractive features of traditional family life. Children were often viewed simply as a source of labor to be exploited and abused. Women were burdened by heavy work obligations and frequent pregnancies (six to eight in the early 19th century). At the same time, their social and legal status was clearly that of second-class citizens, and male domination characterized both society and the family.

Parochialism and Intolerance

Classical theorists often tended to downplay how truly repressive the small community could be toward the expression of individuality. There was an extremely narrow range of acceptable behaviors and beliefs. Superstition and fear of innovation, suspicion of "outsiders," contempt and lack of understanding of intellectual endeavor, and the notion that anything different was necessarily wrong, all are frequently cited as characteristics of belief systems in the traditional rural community (Friedman, 1953:218-231). Treatment of those who failed to conform could be brutal and vicious.

The Myth of Urban Social Disorganization

Just as classical theorists tended to romanticize the small community, they exaggerated the degree to which urban society was disorganized and destructive of close personal ties between individuals. Several decades of research on urban social life reveal that urban society displays much less social disorganization than classical theorists thought. The same research reveals that individuals have worked out a number of strategies to maintain close personal ties with others.

Persistence of Kin Ties

There is substantial evidence that the urban family is not a weak, isolated nuclear one. Rather, the dominant tendency appears to be maintenance of something approximating a modified extended family system. This is not to say that family relationships are the same as in the past. Family members generally do not work together, but leave each other to go to separate jobs. Individuals are less compelled to depend on family for certain services and forms of assistance. Women are in a much better position to function in society independent of their family relationships. Children spend less time around their parents and live part of their lives in a separate social world of school and peer groups. In this sense, the family has less power over individuals because they are less dependent on it (Goode, 1963).

However, most people chose to maintain fairly strong emotional ties with their kin, spend leisure time with kin, and offer assistance to kin in time of need. And, it is worth noting, modern transportation and communication make this possible even for kin who are geographically distant from one another. A whole series of studies indicate that a majority of urban dwellers have regular and frequent contact with their kin. Very importantly, this contact is not limited to emotional ties and social occasions. Extended kin still remain an important source of services and assistance. Child care for a working mother, financial help, care of elderly parents, and the like are all important aspects of contemporary kinship relationships. The result is that both the nuclear family and extended kin remain important sources of emotional support and practical assistance under urban conditions (Litwak, 1965; Sussman and Burchinal, 1962:231-240; Feagin, 1968:660-665; Adams, 1968; Fried, 1973; Fischer, 1982:83-84).

Some qualifications are in order, however. First, there appears to be considerable variation in the strength of kin ties in modern families. Some urban families maintain close relations and others do not. These differences reflect, in part, the particular preferences of individual families. In addition, research suggests that there are differences in kinship relationships based on such things as social class, ethnicity, religion, and region of the country. For instance, kin ties appear to be especially important in working-class, Catholic, "ethnic" neighborhoods (Gans, 1962; Fried, 1973). Second, nothing in what has been said should be construed to mean that urban families do not have problems. They do. Moreover, many of these problems can be traced to the conditions of modern life. The point being made here is that there is nothing uniquely disorganized about urban families which makes them fundamentally "weaker" than those of the past. Urbanization does not necessarily cause the family to break down.

Neighboring and Neighborhoods

Contrary to the classical view, another important source of informal and personal social relationships is the neighborhood. At the most casual level, this involves simple "neighboring." People know each other, provide modest mutual assistance, and may get together socially. In other urban neighborhoods, interaction may be more intense and/or organized. People may have a strong sense of identification with their neighborhood and select a large proportion of their friends from the neighborhood. Many neighborhoods are extensively organized in terms of community groups, social clubs, political organizations, and the like.

How much neighborhood interaction and organization exist varies from a lot to none at all. At one extreme, Jacquelin Zito (Zito, 1974: 243-263) describes a high-rise apartment complex with a large proportion of middle-class working couples in which there is very limited neighboring. At the other extreme, Herbert Gans' classic 1955 study of the West End of Boston describes a lower-class Italian neighborhood which is an extremely well-organized community, with intense and extensive social relationships (Gans, 1962). Similarly, Gerald Suttles found very extensive social organizations within a Chicago slum (Suttles, 1968). Suttles's findings are especially significant because the classical theorists of the Chicago School argued that urban social disorganization would be worst among the urban poor (Zorbaugh, 1929).

How extensive neighborhood ties become in any given neighborhood appears to depend on a number of factors. Physical arrangement can make neighboring easier or harder. In Boston's West End, Gans found that the close-together houses and apartments facing the street made the street the focus of social life in the summer. People sat out on their front porches and steps and it was easy to see each other, talk to one another, and visit informally (Gans, 1962). One recent summary of the research on neighboring suggests that neighboring generally increases as socioeconomic status decreases and proximity (physical closeness), homogeneity of the residents (social similarity), and dependency (need for assistance from others) increase (Wallace, 1980:254-66). Other specific factors which have been mentioned include ethnicity, religion, occupation, family and kinship ties, leisure styles, and patterns of child rearing (Wilson and Schulz, 1978:159-61).

The details of neighborhood research do not have to concern us here, however. The important point is to recognize that, for many people, ties with neighbors are an available source of personal, even intimate, social relationships. Urbanization does not necessarily result in disorganized neighborhoods, even among the poor.

Work-Based Ties

Urban residents may not choose to have close ties with their kin, and they may not have close relationships with their neighbors. That still does not mean that they are isolated in the urban social environment. Work-based social relationships provide yet another means for the urbanite to establish close personal ties with others.

Much has been made of the supposed isolating and alienating effect of work in large-scale, bureaucratically administered organizations. And to be sure, research on work settings suggests that some kinds of modern work are alienating. Workers in certain kinds of mass production industries, where work is unskilled, repetitive, and closely supervised, are likely to experience work alienation (Blauner, 1964). However, a large proportion of the jobs available in urban society are not of that sort. Moreover, even in those relatively alienating work settings, almost a half century of sociological research suggests that workers often develop friendship ties with their coworkers. From the classic Hawthorne Study (Roethlisberger and Dickson, 1939) onward, industrial sociologists have found extensive networks of formal social relationships in most kinds of work organizations.

In some cases, work relationships are limited to the work setting. In other cases, work relationships form an important basis for establishing friendship relationships outside of work. In either case, these relationships again call into question the image of the urban dweller as someone who operates in a primarily impersonal social environment outside of his or her nuclear family relationships.

Membership in Voluntary Organizations

A final source of personal social relationships in an urban setting is widespread membership in various kinds of voluntary organizations. These are formally organized groups which exist to accomplish some specific goal and in which participation is optional on the part of the individual. Examples of such organizations range from the PTA, the Moose Lodge, and the local historical society to political party organizations, taxpayer groups, and professional organizations (like the American Medical Association). Traditionally, classical theorists (who also acknowledged their prevalence in urban society) viewed these groups as an attempt to compensate for the loss of close, primary ties in urban society and emphasized the formal, impersonal nature of these organizations. (People were seen as replacing "primary" ties with "secondary" ties.) More recently, voluntary group participation has come to be viewed as yet another strategy by which urban dwellers actually cultivate informal, personal ties. They participate in the organization not just because they support its formal goal, but because it provides opportunities to develop friendships and participate in social activities (Fischer, 1976:106-117).

As with other sources of close personal ties, different people rely on participation in voluntary associations to different degrees. Most studies suggest that such participation varies with social class: lower-class individuals are much less likely to join voluntary organizations than are middle- and upper-class individuals. Whites and males are more likely to participate than blacks or women. Still, the total involvement in voluntary organizations is impressive. Estimates of overall participation suggest that over half the population participates in voluntary organizations to some degree (Barber, 1957:180-181; Olsen, 1970:682-697; Hyman, 1971:191-206).

The Myth of Urban Stress, Anomie, and Alienation

Attempts to demonstrate that urban life is uniquely stressful, anomic, or alienating have also resulted in findings which are, at best, ambiguous.

The research on this issue has encountered a number of problems. The attempt to assess the extent of such things as urban stress and alienation has been complicated by serious problems of definition and measurement. In addition, the classical view also implies an historical comparison which is hard to establish: the claim of the classical view is that people were happier and psychologically better off in the past. There simply is no direct way to test that claim now, after the fact. Certainly, just as strong an argument can be made that the opposite is the case. One intriguing survey compared levels of "happiness" and "life satisfaction" (with such things as work and family life) between advanced industrial societies and less technologically advanced societies. The results (based on samples in a total of seventy nations) indicated that people in urban industrial societies reported much higher levels of happiness and life satisfaction (Gallup, 1976-77:465-467).

Actual attempts to measure anomie and alienation have yielded findings which are complex and very hard to interpret. As a result, simple generalizations are difficult to make. Certainly, significant minorities of the population seem to display some sorts of alienation and anomie. One urban sociologist has suggested the range of 10 to 20 percent of the population as an estimate of the proportion of people who are socially isolated and estimates that one-third of the population displays some sort of alienation (Butler, 1977:28). However, even if those estimates are remotely close to the truth, it suggests that the majority of the population is not isolated and alienated. Moreover, interpreting the sources of these feelings is even more hazardous. Melvin Seeman, for one, points out that there are several different kinds of alienation which appear to have different sources and are not closely related to one another. In short, people who experience one kind of alienation do not necessarily experience other kinds (Seeman, 1958:783-791). Consequently, sweeping statements about the generally alienating or anomic nature of urban society must be treated as, at best, gross oversimplifications of an extremely complex issue. Indeed, a number of recent evaluations of the available evidence reject the whole notion of a distinctively "urban" alienation and point to the continuing strength of close, personal social relationships. For example, recent research by Claude Fischer indicates that it is true that urban dwellers do feel untrusting toward and isolated from strangers and people unlike themselves. However, Fischer's findings suggest that these feelings do not result in general feelings of alienation because people maintain close, trusting ties with work associates, kin, and neighbors (Fischer, 1976; Kasarda and Janowitz, 1974: 328-339; Berry, 1973; Fischer, 1981:306-316; Fried, 1969:151-171).

The available evidence also indicates that the general indictment of urban life as leading to undue stress and pathological behavior because of urban "crowding" needs to be heavily qualified and reformulated (Baldassare, 1978; Fischer, Baldassare and Ofshe, 1975:406-418). The results strongly suggest that early statements of the "dangers" of living in high-density urban communities both exaggerated and misidentified the nature of the problem.

For one thing, it has proven necessary to distinguish between crowding and density. Density refers to general neighborhood or community conditions in terms of the number of people occupying a given land area (e.g., the number of people per square mile). Crowding refers to conditions within individual households: it is a measure of how many people share a given housing unit of a particular size and/or number of rooms.

Most of the research on the effect of general density has found that high densities have either no negative or only modest negative effects on behavior or mental health (Galle and Gove, 1978:95-132). Simply living in the higher density conditions of cities in comparison to rural areas does not seem to be a significant source of problems for human beings. It is also worth noting that, in any event, densities in urban areas in the United States have generally been declining very significantly during this century (see Chapters 1 and 2).

Research on residential crowding has yielded somewhat more mixed results. A number of researchers have concluded that living in a crowded household has only a very modest influence in creating physical, mental, or social pathologies. These researchers appear ready to dismiss crowding as a problem not meriting serious concern (Fischer et al., 1975). Others, such as Walter Gove, Michael Hughes, and Omer Galle, disagree with this conclusion. They argue that the number of persons per room does affect the number of social demands faced by a person and the person's perception of necessary privacy. Gove, Galle, and

Hughes cite evidence that residential crowding, as a result of these primary effects, is associated with such things as physical and psychological withdrawal, poor planning behavior, poor social relationships in the home, poor child care, poor physical and mental health, and poor social relationships outside the home. Moreover, the independent effect of crowding on many of these problems appears to be as strong as other factors which are generally recognized as important influences on them, e.g., income (Gove, Hughes, and Galle, 1979:59-80).

However, even if crowding does have an effect, it cannot be the basis for a general criticism of contemporary urban life. The sort of crowding researchers have been investigating is greater than the norm for the urban population in the United States. In addition, like density, residential crowding has been steadily declining during this century: the proportion of the population living in housing with more than one person per room has declined to the point where only a small minority live in such housing. (See Chapter 5.)

Hence, the general charge that psychological damage is caused by urban life appears to be unfounded. That is not to deny that significant numbers of people experience stress and feelings of isolation, powerlessness, and the like under modern conditions. However, to place the primary or even the major blame on urbanization and urban social life is certainly premature and probably unjustified.

Anomie and alienation may have been characteristic of cities such as Chicago during periods of rapid urbanization in the early 20th century. This disorganization was due largely to migration of large numbers of single males to the cities from Europe and the rural United States. However, there is no empirical support for theories associating psychological difficulties with urban living under current conditions (Lyon, 1987:103-104; Spates and Macionis, 1987; Poplin, 1979).

More Recent Research

These criticisms of the classical view have led to recent research and theorizing about urban social relationships which attempts to specify how urbanites maintain close social ties. In his "subcultural theory," Fischer notes that cities do not necessarily have negative effects on their inhabitants. Size and density can be seen as providing the number of people sufficient for the development and existence of subcultures, whether they are conventional, unconventional, or deviant. Certain occupations and lifestyles can thus flourish, since enough people with similar interests and activities are present. Fischer concludes that the presence, intensity and diversity of subcultures increase as the size and concentration of people in cities increase. Hence, the larger size and density of a city encourage development of highly organized subcultures, rather than the personal disorganization and loneliness expected by classical theorists (Fischer, 1976).

Harvey Choldin, summing up much of the recent research on neighborhoods, acknowledges that such factors as modern transportation and communication systems weaken neighborhood ties. However, local social life continues, though much of it is now voluntary and differentiated by demographic factors such as family life stage. For example, neighboring is higher in neighborhoods with large numbers of young children. Participation ranges from heavy involvement in local affairs, to more cosmopolitan, city-wide relationships. Recent studies suggest that local uses of the neighborhood are of two types: *instrumental* uses and *social pyschological* uses. Instrumental uses include such things as purchases at local stores and businesses and enrollment of children in schools. Social psychological uses are such activities as involvement in local groups and organizations and identification with and loyalty to the local community. One distinct factor encouraging local involvement is the feeling that the community is threatened with some problem outside itself, such as a proposed freeway that would destroy some or all local housing. Some have argued that "intense neighboring," involving very close relationships of people living in a relatively small geographical area, may well have declined with the emergence of the modern city. Several explanations can be advanced for this change. People moved more frequently. They communicated increasingly by phone with many besides their immediate neighbors. Friendship ties with coworkers increased in frequency. Neighboring came to be limited to home owners, those with children, and people centered on family ties and contacts (Choldin, 1985:272-274, 287-296).

In their research, Wellman and Berkowitz studied neighborhoods in which there was little in the way of vital neighborhood activity. Evident, however, were a great number of community ties. Some of these provided strong support to people, while only a few were local. These researchers concluded that the "social networks" they discovered were best described as "personal communities." Such communities consisted not in local ties, but rather in the way in which informal relationships tied people and families into bonds of friendship and assistance as well as mutual aid. The approach of Wellman and Berkowitz concentrates on the presence both of local ties between people, and also on the ties they have with those in the city and the metropolitan area. The concept of personal community thus enables us to see the whole picture, to take into account that people have both local and also area-wide bonds. The extent and detail of such relationships depend largely on one's social class and occupation. For example, those having higher class rank, such as accountants, lawyers, and engineers, tend to have much more extensive contacts across wider geographical areas. Generally speaking, ties provide identity and belonging, assistance and help, both generally as well as in advancing one's career (Wellman and Berkowitz, 1988:130-131, 134-35). This network approach, noting the continuity of social ties amidst great social and geographical mobility, is also affirmed by Hannerz. Fischer (1982) noted that social involvement varied with community size. In larger communities, people tend to associate more with nonkin, while the reverse holds true for those in smaller places (Hannerz, 1980:171-189, 200-201; Kim, 1981; Fischer, 1982; Marsden, 1987:122-131).

Evaluation

Where does all this leave us? Were the classical theorists simply wrong? Yes and no. Much of what they said about the nature of the change from rural to urban society has some validity. Urban societies are complex, bureaucratic, secular, culturally heterogeneous, and so on. The basic structure of society and the nature of culture has changed in major ways—often in the ways the classical view suggests. Moreover, there are many social settings where the kind of social relationships described by classical theorists predominate: at the checkout counter of the grocery store, the police station, the state license-plate bureau, and the like.

What the classical view failed to recognize was the flexibility of human beings under conditions of rapid social change and their ability (and dogged determination) to maintain close personal relationships under modern urban conditions. The overwhelming majority of urban dwellers have developed a number of "coping strategies" to avoid the impersonality and social isolation which might otherwise result. Most urbanites have some source of intimate social ties: family, neighborhood, coworkers, or group memberships. The majority of people do not live out their lives in large-scale, impersonal social settings. Rather, they live their lives in much smaller and more personal social worlds—often worlds which they actively create or choose for themselves.

At the same time, the classical theorists tended to downplay the tremendous advantages urban life offered the individual. The improved material conditions, individual freedom, excitement, and diversity which the new cities offered were not just minor advantages of urban life. They were (and are) major attractions. The ultimate testimony to these attractions is to be found in the behavior of millions of individuals over the last two centuries who "voted with their feet": they left their rural communities and went to the city. The process continues today in Third World countries.

But we should be careful not to make the opposite mistake from that of the classical theorists, and deny that contemporary urban communities have problems. They certainly do. The remaining chapters of this book are concerned with some of those problems. Others are the more appropriate topics of another book or course. The purpose of this chapter has been to make sure that the tradition of the anti-urban bias would not distort the examination of those problems. Urban societies have problems; so did the societies which preceded them. Rather than dreaming of a golden past of idyllic rural villages which never existed, we need to confront contemporary urban society as it is.

Main Points

1. Urbanization resulted in fundamental changes in the nature of society.
2. The classical view of the consequences of urbanization represented the attempt of early European and North American sociologists to evaluate the differences between rural and urban societies.
3. In the classical view, urbanization resulted in increased size of social units, increased social complexity, and the weakening of kinship ties. These changes in social organization were accompanied by major cultural changes: secularization, rationalization, cultural heterogeneity, and organic solidarity. Social relationships became more impersonal and segmented.
4. Classical theorists evaluated these changes primarily in negative terms. They felt that urbanization resulted in social disorganization, psychological stress, anomie, and alienation.
5. More recent research suggests that the classical view is only partly correct. The basic criticism is that the classical view provides an incomplete view of the nature of rural and urban society and exaggerates the negative characteristics of urban society.
6. This criticism of classical theory is based on a number of specific criticisms of claims made by classical theory.
7. One criticism is that classical theory presents too rosy a view of rural society. Rural society had a number of problems — including poor living conditions, exploitation and conflict, parochialism, and intolerance. In

addition, the family system was not as effective, stable, or close-knit as it has been traditionally portrayed.

8. Another criticism of classical theory is that the extent of urban social disorganization is not as great as portrayed by classical theorists. Urbanites maintain stable, personal, and intimate relationships based on kin ties, neighboring, work-based friendships, and membership in voluntary organizations.

9. Finally, there is no clear proof that urban life is as stressful, anomic, or alienating as portrayed by classical theory.

10. Recent research notes that although traditional neighboring patterns have declined, informal relationships tie people into bands of friendship and assistance.

Key Terms

Alienation   A feeling of powerlessness, meaningless, and social isolation.

Anomie   "Normlessness." A feeling that there are no clear social rules or goals by which to control and direct one's life.

Anti-Urban Bias   The popular perception that cities are places of crime, immorality, loneliness, and impersonality. This bias is reflected in classical urban theory in the description of urban society as the cause of social disorganization, stress, alienation, and anomie.

Classical View of Urbanization   The view, associated with the work of many early sociological theorists, that urbanization results in the destruction of cohesive small communities and the creation of impersonal, socially disorganized, and alienating social relationships.

Cultural Heterogeneity   Lack of agreement and consistency in cultural beliefs, values, and attitudes.

Cultural Homogeneity   Agreement and consistency in cultural beliefs, values, and attitudes.

Division of Labor   The organization of work roles in society into specialized tasks.

Extended Kinship System   A system of family relationships in which close and frequent social relationships and ties based on mutual assistance and obligation are maintained with a large number of kin outside of the nuclear family.

Mechanical Solidarity   Social solidarity based on shared cultural beliefs, attitudes, and values.

Modified Extended Family   A kinship system in which major emphasis is placed on nuclear family relationships but significant ties are maintained with extended kin.

Nuclear Family   A kinship system in which the major emphasis is placed on relationships between the mother, father, and children.

Organic Solidarity   Social solidarity based on a system of exchange relationships between individuals in specialized roles in a complex division of labor.

Sacred Orientation   A cultural orientation in which the justification for an activity or belief is based on an appeal to religious beliefs.

Secular Rationality   A cultural orientation in which the ultimate justification for an activity or belief is an explanation based on logic and systematic observation of measurable phenomena.

Segmental Social Relationships   A network of social relationships in which relationships are specialized by function and the people one knows in different social situations do not know each other.

Social Disorganization   A societal condition in which norms are inconsistent, cultural values are in conflict, kinship and other relationships are weak and unstable, and individuals feel anomic.

Solidarity   The sense of shared identity, cooperation, and agreement which holds a society or community together.

Total Social Relationships   A network of social relationships in which the same people interact with one another in a number of different social situations while occupying a number of different roles.

Traditional Orientation   A cultural orientation in which beliefs and activities are justified on the basis of past practices and beliefs.

Suggested Reading

Choldin, Harvey M. 1985. *Cities and Suburbs: An Introduction to Urban Sociology.* New York: McGraw-Hill, 1985. A well-organized, clear and concise treatment of cities in the United States, especially concerning social and spatial patterns of neighborhoods.

Fischer, Claude. 1976. *The Urban Experience.* New York: Harcourt, Brace, Jovanovich. A landmark work, emphasizing the positive effects of size, density, and heterogeneity.

Fried, Marc. 1969. "Grieving for a Lost Home". In *The Urban Condition*, edited by L. Duhl. New York: Simon and Schuster. A description and critique of the anti-urban bias.

Friedman, F. G. 1953. "The World of La Miseria." *Partisan Review* 20:218-31. A widely-reprinted description of Italian peasant life which thoroughly challenges the romantic view of traditional rural village life.

Shorter, Edward. 1975. *The Making of the Modern Family.* New York: Basic Books. A readable but controversial book which provides an introduction to some of the new social history of the family.

Wellman, Barry and S.D. Berkowitz. 1988. *Social Structures: A Network Approach.* Cambridge, MA: Cambridge University. An insightful set of chapters relating research documenting the nature of networks in urban areas, particularly those of nongeographical nature.

Wirth, Louis. 1938. "Urbanism As a Way of Life." *American Journal of Sociology.* 44:1-24. The most influential summary statement of the classical view of the nature of social life in urban society.

4

Problems of the Urban Disadvantaged

Outline of Topics

Unequal treatment and unequal living conditions are facts of life in all societies. Urban society is no exception. Inequality is a pervasive characteristic of urban social structure. In this chapter, we will examine those aspects and consequences of inequality which have been a particularly major concern of those who study urban problems. Our focus will be primarily on those people for whom inequality is a persistent, ugly reality: blacks[1] and the poor.

Urban Poverty

Obviously, poverty is not just a problem of urban areas. Still, more than 40 percent of the poor in the United States do live in central cities, and their presence is associated with a number of uniquely urban problems. We need to examine who the urban poor are, where they live, and what special problems urban poverty creates. We will then turn to a discussion of attempts by social scientists to understand the problems of the poor and the significance of those attempts for suggesting policies to assist the poor.

Defining and Counting the Poor

It may seem surprising to someone who has not thought about it before, but deciding who is poor in an affluent, industrial society turns out to be a complicated and controversial issue. No one would deny the poverty of someone who lacks sufficient food to stay alive, wears rags, and sleeps in the street. The person is *absolutely* deprived. Even in a rich society like the United States, we see absolute poverty, hunger, and homelessness among a small proportion of our population. But in an industrialized, generally affluent society like ours, the concept of poverty extends beyond those people who cannot obtain a bare minimum level of food and shelter. We consider as "relatively poor" someone whose conditions of life are substantially worse than average and whose standard of living is lower than that considered minimally acceptable by most members of society. Thus, *relative* poverty is the lack of things that most people in a society take for granted as necessary and can routinely obtain.

Defining poverty in relative terms makes it more difficult to decide who is poor and who is not. That is because there is no total agreement on what constitutes an "acceptable" living standard. The definition of "acceptable" depends, in part, on one's perception of what constitutes a generally attainable and reasonable level of living conditions. How much is enough? How much is too little? Where do we draw the line between the "poor" and the "nonpoor"?

The most commonly used definition of poverty is that employed by the federal government. The *official poverty line*, set by the U.S. Department of Health and Human Services, is calculated based on the cost of food. An estimate of what it costs to purchase a minimally adequate diet is made. That figure is then multiplied by three. (The highly questionable assumption is that all other necessities will require not more than twice what must be spent for food.) Thus, in 1989 the poverty line for an individual living in an urban area was $5,980, and for a family of four it was $12,100. Anyone with less income than this is counted as officially poor by the government. Inflation will mean that the poverty line constantly rises. Assuming a 5 percent increase per year would mean that the poverty line would be $16,214 for an urban family of four by 1995.

The official poverty line is only an approximate measure of poverty. It has been criticized, usually for being unrealistically low. Attempts to measure the real cost of a minimally acceptable standard of living have usually yielded income estimates much higher than the official poverty line. For instance, the Labor Department formerly calculated hypothetical family budgets. The "low" or austere budget assumed such things as rented housing, consumption (by four people) of 11 pounds of meat a week, a new suit every four years, a six-year-old car, and virtually nothing spent on luxury or leisure-time activities. The resulting estimate for an urban family of four was a budget that was almost twice as high as the official poverty line (U.S. Department of Labor, 1978).

Another measure that is sometimes used is the *near poor*. These are people living above but close to the poverty line. The census reports on those households receiving incomes up to 125 percent of the official poverty line. If that group is included, the proportion of the population that is poor increases by about 25 percent (U.S. Bureau of the Census, 1989:453).

Thus, even governmental agencies may not agree on exactly who is poor. This lack of agreement means that, at the very least, we need to be cautious about official statistics concerning poverty. The official poverty line represents just one attempt to estimate who is poor and who is not. It is probably a fairly conservative estimate.[2] But since the federal government publishes most of its statistics based on the official definition of poverty, that is the measure most researchers use.

It is also important to note that poor people are not necessarily unemployed. About half of all poor families belong to the *working poor*. They live in households where at least one member works but their income is insufficient to raise them over the poverty level (Levitan and Shapiro, 1987). Whether a working household is poor depends, to an extent, on the number of people in it. For example, in 1989, a person working full-time at the minimum wage earned $6,968 per year. This income, although low, was over the official poverty line for one person. If, however, the wage earner was supporting even one other person, that income put them into poverty.

A related issue is underemployment. Many people who are working can find only part-time jobs. Of course, some people prefer to work part-time and do so voluntarily. An increasing problem for working people in the United States, however, is involuntary part-time employment. A recent study showed that more than half of the 3.2 million new jobs created in the 1980s were filled by people who would have preferred full-time jobs but were unable to get them (Mishel and Simon, 1988:21).

In the last decade, we witnessed a growth in poverty of all kinds, from the "relatively affluent" poverty of those people making less than 125 percent of the poverty level, to the working poor and underemployed, to the extreme poverty of those people making less than 50 percent of a poverty level income. This latter group grew from 8.3 million to 12.8 million persons in the eight years between 1979 and 1987, an increase of 53 percent (Mishel and Simon, 1988:39). Thus, no matter which definition of poverty we use, we must admit that poverty is an increasingly serious problem in the United States.

Given these considerations, how many poor are there and where do they live? During the 1980s, the proportion of the whole population living below the official poverty line first showed a sharp rise—from 12 percent to over 15 percent—then fell somewhat to 13.5 percent. (This is in marked contrast to the 1960s, when the proportion below the poverty line dropped substantially and the 1970s when it remained relatively stable.) In addition, migration patterns of the 1960s and 1970s meant that an increasing proportion of poor people lived in urban areas. In 1959, about 27 percent of the poor lived in central cities. By the mid-1970s, that percentage had increased to 37 percent, and by the mid-1980s, it reached 40 percent (U.S. Bureau of the Census, 1988a). Nonetheless, the official poor are still a minority of central city populations. About 18 percent of central-city residents were living below the poverty line in 1986, compared with 8 percent in suburban areas and 18 percent in non-metropolitan areas (U.S. Bureau of the Census, 1988a).

Concentration of Poverty in Cities

No matter where the poor live, they experience—and create—problems. Being poor is no fun. For instance, besides real material deprivation, the poor are subject to humiliation and social ridicule, and they are more likely to be victims of crime, experience unemployment, die younger, and spend time in jail or a mental hospital (Eitzen, 1978:234-40).

However, the experiences and problems of the poor are not all the same. One difference is that the problems of the poor in cities are different from those of the poor outside the cities, since poverty is more geographically concentrated in urban areas.

We must first remember that most people living in cities are *not* poor, and that most people in cities, even most poor people, do *not* live in neighborhoods characterized by high concentrations of poor people. But the proportion of poor people living in such concentrated high-poverty areas is increasing. This is a disturbing trend because it further separates the poor from the rest of the society. As a result, poor people living in high-poverty areas have fewer ties to nonpoor people and to "mainstream" social institutions than do poor people living outside of these areas. Such isolation has important implications for their opportunities to get out of poverty. A person's knowledge of and ties to the "outside world" are crucial for obtaining employment beyond the bare minimum. Yet these outside ties are difficult to establish for poverty-area residents because of the insular nature of poor neighborhoods. In addition, their neighborhoods typically contain few businesses which would provide good employment opportunities (Ellwood, 1988).

As a result, individuals living in high-poverty areas often work in the local *underground economy*. These are informal or illegal businesses that flourish in areas of concentrated poverty. Jobs in the underground economy include drug dealing, selling stolen goods, prostitution, and organized gambling (such as "numbers" running), as well as working "off the books" at jobs that would be legal (e.g., construction, running errands, or driving unregistered taxis) if they were reported. People work at these jobs because they provide the best economic opportunities in an environment where legitimate work is either not available or not well paid. The fact that the work is illegal, however, means that participants in the underground economy run the risk of getting a criminal record, which makes it even harder for them to obtain regular employment (Sharff, 1987). Of course, not everyone in high-poverty neighborhoods works in the underground economy, but its growth is a sobering result of the concentration of poverty in certain city neighborhoods.

Another important characteristic of poor neighborhoods is that concentrations of poverty vary by racial group. Most poor whites live among people who are not poor. The fraction of poor whites living in high-poverty areas (over 40 percent of all residents poor) is quite small and is remaining constant, while the fraction of poor whites living in areas of moderate poverty (20 to 40 percent of residents poor) has decreased slightly. Among blacks, however, we see a different pattern. While the proportion of poor blacks living in moderate-poverty areas has declined somewhat, the proportion living in high-poverty areas has increased tremendously (Ellwood, 1988:201-202).

This trend is especially pronounced in large cities. The proportion of poor blacks in New York City living in high-poverty areas rose from 15 percent in 1970 to 45 percent in 1980 and in Chicago it rose from 25 percent in 1970 to 50 percent in 1980 (Ellwood, 1988:203). In these types of areas, racial segregation and economic deprivation have combined to form neighborhoods that some researchers call *hyperghettos*, areas with conditions far more extreme than those in normal black neighborhoods (Wacquant and Wilson, 1989).

Special Problems of the Urban Poor

Most of the special problems of the urban poor are related, in one way or another, to their concentration in large, homogeneous neighborhoods. That is why the increasing numbers of the poor in such neighborhoods is so disturbing.

Such geographical concentration has a number of implications. It means that the physical environment, not just one's own housing, is deteriorated and unhealthy. For instance, children can be attacked by packs of rats or develop lead poisoning from old paint flaking off the walls. The squalor of slum neighborhoods is made worse by gutted, open, abandoned buildings, the danger of fire (accidental or set), and inadequate efforts at public sanitation. In poor neighborhoods, the general level of public services is low. Garbage collection, street repair, the level of police protection, the speed with which emergency services arrive, and conditions in the schools are all worse in the poorer sections of our cities. Traditionally, this has been an especially severe problem in Sunbelt cities, where even such basic services as street paving were only grudgingly provided (Lupsha and Siembieda, 1977).

Those living in poor neighborhoods are also likely to experience a number of other problems. Compared to other groups, they are much more likely to be victims of crimes (committed by the poor people around them). Their children are likely to go to neighborhood schools which are not only of poorer quality but also contain mostly other poor children. These children are more likely to have various learning problems, and the peer group pressures are likely to discourage academic achievement and encourage nonconforming behavior. Even relatively simple things can be a problem in a poor neighborhood. Lacking a car, the poor person is likely to have to shop at neighborhood stores which offer a limited range of merchandise at much higher prices than available elsewhere. (See, for example, Caplovitz, 1967.)

Special Problems Created by the Urban Poor

Large concentrations of poor people with poor people's problems in our central cities have created serious problems for those cities.

Poor neighborhoods need more services from government. Social service costs are just part of the problem. Fire protection costs are higher. The need for police protection is greater. The need to deal with deteriorated or abandoned buildings imposes a costly burden on city government. Public transportation is more essential. Children of the poor need more educational services.

At the same time, poor people are not a good source from which to raise taxes. Slum dwellings do not generate much real estate property tax, and poor people do not have much income to tax. This is part of the reason central city governments face growing financial problems (see Chapter 7). It also helps to explain why government services to the poor are of such low quality.

The growing concentration of the poor in central cities also plays a direct and indirect role in the movement of the white middle class and working class away from the central cities. Fear of the poor, mixed with racial fears, and the desire to avoid paying taxes to help the poor may have contributed to the movement to the suburbs (Frey, 1979). This further complicated the central cities' attempts to raise tax revenues and (as we will see) contributed to the process of urban decay.

Understanding Urban Poverty: Two Approaches

The urban poor, given their large numbers and their manifest problems, have been a major focus of research among those concerned with urban social problems. Much of this research has attempted to determine the causes of the problems of the poor. The ultimate hope has been that this research would eventually result in a better understanding of the urban poor which would provide a basis for effective public policies to assist them.

Two general approaches have emerged from research on the urban poor; one stresses the social and economic structure of the society, the other stresses the culture of poor people. Both approaches try to understand why we continue to have poverty in a rich society like the United States. This is a complex question having to do with a number of factors, some very remote from poor individuals themselves (e.g., trends in the national and international economy) and some much closer to individuals (e.g., whether they are married, how much education they have). The structural approach tends to emphasize the more remote factors, analyzing the way the economy and society create opportunities and distribute them, while the cultural approach tends to stress the closer factors, analyzing people's learned attitudes and behaviors and how these help them succeed or fail. The two approaches have different implications not only for understanding what causes poverty but also for attempting to create policies that will reduce the amount of poverty.

The Structural Approach

The structural approach says that poverty is the result of an unequal distribution of opportunity within our society (Beeghley, 1988). That is, the society is *structured* in such a way that there is only a certain, limited number of good jobs to go around. The proponents of this view portray the social structure of the United States as a sort of stubby pyramid, with a few highly desirable, well-rewarded positions at the top; a relatively large but still limited number of acceptable, comfortable positions in the middle; and an equally large number of inferior, undesirable positions at the bottom (including "positions" for the unemployed, as well as for those with bad jobs). They argue that the extent of poverty is to a large degree determined by how many good, middle, and bad positions exist.

One way to see the impact of economic structure on poverty is to observe the increases and decreases in the number of unemployed people as the national economy goes through periods of growth and recession. But proponents of the structural approach examine the quality as well as the number of jobs that exist. They point out that the *types* of jobs individuals hold, in addition to whether or not they *have* jobs, are relevant to their poverty or nonpoverty status. They argue that the increase in the number of working poor in recent years is an indication of a severe structural problem in our economy, caused by a transformation in the types of jobs that are available. Structural theorists hold that the shift from a manufacturing-based economy to a service-based economy and the consequent deindustrialization we examined in Chapter 2 are a major cause of changes in people's economic status. Bluestone and Harrison (1982), for example, argue that it is becoming more and more difficult for people to find secure jobs with good wages, fringe benefits, and opportunities for promotion. The manufacturing jobs that used to provide those opportunities are either being replaced by machines or moved overseas. On the other hand, structural analysts argue, the service jobs that are increasing in number do not provide many opportunities for upward mobility. While a certain proportion of the growing service sector is made up of high-level jobs such as attorneys and computer analysts, a larger proportion is made up of low-level jobs such as janitors and fast-food cooks. Most importantly, the low-level jobs in the service sector do not have career paths leading to promotions. They tend to have very little mobility and act as a "dead end," without opportunities for people to gain experience and move ahead. Thus, in the future, we can expect our society to become more divided into rich and poor, more unequal (Reich, 1989).

Urban poverty has become an increasing problem, according to this view, because of the movement of jobs and industry out of the cities. Whereas in the past, cities were the main areas of job opportunities, today they are attracting fewer employers. Instead, suburban industrial and office parks now contain an increasing proportion of jobs, leaving large areas of the central cities devoid of *any* jobs. Inner city residents without access to transportation may not be able to reach the jobs that do exist. Thus, the changing structure of the economy has affected the geographical distribution of jobs as well as the quantity and quality of jobs available (Kasarda, 1989).

While it may seem that the structural approach deals only with very large-scale, remote explanations for poverty, it also looks at how individuals get "recruited" into positions of poverty or affluence. In particular, structural theorists have pointed to certain institutions, especially schools, as having an enormous impact on people's economic status. They argue that schools act as "gatekeepers," selecting the students who will succeed and fail economically, and contributing to their chances of success or failure at every stage. Although the students' success or failure is supposed to be based on their intrinsic merits (intelligence, ambition, hard work), structural theorists find that school personnel's expectations and attitudes toward a student are heavily influenced by his or her family background, income, sex, race, and ethnicity. Thus, a "self-fulfilling prophecy" often occurs, increasing the probability that a child from a "better" background will be thought of as "bright" while one from a "disadvantaged" background will be thought of as "slow" or "unmotivated" (Ryan, 1981).

The policy proposals that flow from the structural theory are directed toward increasing opportunities for employment. There are two variations, however, one politically more liberal and one politically more conservative. The conservative proposal is for government to cut taxes and regulation as an incentive to businesses to locate in high-poverty areas. An example of such a policy is the establishment of Enterprise Zone programs, in which states give corporations tax breaks in return for building plants in certain inner-city neighborhoods (see Chapter 2). Liberals criticize the program as insufficient, maintaining that the small number of jobs created and the typically low pay offered will not go far toward solving problems of poverty (Goldsmith, 1982).

The liberal proposal is that government should take the responsibility for increasing not just the number of jobs but also their pay and the degree of access to them. That is, government should directly address the issues of economic structure and job distribution. One application of this policy would be the creation of public sector jobs to supplement those in the private sector, especially in areas of high unemployment. Another is regulating the minimum wage, to ensure that employed people are earning above a poverty income. (Although the minimum wage was increased in 1990, the increase was less than needed to restore the 1981 minimum wage level in "real" dollars.) A third policy would be to provide increased access to good jobs to those individuals who have been excluded. This might include access through training programs for those who need credentials, through transportation to job-rich areas for those who cannot reach them, and through government-funded day care facilities for those who are limited in finding work by family obligations. These increased services and opportunities for the poor could be funded by increased taxes on the well-to-do, thus helping to narrow the widening income gap.

The Cultural Approach

The central claim of the cultural approach to poverty is that the poor have a special *subculture* (a set of values and beliefs different from those held by most people in society). In a sense, the poor are seen as operating in a separate social world with a different definition of reality, a different set of rules for behavior, different goals, and different definitions of success. This subculture is seen as being passed on from generation to generation through the socialization of children and as being deeply rooted in the personalities and way of life of the poor. As a result, the poor behave differently and, from the point of view of the rest of society, in an inappropriate and sometimes pathological (sick) fashion.

Different theorists have emphasized different characteristics of this "culture of poverty." However, the classic version derived from the work of Oscar Lewis (1966) emphasizes certain values and beliefs which are seen as shaping the behavior of the poor. The most important of these are "fatalism" (or a lack of aspirations) and "present-time orientation."

By fatalism or lack of aspirations theorists mean to imply that the poor have given up hope for improvement in their lives. The poor do not believe that they can, by their own actions, control what happens to them. They no longer hope for conventional middle-class success. The poor, according to this view, no longer believe in the middle-class "success ethic" that discipline and hard work will lead to a better life. Hence, they see sustained efforts to improve their situation as pointless.

Because they have no long-term goals toward which they are willing to work, the poor, claim these theorists, are unwilling to discipline themselves or plan ahead. Rather, the poor display a "present-time orientation." They live for today — with no concern for what tomorrow will bring. They do not organize their lives. They are unwilling to defer gratification (to sacrifice present pleasure to achieve some long-term goal). Rather, they live from moment to moment, seeking pleasure when and where they can.

The consequences of this view of the world, say "culture of poverty" theorists, are predictably bad. Given opportunities to improve their lives the poor will not take effective advantage of them. Given money, they will waste it on frivolous pleasures. They cannot maintain stable, intimate relationships with others, so family relationships will be unstable. Poor neighborhoods will be socially disorganized: social ties between people in the community will be weak, participation in voluntary organizations will be low, and a sense of community identity and obligations will be lacking.

In recent years, a variant of the cultural approach has focused on one group of the poor, the *urban underclass*. This subset of the poor consists of those not only in extreme poverty and living in concentrated poverty neighborhoods but also highly likely to be living in female-headed families, dependent on welfare as the main source of income, having little history of or prospect for legitimate work, and being heavily involved in crime and drugs. What distinguishes the urban underclass from the rest of the urban poor, in the eyes of researchers, is the families' isolation from mainstream social life and the long duration of their poverty, persisting from generation to generation (McLanahan et al., 1988). (Although underclass members may be of any racial or ethnic background, most of the recent writing on the subject has examined the black underclass. See, for example, Glasgow, 1980.)

The attitudes of the underclass adults and their lack of participation in mainstream society are viewed as a kind of "trap," not only preventing them from getting ahead but also condemning their children to the same fate: dropping out of school, getting arrested for selling drugs, having babies as teenagers. The home and neighborhood surroundings in which the children grow up, according to these writers, place too little importance on work, stable marriage, and education as means of upward mobility.

Where do these subcultural attitudes and behaviors supposedly come from? One well-known explanation sees them as traditional adaptations to life in urban slums. In areas with few real opportunities for upward mobility, cultures develop around the needs of immediate daily survival. The point is not so much that poor people do not *value* working, saving money, marriage, and education but that they see these things (perhaps correctly) as not *possible* for them. They therefore define the seemingly inevitable alternatives (dropping out, unmarried pregnancy, petty crime) as acceptable (Stack, 1974).

A more controversial explanation blames social welfare policy for fostering these "deviant" attitudes and behaviors. In this view, the underclass has become overly dependent on social welfare, especially the Aid to Families with Dependent Children (AFDC) program, which provides cash payments to low-income families with children. Proponents of this view argue that AFDC has destroyed both the work ethic (by providing welfare payments as an alternative to wages) and the stable family (by providing single mothers with incomes) among the underclass (Murray, 1984).

As with the structural approach, the policy proposals stemming from the cultural approach can be either liberal or conservative. In the 1960s, many policies of the national "War on Poverty" were derived from the liberal version of culture-of-poverty theory. The main thrust of the policies was to intervene in the poverty cycle by teaching poor people the attitudes and behaviors they needed to succeed in mainstream society. Many government-sponsored anti-poverty programs, such as Head Start and the Job Corps, were aimed at exposing poor individuals to "middle class" beliefs, values, and experiences. (Others, such as the Model City Program, were oriented toward increasing the level of economic opportunity in poor communities and so were more "structural" policies.) Today, the federal government runs fewer of these programs, but the cultural approach has been adopted by self-help groups in a number of poor neighborhoods. Often associated with churches or religious sects, these groups offer strong support for mainstream attitudes by organizing teenagers against gangs, drug use, and premarital sex and emphasizing education, work, and marriage as achievable goals.

In the past few years, the conservative policy direction has focused on cutting back welfare programs, especially AFDC. Murray (1984) and others argue that the poor will not learn proper attitudes toward work as long as they have acceptable alternatives, such as welfare, on which to rely. By tightening AFDC eligibility and cutting payments, government can ensure that anyone who reasonably could be expected to work will be working. An offshoot of this policy direction is "workfare," which requires welfare recipients to "work off" their payments, thus making AFDC a less attractive alternative to work for all but the truly needy. (There is also a liberal version of workfare; the

Table 4.1 **Facts About AFDC Recepients**

Three out of four live in metropolitan areas.

Three out of four have been receiving AFDC for 5 years or less.

Seven in ten AFDC recipients are children under 18.

Seven in ten adult recipients have two or fewer children.

More than half of AFDC recipients are white.

More than half of the children are fatherless due to death, divorce, or desertion.

One in 25 families receiving AFDC includes an able-bodied man in the home.

Fewer than three out of five people with incomes below the poverty line receive AFDC or any other form of public assistance.

SOURCE: Compiled from Persell. 1987. *Understanding Society;* Currie and Skolnick. 1984. *America's Problems.*

difference is that the conservative proposals are more oriented toward discouraging people from receiving AFDC while the liberal proposals are more oriented toward helping them to enter the paid labor force.)

During the 1980s, conservative attitudes toward the poor dominated the political debate on antipoverty policy. While AFDC and other social welfare programs were cut, the liberal, interventionist policies of the 1960s and early 1970s were virtually dismantled.

Evaluation

What evidence exists to support each of these approaches? Is one correct and the other incorrect? Or can some elements of each be combined to provide a more complete understanding of the causes of poverty?

There is a great deal of evidence to suggest that poverty is, at some fundamental level, caused by the structure of the economy. Take, for example, the increase in the number of poor people during the 1980s. This was not an isolated phenomenon but one facet of a more general trend toward greater inequality, or *polarization*, of incomes in the United States (Bluestone and Harrison, 1988). At the same time that the poverty population was increasing, the numbers of the very rich were also increasing (but not as quickly), and the middle class was shrinking (Bradbury, 1986).

These changes in income distribution were the result of several identifiable trends in the U.S. economy. First, working people's wages did not keep up with increases in the cost of living. When adjusted for inflation, average wages actually declined 7 percent between 1979 and 1987 (Mishel and Simon, 1988:13). During the same period, the incomes of the well-to-do increased rapidly. High level executives' salaries were reported as rising twice as fast as workers' wages, with top corporate executives commonly reaching levels of $5,000 per hour—including all their stock options and other income (*Dollars and Sense*, 1988:11). So polarization in wages contributed to polarization in incomes.

Second, because of deindustrialization, many workers have been permanently laid off from their regular employment. They are "displaced" workers because the jobs they were trained to do have disappeared, and there is little hope that they will become reemployed in the same job. One study showed that of all the workers displaced by plant closings between 1979 and 1983, only 28 percent were able to obtain full-time jobs (or become self-employed) at pay levels comparable to their former jobs (*Dollars and Sense*, 1985).

Third, in recent years, the U.S. economy has been producing many more "bad" jobs than "good" jobs. A study for the United States Senate showed that between 1979 and 1987, more than half of all new jobs created were at or below the poverty level, only 38 percent were at the middle income level, and a scant 12 percent were at a high wage level (*New York Times*, 1988).

Fourth, the good jobs that are being created in cities are mainly in the information-processing industries of the service sector. These jobs have high educational requirements and do not provide opportunities, eve.' at the entry level, for the masses of young unemployed urban dwell ers with low educational levels (Kasarda, 1983).

Finally, the movement of industry to suburbs has aggravated the geographic mismatch between where the most jobs are located and where the most unemployed workers are located, making access difficult. Most people who work in suburban areas, even if they are relatively low-income inner-city residents, drive to work. But among poor, *unemployed* inner-city residents, rates of automobile ownership are very low (Kasarda, 1989:40). Furthermore, since public transit systems are not set up to take people from city neighborhoods to suburban job sites, the urban poor face far greater difficulties in finding and getting to suburban jobs than do suburban commuters who work in the central city (*Chicago Tribune*, 8/14/1989:1,10).

Thus, the structural approach gives us many insights into the larger causes of poverty. It shows how the economy influences the amount, type, and location of poverty in our society. It helps us to understand why we see certain contradictory trends in our cities: increases in homeless people and beggars on the streets at the same time that the market for expensive condominiums heats up and chic new clubs and restaurants open daily.

The structural approach does not, however, give us much information about how *individuals* become poor, stay poor, or become upwardly mobile. It tells us that certain categories of people (members of racial minorities, women and children, people without much education) are most likely to be poor. But it does not tell us why individuals from the same neighborhoods or even the same families, can turn out very differently. From a structural point of view, a great deal of the difference in occupation or income between individuals with similar backgrounds (parents' income, educational level, etc.) is due simply to luck (Jencks et al., 1972).

The cultural approach may help to fill in the missing links between the remote causes of poverty and the ways in which specific individuals or groups become poor. How do people's attitudes and behaviors affect their chances of becoming or remaining poor? Are there systematic differences between the cultures of poor and nonpoor people, and, if so, how do these affect their chances for the future?

Let us begin with the issue of the family style singled out as most likely to make people poor: the single-parent (virtually always female-headed) family. It is undoubtedly true that people living in female-headed families are much more likely to poor than people living in two-parent families, 34 percent as opposed to 12 percent in 1987 (U.S. Bureau of the Census, 1989a:453). They also stay poor longer than other types of families (McLanahan et al., 1988:103). Furthermore, the proportion of families headed by women has been increasing dramatically in recent years, especially among blacks (Sidel, 1986). Does this difference reflect a cultural difference between whites and blacks (for example, a tradition of matriarchal families or a reduced emphasis on the importance of marriage among blacks)? Recent research suggests that most of the difference in marriage rates between white and black women is due not to a cultural preference for single parenthood among black women but to a shortage of "marriageable" black men. William J. Wilson (1987), for example, has shown that there are substantially fewer employed black men available for black women to marry than there are employed white men for white women to marry. Growing rates of unemployment, premature death, and imprisonment among black men, not a cultural rejection of marriage, account for the increase in black families headed by women, Wilson concludes.

A second set of questions addresses the issues of persistent poverty and welfare dependency. To what extent do the poor constitute an "underclass" of people spending most of their lives on welfare, and not trying to get ahead? Some important data on these issues are provided by the Panel Study of Income Dynamics (PSID), which has studied 5,000 families since 1968. One study based on PSID data asked how many of the poor are "persistently poor" (defined as poor for eight or more years out of a ten-year period). The researchers found that, although one quarter of the people in the study were poor *at some time* during a ten-year period, only 2.6 percent were persistently poor (Duncan, 1984:42). Similarly, although about a quarter of the people in the study received some government welfare (AFDC, food stamps, or another form of public assistance) during the period, only 4.4 percent received welfare persistently and less than half of them (2 percent of the total group) derived more than half of their family income from welfare programs (Duncan, 1984:76). The authors of the study conclude that:

> ... [T]he popular conception of "the poor" as a homogeneous, stable group is simply wrong. Although the series of snapshot pictures of poverty provided by the Census Bureau surveys shows fairly constant numbers and characteristics for poor families each year, actual turnover in the poverty population is very high. (Duncan, 1984:60)

Researchers have also studied the issue of individuals' attitudes and their impact on poverty. The cultural approach holds that when people learn attitudes such as fatalism and lack of future orientation within a subculture, those attitudes make them less likely even to try to get ahead. In effect, the culture discourages them from thinking they can succeed. The Panel Study of Income Dynamics examined this question of people's attitudes and their impact on poverty. Since the PSID is a "longitudinal" study, one that traces the same individuals over a long period of time, it lets researchers examine the relationship between people's attitudes at one time and their economic level at a later time. The PSID tested the subjects' achievement motivation, sense of control over their lives, and orientation toward the future. Surprisingly, their attitudes on these dimensions had no relation to their economic success or failure seven years later (Duncan 1984:24-25). This study confirms other research done with smaller groups (Goodwin, 1983).

Should we conclude that the cultural approach to poverty is simply wrong? Not necessarily, but social scientists are beginning to realize that the relationship between social structure, attitudes, and behavior is very complex. Living in a poor neighborhood and growing up in a poor family *can* have an impact on whether people get ahead, but there is no automatic relationship between the two (Mayer and Jencks, 1989). In addition, individuals from the same neighborhoods and even from the same families can grow up with different attitudes toward success and achievement. To complicate matters further, positive attitudes do not necessarily make a person likely to succeed, although consistently negative attitudes must certainly hurt the chances of success.

A more realistic view of the causes of poverty is one that combines three factors. The first is the structural or objective constraints people face (opportunities for good jobs, competition in the labor market, labeling by schools, and so on). The second is the way people interpret their situations through the "eyes" of the cultural groups (family, friends) of which they are a part. The third is the actions they choose based on both of those factors, and, finally, the consequences those actions have for their "life chances." In no sense do these factors guarantee poverty although they may make it more or less predictable in some cases. (See MacLeod, 1987 and Gans, 1968 for more thorough discussions of these points.)

The conclusion we reach is that a distinctive culture is characteristic of only a small proportion of the poor and that it is less a *cause* of poverty than *one means* by which poverty may be perpetuated among some poor people. This is hardly a new idea. The late Oscar Lewis, who originally formulated the culture-of-poverty concept, argued that only about one-fifth of the poor population displayed unique cultural traits (Anderson, 1974). That estimate fits very well with more recent assessments of the size of the underclass.

What about the majority of the poor not in this small subgroup? Most of these poor are people who did not start out in poverty (except if they are children) and frequently get out of poverty when employment opportunities and life circumstances permit (except if they are elderly). Other than that, about all they have in common is low income. Some are the temporarily unemployed who eventually find employment. Those former workers who are permanently unemployed are usually that way because of plant closings or permanent layoffs. Older workers frequently find it difficult to be rehired because of their age. Some of the permanently unemployed are part of the thousands of workers disabled on the job each year. Many single-parent families are poor because they are headed by women (often with young children) who have been divorced or deserted and have, as a consequence, slipped into poverty. Retirement on inadequate social security benefits still (though less frequently than the past) often results in a working-class family slipping below the poverty line. A large proportion of the poor, especially women, are working but receiving wages too low to raise them above the poverty line.

The fact that most of the poor are people such as these (and their children) seems to explain why so many studies have failed to find a majority of the poor displaying culture-of-poverty traits. Most of the poor are not members of a multi-generational impoverished class with a history of welfare dependency and social pathology. They are instead, working class people who have had bad luck and/or are struggling to survive in marginal working-class jobs.

If this interpretation of the evidence is correct, it has important implications for public policy toward the majority of the poor. What they need is not just jobs (many already work), but good jobs, providing an income which will actually get them out of poverty. However, job opportunities will have to be combined with creating conditions in which the poor can take advantage of those opportunities. This would entail doing such things as effectively preventing racial, sexual, and age discrimination, providing education and training opportunities, providing child care for single-parent families, and retraining the disabled. Finally, there is the issue of those who are poor for reasons beyond their control but cannot be employed (e.g., the severely disabled and the elderly). Adequate levels of public assistance are obviously the only way in which their conditions of life could be improved.

There remains the problem of the persistently poor underclass. Fortunately, they represent a minority of those who are poor. However, in absolute numbers there are significant concentrations of these poor in certain neighborhoods of our central cities. What policy response is appropriate for this group depends on a number of considerations. First, to what extent is their behavior really the result of subcultural differences and how deeply embedded is that subculture? Second, to what extent is it possible to design workable programs which will actually have a significant impact on improving their (and, especially important, their children's) lives? These policies will probably have to go beyond providing job opportunities and include ways of convincing young people that they can actually take advantage of them. Unless they see school and work as *viable* routes to upward mobility, young people have no reason not to engage in behaviors like teen pregnancy, gang warfare, taking drugs, and dropping out of school.

An interesting experiment is now going on and may give us increased insight into an effective policy direction. A number of wealthy individuals have "adopted" classes of elementary school children from poor inner-city neighborhoods and promised to pay their college tuition on the condition that they stay in school, avoid drugs, and not become teenage parents. From the preliminary reports, it appears that the students in these classes, exactly like their peers in every other way, are experiencing much higher rates of success in school and fewer arrests than their age-mates (Thompson, 1987).

Observers may ask why we have needed to look to private individuals to take innovative steps toward improving poor people's chances for the future. Unfortunately, as poverty worsened during the 1980s, public policy turned away from attempts to solve the problem. Three faulty assumptions, which are now being re-evaluated, influenced policy in the 1980s. The first was that, as a society, we could not afford to spend money on social programs. As a consequence, public supports such as AFDC, housing subsidies, food stamps, and child health programs were cut back dramatically, reducing the already meager "safety net" that prevents people from falling into destitution. At the same time, however, public spending grew in other areas (notably on an enormous buildup of expensive weapons systems) and the budget deficit actually deepened. The second problematic assumption was that we could rely on economic growth to do away with poverty. Government tax cuts and other "economic stimulus" programs did, indeed, foster growth. The only difficulty is that most of the benefits went to the people who did not need them and few "trickled down" to those at the bottom. The third faulty assumption in the 1980s was that government policy is ineffective in solving problems of poverty. Critics of government programs claimed (falsely) that the antipoverty programs of the 1960s had had no impact on poverty. Meanwhile, in the 1980s, government policy was having a major impact on who was likely to be poor. While consistent increases in government Social Security payments brought down the level of poverty among senior citizens from 25 percent poor to less than 15 percent poor (or about the same poverty level as the rest of the population), cutbacks in AFDC and other child welfare programs helped to raise the level of poverty among children from 15 percent to over 20 percent. Thus, thanks in part to the effectiveness of government policy, children have now replaced the elderly as the poorest age group in the population (U.S. House of Representatives, 1985; Danziger and Weinberg, 1986).

We are compelled to conclude that an effective government policy to address the problems of poverty is both possible and necessary. It cannot be a simple, one-factor type of policy because of the complexity of the problem. At a minimum, it must include:

(1) economic policy to create a sufficient level of jobs with good wages, adequate benefit levels, and opportunities for promotion;

(2) programs of training and education to enable people to gain employment at good jobs as well as the supports (social services, transportation, health care, child care) they need to enable them to undertake and complete the training; and

(3) an adequate social welfare system to provide for those who cannot work, those who are facing temporary drawbacks, and those (e.g., children and young people) whose families cannot provide for them.

The Racially Disadvantaged

As we saw in Chapters 1 and 2, the large (12 percent of the whole population) black population in the United States has come to reside primarily in urban areas. Three quarters of all blacks live in urban areas (mostly in the central cities) and nearly half of all blacks live in the North. Thus, the problems of this disadvantaged group are now primarily concentrated in urban areas. In that sense, the problems faced by blacks have become primarily urban problems. And despite some progress in the last couple of decades, these problems remain severe and deeply embedded in urban life and institutions.

Economic Status

Most whites believe that the recent past has been a period of steady economic advance for blacks and that blacks are finally closing the economic gap between them and the white population. Unfortunately, that is much too simple a view of the recent economic trends in black communities.

The reason that many people think they can see an improvement in the economic status of blacks is that one visible segment of the black community, the black middle class, is improving its economic standing. The incomes of middle class black families have been rising, and the incomes of younger black couples in which both husband and wife work are now approaching those of comparable white families. An important reason for the gains of the black middle class is that in recent years, education has had an increased payoff in earnings for blacks. This means that, for every year blacks stay in school, they are likely to earn a salary or wage closer to that of white workers with the same education. While black workers are still, as a group, paid less than whites with similar educational levels, these wage differences have been decreasing, and have decreased the most among workers with college degrees (Farley, 1984:126).

By many other criteria we can examine, however, the economic position of blacks shows less improvement, or, in some cases, deterioration. Average family income levels are one example. In 1950, black family median yearly income was 54 percent as high as white income. (In other words, the average black family had an income only about half as large as a white family's.) Things did improve somewhat beginning in the 1960s. By 1969, black family median yearly income was up to 61 percent of white family income. But that trend did not continue. By 1977, the position of black families relative to whites had declined to 57 percent, and by 1987, black families were making only 56 percent of white families' incomes, only slightly better than in 1950 (U.S. Bureau of the Census, 1989b: 721, 723).

But these trends in family income levels provide only a partial picture of the actual situation. Average family incomes are the statistical result of a number of different and sometimes contradictory influences, such as whether people are employed, how much their wages are, how many people in the household are working, whether there is income from anything other than wages (such as government payments, alimony, or interest), and a number of other factors. If we look only at wages of employed workers, for example, we find that black workers' wages are getting closer to those of white workers. This is especially true of employed women (Farley, 1984:58). If we look at unemployment levels, however, we find that blacks are even more likely to be unemployed compared to whites than in the past (U.S. Bureau of the Census, 1989b:393). In addition, once laid off, black workers tend to be unemployed longer and have a harder time finding new jobs than white workers (U.S. Bureau of the Census, 1989a:5,6). Unemployment has become especially severe among younger urban black males, many of whom are not even counted as unemployed because they have stopped looking for work. Instead, they are counted as "not in the labor force."

Perhaps the most sobering statistics about the economic differences between blacks and whites are those relating to poverty. Throughout the past two decades, the poverty rate among whites has fluctuated between 8 and 12 percent of the population. But the poverty rate for blacks has fluctuated between 30 and 35 percent. Almost half of all black children are now being raised in poverty, and a black child born in the United States is three times as likely as a white child to be poor at some time in her or his life (U.S. House of Representatives, 1985). Racial differences are even more pronounced among the subgroup of people who remain in poverty over long periods of time. While blacks make up about 30 percent of all the poor, they constitute over 60 percent of those who are persistently poor (Duncan, 1984:61).

Thus, when we ask how blacks are doing relative to whites, we get different answers depending on which group of blacks we are discussing. Many sociologists now think that *economic polarization*, the widening of the gap between the rich and the poor, is one of the most important trends affecting the black population. As we saw earlier, economic polarization has been occurring among the entire population of the United States, but some analysts argue that it has been taking place even more rapidly among blacks than among the population as a whole.

One factor that seems to be related to economic polarization among blacks is changing family structure and the different impact that has had on white and black families. We have already seen that single-parent families are more likely to be poor than two-parent families. The black middle class is largely composed of highly educated, well-paid workers living in families in which both the husband and the wife are employed. The black poor are increasingly likely to be living in families headed by a single mother. Much of the decline in incomes of black families relative to whites was caused by the increase in the proportion of black families headed by a woman (Farley, 1984:147). Unfortunately, this fact has consequences for the future as well as the current living standard of poor black families. These single-parent families are not only more likely to be poor than two-parent families, but they also tend to stay poor for longer periods of time (McLanahan et al., 1988:103).

Another important factor affecting economic polarization, especially in urban areas, is the changing availability of job opportunities for workers at different educational levels. When we examine the employment trends in the large cities, we see that many low-level jobs have been eliminated or cut, while at the same time, the educational requirements for entry-level jobs, especially in the information-processing industries, have increased. Although blacks as a whole are catching up to whites in educational achievement, the proportion of urban blacks without high school diplomas is far higher than that of urban whites, and the proportion of urban blacks with some college education is far lower than that of urban whites (Kasarda, 1983:28).

Overall, negative trends in the economy tend to hurt blacks more than whites. During the recessions of the 1970s, for example, black workers were more likely than white workers to be laid off because they were concentrated in the less-skilled, low-wage, non-unionized jobs which were most affected by work force cuts (Farley, 1975). Remember also that black workers are heavily concentrated in Northern central cities. As basic changes in the economy have moved manufacturing job opportunities from the North to the South and West, the industries most affected have been those employing the largest numbers of black workers (Wilson, 1987:100-102). At the same time, wages for the types of jobs held by black workers, especially because they are less likely to be unionized, have tended not to keep up with inflation.

Racial discrimination also affects blacks' economic position. Although for the past thirty or more years, racist attitudes among whites (or at least the proportion of the population admitting to them) have been declining, many patterns of racial inequality persist. Because of past discrimination in hiring, for example, employed blacks are often "low-seniority" workers. Since they have been working at their jobs for a shorter time than their white counterparts, they are more likely to be laid off when the company cuts its work force. Past discrimination also means that there are large numbers of older black workers who were locked into low-wage, low-skill jobs when they were younger. Denied access to education, training, and the chance to work at jobs which would improve their skills, their opportunities now are severely limited. Another consideration is that residential segregation can limit economic opportunity, especially among the very poor. Those extra poor, socially fragmented inner-city black neighborhoods that have been called "hyperghettos" are affected by economic problems more intensely than are other types of neighborhoods. When the economy is bad, they are hurt worse than other areas, yet when the economy recovers, they recover less than other areas (Wacquant and Wilson, 1989). Finally, black workers are still paid less than white workers with the same education, even though the pay difference is gradually decreasing (Farley, 1984).

Many of the economic gains blacks have made are at least partly the result of social policy. Antidiscrimination legislation, although not always effective, has helped blacks and other disadvantaged groups take advantage of many educational and employment opportunities formerly closed to them. Other government policies have aided blacks in their struggles to overcome discrimination in business. Equal opportunity hiring and promotion programs, guidelines that spell out affirmative action procedures for companies seeking contracts with the federal government, and legislation mandating local governments to do a certain amount of business with minority-owned firms are some examples. Some analysts argue, however, that since blacks' gains have been based more on government actions than on actions of the private sector, their position is more fragile than most people realize (Collins, 1983). In any event, it is clear that for the foreseeable future, the United States will continue to see strong economic divisions between the majority of blacks and the majority of whites.

Education

Sadly, the continuation of black economic deprivation has occurred despite major gains in the amount of education being obtained by black children. The gains have been most spectacular in terms of the proportion of blacks completing high school. In 1960, 38 percent of black young adults and 60 percent of white young adults had completed high school. By 1987, the black percentage was 83 percent and the white percentage was 87 percent. Clearly, the education gap between blacks and whites at this level has been closing. Progress at the level of a college education was slower, although still significant. The percentage of young adults (age 25-34) who completed college increased during the 1960-74 period among both blacks and whites. In 1960, about 5 percent of the black young adults and 12 percent of the whites had received a degree. By 1987, the figure for blacks was 11 percent and for whites 23 percent (U.S. Bureau of the Census, 1989a:30).

The fact that black children now attend school for almost the same length of time as white children does not necessarily mean that the educations they receive are identical. Reynolds Farley (1984:22) points out that black students are more likely than white students to be one or more years behind the proper grade for their age, and, as a group, to get lower scores on standardized achievement tests than white students. In addition, an overwhelming difference between black and white students' educations stems from the fact of continued racial segregation in the schools. Hence, blacks are still likely to be consigned to schools in the central-city school districts which are predominately black.

That is a problem for several reasons. School integration has been a constitutionally mandated goal of government policy for a generation. Continued segregation represents evidence of a serious failure of public policy. Continued segregation in the schools is symbolically important too. Segregation in the schools is highly visible evidence of our society's failure to operate in a racially blind fashion.

The educational and social effects of continued segregation as opposed to integration in the schools is a matter of some debate among social scientists. It is generally acknowledged that the overall quality of the schools which most blacks attend is lower (Coleman, 1966). However, Christopher Jencks (1972) and others have argued that the evidence available indicates that the school quality differences which exist are not, by themselves, very important in determining future academic achievement or career success. On the other hand, research does suggest that schools with a high percentage of middle-class students have a social atmosphere (e.g., peer group pressure) which encourages academic achievement. This in turn suggests that integration in which lower-class black students attend a predominantly white, middle-class school may foster academic achievement among the black students. However, attempts to show that this does indeed happen have not always yielded the expected results (though there is agreement that white students' performance is not impaired). Similarly mixed results have been obtained in regard to the effect of integration on racial attitudes of both blacks and whites attending integrated schools (Armour, 1972). While the controversy continues, much of the available evidence seems to be that integration does not automatically improve performance or attitudes, but under the right circumstances, it can yield desirable educational outcomes (Mayer and Jencks, 1989).

What is clear is that attempts to integrate schools over the last few decades have yielded incomplete and often temporary results. To understand what has happened, it is necessary to distinguish between two kinds of school integration: *within-district integration* and *between-district integration*. Within-district integration refers to integration between schools in the same school district, while between-district integration refers to integration between schools in different school districts.

Almost all efforts at integration in the United States have been limited to within-district integration. The result, by the early 1970s, was a significant increase in the proportion of black students attending integrated schools. However, the greatest increases in integration occurred in smaller, isolated school systems. In these school systems, small size and isolation made stable integration more likely. If a system has only two high schools, for example (one predominantly black), moving students between the two schools (or closing the black school, a frequent approach) yields a high degree of integration. And, very importantly, white students in the newly integrated schools have no other (public) school to which to go. Consequently, the integrated situation will be a relatively stable one. Thus, small-town and rural school systems have become the most integrated ones (Coleman and Kelly, 1976).

Large central-city school districts (which serve most of the urban black population) achieved much more limited integration. This occurred for several reasons. Many central cities made only limited attempts to achieve integration: not all schools in the system were equally affected. Many schools stayed "lily white" or experienced token integration. The schools which experienced extensive integration in the city tended not to stay integrated, because the whites quickly left. They could do so because there were predominantly white schools to which to flee. In other cases, extensive city-wide busing plans were tried. After initial problems, substantial degrees of integration in central city systems were achieved. However, in many cases integration has proved to be temporary. The continued movement of white families to the suburbs has meant that there are simply fewer and fewer white children available to participate in attempts to integrate the schools, and resegregation has occurred. Whether enforced busing actually contributed to the white move to the suburbs is a matter of some controversy. The available evidence is contradictory, but it may have added somewhat to existing trends (Farley, 1984:24).

There are also significant differences in desegregation among the large cities—differences related to the ways in which desegregation plans have been adopted. In Southern cities such as Atlanta, Memphis, Dallas, and New Orleans, the progress toward desegregation has been dramatic. This is at least partly due to the aggressive stance of the courts on enforcing strong desegregation plans. Many Northern cities, such as New York, Chicago, and Philadelphia, have had no court-ordered desegregation and have experienced either steadily high or increasing levels of school segregation. In those cities outside of the South where court-ordered programs have been implemented (such as Los Angeles, Milwaukee, and Indianapolis), school segregation has decreased (Farley, 1984:25).

A second difference between desegregation plans is that in the few cases where between-district desegregation has occurred, it has been more successful than in those cities using within-district desegregation. Two good case studies are Nashville and Jacksonville. In each case, the school district of the central city was merged with the school districts of the surrounding communities in the metropolitan area. As a result, these two school districts include all of the students in the metropolitan area. They therefore have an overall school population more closely resembling the racial mix of the whole metropolitan area (majority white) rather than that of the central city (majority black). This expanded pool of white students makes it easier to achieve racial balance in the schools. At the same time, white families cannot move to the suburbs to find all-white schools, since the suburban schools are part of the same system as the city schools. As a result, Jacksonville and Nashville have been the most successful of all cities at reducing the separation of black and white students (Farley, 1984:29). Since school segregation today is mostly the result of blacks and whites living in different *school districts* (not, as previously, their living in different *neighborhoods* within the same school district), between-district or merged-district desegregation programs are probably the only effective avenue for decreasing school segregation. Unfortunately, in some cities outside of the South where these plans have been proposed, they have been blocked by suburban communities whose residents want their schools to remain virtually all white.

In the past few decades, most policy proposals have emphasized desegregating schools as a way of increasing the quality of the educational experience for black students. However, achieving integration is not the only way of improving education for blacks, and the evidence is mixed on whether (and to what degree) going to school with whites improves the "life chances" of black students. Some black scholars advocate de-emphasizing school integration and concentrating instead on improving education in the many predominantly-minority schools of our cities. They propose measures such as decreasing the size of schools, involving parents and community members (for example, in tutoring and after-school activities), and developing new methods of teaching and evaluation for black students (Robinson, 1987; Bakalis, 1987; *Chicago Tribune*, 5/24/1989:1,24). The question left for us to weigh, then, is not whether school desegregation is possible, or whether it increases the achievement of black students, or whether it is the only avenue to increasing the quality of education for black students. Even if we were to answer no to the above questions (which would by no means be justified by the evidence social scientists have gathered), we still need to weigh whether school desegregation may be an end in itself—a public commitment to decreasing racial isolation, indifference, and antagonism in our society.

Housing Segregation

Within-district school integration efforts have been frustrated in part because of a fragmented system of independent school districts serving racially segregated residential areas. As should be obvious to even a casual observer, neighborhoods in the United States remain highly segregated by race. There have been some changes in the extent of residential segregation over time, but the changes have been small and the overall degree of segregation remains high. Most research suggests that there was some increase in overall residential segregation in the 1940-50 period and some decrease in 1960-70. However, the decrease in the 1960-70 period was concentrated in smaller metropolitan areas with small black populations. In large metropolitan areas where most blacks live, segregation increased (Taeuber and Taeuber, 1965; Van Valey et al., 1977). During the 1980s, the United States as a whole showed a modest decline in segregation, but the central cities remained highly segregated by race (Farley, 1987).

How segregated are the cities of the United States? As of the 1980 census, on the average, only 12 percent of whites and 18 percent of blacks in the largest 28 metropolitan areas lived in neighborhoods that included members of the other racial group. In the most segregated cities, only 5 percent of whites and 7 percent of blacks had interracial neighbors, while in the least segregated cities, 34 percent of the whites and 31 percent of the blacks had interracial neighbors (Taeuber, 1983). There is some regional variation to the general patterns. Cities in the Midwest are the most segregated cities, while those in the West are the least segregated. Southern and Eastern cities are moderately segregated (Farley, 1987).

Of course, as we have seen in Chapter 2, since 1970 there has been an increasing rate of black suburbanization. However, that does not necessarily mean that the suburbs are becoming integrated communities. The percentage of blacks in the suburban population nationwide rose from 16 percent in 1970 to 21 percent in 1980 (Farley, 1987), but black suburbanization did not occur equally rapidly in all cities. A high proportion of the increase in black suburban dwellers was due to large changes in only a few metropolitan areas, and a full 9 percent of the increase in black suburbanization took place in *one* suburban community, Prince Georges County, outside of Washington, DC (Orfield, 1986).

In addition, the available evidence indicates that most black suburbanization results in the resegregation of blacks in suburban locations. It does appear that the traditional pattern of black suburban settlement has changed. Traditionally, blacks tended to be concentrated in semi-rural enclaves or in segregated communities in older industrial "satellite" towns. The new pattern of settlement is more varied. Some black suburbanization consists of central city black neighborhoods simply spilling over into the inner ring of older suburbs. In other cases, particular sections (often older, less desirable ones) of the suburbs are undergoing racial change and being converted into predominately black communities, experiencing problems similar to those of inner city ghetto areas (Schneider and Logan, 1982). About the only exception to these patterns may be among the most affluent blacks, who do seem to be achieving a more dispersed pattern of residence in predominately white areas.

What accounts for this continued pattern of residential segregation by race? It is highly doubtful that this pattern exists because blacks prefer to live in separate neighborhoods. The pattern of residential segregation runs counter to expressed black desires and causes real hardship for black families. Surveys of urban blacks consistently indicate than an overwhelming majority would prefer to live in integrated neighborhoods (Darden, 1987). In addition to desiring integration itself, many blacks want to obtain better housing and services than those available in predominantly black areas. The evidence indicates that, regardless of income level, blacks obtain housing which is of lower quality than that obtained by whites at similar income levels and pay as much or more for that housing (Jackman and Jackman, 1986). It is no wonder, then, that black residents express higher levels of dissatisfaction with their neighborhoods than do whites in the same metropolitan areas (Darden, 1987).

If segregation cannot be explained by blacks' preferences, neither can it be explained by black poverty. Blacks are not concentrated in the central cities simply because they cannot afford housing in the suburbs. In city after city, studies have shown that if families bought or rented their housing solely on the basis of their incomes, racial segregation would decline dramatically. In our large metropolitan areas, only a fraction of the middle-class blacks who can afford to live in the suburbs actually live there. And only a tiny fraction of poor whites have poor blacks as neighbors (Yinger, 1979; Kain, 1987). In fact, it is one of the sad ironies of urban housing markets that, for a given level of housing quality, black families usually pay higher prices than white families living in comparable housing (Yinger, 1979).

What then accounts for the continuation of residential segregation? The overwhelming weight of sociological opinion is that widespread, systematic (though covert and subtle) racial discrimination in housing continues to occur in the United States. It may be illegal, but literally millions of whites are finding ways to get around the antidiscrimination laws.

On the face of it, this may seem a curious conclusion given what is known about the change in white racial attitudes. In the last few decades, most surveys have indicated that acceptance of the basic principles of integration, equal opportunity, and racial justice has increased steadily. For example, the percent of whites supporting local laws barring racial discrimination in housing sales rose from 34 percent in 1973 to 46 percent in 1983 (Schuman et al., 1985:88). Given this change in racial attitudes, why would we not find more rapid progress toward housing desegregation?

The answer appears to be that simply agreeing with the principle of integration is not enough to prevent discriminatory behavior in regard to housing. Housing discrimination rests on a complex of beliefs, perceptions, and preferences. The white middle class has a strong preference for neighborhoods in which people like themselves predominate. A few people can be different, but they must be a small minority of the people in the neighborhood (Downs, 1973). The problem is that most whites regard most blacks as people very different from them. Blacks are perceived not just as poor, but as having different (and undesirable) character traits and cultural traditions. Many whites believe that black entry into a neighborhood will bring higher crime rates and lower property values (Taub, et al., 1984). Many whites also believe that the movement of even a few blacks into a neighborhood guarantees that the neighborhood will become predominantly black very soon thereafter.

A good deal of evidence shows that these beliefs are unfounded, or at best half-truths. Black residents moving into predominantly white neighborhoods are similar in most social characteristics (education, occupation, income, family type) to their white neighbors (Scott, 1983). In addition, several studies show that there is no predictable relationship between racial change and property values in neighborhoods. Sometimes property values decline, but they are just as likely to increase (Laurenti, 1960; Yinger, 1987). There is also no evidence that integrated neighborhoods will inevitably become all black (Saltman, 1989). Sometimes these beliefs, however, can act as self-fulfilling prophecies, actually producing the feared outcome. If large numbers of people put their houses on the market at the same time, the prices *are* likely to decline; if whites flee from a neighborhood, it *is* likely to become increasingly populated by black households, and so on. Thus, an underlying white uneasiness about "changing neighborhoods" (even when not expressed openly as racial prejudice) can be a powerful force affecting where people of different races live.

The result, despite laws to the contrary, is that whites have contrived a number of ways of maintaining segregation through discriminatory practices. Documenting these practices is difficult because they are informal and secretive to avoid the possibility of legal prosecution. (In fact, it is hard to prove, in court, that they are intentionally discriminatory.) Yet, they quite clearly occur. Two examples will illustrate the nature of the problem.

One widely reported practice is that of "steering" prospective customers by real estate agents. Real estate agents in some cities make it a practice to encourage blacks to look at housing in black or "changing" neighborhoods; that is, neighborhoods with a growing black population (Pearce, 1978). The techniques range from subtle (e.g., only mentioning houses in particular neighborhoods) to not so subtle (e.g., missing appointments with black customers or leaving through the back door when blacks appear). Similarly, the agents assume whites will not be interested in housing in integrated neighborhoods and act accordingly. Thus, in most large cities, a "dual housing market" exists: a situation in which black and white homeseekers have very different choices for housing available to them. Real estate agents in these dual markets often act as the gatekeepers who channel people into the "proper" areas.

More blatant and uglier is the very real threat to blacks of white violence if they do manage to surmount discriminatory barriers and move into a white neighborhood. Violent episodes, on the increase in the past decade, create real fear among blacks (Logan, 1988). Research in Detroit indicates that although blacks were almost unanimous in preferring integrated neighborhoods, they perceived strong white hostility toward blacks in the suburbs and were fearful of being the first black family to integrate an all-white neighborhood (Farley, et al., 1978).

Figure 4.1 **Major Causes of Residential Segregation**

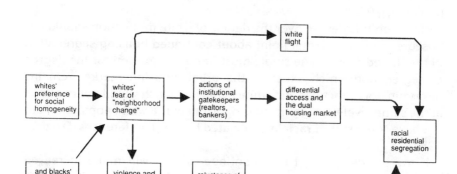

Besides practices which serve to keep blacks out of white neighborhoods, segregation continues because whites tend to leave central city
neighborhoods into which blacks have moved. There is some debate
as to the reasons for this phenomenon.

Some observers have found evidence that the resegregation of some
neighborhoods (to all black), once blacks move in, has been the result
of white flight fueled by fear. They argue that the entrance of black
residents, beyond a certain proportion, sets off fear of neighborhood
deterioration among whites, who then decide to leave in large numbers
(Guest and Zuiches, 1971). In some cases, this white flight is hastened
by real estate speculators manipulating residents' fears to increase sales
activity. This (illegal) sales practice consists of systematically canvassing
neighborhoods in which a few black families live and informing the white
residents that their neighborhood is "changing" and the property values
are about to fall dramatically. The speculator offers to pay cash for their
homes if they will sell immediately at a price under normal market
values. In a panic, the whites sell out. The speculator then turns around
and sells to black families at inflated prices, making a large profit.

Other observers have placed much less emphasis on the role of racial
fears and white flight as a cause of resegregation. Research by Molotch
suggests that resegregation is not so much a matter of racially motivated
flight from a neighborhood as it is a matter of the failure of whites to
move into a changing neighborhood. As housing units become vacant

in the normal course of events (such as a family being able to afford better housing and moving) only blacks move into the neighborhood (Molotch, 1972).

However, this debate over the details of white motivation should not obscure the fundamental point about continued housing segregation in the United States. The single most important reason for the degree of segregation which exists in the urban housing market remains discriminatory practices and white behavior, which would not continue at the same level if a significant proportion of the white population did not have some sort of racially motivated housing preferences (Darden, 1987).

If the trends of the 1980s continue, blacks will make increased progress on two dimensions of housing: improving the quality of their housing compared to whites and increasing overall integration, especially in the suburbs. If present trends continue, however, our largest cities will remain highly segregated and may even become more segregated in the future.

The New Immigrant Groups

An important new development in the 1980s was increased foreign immigration into the United States. Because of changes in U.S. immigration laws and economic or political conditions in other areas of the world, hundreds of thousands of immigrants arrived, especially from Asia and Latin America. They have, to a great extent, settled in the largest metropolitan areas of the United States. The city with the highest proportion of recent immigrants is Los Angeles, which has been called "the new Ellis Island" (Woolbright and Hartmann, 1987), but sizeable numbers of newcomers have arrived in most large cities.

Latin American immigrants have come in large numbers from Mexico, Central America, and Cuba. (Puerto Ricans are not actually immigrants since Puerto Rico is legally part of the United States.) They, along with smaller numbers from South America, the Caribbean, and Spain, are counted together in the Census as "Hispanic." Together they constitute the fastest growing ethnic group in the population (Darden, 1986). Taking the group as a whole, the socioeconomic status of Hispanics, based on such measures as income and rate of unemployment, is slightly higher than that of blacks but still well below that of whites.

Hispanic immigrants' settlement patterns vary depending on their country of origin. While Cubans tend to be concentrated in suburban areas, Puerto Ricans are mainly central city dwellers and Mexicans are found predominantly in rural areas. The regions of residence also vary greatly, with Cubans located disproportionately in the South and Mexicans in the Southwest. Puerto Ricans are the most segregated from whites and have the lowest socioeconomic status of all of the Hispanic subgroups (Woolbright and Hartmann, 1987), except possibly for illegal immigrants from Mexico (Wilson and Aponte, 1985).

Immigration to the United States from Asia exploded in the aftermath of the Vietnam War. Because of political and economic changes in Asia, significant numbers of people chose to migrate to the United States from Vietnam, Laos, Cambodia, Korea, the Philippines, China, Taiwan, Hong Kong, and even Japan. Like the Hispanic groups, the Asian groups from different nations vary in their socioeconomic status, degree of segregation, and region of settlement. The Chinese (including those from Taiwan and Hong Kong) are the most highly urbanized, while Koreans have a large proportion (over half) living in suburban areas. As a group, Asian immigrants have disproportionately settled in the Western United States, but while 80 percent of the Japanese are located in that region, fewer than half of the Koreans and Vietnamese are living in the West (Woolbright and Hartmann, 1987).

One interesting and perplexing phenomenon sociologists have explored is the apparently greater success the new immigrants have achieved in the United States compared to that of blacks. Although there are significant internal variations, as a group both Hispanic and Asian immigrants have more rapidly dispersed into white areas and have achieved a higher standard of living relative to whites than blacks (who have been here much longer) have been able to achieve. This is partly the result of lower (although still significant) levels of housing and job discrimination against Hispanics and Asians. However, several other factors have been identified as contributing to their higher success rate.

For one thing, certain countries' immigrants have been drawn from the most educated, skilled, and wealthy segments of the native population. Most Cubans who left immediately after the revolution in 1959 and Vietnamese who left during the revolution in the early 1970s fall into this category. When they arrived, even without a knowledge of English, they had the education and financial resources to establish themselves in the middle class (although many could not obtain as high a level of occupation as they had had in their native country).

A second factor in their favor has been the tendency to form *ethnic enclaves*, ethnically homogeneous neighborhoods in which housing, businesses, and all economic activity can be dominated by a single ethnic group (Light, 1972). Groups such as the Chinese and Koreans have been very successful at establishing businesses run by and for members of the ethnic group. This not only provides jobs to the group's members, it also circulates members' money within the ethnic community rather than paying it to outsiders. New immigrants have frequently used strong family and kinship networks for economic advantages such as borrowing money at low interest rates, hiring free (or low-paid) workers, getting free child care, and living in groups to save on rent (Kasarda, 1989). Finally, many recent immigrants come from ethnic groups in which attitudes of extreme frugality and even self-exploitation are common. Almost no sacrifice of self or family members is too great when the goal is entrepreneurial success (Wong, 1982). These ethnic-based strategies have either not been available to most blacks or have not been applied consistently enough to enable blacks to move ahead economically as rapidly as the new immigrants.

Main Points

1. The number of poor people cannot be definitely determined since poverty can be defined in different ways. The official count probably understates the true number of people in poverty.

2. Poverty can result not only from the lack of work but also from being employed at jobs that do not pay adequate wages.

3. Although most urban dwellers are not poor, there is an increasing tendency for poor people to be found living in neighborhoods where the majority of the population is poor. This is especially true for poor blacks.

4. There are two sociological approaches to explaining poverty. The structural approach stresses the ways in which jobs and income are channeled by social institutions. The cultural approach stresses the ways in which individuals learn behaviors that contribute to making or keeping them poor. Each of the approaches has different implications for reducing the amount of poverty. Some combination of both will probably be necessary to address the problems of the different groups of the poor.

5. Racial inequality continues to be a serious problem in United States cities. Although blacks' educational achievement is approaching that of whites, blacks' income levels remain substantially lower than those of whites.

6. Within the black community, there has been a tendency for increased polarization into a successful, educated group on one hand and a growing impoverished group on the other.

7. Many schools that were desegregated in the 1960s and 1970s have become resegregated. Smaller school districts and those systems that merge city and suburban schools have the best records regarding school desegregation.

8. Residential segregation by race is still very pronounced in U.S. cities. Blacks and whites do not have access to the same housing; rather a "dual housing market" operates in most metropolitan areas.

9. Housing segregation cannot be explained mainly by racial differences in income nor by blacks' preferences for living with other blacks. Any explanation must include racially motivated preferences and choices of whites.

10. Immigration into the United States, especially from Asia and Latin America, is having an important impact on our cities, since the majority of new immigrants are settling in metropolitan areas.

Key Terms

Between-District Integration   Integration of students across school district lines.

Cultural Approach to Poverty   A theory which claims that the behavior of the poor is the result of socialization to different, pathological values.

Ethnic Enclaves   Neighborhoods in which a single ethnic group controls most housing and businesses.

Hyperghettos   Minority neighborhoods whose high degree of racial segregation is accompanied by extreme poverty.

Official Poverty Line   The most commonly used estimate of the amount of income necessary to escape poverty. It is generally considered a low estimate.

Polarization of Income   The increasing gap between the rich and the poor.

Structural Approach to Poverty   This theory holds that poverty is the result of the unequal distribution of resources and opportunities within the social structure.

Underground Economy   Jobs that are either illegal or unreported to authorities, also called the "informal economy."

Within-district Integration   Integration of the students within a single school district.

Working Poor   That subgroup of the poor who work full time but at wages too low to put them over the poverty line.

Suggested Reading

Bluestone, Barry and Bennett Harrison. 1988. *The Great U-Turn*. New York: Basic Books. A description and analysis of increasing income polarization in the United States during the 1980s.

Ellwood, David. 1988. *Poor Support: Poverty in the American Family*. New York: Basic Books. A survey of the problems and policies relating to poverty.

Farley, Reynolds. 1984. *Blacks and Whites: Narrowing the Gap?* Cambridge, MA: Harvard University Press. A fact-filled comparison of the socioeconomic status of blacks compared to whites.

MacLeod, Jay. 1987. *Ain't No Makin' It*. Boulder, CO: Westview Press. An ethnographic study of two groups of poor teenagers in an inner-city neighborhood.

Saltman, Juliet. 1989. *A Fragile Movement: The Struggle for Neighborhood Stabilization*. Westport, CT: Greenwood Press. An analysis of the factors contributing to stably integrated neighborhoods.

Tobin, Gary, ed. 1987. *Divided Neighborhoods*. Newbury Park, CA: Sage. A good overview of current research on housing segregtion.

Wilson, William J. 1987. *The Truly Disadvantaged*. Chicago, IL: University of Chicago. An important study of poverty among urban blacks.

Endnotes

[1] There is some disagreement over the preferred terms for racial groups in the U.S. We have chosen to use the term "black" because it is broader than "Afro-American" (including, for example, people whose background is Jamaican) and narrower than "people of color" (excluding, for example, people with an Asian heritage). In this way, we use it as an approximate parallel to "white."

[2] In its early years, the Reagan administration proposed an alternative way of measuring income that results in even fewer people being counted as officially poor. Under this proposal, the cash value of government services (such as Medicaid or food stamps) a household receives is added to its income. More than one-third of people in poverty automatically become "nonpoor" when these "in-kind" payments are added to their incomes. This proposal caused much controversy, with the result that the government now counts and reports income both with and without the in-kind payments. Sociologists continue to use cash income as the basis of their calculations. For a good discussion of this issue, see Beeghley (1983).

5

Housing and Urban Decay

Outline of Topics

H ousing represents one of the largest expenditures in the average family's budget. When purchased, it is the largest purchase most people make and constitutes their most important asset. It is also a basic material necessity. Weather-tight, physically safe, sanitary, and affordable housing is something everyone needs. At the same time, the housing people can afford in terms of its comfort, convenience, and aesthetic qualities is a major determinant of a family's standard of living and quality of life. Additionally, housing is an important social symbol which reflects social rank and prestige. As a consequence, the condition, cost, and availability of housing is both a critical concern to individuals and a major indication of material well-being in society. And to be deprived of adequate housing is a major form of deprivation and disadvantage.

Our discussion here will be limited to two major problems which urban areas face in regard to housing. Our first concern will be with the nature and extent of, and trends in, urban housing deprivation. We will then turn to the related problem of housing decay and neighborhood deterioration.

Housing Deprivation

A person can experience two kinds of housing deprivation, either separately or in combination. First, a person can be deprived in terms of the quality of the housing he or she occupies. Quality can be defined in either absolute or relative terms. Absolute deprivation consists of housing which does not meet minimum standards in relation to such things as space per person, structural soundness, cleanliness, and sanitation. Relative deprivation consists of not being able to obtain housing which meets one's expectations in terms of life-style preferences, aesthetic preferences, and prestige needs. For example, in the United States the middle-class ideal has traditionally been ownership of a large, detached single-family home on a spacious lot.

The other form of deprivation is deprivation caused by the high cost of housing. Such deprivation exists when people find themselves with no alternative but to pay such a large portion of their income for housing that their ability to purchase other necessary items is substantially impaired.

Housing Quality

One of the great accomplishments of this century has been that the overall quality of urban housing has improved markedly and the portion of the urban population living in low-quality housing has decreased.

Precisely how much things have improved, however, is not something which has been measured very successfully. Census measurements of housing quality have been crude, unreliable, and inconsistent. The basic distinction has been between housing which was *substandard* (variously defined) and housing which was not. The determination of what constituted substandard has included (in various censuses) attempts to evaluate structural soundness, the presence of working plumbing, and the extent of crowding (number of people per room). It is recognized as a very primitive attempt to measure housing quality. As a result, census figures on housing probably understate the amount of bad housing and tell nothing in detail about changes in housing that is not substandard (Hartman, 1975). Other attempts to measure housing quality have been sporadic and have not generated information which can be compared over time.

Still, all the available evidence consistently points toward substantial improvement in housing quality over the long term. Changing census definitions over time prevent comparisons of the proportion of housing rated substandard. However, some comparisons are possible. For example, in 1940, 29 percent of all families living in rental housing were in "crowded" housing (defined as more than one person per room). Only 4 percent of these families lived in crowded housing by 1983 (Schwartz et al., 1988:31). Similarly, up until the early 1970s, the "quality" of new homes (defined by size, number of bathrooms, attached garages, central air conditioning, and the like) had almost steadily increased from the 1940s onward. Also, the proportion of people living in homes they owned themselves increased. In 1900, 47 percent of the population owned their own homes. In 1985, 64 percent were homeowners (Schwartz et al., 1988:8). Thus, during this century urban areas have seen a major decline in grossly inadequate housing and significant increases in the quality of housing occupied.

This overall increase in housing quality does not mean that our housing problems have been solved. Progress toward eliminating substandard housing has slowed in recent years. In its 1983 *Annual Housing Survey*, the U.S. Department of Housing and Urban Development (HUD) found that almost 10 million families were living in inadequate housing. Of these, 7.5 million were in structurally unsound housing and an additional 2.25 million were in housing which, although sound, was overcrowded (Schwartz et al., 1988:32). Note that some of the 7.5 million in the unsound housing were also overcrowded, but that figure was not reported separately.

Housing quality also varies depending on the population group to which the household belongs. While homeowners in general enjoy better than average quality, renters suffer from worse than average housing quality. Those groups with the least adequate housing, according to the Census, are low-income renters, blacks, and Hispanics (Gilderbloom and Appelbaum, 1988:20).

Federal policies that have been developed to deal with inadequate housing have primarily addressed the problem by removing inadequate units from the housing stock. Beginning with programs in the 1930s to build public housing, legislation linked the production of new subsidized housing units to the demolition of an equal number of substandard units. Later in the 1950s and 1960s, slum clearance became a major urban policy goal, and cities used federal funds to demolish housing that was considered "blighted." While this type of policy was effective in decreasing the number of substandard housing units, it was not necessarily effective in replacing them with low cost, adequate housing. So some of the statistical improvement in the housing stock was gained by an overall reduction in the supply of low-cost housing (National Commission on Urban Problems, 1968).

Zoning and Housing Quality

One of the hidden factors complicating the issue of housing quality in urban areas is the role of suburban zoning ordinances in distributing different types of housing. In most metropolitan areas, at least some suburban communities practice *exclusionary zoning*. By requiring builders to use a sizeable housing lot (often a half acre), large square footage plans for new homes, and sometimes even particular building materials, existing residents ensure that only the well-to-do can afford to move in. Some areas institute outright bans on certain types of housing: mobile homes, attached single-family dwellings (e.g., townhouses), or apartment houses. The result is that these towns literally become exclusive — that is, they exclude those families whose incomes do not allow them to live in their upscale type of housing. As a result, in most metropolitan areas, low-cost housing is highly concentrated in the central cities. This concentration limits the kinds of neighborhoods from which low-income households may select their housing and narrows the choice of neighborhood amenities such as schools, shopping, and recreational facilities that are attached to the housing decision.

In recent years, several states have begun to limit exclusionary zoning and to encourage or require communities to allow low-cost housing to be built within their boundaries. In New Jersey, for example, a State Supreme Court decision (called Mount Laurel II after the community that was allegedly practicing exclusionary zoning) required that all towns develop plans to construct low-cost housing. Each suburb was to take its "fair share" of units based on the size of the town and the amount of buildable land available. The mechanism used in New Jersey, as well as in California and other areas, to achieve the integration of low-cost units into suburban areas is called, appropriately enough, *inclusionary zoning*. By this mechanism, new housing developments must include a certain proportion of low-cost units in order to be approved for construction. If developers want to build, for example, 50 houses, about 10 of them (usually 20 percent of the total) must be priced for low- and moderate-income families. In the first ten years since exclusionary zoning was abolished in New Jersey, an estimated 12,000 new units of high quality, affordable housing have been built or are planned (Mallach, 1988).

The significance of this legal change is that it increases housing choices for many families and allows access to the suburbs for many who were formerly "priced out" of those areas. Eliminating exclusionary zoning is hardly a panacea for housing quality problems, however. Not everyone wants to or can move to the suburbs, and even if more households do move out of the central cities, attention must be given to increasing the quality of deteriorated housing for those who remain.

Housing Costs

In the past, gains in housing quality were the result of two long-term trends. First, the trend was toward very large increases in average real purchasing power in the general population. One of the major things people did with this rising purchasing power was to upgrade the quality of their housing. The second basic trend, reinforcing the first, was that the cost of new housing increased at a slower rate than average income from 1945 until 1965 (Stone, 1986).

Since 1965, however, these trends have reversed. Real purchasing power has not increased, and the cost of housing has risen more rapidly than income. The result has been a growing problem of cost deprivation in housing, in which a growing proportion of the population either cannot afford the kind of housing to which they have become accustomed or must devote much more of their income to housing.

Housing price increases in recent years have been extremely rapid. In 1970, the median rent in the United States was $108. By 1985, it had tripled to more than $350. Homeowners fared even worse than renters: the median sales price of new homes quadrupled, going from $23,000 in 1970 to more than $92,000 in 1986. But these *average* increases in housing prices mask the differences among regional housing markets. While the housing prices in the middle of the country rose only modestly, those on the coasts soared. In just the five years between 1983 and 1988, the median price of existing single-family homes in Boston rose from $82,000 to $183,000. In Orange County, California, the average new house cost over $200,000 by 1988. Rents in both Boston and California, pushed by housing prices, rose at twice the national average between 1980 and 1989 (Sternlieb and Hughes, 1986; Case and Cook, 1989).

The housing price increase has been so profound that it has changed our very definition of "reasonable" housing costs. Until the mid-1970s, economists and realtors used a guideline for rent or housing payments of 25 percent of a household's income. Housing prices have risen so much faster than incomes that the 25 percent rule has now been raised to 30 percent. Even if we use this higher figure to define "comfortable" housing payments, however, we find that about a third of all households are paying an excessive amount for their housing. Among renters, nearly a quarter pay *more than half* of their income for rent (Schwartz et al., 1988:18,31).

There were several reasons for these increased costs since the mid-1970s. The single most important factor in the increased price of new houses was the cost of land. However, costs of material, labor, and financing (i.e., mortgage rates) rose almost as quickly. The tremendous demand for housing also created upward pressures on the price. The baby-boom generation was in the family formation period, and that meant a huge increase in the number of young families looking for housing. The rental housing market was caught in a particularly vicious circle. High financing and construction costs, changes in the tax law, and a lack of people able to pay the high rents necessary to make a profit from new units, all made new construction less profitable. So fewer units were built. The resulting shortage of rental units drove rents up further. At the same time, people unable to purchase single-family houses turned to the option of purchasing condominium apartments (partly to escape rising rents). They made "condo conversion" profitable: landlords could make more money by selling their units to their tenants as condominiums. This further tightened the supply of rental units and drove up the price. In some cities, owners and developers have taken advantage of the tightening market to force existing tenants to purchase their units at grossly inflated prices.

The overall impact of these changes in the housing market has been to produce an increase in the supply of higher-priced housing and a decrease in the supply of lower-priced housing. Thus, although housing units are being produced, they are not concentrated in the price range where most buyers or renters can afford them. Indeed, the average income family has not been able to afford to buy the average priced home since 1975 (Schwartz et al., 1988:10).

While the supply of low-cost units has been decreasing, the number of low-income families has been increasing. Between 1973 and 1983, the number of households with incomes under $10,000 increased by one-third, while the number of apartments renting for less than $250 a month (in 1983 dollars) fell by one-fourth (National Housing Task Force, 1988:15). Thus, analysts have now come to the conclusion that the main housing problem in the United States today is not the overall supply of housing but the short supply of *affordable* housing. In short, we have developed an *affordability crisis.*

The "Housing Have-Nots"

According to a recent study released by the Joint Center for Housing Studies at Harvard University (Apgar and Brown, 1988), "America is increasingly becoming a nation of housing haves and have-nots." The description, however chilling, appears to be accurate. When we compare different population groups, we find that certain groups are doing quite well with their housing while others are bearing the brunt of the affordability crisis.

The group that has been hurt the most is the poor. Between 1978 and 1983, median rents for the very poor rose 82 percent, compared to an increase for all income groups of 51 percent. Among this group, households with less than $3000 income in 1983, the average rent payment was 60 percent of the household's income. On the other hand, affluent renters with incomes over $75,000 paid only 10 percent of their incomes in rent (Gilderbloom and Appelbaum, 1988:23-24).

Another group that has been disproportionately affected by the rising cost of housing has been households headed by women supporting one or more dependents. Women heads of households are more likely to be renters and are more likely to be poor than male household heads or single adults. While many two-parent families have been able to keep up with housing prices by becoming two-earner households, women-headed families obviously do not have that option. In fact, as a group, women-headed renter families experienced a 12 percent *decrease* in their incomes between 1975 and 1985 while their rents rose 20 percent during the same period. Besides high housing costs, women often face discrimination which further limits their housing choices. Although technically illegal, it is common for landlords to reject women applicants, especially those with children (Pearce, 1990).

Surprisingly, young people form the third group of those hardest hit by housing costs. Young adults who entered the labor market during the difficult years of the late 1970s and early 1980s saw their incomes stagnate while housing prices literally ran away from them. In every year between 1980 and 1986, the rate of homeownership among households headed by persons under 35 showed large decreases, with the steepest drop-off among householders under 30. Much of this drop-off is due to the size of the downpayments needed to purchase homes. In 1985, a 20 percent downpayment on the average home amounted to $15,000—a huge sum for a young person (or family) to have saved (Schwartz et al., 1988:10-11). Many young people who chose to buy at the high prices of the 1980s have put so much money into their property that they have become, in the terms of one economist, "shelter poor." That is, although they are technically not poor, once they have made their house payment, the remainder of their income is insufficient to meet their other needs (Stone, 1986).

The Homeless

The most dramatic consequence of the housing affordability crisis has been the appearance of an increasingly large group of people without permanent homes. Although homelessness is a problem in rural and suburban areas, it is, like so many social problems, more concentrated and more visible in cities.

The most visible groups of the homeless, the bag ladies, winos, and beggars, have given many people a false impression of the nature and extent of homelessness. The homeless are a highly diverse group with many different specific paths by which they became homeless. What they all share, as Jonathan Kozol (1988) has so eloquently pointed out, is that they all lack a place to live. Some, approximately one-third, have a psychiatric problem or a drug or alcohol dependency that prevents them from functioning normally or working on a consistent basis. Others are perfectly "normal," middle- or working-class people who have lost their housing due to a traumatic event: a house fire, a severe illness, a divorce, or loss of a job. A large and growing proportion (estimated at about another third of the total) are mothers of small children who either have been denied (or cut from) public assistance or whose payments are too low to pay the increasingly high rents in urban areas.

Homelessness is a relatively *new* problem, a new manifestation of poverty in our society. Although there have always been poor people, people who needed psychiatric help, and single mothers, these groups did not suffer from homelessness in large numbers until the 1970s. Economic trends during the past twenty years, and particularly the virtual disappearance of the cheapest types of housing, have precipitated the large-scale homelessness we see today. The rising housing prices that have affected all segments of the population have literally driven out many low-income households, as landlords have been able to charge higher rents. Some alternative types of housing, like the old single-room-occupancy hotels (SROs) favored by many single, elderly people, have been demolished or converted to luxury apartments. An additional factor leading to increased homelessness has been the deinstitutionalization of large numbers of psychiatric patients without adequate supervision to ensure their re-integration into community life. Thus, a number of independent factors: higher housing costs, stagnating incomes, increasingly stringent welfare programs, housing demolition, and psychiatric policy, converged in an unfortunate manner in the 1970s and 1980s to produce increasing homelessness (Bingham et al., 1987).

Policy responses to homelessness have been, by all accounts, inadequate. On the federal level, there has been virtually no policy directed toward the homeless, save for some "emergency" funds which were largely directed toward soup kitchens. Local governments have had to deal with the homelessness problem on their own, and they have done so in wildly different ways. Some cities have passed ordinances to get rid of their homeless by preventing them from sleeping in public, begging, and scavenging in dumpsters, or even by giving them one-way bus tickets out of town. Others have provided temporary shelters but have kept the facilities stark and primitive so that they do not attract larger numbers of homeless from other areas. A few cities have established comprehensive policies ranging from alcohol and drug counseling to job placement to housing subsidies. Others have tried to prevent homelessness by intervening to prevent evictions.

Despite the best efforts of local officials, churches, and nonprofit agencies to help homeless people cope with their situation, the problem of homelessness can be fundamentally solved only when the homeless are able to find permanent, affordable housing. Many analysts (e.g., Swanstrom, 1989) argue that this will require a concerted policy by the federal government to increase the supply of affordable housing.

Government Housing Policies

In the last four decades, the federal government has attempted to reduce housing deprivation through a number of different programs. One set of programs was designed to help more affluent working- and middle-class families purchase single-family houses. Another set of programs attempted to reduce the absolute housing deprivation of the poor (and, thereby, eliminate slum housing).

Assistance to the Nonpoor

Since the 1930s, the federal government has provided major assistance to those seeking to buy housing. Most of these subsidies have gone to the more affluent. The single most costly part of the program has been the income-tax deduction allowed for the cost of interest on a mortgage, combined with deductions for state and local property taxes. In 1988 alone, the cost to the federal government, in terms of lost taxes, of these deductions was $40 to $50 billion. (That compares to $10 billion spent on housing subsidies for the poor and a total federal housing budget of $64 billion in 1988.) The more affluent a person is, the larger the total amount of the subsidy: in 1988, two-thirds of all homeowner tax deductions went to households with incomes over $50,000 (Working Group on Housing, 1989:19). This is due partly to the fact that the more affluent tend to buy more expensive houses and thus pay more (deductible) mortgage interest than the less affluent. A second reason is that since the incomes of the affluent are taxed at a somewhat higher rate than those of the less affluent, the deductions represent a greater tax savings to people at higher income levels. The homeowners' tax deduction is so much larger than the other federal housing subsidies that the amount for the single year, 1980, of the tax subsidy exceeded the total of all federally-assisted housing programs from their beginning in 1937 through 1980 (Dolbeare, 1983).

In addition to this subsidy, the other major subsidy to home buyers has been the FHA and VA mortgage programs. Because the government insured the loans, private lending institutions were willing to provide relatively low-interest, low-down payment mortgages to home buyers. This program primarily subsidized suburban housing construction and played a major role in suburbanization after 1945. (See Chapter 1.) Changes in the FHA program in the 1970s meant that some less affluent families in central cities began to participate in the program, but the bulk of the loans have continued to go to the nonpoor. The federal government also plays a major role in making sure that adequate funds for mortgages are available in the banking system.

In the past at least, this part of the federal housing program (the most expensive part) enjoyed major success. It played a central role in the post-1945 housing boom which created the suburbs and made possible an increase in home ownership in the population. It generated a tremendous amount of housing. While its direct beneficiaries were the more affluent, its supporters argued that the middle class and poor would also benefit from these programs. As each well-to-do family moved into new housing, its former residence would become available to another (presumably less affluent) family, which would in turn vacate its former residence, and so on. Thus, a "vacancy chain" would be created by which housing of each higher income group would "filter down" to each lower income group. Critics such as Dolbeare (1986) point out that these programs are an expensive and inefficient way of producing housing, as well as a boon to those who need help least. They are, however, politically popular precisely because they benefit those groups (the middle class and affluent) with the most political influence.

Assistance to the Poor

The set of programs designed for the poor has always had much more limited success. These programs have taken two major forms: (1) the construction of housing and (2) the provision of various housing subsidies to the poor.

From the 1930s through the 1960s the primary focus of federal programs to help the poor obtain decent housing was the construction of low-income housing projects. The initial, very small program of low-rise projects of the 1930s housed very few poor people, but met with modest success. Most of the people they housed were the "temporary poor" of working class people left unemployed in the Depression. In general, they were well maintained and did not have major problems of vandalism and crime.

This limited success was followed by the decision to construct large-scale public housing projects. Officials hoped to provide a significant amount of decent housing for the poor at a reasonable cost to the taxpayers. It soon became apparent, however, that these two goals were in conflict with each other.

The main problem was that sufficient funds were never provided to ensure the success of the program. This had many repercussions. While public housing construction was funded by the federal government, the operation of the buildings was left mainly to the cities and towns in which they were located. That meant that, like private landlords, the local housing authorities in charge of public housing projects had to take in enough in rents to cover their expenses such as utilities, maintenance, and administration. At the same time, however, changes in federal regulations (and in the private housing market) transformed the clientele living in public housing from the Depression-era temporary poor to the poorest of the poor. While operating expenses for public housing rose throughout the 1960s and 1970s, rents were nearly frozen due to the extremely low incomes of the residents and legal limitations on the percent of their income they were allowed to pay for rent. As federal operating subsidies fell farther and farther behind what was needed, many local housing authorities could not meet the necessary expenses for maintenance and security. These "problem projects," usually located in very poor parts of larger cities, became not only eyesores but also dangerous to their inhabitants. (Rachel Bratt, 1986, gives an excellent history of the public housing program.)

Funding problems were compounded by serious design failures. It was believed cheapest to build large projects of high-rise buildings. Public housing built during the 1960s tended to be clusters of high-density apartment blocks, separated by large open spaces. Designers gave little effective attention to creating structures which provided safe public space, adequate meeting and shopping areas, access to transportation and places of employment, and means for parents to keep an eye on their children. Political pressure also guaranteed that public housing reinforced housing segregation by being located in low-income, black neighborhoods. The most notorious example of the failure of this type of cheap, large-scale "warehousing" of the poor in public housing was St. Louis's Pruitt-Igoe project, which became so deteriorated and dangerous that it was demolished less than twenty years after it had been built. (See Rainwater, 1970 for a description of these problems.)

Another important problem of the large-scale public housing projects is that they have often been regarded as visible symbols of poverty for many of those who live in them. A certain address can immediately mark and stigmatize children in school, jobseeking adults, and social service clients as different and undesirable. These negative attitudes so common in the United States are largely absent in Europe where public housing is more widespread, serves a broader cross-section of the population, and is better integrated into the community (Popenoe, 1985).

In fact, in the United States as well, many public housing projects are highly successful. The most popular and successful are those reserved for senior citizens, but many people do not know that these projects are part of the public housing program. Other successful types of projects are the small (under 100 units) developments that have made up most of the public housing construction since 1980 and the "scattered site" developments in which individual units of public housing are located among the private housing units in residential neighborhoods. Recent evaluations of public housing have shown, however, that the absolute size of the project is less important than how it is managed and how it compares to other available housing. In New York City, for example, there are over 174,000 public housing apartments, most in high-rise buildings, but the waiting lists for rentals far exceed the numbers of available units. As one report stated, "Nobody likes public housing except the people who live there and those who want to get in" (Bratt, 1986:343).

Starting in the late 1960s, the federal government began moving away from building publicly owned and operated housing. Instead, it initiated a number of programs that encouraged private landlords to make additional apartments available for low-income households. One aspect of this new strategy was a mortgage construction subsidy. Under programs such as Section 221 (d)(3) and Section 236, housing developers received low-interest mortgages subsidized by HUD. In return, they had to agree to rent to low-income households for a certain period of time (usually about 20 years). While these construction programs helped augment the stock of low-cost housing, they were only temporary additions to the low-cost inventory. As the time limits have expired, and as market conditions have changed, many landlords have chosen to convert their apartments from subsidized to market-rate units, raising rents as much as 300 percent. Other landlords have gone into default, since they were using these projects mainly as a tax write-off. Because of these complications, an estimated half a million apartments may be lost from the stock of low-cost housing, under these two programs alone, by the year 2000 (Hoff, 1988; Yates, 1988).

Another way in which the federal government changed its housing subsidy strategy was by giving rent subsidies to tenants seeking housing in the private market. The chief program developed for this purpose was the Section 8 rental assistance program, begun in 1974. Under Section 8, landlords charge the approved "prevailing market rate" for apartments, while the low income tenants pay a proportion of their income for rent (originally 25 percent of their income, now 30 percent), and the federal government makes up the difference. Such direct rent subsidies were supposed to provide more flexibility for tenants and a cheaper, less bureaucratic alternative to public housing. Since both tenants and landlords have to apply to be accepted to Section 8, however, it proved to have its own bureaucratic problems. Moreover, since fair market rents have increased dramatically, the price of the subsidy has skyrocketed. Critics argue that in some areas, rent subsidies have actually contributed to pushing up rents since they have allowed landlords to charge low-income people higher rents than they would otherwise have been able to pay. In other areas, government approved "prevailing rent levels" have not kept up with actual rents in recent years, discouraging landlords from entering the program. Thus, of the many low-income households eligible for Section 8 subsidies, only a fraction apply, only a fraction of those who apply are approved, and only a fraction of those approved can actually find an apartment at the approved "prevailing market rate" (Working Group on Housing, 1989).

A new version of the rent subsidy strategy, a housing voucher system, is being pursued by the Bush administration. Like the Section 8 program, the housing voucher pays the landlord the difference between 30 percent of the tenant's income and the approved prevailing market rent for an apartment in a given area. The chief difference is that while Section 8 certificates can be used only for approved apartments at approved rents, vouchers can be used for any apartment at any price. The voucher program has been operating on a demonstration basis since 1982. A preliminary study released by HUD shows that it has helped push rents even higher, since landlords have no limit on what they can change under the voucher system. The HUD study concludes that the dollar amounts of the subsidy per household are $23 a month more than those under Section 8, and that the households using vouchers are actually paying $32 a month more on their rent (Widrow, 1987).

During the 1980s, the Reagan administration instituted a number of profound changes in the direction of national housing policy. These changes were expressly designed to reduce government intervention in housing and to rely more on the private market to provide housing. Probably the most significant of these changes was the decision to cut back the public housing program by not producing any new units and by selling existing units either to tenants or to private landlords. A related policy change was to raise the rents in subsidized units (public housing or Section 8) from 25 percent to 30 percent of tenants' incomes. Spending for HUD programs overall was drastically reduced. It fell from about 7 percent of the federal budget in 1978 to 1 percent in 1987, making housing the most severely affected of all the social programs cut during the Reagan era (Schwartz et al., 1988:47). Citing "too much government regulation," the administration unsuccessfully tried to get cities and states to rescind local rent control laws, threatening to withhold federal community development funds if they did not comply. In line with its market-oriented philosophy, the Reagan administration's overall policy has been to rely on the *trickle-down effect*: the notion that by subsidizing housing for the non-poor, the poor would eventually benefit.

New Policy Directions

As a result of both the private market's failure and the federal government's wholesale withdrawal from the arena of low-cost housing, nonprofit groups have increasingly taken on the role of housing developer. Local governments as well as community organizations, churches, and labor unions have been forming or supporting nonprofit corporations to produce subsidized housing. While state and local governments may provide some funds, other sources such as charitable foundations and individual contributions (of money, materials, and labor) are often used for support, and the amount of housing being constructed is naturally very limited. Supporters of the nonprofit housing sector use the example of Canada, which has channeled government housing funds through nonprofit organizations for the past twenty years, as a model for the United States to follow. While Canada still has some housing problems, it has been able to produce more than 300,000 well-designed subsidized units which integrate lower- and middle-class residents, carry little social stigma, and cannot by law be sold to private owners or converted to condominiums (Dreier, 1989).

While government policies have stressed private home ownership for the nonpoor and private rental apartments for the poor, many housing activists argue for a broader range of housing options. Some examples of innovative housing designs include *congregate housing* in which individuals have private rooms but share living and dining areas, and *co-housing* in which households have private units (apartments or townhouses), but share recreational space, laundry facilities, and often a communal dining room in addition to their own kitchen. Congregate housing is popular among elderly people who want to combine independent living with a supportive social environment. Co-housing (more common in Scandinavia, but growing in the United States) is preferred by younger households desiring the privacy of their own home but not the isolation of the typical single-family house (Dennis, 1989). In addition to variations in design, options in tenure, other than simply homeowner and renter, are becoming available. These include co-operative ownership, in which a number of persons jointly own one or more buildings, and shared mortgages, in which the mortgage is "shared" between one person (normally low-income) who lives in a home and a second person (normally middle- or upper-income) who is able to benefit from the tax deduction on the mortgage. Housing analysts such as Peter Marcuse and Emily Achtenberg (1986) hold that more varied forms of tenure and socially, rather than privately, controlled housing are necessary if we expect to house everyone adequately.

Evaluation

The record of government housing policy has been a mixed one. It has had substantial success, although at great cost, in helping the nonpoor obtain single-family houses. It has devoted fewer resources and had much less success dealing with the housing problems of the poor, who face worsening conditions in regard to both the quality and the cost of the housing they occupy. However, the government effort to assist the poor cannot be judged a total failure. Significant numbers of the poor have either been moved to better housing or received economic assistance in meeting their housing needs. The most obvious evidence that government housing programs work is the fact that, as spending has decreased, housing problems, especially homelessness, has increased. Since the private market cannot provide adequate housing for low-income families, government intervention will be necessary for the foreseeable future.

Urban Decay

Urban residential decay is the process by which the physical condition of housing in a whole neighborhood or major section of a community deteriorates. Fundamentally, it is a reflection of two basic facts. First, urban areas are home for large numbers of poor people who can afford to spend very little for housing. Second, in a profit-oriented society such as ours, housing is produced (built, mortgaged, rented out) only if it will make a profit for someone.

Even as the overall quality of housing in metropolitan areas has risen, the central cities (home for the poor and centers of low-rent housing) have experienced declines in the quality of their housing stock. They have been decaying. In a few of the worst hit cities, that decay has spread to a majority of the neighborhoods. All central cities, however, have experienced some decay in the last few decades. A number of factors have contributed to or accelerated that process.

Causes of Urban Decay

The age of the housing stock in the central cities makes central-city neighborhoods vulnerable to decay. Simple age does not guarantee decay, of course. Old housing is often structurally sound and repairable. However, most of the housing in our Northern central cities was built prior to 1930. At the very least, that means higher maintenance and heating costs. Older structures also lack the amenities that became popular after 1945, such as large yards, garages, and multiple bathrooms. The older housing is also often multiple-family rental housing which has fallen out of favor in recent decades.

After World War II, the vast majority of the new housing being constructed was in the suburbs. The suburban exodus from the cities, which had begun in the 1920s, accelerated. Older, urban housing gradually lost its appeal as middle-class housing, and less affluent families began to move in. Landlords could not charge as much rent to cover operating expenses, maintenance, and financing costs. Less affluent homeowners could afford to do less maintenance. Initial deterioration began.

However, the rate of that deterioration was much accelerated after 1945 by the in-migration of the rural poor. At the same time that the middle-class housing market was weakening in the cities, there was a tremendous demand for low-rent housing. The old slum neighborhoods could not accommodate the new wave of the poor. Thus, the stage was set for rapid conversion of neighborhoods for use by low-income families.

However, the process of urban decay should not be viewed as a simple combination of an aging housing stock, "natural" market forces, and demographic trends. Government policy had the effect of encouraging, even forcing, the pace of slum creation. As we have seen in Chapter 1, government policy heavily subsidized the middle-class movement to the suburbs. Failure to help the poor obtain housing guaranteed a market for cheap, deteriorated housing. FHA lending policies made it difficult to obtain mortgages in older neighborhoods. Highway construction and urban renewal destroyed substantial quantities of low-income housing, forcing the poor to look for new neighborhoods. Little governmental assistance was available for rehabilitation of old housing in the 1950s and 1960s. Local government contributed to the problem by its real estate property tax policies. Owners of older buildings faced higher real estate taxes if they made substantial improvements which increased the assessed valuation of their property.

Banks and other major lending institutions also contributed to the decline of many inner-city neighborhoods. Beginning in the 1940s, banks began to *redline* or disinvest in many central-city neighborhoods. This meant that they would not give conventional long-term, low-interest mortgages to people seeking to purchase homes and rental properties in older neighborhoods, and especially neighborhoods with a large proportion of nonwhite residents. Only people who were willing to pay higher interest, larger down payments, and larger monthly payments over a short period could obtain financing. The result was that average families and investors were not able to purchase housing in many central-city neighborhoods. While government agencies such as the FHA theoretically could have stepped in to provide financing in these neighborhoods, they did not. The FHA's criteria for mortgage lending were based on the same assumptions as those of the private banks (Bradford and Marino, 1977). This further depressed the market for urban housing and also favored the involvement of real estate speculators (who had access to financing) in older central-city neighborhoods.

The Role of Speculators

Destroying a neighborhood proved to be profitable to various kinds of real estate speculators, at the expense of the existing residents of the neighborhood. That speculative activity took a number of forms.

Conversion of rental property to slum use was one form of profitable activity. One very common strategy was for high-income investors to use the purchase of old apartment buildings as a tax shelter. Investors bought old buildings cheaply on high interest, short-term mortgages. To cover the cost of the large mortgage payments they would do almost no maintenance and would subdivide the apartments to create more rental units, "milking" the buildings by running them down. Hence, the buildings would generate enough money to pay the mortgages and, perhaps, even generate income for the owners. However, the real payoff for the owner came from the Internal Revenue Service. For tax purposes, buildings are assumed to decline in value over time, an accounting device known as *depreciation*. The amount the buildings depreciate each year would be counted as a business expense since the owners would be, on paper, losing the value of their investments. Thus, even though the owners would not lose any cash income, substantial "paper" losses caused by depreciation could be subtracted from their taxable incomes. When the buildings were fully depreciated, they could still be sold for enough to cover the initial down payments. Thus, the investors did not lose any actual money but saved substantial amounts of income tax. The buildings, neglected and overused, rapidly deteriorated. (Changes in the tax laws over the past 20 years have alternately made this type of tax write-off easier and more difficult for investors to claim.) Banks have also found these speculative practices profitable because of the high interest rate they charged speculators to take out mortgages on properties that they would not have lent on otherwise — that is, areas that were redlined for purposes of homeownership (Downie, 1974).

Another very profitable speculative practice was that of *contract selling*. Speculators would buy up houses at distress prices in changing neighborhoods. They would then resell the houses to families "on contract" at a high price. In a contract arrangement, the seller retains legal title to the house until the full amount of the loan is repaid. If the buyer fails to make even one payment, the seller gets the house back and keeps all the money already paid. Thus, there is little risk for the seller. At the same time, the amount of interest that can be charged on the loan is much higher than on a conventional mortgage. Thus, the seller can sell an overpriced house, receive very high interest, and incur very little risk. The buyer has high payments, is responsible for the maintenance of the property, and has no security. Why did people buy on contract? Because they had no choice. Until the 1970s the FHA would not usually insure mortgages in these neighborhoods, and the banks had redlined the neighborhoods. Where did the speculators get the capital necessary to purchase all the houses and make the high interest loans? Ironically, the same banks who had redlined the neighborhoods were often the source of capital (Palen, 1975).

A final cause of urban decay, not found in all areas but very dramatic and devastating where it does occur, is the deliberate destruction of property through arson. When landlords are unable to make money on their buildings through the normal rental process, they may resort to burning them for the insurance money. Arson-for-profit frequently occurs in neighborhoods with high degrees of absentee ownership, abandoned buildings, housing code violations, and overdue property taxes, where owners are taking the "final step" with their slum properties. Other areas that may experience arson-for-profit are those undergoing gentrification. Here a fire serves the useful purposes of evacuating current (usually low-income) tenants and providing an insurance payment which can help finance renovation of the building for a more upscale clientele at higher rents. Arson is a serious problem in many large cities, displacing tens of thousands of residents and taking more than a thousand lives each year (Working Group on Housing, 1989:9).

The Consequences of Urban Decay

Quite obviously, urban decay results in the deterioration of large portions of the residential areas in the cities. It means that the poor continue to live in bad housing. However, that is not the whole story.

Ultimately, urban decay results in the destruction of large numbers of housing units. This is another way of saying that the end of the process of urban decay in a neighborhood is usually abandonment. Abandonment has reached epidemic proportions in our central cities.

As a neighborhood runs down further and further, a number of things occur. The buildings deteriorate until they are barely habitable. Those who have any economic resources move to slightly less decayed neighborhoods in search of better housing. To attract any tenants at all, landlords have to decrease their rents. In turn, this leads the landlords to further decrease the level of maintenance and services. Unworkable plumbing, broken windows, collapsing stairs, unrepaired furnaces, lack of heating fuel, and broken wiring, become more and more common in the buildings. Building owners drop any pretense of trying to pay their taxes to the city, and the city's service levels are often cut in response. The residents of the neighborhoods become almost exclusively the poorest of the poor. Vandalism, crime, juvenile gangs, and unsanitary conditions in the buildings and the streets make the neighborhood a nightmare in which to live. The stage is then set for abandonment.

When this stage of decay is reached, it is no longer possible to make a profit out of a slum rental property. Rents are too low, and vacancy rates are too high, so that the costs of keeping the building open at any level of adequate services exceed what the owner can make from the rent. The building has been "milked dry." At this point, many owners default on the mortgage and walk away from the building; they may even "disappear" through a scheme such as owning the building through a "dummy" corporation, which simply goes out of business with no assets left to seize. The city takes over ownership of the property because of the many years of back taxes owed on the building, boards it up and schedules it for demolition at city expense. The buildings remain as burned-out or vandalized shells until the city can afford to bulldoze them. The city ends up the owner of acres of vacant rubble in a depopulated neighborhood.

This reduction in the number of housing units through abandonment has had two important results. It has contributed to the shortage of housing (especially rental housing) in our urban areas at a time of inadequate construction of new housing units and rapidly rising housing costs. (Many abandoned housing units were salvageable prior to reaching the final stages of decay.) At the same time, it has withdrawn from the tax rolls of our central cities significant numbers of formerly tax-producing properties. Thus, abandonment has contributed to "tax-base erosion" which is part of the reason central city governments face a continuing, serious financial crisis. (See Chapter 7.)

Policies Addressing Urban Decay

The federal government began to address the problems of housing deterioration in the 1930s when Congress passed its initial public housing legislation. The emphasis of federal policy for the first 30 or more years was on eliminating deteriorated housing by demolishing it. This so-called "bulldozer approach" reached its peak in the *urban renewal* program administered by the federal government between 1949 and 1974.

Under the urban renewal program, cities were given federal money to identify slums, raze existing buildings, and prepare the land to be sold to private developers. Many older, northern cities such as Chicago, Boston, New Haven, Newark, Philadelphia, St. Louis, New York, Washington, Pittsburgh, and Detroit bought and demolished great tracts of property in the late 1950s and throughout the 1960s. Officials hoped that by cleaning out slum properties they would prevent blight from affecting sound neighborhoods and would attract developers to build new, more modern housing in the central cities. Despite legal restrictions, however, urban renewal land proved to be more valuable to developers as sites for non-housing related uses and more valuable to city officials as space for central business district growth. Thus, much of the low-income housing torn down was not replaced with new housing. Rather, the cleared land was used for convention centers, university expansions, parking lots for the downtown business buildings and (ironically) luxury housing (Kleniewski, 1984). Frequently, the neighborhoods destroyed were not even the worst slums, but fairly stable working-class ethnic neighborhoods. The net result was that the modernization of downtown areas was obtained through the forced displacement of low-income people, reduction in the supply of low-income housing, and destruction of potentially salvageable neighborhoods (Gans, 1962). Despite some belated efforts to provide relocation assistance after early gross abuses, this program also often created real hardships for the people living in the neighborhoods slated to be demolished: difficulty finding affordable replacement housing, disruption of social ties, moving costs, and psychological stress (Fried, 1969).

In the mid-1970s, the urban renewal program was discontinued and another federal program, *historic preservation*, was begun as a way of addressing urban decay. Realizing that the urban renewal approach had destroyed many usable buildings, Congress enacted a provision of the tax code allowing investors to get federal income tax deductions for renovating historically certified buildings (Logan and Molotch, 1987:175-178). The goal of this policy was to save many older buildings which, under urban renewal, would have been demolished and to convert them to modern uses; e.g., warehouses to offices or manufacturing lofts to apartments. The Historic Preservation Act was successful in saving many buildings and providing subsidies for their renovation. The program, however, has done little to stem overall urban decay, nor has it helped provide housing for low-income people. Since it is designed to benefit investors, it does not provide assistance to homeowners and, indeed, much of the benefit has gone to developers of commercial properties rather than residential properties.

Government programs aimed at reducing urban decay have, according to critics (e.g., Smith, 1986), merely moved it around. They may remove slums from one area but often force the former residents of those areas to crowd into other neighborhoods, creating new slums. They have brought some young, white middle-class households into the city, but they have displaced many low-income households of various races and ethnicities from their traditional neighborhoods by driving up rents and property taxes. While local officials may be happy to see the property values (and thus tax revenues) increase in gentrifying areas, they inevitably have to face property decline somewhere else as low-income people move on.

Recently, two new kinds of programs have been initiated to provide more resources for housing *without* displacing low-income residents. The first, the Community Reinvestment Act, passed by Congress in 1977, requires federally chartered banks to "... help meet the credit needs of the local community in which they are chartered ..." (Schwartz et al, 1988:233). Thus, it addresses the problem of redlining by allowing community groups to review banks' lending policies and to challenge their applications for merger, expansion, or re-chartering if they are found to have discriminatory lending practices.

The second new program, a local rather than a federal policy, is the practice of *ownership transfer* that allows ownership of rental properties to be transferred from the owner to another person (or group) under certain conditions. One such condition, prevalent in many areas, is that landlords may be chronically behind in their tax payments. Tenants in New York City can now force the city to take over tax-delinquent buildings (which, although legal, the city governments have been reluctant to do in the past) and can form a tenants' association to run, or even buy, the buildings themselves (Working Group on Housing, 1989). Another condition for transfer of ownership, now permitted in ten states, is an owner "milking" a rental property. If tenants can document consistent lack of repair that poses a hazard to residents, they have grounds to ask that the building be put into receivership and that their rents go into a fund for repairs rather than to the owner. Although landlords can decide to pay for the repairs and thus retain ownership of the buildings, if they choose not to pay, the tenants have the option of buying the building (Morrissy, 1987). The value of the Community Reinvestment Act and the Ownership Transfer programs is that they give the residents of low-income communities some leverage over the outside groups and individuals (in this case, banks and absentee landlords) affecting their housing conditions.

Evaluation

Urban decay is more than a problem of blight or property deterioration. It is rooted in two facts about United States cities: first, that there are significant numbers of people who do not have enough income to pay for adequate housing, and second, that the people who own and manage property do so mainly to make a profit. (See David Harvey, 1973, for more on this subject.) Programs oriented toward physically improving property often have the effect of displacing low-income people to other locations and, in effect, creating new slums. Government policy seriously aimed at solving these problems must be oriented toward obtaining a more equal distribution of income and better access to decent housing for everyone. Otherwise, cities will continue to look like mosaics, with some good areas and some bad areas intermixed, and with new investments in one area implying withdrawal of resources from another area.

Main Points

1. Housing quality has improved, on the average, in the past 50 years. Improvements have been accomplished mainly by removing substandard units from the housing stock.
2. Gains in housing quality have to be weighed against increasing housing costs, however. Housing costs during the 1970s and 1980s rose more rapidly than people's incomes, creating an affordability crisis for low- and even middle-income households.
3. Rising costs have disproportionately hurt young people and women and have contributed to the increase in homelessness in urban areas.
4. The largest federal housing assistance program, the homeowners' tax deduction, is designed to benefit the nonpoor. Households making more than $50,000 a year receive two-thirds of its benefits.
5. Housing programs for the poor, mainly public housing and rent subsidies, have been chronically underfunded by the federal government, and have achieved only limited successes.
6. During the 1970s and especially the 1980s, federal housing policy moved toward relying on the private market to provide housing rather than having government help provide housing.
7. Not-for-profit corporations have become important housing providers, especially for poor people, since neither the private market nor the government is currently providing adequate low-cost housing.
8. Urban decay has been a significant problem for cities since the 1940s when suburban growth began to outstrip city growth. Deliberate property destruction for profit often speeds up the process of decay.

9. Decay and abandonment have contributed to the loss of many viable buildings and residences in urban areas.

10. Government policies addressing decay have been shifted from programs emphasizing demolition of decayed buildings to those stressing rehabilitation and reuse. They do not, however, address the real sources of urban decay, e.g., income inequality and the market for property.

Key Terms

Abandonment   The final stage of residential decay in which building owners burn or abandon their buildings and residents flee leaving the neighborhood a depopulated wasteland.

Contract Selling   The speculative practice of selling homes "on contract" at inflated prices and interest rates in which the seller retains title and the buyer faces both high costs and repossession without compensation in case of default.

Exclusionary Zoning   The practice of allowing only certain (usually expensive) housing to be built within a community.

Historic Preservation   A government program that gives tax incentives to developers to rehabilitate older properties.

Inclusionary Zoning   The practice of requiring a certain amount of low-cost housing to be built in growing communities.

Public Housing   A government program to construct and operate rental housing.

Redlining   The practice of refusing to provide conventional mortgage financing for the purchase of housing in particular neighborhoods.

Residential Decay   The process by which the physical condition of housing in a whole neighborhood or major section of a community deteriorates.

Shelter Poverty   A form of housing deprivation in which people find themselves with no alternative but to pay such a large portion of their incomes for housing that their ability to purchase other necessary items is substantially impaired.

Trickle-Down Effect   The federal government policy which relies on the notion that by subsidizing housing for the nonpoor, the poor would eventually benefit.

Urban Renewal   The major federal slum clearance program.

Suggested Reading

Bratt, Rachel, Chester Hartman and Ann Meyerson, eds. 1986. *Critical Perspectives on Housing*. Philadelphia: Temple University. A comprehensive collection of articles analyzing housing problems and policy.

Kozol, Jonathan. 1988. *Rachel and Her Children*. New York: Fawcett Columbine. A fascinating study of homeless people living in a welfare hotel in New York City.

Schwartz, David, Richard Ferlauto, and Daniel Hoffman. 1988. *A New Housing Policy for America*. Philadelphia: Temple University. Policy proposals advocating increased government involvement in housing.

Shelterforce, a monthly magazine of housing. Published by National Housing Institute, 439 Main St., Orange, NJ 07050.

Working Group on Housing, 1989. *The Right to Housing: A Blueprint for Housing the Nation*. Washington, DC: Institute for Policy Studies. An introduction to housing problems and policy for a general audience.

6

Transportation

Outline of Topics

A number of years ago, a Gallup poll of city dwellers asked the question, "What do you regard as your community's worst problem?" People ranked transportation-related problems as worse than education, poor housing, and high taxes (*Washington Post*, 6/15/1975). Even now most people, it seems, are dissatisfied with urban transportation. For the majority of the urban population, the underlying problem is a car culture, which resists and overwhelms all alternatives. Most commuters do not want to adhere to fixed routes and schedules, whether they be buses, car pools, or van pools (Ibata and Kamin, 1990).

What we will discover in this chapter is that transportation is, indeed, an urban problem. However, the nature of the problem is much different from what most people think. The fact is that, compared to other times and other places, the American urban transportation system is a very fast, flexible, and convenient system (except for some groups). The real problem is not how well the system moves people (which it does very well), but the huge and increasing costs and problems the system creates in exchange for the flexibility and convenience it provides.

The Contemporary Urban Transportation System: The Automobile

In the typical large American city of seventy-five years ago, a very different pattern of urban transportation existed than exists today. Automobiles were still relatively rare. Walking and riding slow-moving electric trolleys were the primary means of transportation for the average citizen. (A few cities had faster subways and elevated trains.) Most transit lines radiated out from the central business district, and, as a result, getting places other than downtown on public transportation was a slow and complicated process. Main streets and downtown areas were at least as congested as they are today. Traffic moved slowly, as clumsy, underpowered trucks, horse-drawn wagons, cars, trolleys, and pedestrians tried to get around each other. The automobile was being hailed as a solution to a very serious hazard to health and pedestrians: horse manure on the streets. As we have already seen, these transportation difficulties resulted in cities which were compact and densely settled as a way to minimize distances between work, home, stores, and places of recreation. Since that time, urban transportation has undergone fundamental change.

The story of urban transportation in this century is basically the story of the rise of the automobile to almost total dominance as a means of moving people. As recently as 1940, public transit was still responsible for about 30 percent of all *passenger miles* in urban areas. (A passenger mile is defined as one person traveling one mile and is a measure of transportation use.) By 1970, public transit accounted for only 6 percent of the passenger miles, and the automobile was responsible for the other 94 percent (Kemp and Cheslow, 1976:289). By 1983, mass transit included less than 3 percent (*Personal Travel in the U.S.*, 1986:E134). While annual person trips by automobile actually went down a little (from 85.1 to 81.5 percent during the period 1969-1983), the proportion of journeys by light trucks doubled, from 5.6 to 11.6 percent. This last shift points to trucks being used increasingly as personal use vehicles. The share of trips by public transit, already very low, dropped from 3.4 to 2.6 percent during the same period of time (*Summary of Travel Trends*, 1985).

The decline in mass transit use is even greater when we consider that the number of people living in urban areas is increasing. There were several reasons for this almost total takeover of urban transportation by cars in the post-1945 period.

Probably the most important reason was that car ownership and operation finally became affordable for all but the very poor. As recently as 1950, 41 percent of all families did not own a car. By 1970 only 17 percent did not own one (Kemp and Cheslow, 1976:290-291). Cars made up about 75 percent (110 million) of the 146 million increase in motor vehicle registrations from 1944 through 1986. Retail sales of autos accounted for over 70 percent (about 11 million) of all vehicles sold in 1985 (*Our Nation's Highways*, 1987:8-9).

As we have seen, this nearly universal car ownership played a major role in suburbanization. In turn, suburbanization encouraged increased car use. The majority of the urban population now lives in low-density suburbs. In addition, about two-thirds of new jobs emerging in the United States from 1960 to 1980 were located there. Consequently, by 1975 a majority of all urban workers lived in the suburbs, but only about a third of them commuted into the central cities (U.S. Bureau of the Census, *Journal to Work*, 1979). For reasons discussed later in this chapter, traditional mass transit just did not fit in with changing commuting patterns.

Government also played a role by encouraging car use and discouraging mass transit. The role of the Interstate Highway System was especially important in the development of the contemporary urban transportation system. The decision to route these highways directly through most urban areas and to add various beltways (circling routes) and short connectors in urban areas turned the program into a disguised way of subsidizing urban expressway construction. With the Highway

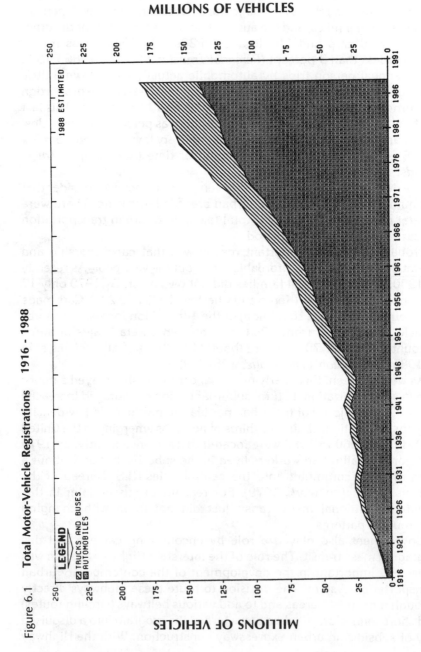

Figure 6.1   **Total Motor-Vehicle Registrations   1916 - 1988**

SOURCE: *Selected Highway Statistics and Charts 1987*, FHWA-PL-89-001, U.S. Department of Transportation, Federal Highway Administration, p. 7.

Trust Fund picking up 90 percent of the cost of construction, the temptation to build expressways to provide urban transportation was almost irresistible for state and local governments. It was simply the cheapest way, from the point of view of these governments, to deal with urban transportation needs.

While government lavished money on expressways, public transportation was allowed to languish. No federal aid to urban mass transit was available at all until 1961. Initially, the funds provided were very modest and limited to the construction of new facilities and the purchase of new equipment. That meant the local government still had to bear a relatively heavy burden of operating costs which made mass transportation more of a drain on local and state governments than highway construction (Congressional Quarterly, Inc., 1978).

Real attempts at giving support to urban mass transit began with the Urban Mass Transportation Act of 1964. This legislation, designed to aid urban development, authorized grants of up to two-thirds of construction, as well as reconstruction and acquisition of facilities and equipment. A single mass transit authority was created in 1968, the result of a reorganization plan dividing resposibility for urban mass transportation between the Department of Transportation and the Department of Housing and Urban Development (Weiner, 1988:45-46, 54; *Beyond Gridlock*, 1988:54-59, 62-63). During the 1970s the federal government increased its support of public transportation. A few new rail transit systems (e.g., in Washington, D.C., San Francisco, Atlanta) were opened. In some of the newer, growing cities, which had relied almost exclusively on private cars for transportation, some efforts were made to provide government-operated, subsidized public transit for the first time (Kemp and Cheslow, 1976:283; Congressional Quarterly, Inc., 1978).

However, this increased federal effort never came close to matching that devoted to highways. Moreover, federal expenditures for infrastructure, including mass transit, went down by almost 20 percent in actual dollars between fiscal 1980 and fiscal 1991. The Bush administration plans to reduce this by 10 percent more by 1995. Between 1960 and 1987, the federal share of spending for all infrastructure dropped from 31 percent to 23 percent of total expenditure. State expenditures declined from 29 to 24 percent. Local governments increased their outlay from 41 to 53 percent. There is little indication that the federal effort will increase markedly in the near future. While Secretary of Transportation Skinner's 1990 transportation proposals emphasized the urgent priority of the United States transportation system, he proposed that federal funds for urban transit be reduced. To meet transit needs, he suggested that state and local governments increase their contributions. Recent administrations thus have placed little emphasis on maintaining national infrastructures generally, and in particular, transportation (Broder, 3/11/1990).

Government policy can also be seen as having indirectly contributed to the growing reliance on the automobile. As we have already seen (Chapter 1), government played a major role in subsidizing the construction of suburban housing and the relocation of employment to the suburbs.

Perhaps less important, but still significant, is the evidence that powerful private interests benefited from and successfully worked for the destruction of mass transit in some cities. The most famous example was the role of General Motors, Firestone Tire, and Standard Oil of California in eliminating electric streetcar systems for several cities. These companies contributed money to "holding companies" which bought the privately owned transit companies in cities such as Los Angeles and converted them to diesel buses (which GM made). As one critic has written:

> Diesel buses have 28 percent shorter economic lives, 40 percent higher operating costs, and 9 percent lower productivity than electric buses... In short, by increasing costs, reducing revenues, and contributing to the collapse of hundreds of transit systems, GM's dieselization program may have had the long-term effect of selling GM cars (Snell, quoted by Brown, 1979:14).

More generally, the so-called "highway lobby" has been credited with a major role in encouraging highway construction and blocking funds for mass transit. This group consists of the large highway construction contractors, automobile makers, oil companies, trucking companies, and automobile supply companies who have a major stake in continued highway construction and car use. It is generally recognized as one of the better organized and funded lobbying groups in Washington (Brown, 1979: 14).

One final note about automobile dominance is in order, however. The national patterns we have been examining tend to hide the fact that, in some cities, mass transit is still a significant form of transportation. A few of our older, larger cities have "inherited" quite extensive mass transit systems which still move large numbers of people. Most notable are the cities of New York, Boston, Philadelphia, and Chicago. These systems were built prior to 1920 and have remained in use for a number of special reasons. Two of the cities are major centers of corporate headquarters which require movement of large numbers of office workers to downtown locations. All of them experienced most of their growth prior to the appearance of the automobile. As a result, their basic

Figure 6.2   **Highway Expenditures By All Units of Government**

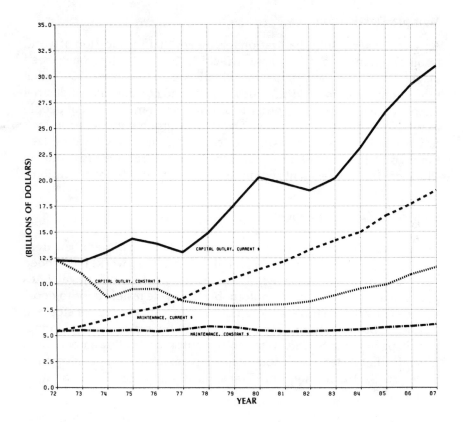

SOURCE: *Selected Highway Statistics and Charts 1987,* FHWA-PL-89-001,
U.S. Department of Transportation, Federal Highway Administration, p. 20.

physical structure is such that automobile use is usually inconvenient. In addition, these cities were willing to subsidize the continued losses of their transit systems to keep them going (Kemp and Cheslow, 1976:297).

Other Characteristics of Urban Transportation

The combination of suburbanization and heavy automobile use has, in turn, had a number of other consequences for the nature of contemporary urban transportation.

Multiple Destinations

As we have seen, suburbanization has meant that the location of work, retail shopping areas, recreation facilities, and the like have been dispersed to a large number of widely separated locations. Radial movement to centrally located downtowns and concentrated industrial districts is a much smaller proportion of the total movement of people in urban areas than previously. The typical urban commuter, in fact, drives from a suburban residence to a suburban work location (see Figure 6.3). In many urban areas, there is even a "reverse rush hour" in which central city residents commute to dispersed suburban locations.

Increased Travel Distances

The spread-out, low-density, and decentralized nature of suburban areas also means that the distance traveled (especially to work) has tended to increase in most urban areas. Despite this fact, however, travel times have not increased as much. Automobiles provide faster "door-to-door" service because the traveler does not have to walk to a transit stop and wait for a bus or a train. Generally, automobiles also average higher travel speeds. Hence, the switch to the automobile allowed people to travel further distances without major increases in the time devoted to travel (U.S. Department of Transportation, 1972 Transportation Report:197).

Approaching Gridlock?

However, despite the past success of the urban highway in moving people, more recently, in a number of urban areas, the highway system has not expanded rapidly enough to keep up with the growth of traffic.

Figure 6.3
Urban Movement Patterns in 1920 and 1990

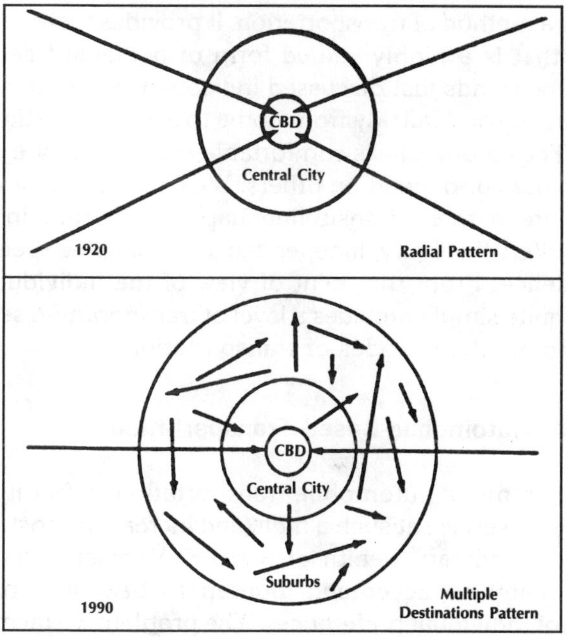

The result is the increasing occurrence of *gridlock*: during peak commuting hours the number of cars attempting to use the highway system exceeds the capacity of the system. Cars are increasing in number twice as fast as people. While there has been a growing use of highways, there has been at the same time a steady decline of funds spent for new construction as well as maintenance. The rapid increase in inter-suburban commuting is a major source of the problem. Suburbs have few main arteries, and thus a rapid and efficient flow of traffic is inhibited (*Time*, 9/12/1988:54; *Chicago Tribune*, 2/18-20/1990:1,1).

Evaluating the Urban Transportation System

How should these changes in urban transportation be judged? That depends on what standards one uses to judge them. In some respects the urban transportation system works very well. In other respects our automobile-based transportation system verges on a national disaster.

The Benefits of Automobile-Based Transportation

For the vast majority who now own automobiles, the automobile serves them well as a method of transportation. It provides them with a degree of mobility that is a highly valued form of personal freedom in our society. As the trends just discussed indicate, with minimal effort, we can move directly and quickly from home to another location whenever we want to. The automobile is comfortable and private. We do not have to wait for others or depend on others. We can live where we want to, not just where a mass transit line happens to run. In short, the automobile offers flexibility, independence, reasonable speed, comfort, and convenience. From the point of view of the individual user, the automobile quite simply provides a level of transportation service which is superior to all other modes of transportation.

The Costs of Automobile-Based Transportation

The basic dilemma of automobile transportation is that it delivers its superior level of service at such a high (and increasing) cost. In the past, given the extraordinary wealth of American society, that high cost seemed to many an acceptable burden to bear in return for the satisfaction of individual preferences. The problem we face now is that the costs of continuing to rely on the current approach to urban transportation may be finally exceeding our ability to pay.

The cost of automobile transportation was not much of a problem for individuals in the first two decades after 1945. Personal income was rising, and people were willing and able to pay the costs of car ownership and operation in return for the tremendous convenience and mobility the car offered. Even under these relatively favorable economic conditions, relying on a car for transportation was quite expensive. However, in the last decade costs have continued to rise rapidly, and real purchasing power has stagnated as inflation matched or surpassed wage increases, especially for low and moderate income workers. Depending on the size of the vehicle, expenses for 1990 models ranged from 33 to 44 cents a mile, as compared to the 30.6 to 42 cents a mile for 1988 models. While gasoline costs rose only slightly, such expenses as insurance, financing, and depreciation went up sharply. Costs of owning and operating an automobile in 1990 ranged from $3300 to $4400 annually (Mateja, 1990). Transportation by car is indeed a relatively expensive operation, involving not only purchase costs and repairs, but also, ultimately, replacement. Of course, there is no guaratee that gasoline price rises will remain moderate. This became apparent in mid-late 1990 when the Iraqi invasion of Kuwait caused gasoline prices in the United States to soar.

In addition, we should not look at the cost of an automobile-based transportation system only from the point of view of the individual. Because the automobile is the most expensive mode of land transportation, our reliance on it means that as a society we spend more of our national income on transportation than other, less auto-dependent societies.

The costliness of the automobile to the whole society is probably best illustrated by the demands it places on our scarce and expensive energy supplies. Indeed, this is probably the single most serious problem with continuing our present approach to urban transportation. The United States now imports about half of its oil, and domestic production is projected to decline dramatically in the 1990s. Oil imports were a major cause of our massive trade deficit in the 1980s. Increasing dependence on foreign oil leaves the United States more vulnerable economically to disruptions in foreign production. A real roadblock to reducing energy costs has been the tendency for Ford and General Motors to concentrate on big cars, in order to increase profits. There was also a lag of consumer interest in fuel efficiency. Low fuel prices in the 1980s resulted in both consumer and producer losing interest in fuel economy. At the same time, taxing policies, while restricting consumption somewhat, were not geared toward discouraging the purchase of less efficient cars (Renner, 1989:103-106).

Automobiles also continue to be a major source of urban air pollution, despite the addition of pollution control devices. Between 1976 and 1986, American lead emission decreased 94 percent. Though lead levels in people decreased by one-third, lead is now felt to have effects at much lower levels than formerly believed. Exhaust control devices work very effectively to decrease other pollutants, but do not work well if not maintained, or if the engine is cold. The immense growth in traffic has greatly dulled the effectiveness of pollution control attempts. For example, in the 1970s U.S. emission of carbon monoxides decreased by one-third, but leveled off dramatically in the early 1980s. This change was due largely to increases in traffic as well as higher speeds. In addition, the U.S. Environmental Protection Agency has not been enforcing the ban on federal funding for highways and industrial construction in areas not obeying pollution regulations. The Reagan administration sharply cut or ended government research and development funding for development of engines and engine parts that could seriously reduce pollution. Alternate fuels don't offer a simple solution. The use of methanol can reduce some pollutants, but if it is produced from coal, methanol can result in increased emissions

(Renner, 1988: 42-45; Renner, 1989:108-109). A ray of hope may be present in the recent decision of environmental commissioners in eight Northeastern states to adopt the strict California motor vehicle standards. This action is additional evidence that the states have taken the lead in the fight against pollution, in marked contrast to the federal government in the 1980s (Lieberman, 1989:19). The passage of new federal environmental proctection laws should also help curb emissions.

The automobile also has contributed to urban decay. It played a very significant role in suburbanization, thereby accelerating the decline of downtown retail business and central-city residential neighborhoods. The interstate expressway system, begun in the late 1950s, accented this trend, enabling easy access both to adjacent suburbs but also to local newly-built suburban industrial plants, offices, and shopping centers. The suburbanization process was (and is) very closely linked to the building and proliferation of roads, and the geometric increase in the number of automobiles (Palen, 1987:118, 182-187).

It also should be kept in mind that not everyone enjoyed in the convenience and mobility which conversion to an automobile-based transportation system provided for the majority of urban residents. The poor, blacks, the elderly, and (to a lesser extent) the handicapped still rely heavily on public transit. (The handicapped can use public transit less because of physical barriers which make public transit hard to use. In the absence of someone to drive them, what that means is that they are simply rendered immobile.) Indeed, with the influx of the poor into our cities in the 1950s and 1960s, the absolute number of families without cars in metropolitan areas increased by about 350,000 (Kemp and Cheslow, 1976:290). By 1975, 41 percent of all urban black households were without cars, and black workers used public transportation three times as often as white workers (Bureau of the Census, *Journey to Work*, 1979).

What this means is that one of the real problems for many of the urban poor, elderly, and handicapped is that they face major obstacles to mobility. Given the limited nature of mass transit systems in all but a few cities, they may have to undertake long walks to reach transit lines, endure tedious rides in slow-moving, infrequently scheduled buses; long waits to make transfers; and pay increasingly expensive fares. In many cases, this dependence on public transit means that these people simply cannot get to many places (especially in the suburbs) or travel at certain hours of the day. This is an especially severe problem for the working poor. As we have seen, employment opportunities have become increasingly limited in central cities. The suburbs are where a large portion of the jobs, especially the good jobs, are located. Lacking cars, many of the poor have simply been unable to go where the jobs are.

Transportation Alternatives

As a result of these problems, there has been a growing concern to find a way to make urban transportation more efficient and effective for all groups in the population. The difficulty is that of finding a system which will actually meet contemporary transportation needs. How can we find a system which will provide something which approximates the kind of superior mobility to which we have become accustomed and also move large numbers of people efficiently?

Traditional Mass Transit

Most of the public discussion of how to improve urban transportation has centered around creating new public mass transit systems. Generally such systems are conceived as being cleaner and faster versions of the kind of mass transit systems already operating in some of our central cities. The choice usually discussed is seen as being between publicly supported and subsidized rail systems (e.g., subways or surface rail rapid transit) or "line bus" systems (large buses following a fixed route). The popular view seems to be that if you provide people with good, cheap, fast subways or buses, they will leave their cars at home. A survey taken by a metropolitan bus system found, in contrast, that 9 out of 10 people surveyed felt that mass transit was less convenient than driving. Over half surveyed felt that bus trips were too long. Low bus ridership seems to be due to low population density in suburban areas (Ibata and Kamin, 1990).

The solution of urban transportation problems will not be simple. The idea that building traditional mass transit systems will provide a relatively quick, efficient, and effective way to move a major portion of the urban population neglects a number of problems which traditional mass transit has as a means of moving people in modern urban areas.

Traditional mass transit systems have generally been designed on the assumption that people will walk to the transit line. In addition, to make transit attractive to people, service on a given route must be frequent: people will not wait long periods of time or change their work habits just to use mass transit. As a result, each mass transit route must attract a large number of people to justify the number of trains or buses to be run. There is no efficiency in running a train or large bus almost empty. The problem is most severe in the case of rail transit. The huge cost of building the rail system means that a very large number of people have to use it to justify the cost of construction. One estimate is that each rail line must carry 25,000 people a day.

As we have seen, the suburbanization process resulted in urban areas of low population density. Single-family houses on large lots mean that a relatively small number of people are spread over a relatively large area. Under these conditions, the problem low density creates for mass transit should be obvious. Not enough people live within easy walking distance of the mass transit route to provide enough passengers to justify the cost of frequent service (in terms of fuel, equipment, or labor costs). The only place this is not a problem is in the large, old central cities with high densities and inadequate highway systems. It is no accident that it is there that traditional mass transit systems have fared best in competition with the automobile. The problem of low density is worst in those areas which now contain the majority of our urban population: suburbs and the newer metropolitan areas of the South and West.

Traditional mass transit also is designed to serve a centrally located downtown or other location which attracts a very large number of people. People are picked up along the route and deposited in one central location. Yet, current urban transportation patterns based on car use have evolved toward people going to a very large number of dispersed locations. Only a minority of workers and shoppers now head for the central business district.

Moreover, there is no simple way to restructure traditional mass transit to serve dispersed locations. Again, we run into the requirement that each route in the system must carry large numbers of people to be efficient. Not enough travelers are going to the same locations to meet this requirement.

Surface rail and subway systems present another problem: they are monumentally expensive to construct. For surface rail systems, land must be acquired at a very high cost. Subway tunnels are very expensive to dig. In addition, rail, control systems, maintenance yards, and rail cars are all very expensive. Again, what this means is that a large number of people must use the system to make it economically viable.

There are other financial barriers to be overcome. To attract users, fares have to be kept low. Partly, this is because people do not calculate the true cost of operation when they compare using their cars to mass transit. They usually think only in terms of the gas and other basic operating costs of their cars. Also, they consider the obviously greater convenience of traveling by car. Hence, only very low fares are likely to attract riders to transit systems. Generally speaking, the fares have to be set so low that they do not generate enough income to cover the cost of constructing the system. In fact, most systems require subsidies to cover operating costs. The result is that actual users of the system do not pay for it.

This need to subsidize the huge cost of a rail system makes for several problems. For reasons already discussed, only a small minority of urban residents are likely to use and directly benefit from the system. Thus, the net gain to the whole community really is relatively small. On the other hand, new subway systems in a number of cities, for instance San Francisco and Toronto, have resulted in a very considerable expansion of business and economic development ("Big City Metro," 1990).

It should also be kept in mind that constructing a rail system, like constructing an expressway, can be very disruptive to the areas through which it passes. It is true that real estate values go up along such a line (especially near the stations) because of the increased attractiveness of the land for commercial development. However, that is not much consolation to the neighborhood residents. Moreover, the period of construction can destroy small merchants, and surface rail systems bring with them noise and visual blight which can make an area very unattractive for residential use.

There is simply no escaping the fact that the automobile is the most attractive and convenient method of urban transportation from the point of view of the user. Despite the stereotype of the frustrated commuter trapped in a traffic jam, most people actively prefer to travel by automobile. Despite the high cost of automobile use, many people are likely to be able to afford to commute via automobiles for a long time to come.

In contrast, traditional mass transit is relatively inconvenient to use. The choice of destinations is limited. It is crowded during rush hours. People worry about riding transit at night because of the fear of crime. Commuters have to walk to the transit line and wait for at least a short period of time. Lumbering buses trapped in traffic are much slower than traveling by automobile. Many of these inconveniences are minor. Some of them can be partially corrected by proper transit design and operation procedures. Automobile use is likely to become an unacceptable economic burden to more people. But the basic fact remains that people who use traditional mass transit tend to be those people who have no other choice. Those who have a choice, opt for the automobile. People have grown up in a setting where cars are the only way to get from one place to another. It is harder, therefore, to convince people to use public transportation. A recent survey in the Chicago suburbs revealed that 90 percent of suburbanites feel mass transit is not as convenient as the automobile. This study also showed that two-thirds resented fixed schedules (Ibata and Kamin, 1990).

Hence, the traditional approaches to mass transit are not likely to attract a large number of riders who voluntarily choose to leave their cars at home. Major new approaches to making transit attractive and convenient will be required.

Finally, recent legislation on behalf of the handicapped raises the issue of providing them with equal access to the mass transit system. Equal access assumes that the quality of service will not change when access is made possible. Such availability will increase transit costs in a number of ways. Equipment expenses, as well as access at stops, for both suburban trains and subway cars as well as buses, may well skyrocket. Ridership of those not needing such assistance may decline considerably, due to the longer time schedules necessitated by greater loading time required for handicapped riders. This decline might be especially apparent during rush hours. Fares may very probably increase, to compensate for decreasing ridership. (Houston, 1989; Walberer, 1989; Washburn, 1989; *Wall Street Journal*, 11/20/1989:A-14).

The end result is that there are growing doubts about the usefulness of rail transit systems as the primary transit system for most urban areas. Certainly, these systems will have to be limited to those few cases where the rail system can move very large numbers of people and provide major advantages to justify the high initial cost. Moreover, the cost must be compared to other alternative systems of transportation, such as bus systems, which may provide more flexibility at a lower initial cost. City governments do not have an infinite amount of money to spend on public transportation. Even if a traditional rail system will ultimately pay for itself (over a twenty- or thirty-year period), the question remains whether another approach would cost less to begin with, move as many people, and, hence, pay for itself sooner. As we will see later in this chapter, there is a good possibility that such alternative approaches exist.

Do all these problems mean that traditional mass transit has no role to play in urban transportation? Not necessarily. Such transportation probably will play a limited role in urban areas. There are things that traditional mass transit does very well. It does move large numbers of people efficiently to a downtown location. In the old, large central cities of the North, traditional mass transit can move large numbers of people. With increasing numbers of middle-class workers who work in these downtown areas choosing to live in central city residential neighborhoods, traditional mass transit could enjoy a modest revival of popularity. In the lower-density, more dispersed sections of newer urban areas, however, traditional systems will probably play a much smaller role (Shannon, 1980). In the foreseeable future, therefore, such systems will not move a majority of urban travelers. Rather, traditional mass transit must be seen as just one part of a larger transportation improvement strategy.

The Mixed-Systems Approach

If the public is to have real alternatives, transit networks, appropriately including various types of transit, must be designed in the context of urban planning. For example, this can be done by synchronizing schedules of different modes of transportation, and by structuring convenient transfers from one type of system to another. A multiple approach, using several different forms of mass transit in conjunction with each other, can make mass transit much more attractive and efficient. This in fact has been done in a number of places (Renner, 1988:47, 49-51; Barry, 1989; Koepp, 1988; Work, 1987). Such a comprehensive approach would enable the user to have the best of many worlds: the combining of cars and other forms of transit according to one's personal, daily needs. To reduce auto congestion, transit alternatives should be focused on the needs of the various transit populations. Projects for discouraging auto use should be worked out with the participation of those affected. This indeed *must* be done if such plans are to really be effective (Kapinos, 1989; Prewda, 1989; Renner, 1989:111; Work, 1987). A number of proposals have been put forward to combine more efficient automobile use with more innovative forms of public transit and some use of traditional mass transit. This is what might be called the *mixed-systems approach*. Some of the elements of such an approach which have been suggested include: redesigning the automobile, changing car use pattens, altering mass transit, and transforming consumer preference.

Suburban sprawl requires the automobile as a primary mode of transportation. There is a huge fixed investment in the existing "built environment" of our suburbs, and that environment has been designed for auto use. Hence, the problems of energy use and pollution will have to be addressed, in part, by the introduction of much more efficient cars. There was a considerable emphasis on small, fuel-efficient cars after the Iranian oil crisis of 1979 (Lave, 1979:39-52). As the price of gasoline leveled off and actually declined during the 1980s there was an accompanying desire for larger and more prestigious vehicles. While small, fuel-efficient automobiles are definitely a large percent of production, an increasing number of new models were larger and less fuel-efficient. The notion of the car as a status symbol returned, especially for the younger, wealthier buyer. American buyers are more likely to prefer showier cars (Renner, 1988:33; Greenwald, 1990). However, the potential savings derived from converting the national car fleet to more fuel-effiicent vehicles is immense. Very small, fuel-efficient cars could meet most individual needs in urban areas as well as bigger cars do now. Additional benefits of the conversion would include being able to accomodate more vehicles in existing parking facilities and, to a lesser extent, on the highways.

Most urban dwellers drive to work alone (U.S. Bureau of the Census, 1979; *Personal Travel in the U.S.*, 1986). Just increasing the average number of people per car to two would reduce the total number of cars during rush hour in most urban areas by about 40 percent. The result would be a reduction in energy use, pollution, congestion, and the need for more highways. The benefits to individuals would also be substantial. The cost per trip would be reduced by almost half. The need for a second automobile would be reduced, while the flexibility and convenience of door-to-door service provided by the car would be retained.

A number of programs to promote car pooling have been developed. Companies in Southern California have provided incentives for employees to join pools. A 1987 study found that when several companies paid employee expenses for parking and car pool expenses, worker participation increased to over 50 percent of their staff. The success of such an approach in this region may be due to tough legislation designed to reduce the number of employees driving to work without passengers, the alternative being the payment of stiff fines (Ibata and Kamin, 1990). Presently there are over 2,000 van pools in the Northern Virginia suburbs of Washington, D.C. However, results are not uniformly hopeful. Some large businesses in the Chicago suburbs have organized TMAs (transit management associations) to promote van and car pooling, by enlisting the participation of local businesses and companies. To date, only about 1 percent of the employees have participated. A contrast is the response of a branch of Sears and Roebuck, whose car and van pool effort netted 40 percent of workers (Ibata and Kamin, 1990). A significant number of drivers using the San Francisco Bay Bridge drive in lanes designated for car pool use, first placing dummies in their cars to simulate riders (*Chicago Tribune*, 5/13/1989:1,8; Work, 1987).

At the same time that we can change car use patterns, the traditional form of mass transit may not attract many passengers, but it is possible that the system could be changed so that a gradually increasing share of urban travelers might be attracted to a modified system — especially in the case of those traveling to central locations. Most proposals of this sort involve the use of various forms of buses, rather than rail systems. Buses have the advantage of being able to travel flexible routes and requiring smaller initial investment than rail systems.

One of the chief disadvantages of traditional bus service is that it is so slow. One possibile solution is the creation of special bus lanes on urban expressways to allow for express bus service. A number of cities have already created such lanes. In one variation of this approach, the bus makes a passenger pick-up "loop" in a suburban area and then runs at high speeds downtown. The "park-ride" approach involves passengers driving to the central pick-up areas, parking their cars, and finishing the trip by bus. This approach also works to feed passengers from suburban areas onto commuter rail lines or subway systems at the edge of the city. The park-ride concept has the dual advantage of allowing frequent, high-speed service and overcoming the problem of low population densities in the suburbs. It is also a very efficient way to use the existing freeway system. An excellent example of such an approach is that of metropolitan Toronto. Synchronizing of schedules enables convenient transfer between different routes as well as different modes of transit. Such multi-destinational systems work well in a number of North American cities (*Transit in Toronto*, 1987; Renner, 1988: 49-51).

The so-called "minibus" (large passenger van) system has also been suggested as a possibility — usually for smaller urban areas. These vans can pick people up from at their homes, either by being radio dispatched in response to a telephone call or by a prearranged schedule, and then deliver the passengers to some common location (an office complex, a subway station, a large factory, etc.) The small size of the van minimizes the time spent collecting people and could allow the creation of a system which serves many dispersed locations. In effect, the system would function something like a car pool, except that people would not provide their own vehicles and there would be more people per vehicle. Where such a system feeds into an existing traditional mass transit line, it could provide enough passengers to justify the operation of high-speed rapid transit and overcome the problem of low density in suburban areas. Finally, another suggested role for the minibus system is that of providing flexible, door-to-door bus service to the handicapped and elderly. This would save the expense of modifying the whole transit system to allow for special access facilities and could provide, if properly developed, higher quality service (Department of Transportation 1972; 214-218).

One approach used in some smaller cities across the United States to help those handicapped and/or needy to obtain transportation is the cab subsidy. Those eligible register with the city and are issued a card and a number. Riders are limited to a certain number of trips per month. Those using this system pay the company either a lower or subsidized fare. The balance is paid to the company by the city every month. The city, in turn, receives state and federal subsidies. This approach has the advantage of using existing equipment and personnel while at the same time providing affordable service to the user (Bolton, 1989).

Other solutions also involve using resources already available. For example, it might be possible to use interstate corridors as sites for metropolitan trains connecting suburbs. Abandoned and underused rail freight lines could also be put to use. These approaches could provide a more rapid means of getting people from one suburb to another in an era in which an increasing number of jobs (and traffic problems) are in the suburban area (*Chicago Tribune*, 2/27/1989:1,10).

Not all mass transit should be downtown-centered. The PACE system (Chicago suburban bus service) is an example of this philosophy. This agency has proposed building a center in Schaumburg, a suburban office center northwest of Chicago. This facility will be designed to combine a number of transit types: a bus depot, taxi and limosine stands, a large garage for cars, and car rental agencies. Buses terminating at this center would operate as links for nearby suburbs to office buildings and an adjacent mall. Direct bus service will be available both to Chicago and O'Hare Airport, as well as to convention centers and hotels (*Chicago Tribune*, 3/22/1989:1,12). PACE has also started an express service linking southern and western suburbs. This is a first step in linking suburbs distant from one another. Those needing work and living in the south suburbs can thereby get to the many jobs available in the west suburbs. PACE promotes cooperation and communication of employment services and employers in both sets of suburbs (*Chicago Tribune*, 8/14/1989:1,10).

Argonne National Laboratory has developed a plan whereby supertrains capable of speeds of 300 miles per hour could be used to connect cities within 100 to 500 miles of each other. Such an approach, using interstate highway corridors, would eliminate the need for short-distance air routes. This plan could greatly decrease airport congestion and the possibility of accidents, as well as eliminate pressure for expanding existing airports and building new facilities. The money saved would more that cover the cost of the new rail systems. The airlines may in fact integrate their operations with such high-speed rail systems (Johnson et al., 1989).

There are a number of programs throughout the nation that are making attempts to provide access to good transportation. Most prominent are efforts to adapt existing systems and equipment so that the physically impaired can use them more easily. Important also are those trying to help people unable to travel from more remote areas of the nation to larger population centers. The Greyhound Rural Connection Program is designed to provide such access. Recently, Greyhound developed a system linking passengers in rural and small towns with larger urban areas. Local feeder systems work with the Greyhound inter-city system via coordinated schedules. This approach, already partly in place, is to be expanded for the whole nation (*Reconnecting Rural America*, 1989:27-34).

Rapid increases in the cost of car use could provide a major incentive for people to use systems such as these. However, most discussions of urban transportation have concluded that changes in the mass-transit system to make it more attractive will have to be linked to changes which make car use less attractive and convenient.

The basic goal of such a policy would be to reduce single-occupancy car use in favor of either public transportation or car pooling. Obviously, care would have to be exercised to assure that such policies would not simply discourage car use to one particular location. Restricting car use in downtown areas, for example, might simply encourage relocation of stores and places of employment to suburban locations.

A number of policies are possible. Special lanes can be designated in freeways for vehicles with several passengers. Fees for low-occupancy or single-rider vehicles can be levied. Access fees can be charged for use of congested roads (Renner, 1988: 49).

Clearly, approaches such as these would take time to implement, encounter some public resistance, and involve substantial, regionally-based planning. However, overall, the mixed-systems approach should have several advantages. It would retain much (but not all) of the flexibility and convenience of the present system. It can be adapted to our low density, suburban pattern of land use. Hence, it would not require rapid, massive changes in residence, work, and travel patterns. That means it could begin to be implemented now, and we could begin to reap the benefits of increased efficiency sooner. Also, many of the changes do not require massive capital investments by government. At the same time, it is an approach that can be introduced gradually, and costs can be spread out over a number of years. Finally, it is a flexible enough approach that it can be tailored to the specific needs of each urban area. However, such a strategy does require some significant federal and state expenditures and, just as importantly, coordinated government planning and intervention. Whether such a government effort is likely to be forthcoming in the near future seems dubious, given current efforts to reduce government expenditures and to rely increasingly on private economic initiatives to provide services.

The city of Toronto offers us one model of an integrated transit system. Many of Toronto's subway stations provide commuter parking as well as fast transfer to surface routes (both bus and light rail). Dial-a-bus systems provide service to commuter trains. Parking is available for either the entire day, or for short-term use. Since 1963, the policy of expanding and updating transit systems to effectively serve established and growing sections of metropolitan Toronto has been followed. This plan has made it possible for 95 percent of this area's residents to be within half a mile of some transit route (*Transit in Toronto*, 1987).

Evaluation

To a large extent, modern urban areas are a creation of the automobile. This is even more true of our newer urban areas in the Sunbelt and Mountain states. Patterns of land use, the single-family suburban house, the shopping center, and a life-style based on easy mobility all have resulted from nearly universal car ownership. But many urban problems and much of our wasteful energy practices are also attributable to the automobile. Central-city decay, pollution, the decline of public transit, rising transportation costs, visual blight, neighborhood destruction, and much suffering and death from auto accidents are part of the legacy of our decades-long love affair with the automobile. It now appears that this love affair has finally become too costly to continue.

The next few decades will probably be a period of transition in urban transportation. Significant new approaches will have to be tried. In the long run, these changes in urban transportation will probably have as major an impact on urban form and urban living as did the automobile in the last half century.

Main Points

1. Contemporary urban areas rely almost exclusively on the automobile for transportation—despite some recent revival of public transportation in some cities.
2. Automobile dependence came about as a result of increasing car ownership, suburbanization, government subsidies of highway construction, government neglect of public transit, and the influence of special interests.
3. The combination of heavy car use and suburbanization has meant that people travel more often, for more reasons, to more dispersed locations, longer distances away, and at higher speeds. However, rapidly rising traffic volume threatens gridlock in some urban areas.
4. The automobile has meant a high degree of mobility and convenience for most urban residents.
5. However, the superior transportation of the automobile has been bought at a high cost in terms of economic waste, energy inefficiency, pollution, urban decay, and the creation of a group of "transportation disadvantaged."

6. Traditional mass transit has a number of problems which limit its usefulness in contemporary urban areas. These problems include those associated with low population densities, multiple destinations, high construction costs, consumer resistance, and dubious benefits to the transportation disadvantaged.

7. An alternative approach to urban transportation needs is the "mixed-systems" approach. Such an approach would include redesigning the automobile, changing car-use patterns, more innovative approaches to mass transit, and changing consumer transportation preferences.

Key Terms

Gridlock   The severe traffic congestion and extremely slow travel speeds caused by traffic volume greater than the capacity of the highway system.

Mixed-Systems Approach   The strategy of designing an urban transportation system which employs a number of different modes of transportation to meet the needs of different areas and groups of travelers.

Multiple Destinations   The pattern of contemporary urban travel in which urban travelers are moving to a large number of widely dispersed destinations.

Traditional Mass Transit   A system of transportation which relies primarily on the use of high-speed rail cars and fixed-route line buses.

Transportation Disadvantaged   Those persons having less mobility, because they are not able physically or financially to drive cars.

Suggested Reading

Johnson, L. et.al. 1989. *Maglev Vehicles and Superconductor Technology: Integration of High-Speed Ground Transportation Into the Air Travel System.* Lemont, IL: Center for Transportation Research, Argonne National Laboratory. A description of a plan to cut down on the crowding of airports by constructing a new type of rail system replacing short airplane flights.

Kapinos, Thomas. April 1989. "Attitudes Toward Mass Transit." *Mass Transit:* M/T 10-15. An outline of views of the public and their implications for mass transit planning.

Kemp, Michael and Melvyn D. Cheslow. 1976. "Transportation." In *The Urban Predicament*, editors W. Gorham and N. Glazer. Washington, DC: Urban Institute. A reasoned overview of urban transportation problems which considers alternative policy approaches.

Kirby, Ronald et.al. 1975. *Para Transit: Neglected Options for Urban Mobility.* Washington, DC: Urban Institute. Some suggestions for innovative alternatives to traditional mass transit.

Reconnecting Rural America: Report on Rural Intercity Passenger Transportation.
1989. Washington, DC: U.S. Department of Agriculture, Office of
Transportation. Traces recent attempts to restructure a national bus system,
with attention to both rural and small-town systems, and their relation to
intercity systems.
Renner, Michael. 1988. *Rethinking the Role of the Automobile.* Worldwatch Paper
84. Washington, DC: Worldwatch Institute. Updated information on the
evolving role of cars in developing and developed nations, with a focus on
environmental effects.

7

Urban Political Systems

Outline of Topics

U rban residents rely heavily on the services provided by local government. The overall quality of life, as well as the health, safety, and economic opportunities of most urban residents depend partly on how efficiently and effectively local government delivers a wide range of services. The next chapter will examine how well local urban governments are doing in providing specific services. However, before we can consider those services we need to understand something about the general nature of urban government. In particular, we need to examine how responsive local government is to the demands placed on it by its citizens. That depends on the structural constraints which limit what local governments can do and how they go about doing it and the distribution of political influence in the community which determines to whom government is most likely to respond. Our discussion will conclude with an examination of one issue which vividly illustrates both the role of structural constraints and the distribution of influence in how local governments operate: the recurrent problems of urban government finance.

Structural Constraints on Urban Government

The structural constraints on local government refer to a relatively fixed set of conditions which limits what they can attempt to do. Some are a reflection of the formal legal organization of government in the United States. Others are a result of our capitalist system of economic organization.

Limited Authority

The authority (the legal right and responsibility) to carry out local government activities has been limited by state legislatures in several ways which strongly influence what local government does, how it does it, and how it pays for what it does. These limitations, in turn, have often created difficulty when urban governments have attempted to respond to a rapidly changing set of urban problems.

The tasks local urban government undertakes are essentially assigned to it by the state legislature. In general, the long-term historical trend has been for state legislatures to require that local government provide more services and to specify in greater detail the nature of those services (Gluck and Meister, 1979:211-212). In some states, for example, certain social services must be provided by local government. The result is that a large proportion of the budget of local government usually goes to provide services which are required by state law. Conversely, local government is not allowed to perform other activities which the states have reserved for themselves. Pollution control, for example, may be a state responsibility.

State legislatures also generally determine the basic form local government can take: for example, how much authority the mayor can have, the make-up and form of election of the city council, and how independent the school board is from the city council. In addition, states have increasingly specified in great detail how local government agencies are to be operated. For example, many states specify such things as the number of days schools are to be open, qualifications for police officers, civil-service procedures for government employees, and the nature of zoning procedures.

Finally, the type of taxes a local government can impose are usually strictly limited by state government. In practice, what this has meant is that local government relies very heavily on the real-estate property tax for its tax revenues. Other major sources of tax revenues are generally reserved by the state. As we will see later in this chapter, this reliance on the real estate property tax has been one source of the financial difficulties of many cities.

These limitations on local government arose for a variety of reasons, some of them very good ones. Some restrictions date back to the 19th and early 20th centuries. State legislatures were controlled by representatives from rural areas. These rural representatives were fearful (partly because of the large number of foreign immigrants in the cities) of the growing size and economic power of the cities. Accordingly, they sought to impose limitations on the political power of the cities and maintain rural dominance over state government. Other restrictions grew out of a concern that local government was not performing needed services in an adequate, equitable, or efficient way. States intervened to correct the situation by forcing local governments to undertake certain activities and mandating the level of service to be provided. In other cases, city governments were dominated by powerful and corrupt political machines, and state governments stepped in to control local corruption (Gluck and Meister, 1979:71-96).

However good the intentions of such limitations, they have often created problems for local government. The actual freedom of action of local government officials is quite limited. They have a limited ability to raise revenues and much of that revenue is committed to required programs. The ability to develop new programs, change priorities among existing programs, and respond to citizen demands and complaints is therefore not great. Local government is thus relatively inflexible in terms of the activities and programs it can undertake. That means that it also tends to be relatively unresponsive to changing citizen needs and expectations.

Not surprisingly, as new urban problems confronted urban governments in the post-1945 period, they often appeared paralyzed. They lacked both the resources and the authority to do very much to deal with the developing problems, even in those rare cases where there were both popular support and the political leadership to back new initiatives (Gluck and Meister, 1979:12-15).

New programs, and the funding for them, had to come from state and (increasingly) federal government. During the 1950s and 1960s both federal and state urban policy primarily took the form of programs either directly administered or tightly regulated by state and federal agencies. For instance, most of the urban renewal projects begun in the 1950s were dependent almost exclusively on federal funds, and each project required detailed approval at the federal level. These sorts of efforts reached their peak in the 1960s under the auspices of the Johnson administration's "Great Society" program. This only served to diminish further the independence and significance of local government. And, for better or for worse, it meant that urban policy and programs were determined mostly at the state and federal level, rather than locally. To a very large extent, what constituted urban policy in the United States had become essentially a federal responsibility. In addition, the growth of federal welfare programs created another set of "de facto" urban programs in the large central cities with major concentrations of the poor.

In the 1970s the federal government attempted to provide money to urban governments with fewer restrictions on how it was spent. For example, the *revenue sharing* program essentially transferred federal money directly to cities for use in their general budgets with few stipulations on how it was to be spent. This may have increased local policy autonomy somewhat in the short-term. However, it also made local budgets increasingly hostage to decisions made in Washington. We will see later in the chapter how devastating this growing fiscal dependency proved to be when both unrestricted federal grants and more strictly controlled federal urban programs were cut in the late 1970s and 1980s.

This dependency on state and federal government has become so pervasive that Warren (1956) argues that local government agencies have essentially become tied to agencies at the higher levels of government. These "vertical ties," he argues, have become more important than decision-making at the local level in determining what local government does. Similarly, both Alford and Friedland (1975) and

Gottdiener (1987) characterize local government as now in an essentially dependent relationship with the higher levels of government. This dependence has increasingly rendered local politics and decision-making less and less relevant to understanding what local government does.

One of the major policy initiatives of the Reagan administration was the set of proposals which were labelled the *new federalism*. These explicitly sought to address the growing federal role at the state and local level. They involved consolidating funding for a myriad of federal programs for states and localities into large block grants (e.g., all programs relating to transportation). States or localities were to be free to allocate money for specific programs within "blocks" as they saw fit. Overall funding was simultaneously to be very substantially reduced. The policy was billed as a way of increasing state and local autonomy in relation to the federal government. It was never fully implemented because it was viewed by opponents (in Congress and state and local officials) as a disguised way of destroying many of the social programs created in the 1960s and 1970s. The fear was that drastic funding cuts could not or would not be made up at the local level. In addition, there was concern that programs targeted towards the poor and minorities would suffer the most because of their lack of political power at the state and local level. As we will see, the major funding cuts that did occur and the partial implementation of block grants that Congress approved appear to have had that result. It can be argued, in addition, that any increased autonomy (mostly obtained at the state level) was counterbalanced (especially at the local level) by the constraints imposed by reduced federal funding (Fainstein and Fainstein, 1989).

Finally, it should be pointed out again that many federal decisions on general national policy can also be regarded as a form of "urban" policy-making which fundamentally shapes the problems and opportunities faced by local government. For example, we have seen how federally supported mortgage loan guarantee programs (FHA and VA) helped determine both the form and extent of post-1945 suburbanization. The role of the federal government in shaping the economic changes of the 1970s and 1980s (discussed in Chapter 2) provides another example of "indirect" federal urban policy-making.

Fragmentation

American metropolitan areas are governed not by one local government but by many. The list of local government units is almost endless: city governments, suburban governments, county governments, sanitation districts, pollution control authorities, and so on. The typical large metropolitan area is governed by several hundred, usually autonomous, government units whose jurisdictions frequently overlap.

This fragmenting of local government authority has occurred for a number of reasons. Rapid urban growth meant that urban populations quickly spread out beyond central city boundaries. In the 19th and early 20th centuries cities responded by annexing these new urban areas. Cities grew very rapidly both in terms of their geographical area and population. However, except in some areas of the South and Southwest annexation was soon stopped—usually by state legislatures (see Chapter 1). Urban reformers early in this century added to fragmentation by advocating the creation of numerous independent boards and agencies to encourage citizen control and weaken the power of the corruption-ridden city political machines. Also, as problems such as transportation and sanitation became regional, independent agencies (e.g., the New York Port Authority) were created to provide special services to those areas. Finally, state and federal programs to provide services to local areas added yet another set of government agencies, independent of local control and, often, of each other (Gluck and Meister, 1979:155-56; Greer, 1962; Wood, 1964).

Most observers have argued that one result of this fragmentation is poor coordinating and planning between the various government agencies attempting to deal with problems that affect a whole metropolitan area. Each governmental unit jealously protects its jurisdiction and attempts to work out solutions to problems, often with only minimal concern either for what other agencies are attempting to do or for the needs of the area as a whole (Lineberry 1970).

Critics of fragmentation have also claimed that it leads to inefficient delivery of services. There may be unnecessary duplication of services. For instance, both city and county government may operate police forces and build jails to serve much of the same area. Many small departments (e.g., police, fire, water) may not be as efficient as one large centralized department (Wood, 1964).

Another frequently cited result of fragmentation is that the quality and level of services will vary substantially within a metropolitan area. For example, the financial difficulties of the central cities, in part a result of the loss of more affluent taxpayers to the suburbs, have resulted in a disastrous deterioration in their public schools. Within the suburbs themselves, some localities with less affluent residents may find themselves unable to provide even such basic services as sidewalks, sewers, or a professional fire department. Meanwhile, nearby suburbs with affluent residents can enjoy elaborate public services. These service differences point out again that the suburbs are not homogenous, middle-class "bedroom" communities, but include some communities of predominately working-class and poor residents. As a result, suburban governments have varying abilities to raise revenues and provide services (Logan and Schneider, 1981; Wood, 1964). Mark Gottdiener (1987:198) contends that this inequality in the ability to provide services also becomes self-perpetuating. Poorer communities are unable to attract more affluent residents and desirable businesses because of their inferior service provision. The resulting weak tax base makes it impossible to improve services.

In addition, Newton (1976; 1978) argues that there is a direct relationship between fragmentation and the very low level of citizen participation in urban politics. Fragmentation means that each small political unit is unable to address the major problems of the metropolitan area. Hence, local politics only addresses the more minor problems within each small jurisdiction. These issues do not evoke much interest on the part of the citizens. A case study of suburban politics by Gottdiener (1977) supports Newton's claims.

Small governments are also inherently less powerful in their dealings with higher levels of government. They have limited resources and small staffs. Moreover, they represent only a small fraction of the population of their urban area.

These criticisms of fragmentation have generally been cited by urban reformers as the reason for the creation of metropolitan-wide governmental units for at least some local government service functions. However, a number of researchers have called the critique of fragmentation into question (e.g., Ostrom, 1983; Bish and Ostrom, 1973; Popenoe, 1985; Parks and Oakerson, 1989; Stein, 1989). They note that there is little evidence that centralized, metropolitan service departments are actually more efficient. Indeed, small service units may often be more efficient. Moreover, they argue that small government units may be more responsive and accessible to citizens and provide people with a form of local autonomy which they prefer. As a consequence, the overall distribution of services in a metropolitan area may better reflect citizen preferences because of fragmentation.

The controversy over the merits and limitations of metropolitan government is likely to remain primarily an academic argument. There have been very few successful government consolidation efforts. Political opposition to government consolidation is widespread. Local officials whose power or positions might be threatened often oppose consolidation. Public opposition to consolidation appears to be strong (Baldassare, 1989). That opposition has a number of sources. For example, suburban residents may be concerned that their taxes will be raised to support central city services or that busing to achieve racial integration would be mandated in a consolidated school system. Both suburban and central city residents may fear the loss of political autonomy.

Increasing Capital Mobility

As was pointed out in Chapter 2, the United States economy has come to be increasingly dominated by large corporations serving a national and/or international market, often from a large number of geographically dispersed facilities. Modern communications and transportation systems allow administrative control to be exercised far from centers of administration. Fewer and fewer corporations are tied to a single metropolitan market. There is less reason to locate in one particular urban area because of geographic factors, quality of labor supply, physical infrastructure, or transportation facilities. For an increasing number of corporations, there are numerous urban areas which are more or less interchangeable in terms of their desirability as places to locate their facilities . At the same time, pressures created by increasing international competition have made the search for more cost-effective locations a major corporate priority. For example, the last two decades have witnessed a major further dispersal of the auto industry away from its traditional location in or near Detroit (Kantor, 1987:506-507).

As a consequence, urban areas find themselves in an increasingly fierce competition for corporate investment. Indeed, the fragmentation of metropolitan government means that even within a given urban area, local governments compete with each other. This puts large corporations in a very favorable bargaining position. They can demand subsidies, tax relief, favorable regulatory policies (e.g., zoning laws), and other special treatment as the price for deciding to locate in a particular urban area (Kantor, 1987:507; Gottdiener, 1987:199). For example, in 1989, Chicago and the state of Illinois (representing the Chicago area) found themselves in an intense bargaining war with other metropolitan areas to obtain a commitment from Sears Corporation to locate a major portion of its central headquarters operations (previously all centered in Chicago) in their areas. (Suburban Chicago "won," after agreeing to major subsidies to Sears.)

Such competition is a major constraint on the actions of local government. Loss of corporate investment to more aggressive competing localities is increasingly possible. As a consequence, local leaders have come to see protection and expansion of the local economic (and tax) base as a central priority of government, even if it means paying less attention to other pressing needs or citizen demands. Corporate preferences and concerns tend to be given precedence. Various schemes to attract corporate investment consume a major portion of governmental effort and resources (Kantor, 1987:510-511; Molotch, 1988:32-35; Logan and Molotch, 1987:57-62).

The Requirements of a Capitalist System

A number of "neo-Marxist" sociologists have suggested that the most fundamental constraint on urban government (as well as all other levels of government) in the United States derives from the nature of capitalism itself. In this view, a capitalist system has certain fundamental requirements if it is to continue to operate. The activities of local governments are seen as necessary to meet some of those requirements. Hence, there are some things which urban government simply *must* do.

The most common form this argument has taken is associated with the so-called *structuralist* neo-Marxist theory of how the political system operates (see O'Connor, 1973; Habermas, 1975). These theorists contend that modern capitalism has become increasingly dependent on government action. In this view, corporate profitability has come to depend upon obtaining government subsidies (e.g., labor force training at public expense, government supplied infrastructure, and special tax breaks). This is the so-called "capital accumulation" function of government. Consequently, not only are local governments motivated to attract capital investment by assisting corporations, the survival of the capitalist system depends on it. In addition, government is also called upon to alleviate some of the consequences of corporate activity (e.g., pollution, periodic unemployment, and inadequate housing for the poor). In part these activities are imperative to assure the survival of the labor force needed by capitalist enterprises (again, assisting "capital accumulation"). No less important, they also reduce public discontent caused by the negative consequences of corporate action. Controlling discontent is the so-called "legitimation" function of government. Thus, action to assist in capital accumulation and legitimation on the part of government at all levels is one of the "imperatives" of capitalism.

A different view of what government, of necessity, must do to preserve capitalism is offered by Gottdiener (1987). He contends that there are two levels or tiers of government operation. The first tier is constrained by the requirements of capitalism. This tier enforces the system of private property and wage labor which is the fundamental defining characteristic (and requirement) of a capitalist economy. It does so through its "social control" activities (i.e., the police and legal system). For example, local government cannot allow strikers to seize or destroy corporate property during a labor dispute. Gottdiener does not deny that the activities specified by the structuralists *may* be undertaken by urban governments. However, he does not see them as a fundamental requirement for the survival of capitalism. Rather, they are activities undertaken in the second tier of government operation, which affects the distribution of wealth rather than the more fundamental system of private property. Gottdiener contends that what determines the policies of government at this second level depends on the struggle for influence over government by various groups in the community. It is to this influence system that we now turn.

Pressures on Urban Governments: The Influence System

The policies pursued by urban governments are not determined completely by the structural constraints which they face. Those constraints simply represent the general environment in which decisions are made. Within the limits imposed by that environment, urban governments enjoy considerable potential latitude in adopting specific policies.

In principle, the formal procedures of electing public officials by universal suffrage is supposed to assure that public decision making reflects the distribution of preferences among citizens. However, few scholars of electoral systems believe that elections actually achieve that result. They fail to do so for a number of reasons. For example, in local elections, only a small (unrepresentative) minority (less than 20 percent) normally bother to vote. Voters tend to be poorly informed, and their sources of information are limited. Elections provide limited candidate choice and rarely provide citizens with clear issue choices. Once elected, officials need not be bound by their campaign promises. Many policy decisions are really made outside of public view and/or by appointed civil servants (Marger, 1987:227-254). In short, elections are, at best, "crude blunt instruments" of popular control.

More crucial to policy outcome than the formal system of elections is what might be called the "informal structure of power." The informal structure consists of a system of political "influence" relationships. Influence is a kind of political power which exists outside of the official framework of authority created by laws or government charters. It consists of the ability to affect the decisions of government without going through the procedures (e.g., voting) called for by the system of laws. For example, if a wealthy individual can obtain a tax reduction by making a large campaign contribution to a politician, we say that the person has political influence.

In general, social scientists have seen influence in group terms. Various groups are seen as having common interests and certain resources which allow them to exercise influence to achieve goals which serve their interests. A number of such groups can be identified in any urban political system.

Business Leaders

There can be no doubt that local business leaders exercise considerable influence on local government. (Just how much we will discuss in a moment.) They have the ability to make substantial campaign contributions, and they have both the information and the political skills necessary to become involved in local politics. In addition, the local press, radio, and television will tend to reflect the interests of business either because they are owned by local business interests and/or because they do not wish to offend local advertisers. Business leaders also have considerable prestige in most communities so that they are able to affect public opinion. Business leaders are frequently asked to serve on government commissions and advisory groups because of their leadership skills and prestige. Finally, they are often in a position to directly affect the economic health (and tax base) of a community since they are major employers. In some cases, this includes the ability to move their businesses out of the community if local government policy on such issues as zoning and taxation is not to their liking. We have already seen that this is not an idle threat, as the older central cities in the North have discovered.

Formally Organized Interest Groups

Every urban area has a large number of organized groups which attempt to influence local government. These include such groups as labor unions, professional groups, charitable organizations, civic-improvement associations, neighborhood improvement associations, and the PTA. Frequently, they have, or are in the position to collect, money from their members to make campaign contributions. They can get their members to vote for candidates endorsed by the leadership. They also can be a source of campaign workers (a very important role that many labor unions play), and their leaders can often attract media attention and influence public opinion. Many of these organizations (e.g., charitable groups) also provide a political platform for business leaders, who often are the leaders of these voluntary organizations.

Government Officials

In the last decade scholars have paid increasing attention to government officials as a group with political interests and the resources to pursue them. At the very least, they have an interest in increasing their own power and privileges. The primary means of doing so is to expand the scope, power, and resources of government itself. Besides their formal authority, such officials also possess specialized knowledge about what government is doing and how government operates. They can use this information to their own advantage. Elected office also is a "bully pulpit" (in T.R. Roosevelt's famous phrase) from which to influence public opinion. Moreover, they have easy access to other influential people in the community.

Local Government Employees

Especially in larger cities in the North, government employees have emerged as a major political force. As the (somewhat ironic) result of efforts to prevent corruption and favoritism, many local government employees have civil service protection and cannot be threatened by loss of their jobs or promotions by elected officials. Moreover, elected officials depend on the permanent bureaucracy for the specialized knowledge and skill needed for planning and implementing policy. City employees also provide very visible and critical services which can be disrupted to put pressure on elected officials and the public. Thus, for example, the police can develop "blue flu" (call in sick in large numbers) or write large numbers of parking tickets to press their demands. Of course, in some cities, government employees also exercise influence as formally organized interest groups through their labor unions. Consequently, public employees are in a position to block policies of which they disapprove and make demands for the recognition of their economic interests. For instance, when the first black mayor of Gary, Indiana, was elected, he had considerable difficulty changing government operations because of the opposition of the city bureaucracy and, very importantly, the police.

Unorganized Voting Blocs

Most urban areas have at least some divisions in the electorate based on such things as ethnicity or religion. Often these groups are represented by informal groups. Even when they are not, they may tend to vote together as a bloc based on a sense of shared identity, interests, and tradition. Hence, elected officials may feel obliged to make special efforts to please these groups in hopes of obtaining their support. The result is that their concerns may carry more weight than other, less homogenous groups which are less likely to vote together. For example, in most cities, middle-class voters have an influence on local government much greater than their sheer numbers in the electorate might suggest. This is because middle-class voters are much more likely to be informed and concerned about local political affairs and are much more likely to vote. In contrast, lower-class voters are much more likely to be politically apathetic and, hence, their concerns and problems can be more safely ignored by local government. (However, some observers feel that the large numbers of welfare recipients in the central cities may have become a significant voting block, despite low voting turnout, simply because of their large numbers and their dependence on government.)

The Elite-Pluralist Debate

How much influence do these various groups have? In the last few decades, social scientists have made a major effort to determine the relative weight of the various groups in the political influence system at the local level. In the 1950s and 1960s this research took the form of "community power studies." Two contradictory views developed: the *pluralist* and the *elite views.*

Pluralists argued that influence is fairly widely distributed between various segments of the community (Dahl, 1961; Polsby, 1963). These segments were viewed as being represented by some more or less organized groups (which pluralists called *interest groups*) which actively work to try to influence local government in favor of the people they represent. Interest groups were seen as fairly representative of the range of political concerns in the community: most people have their interests protected by at least one, and usually more, organized interest groups.

Pluralists argued that the political leadership of a community is usually not unified on most issues. Different leaders are important for influencing different government policies. Community leaders represent different groups, and these groups have clearly different goals and concerns. For instance, Robert Dahl, in his classic study of the city of New Haven, identified three critical local issues (school decisions, urban renewal and political nominations) and found different sets of leaders attempting to influence government on the different issues.

Moreover, each interest group has some effective means for exercising influence in areas which are of concern to it. Hence, the pluralists contended that no one group or its leaders is powerful enough (or even interested enough) to dominate local government on every issue. Local policy, as a consequence, was seen as a compromise between a limited set of interest groups. Faced with conflicting demands of the different interest groups, government officials and politicians try to find a compromise that is acceptable to all the involved groups. Thus, according to the pluralists, the role of political leaders is that they function as "honest brokers" (negotiators) who put together coalitions (alliances of interest groups) backing a compromise policy. Government officials themselves were seen as relatively neutral participants who simply seek to keep the various interests satisfied. No one group gets everything it wants, but almost everybody has some indirect influence on government policy. It is not a perfect system, said the pluralists, but one that is reasonably responsive to citizen desires.

For pluralists, the big danger from this sort of system is not that it is undemocratic, but that it may lead to paralysis and stalemate. The various groups' positions may be far apart, and they may so effectively block each others' influence that no policy compromise can be achieved. Hence, no government action at all can take place. This sort of problem is most likely to arise in the case of major issues which affect many groups and where the issues involved are extremely controversial ones. Under these conditions the politics of compromise may become the politics of inaction and drift. Thus, the dilemma of the influence system is that the very thing that makes the political system democratic may also render government incapable of acting on the most important issues it faces.

Elite theorists of community power (e.g., Hunter, 1952) did not necessarily deny that the groups the pluralists talk about exist and function the way the pluralists said they do. The key difference in the elite view is the notion that one group has overwhelming political influence, and the other groups are of only secondary importance. This dominant group, the power elite, is usually identified as consisting of major business leaders in the community: for example, bankers, newspaper owners, real estate developers, owners of large retail enterprises, and executives of large local corporations.

The basis of this elite's power, said elite theorists, is shared interests, coordination of political activities, and the possession of resources which can be used for maintaining political dominance.

According to elite theory, members of the elite have a sense of shared interests based on their economic and social positions. Simply put, they want a "good business climate" in the community. The goal is to minimize local government interference in their business operations (including keeping taxes low) and to obtain services which benefit local business activity (e.g., "reasonable" zoning policies).

Given their shared interests, the elite can be expected to work together to achieve them. Through informal meetings, regular social contact in clubs and organizations, and even secret political strategy meetings, they develop common positions on issues. Often, they attempt to stay out of the political limelight and work through other people who function as their representatives. Thus, leaders of charitable organizations, local politicians, and the like really are only representatives of powerful community leaders who prefer to work behind the scenes.

Elite efforts are more consistently successful than the efforts of other groups, argued the elite theorists, because the political resources they control are much greater than those of other groups. They have more money to contribute. Media control is in their hands. The economic fate of the community can be fundamentally affected by their business decisions. In a real "showdown" they have more ability to protect their vital interests than do other groups.

The consequences of elite influence is clear, said elite theorists. Local government policies tend to reflect elite interests and concerns. For instance, money may be appropriated for urban renewal, but the money will go for improvements for the downtown business district and the housing needs of the poor will be ignored or given only minimal attention. Parking lots and convention centers will be built, expressways will cut through working-class neighborhoods, and business interests will be the prime beneficiaries.

The problem created by elite control is therefore seen as that of the subversion of democratic control. Behind the noise of election campaigns, conflicts in city council, and the demands of the contending interest groups, a small group of business leaders actually chart the political course of the community. Government is viewed as a creature of the business elite, rather than a reflection of general community interests and desires.

Evaluation

Which view is right? There is no simple answer to that question. As Walton (1966) pointed out, the two approaches use different methods to reach their opposing conclusions. Elite theorists use the "reputational" approach to identify the elite, and pluralists use a "decision-making" approach to determine which groups participate in making policy. Thus, the conclusions of the two theoretical approaches appear to be a consequence of the methods of research they employ. As long as there is no clearcut way to decide which method is better, there is no way to decide which theory fits the evidence best.

Some researchers have attempted to get around this stalemate by concluding that the whole theoretical debate between the pluralists and the elite theorists is essentially ideological and really misses the point. Rather than insisting that urban government is always either pluralist or elite in structure, these researchers suggest that how much a community is pluralist or elite in structure is a matter of degree, and communities vary quite a bit in the nature of their influence structures. Hence, some communities may have relatively strong political elites, others may be primarily pluralist, and still others may fall somewhere in between. Thus, the degree to which local political influence is centralized in the hands of an elite is highly variable. Urban governments can be ranked on a continuum (a graduated scale) from high to low in terms of how centralized political influence has become. The task of research on urban influence then becomes to identify characteristics of cities associated with high or low centralization and how the degree of centralization affects policy decision making (Clark, 1968).

More recently, a number of theorists have attempted to combine and/or modify the pluralist and elite perspectives in various ways to develop a general theory of influence at the local level. All these new theoretical approaches recognize a role for conflict and contention between competing interest groups at the local level. All of them also identify a special role played by a particular elite group. However, how they treat the role of nonelite interest groups and their depiction of the nature and behavior of elite groups varies considerably. To illustrate these various new approaches we will briefly examine three recent theories: (1) state managerialism, (2) the city as growth machine, and (3) the two-tiered state.

More Recent Theories

Pluralist theory views government officials as relatively neutral brokers between interest groups. Traditional elite theory treats those officials as essentially passive agents of business interests. The emergence of what is called the "neo-Weberian" approach calls both of those views of local government into question. This theory is usually called *state managerialism* (Gottdiener, 1987:66).

Theorists employing this approach (e.g., Pahl, 1977; Lipsky, 1976; Block, 1980) argue that government officials (state managers) represent an independent "interest group" which seeks to influence public policy to benefit itself. Most of these theorists argue that what state managers want is an increase of their own power and the resources under their control by expanding the role of government. They are free to pursue their own goals because authority over the government administrative apparatus provides them with resources which allow them to free themselves from control from groups outside of government. For instance, they have access to specialized knowledge on government operations which no one else possesses. Civil service bureaucrats are protected from easy dismissal, and they are given considerable latitude on how they perform their tasks (Gottdiener, 1987:66). The result, argue these theorists, is that the characteristics of local government organization and the preferences of state managers play a powerful independent role in shaping the nature of urban government policy. For example, Pahl (1977) argues that those groups that are best able to deal with complex bureaucratic rules and procedures will get the most resources from local government simply because officials find it less difficult to deal with those groups.

State managerialists differ, however, in how they view the relationship of state managers to other groups. Some implicitly seem to assume that there is an essentially pluralist system in which state managers enjoy an especially strategic position to determine the nature of policy (e.g., Lipsky, 1976). Others (e.g., Block, 1980) argue that business interests are the chief group putting pressures upon and constraining the behavior of state managers. State managers dare not pursue policies which so threaten business interests that they become unwilling to invest in the economy. At the same time, other citizen groups cannot be completely ignored. State managers need at least the grudging support of average citizens, if for no other reason, than to avoid mass political discontent and disorder. Hence, state managers will sometimes, especially in times of crisis and impending mass discontent, adopt policies favorable to average citizens, even if it runs contrary to the immediate interests of business.

A much different view is provided by Molotch (1988) and Logan and Molotch (1987) who argue that urban governments function as *growth machines*. While it has significant similarities to the traditional elite view, this view represents a major modification of that earlier approach. It also incorporates many of the basic insights of another major recent approach to urban politics called the "political economy" perspective. These theorists also acknowledge at least some role for the citizen interest groups of pluralist theory.

The "growth machine" consists of those interest groups that have the most to gain from rapid economic growth in a given local political jurisdiction: real estate developers, local business leaders, and providers of professional services, financial institutions, and newspapers. All such groups stand to obtain major direct financial benefits from local growth. Even local universities, cultural centers, and social service agencies are likely to view growth as a source of increased students, clients, and patrons. On the other hand, there are many groups that are not the direct beneficiaries of development and do not participate in the growth machine. Large corporations not headquartered in the area and/or having operations in many locations have little stake in the success or growth of one area: they can locate anywhere. In addition, Logan and Molotch argue that rapid local growth is probably not in the interest of most average citizens. Growth increases such things as housing costs, congestion, pollution, crime, and taxes. While all groups suffer from these problems of growth, only those in the growth machine reap major benefits. For example, poor people may not benefit from increased job opportunities because many of the new jobs go to better qualified migrants. An increasing tax burden may fall mostly on homeowners.

Why does the growth machine have its way, even if the benefits of growth are spread among the interest groups so unevenly? Logan and Molotch answer with an essentially elite theory answer. The growth machine, through such things as campaign contributions and control of the media, has a major say in the selection of the political leadership.

However, Logan and Molotch do not consider their theory as simply an extension or refinement of elite theory. Rather, they present it as a synthesis of previous theorizing. They acknowledge that factors emphasized in other theories, including pluralism, limit the power of the growth machine. These factors are outside constraints on the growth machine. The most important of those constraints is that identified by "political-economy" theorists: the danger that corporate capital will either fail to invest or remove its capital investment to more attractive localities. We have already discussed the implications of this constraint. They regard other constraints as much less important in affecting the actions of the growth machine. They accept the notion that the competence, unity, and preferences of state managers may have some minor influence on the success of the growth machine coalition. The least effective constraint, they argue, is the impact of the efforts of average citizen groups: established interest groups, voting blocks, and political movements. Their successes in opposing the growth machine are likely to be limited in scope (achieving minor concessions) and short-lived (once the group disbands).

Finally, Gottdiener (1987) has proposed a theory which he regards as a balanced synthesis of recent theorizing about the local state, which he calls the *two-tiered theory of the state*. As we have already discussed, the first tier refers to those state activities directly constrained by the requirements of a capitalist system. The second tier refers to state activities which affect the distribution of wealth in society (e.g., tax policies, the provision of services to different groups, and government subsidies). Contrary to most neo-Marxist theorists, Gottdiener does not regard the second tier as being directly constrained by the requirements of the capitalist system. Rather, policy outcomes in the second tier are the result of the conflict among three general groups: state managers, business interests, and citizen groups. To further complicate the struggle between these groups, each of them is frequently divided into factions pursuing their own interests. For example, public employees may seek to increase their wages and job security, creating problems for elected officials. Thus, Gottdiener proposes a model of conflict which has some similarities to the pluralist view. However, agreeing with the managerialists, he treats state managers as having their own set of interests, rather than treating them as neutral coalition builders (the pluralist view).

What determines the outcome of this three-way conflict? No one group is automatically the winner. The sort of government policy that results depends on a number of factors which Gottdiener calls "constraints," "unifying factors," and "canalizing factors."

Gottdiener identifies several constraints relating to the organization of local government. The methods the state uses to implement policy limit what the state will end up doing. For example, what kinds of taxing power does local government have or not have? The formal and informal arrangements that have developed for citizens to control government officials are also constraints. For example, local governments in which a directly elected mayor controls the routine administration of the city provides a different kind of citizen control than one in which city council appoints a full-time, professional city manager. The organization of the government bureaucracy also varies in ways that effect the outcome of local politics. For example, if city employees' jobs are protected by a strong civil service system, they are less affected by the preferences of elected officials and can use their autonomy to pursue their own interests.

Gottdiener also recognizes the constraining effects that different forms of economic organization have had on local governments over time. For example, in the past, when almost all businesses were locally owned, business interests were much more dependent on and affected by the decisions of local government. Now, large national and multinational corporations' interests are much less influenced by political decisions in any particular locality.

However, while the variations in governmental and economic organization have affected political outcomes in meaningful ways, Gottdiener argues that the "unifying" and "canalizing" factors have generally favored success of business organizations over other groups. "Unifying factors" are essentially areas of general consensus among the various groups. They both provide a definition of what political conflict should be about and limit what will be considered as a politically relevant question. Gottdiener identifies two unifying factors: the belief that encouraging economic growth benefits everyone equally and agreement that government should limit its activities to providing certain services (but not do such things as regulate corporate investment decisions). "Canalizing factors" refer to the distribution of political resources that groups bring to the political process and the institutional arrangements and ideologies which shape the way they use those resources. Gottdiener argues that corporations command the most resources, and that local politics is conducted in such a way that cooperative relationships tend to develop between business leaders and political leaders.

Thus, Gottdiener argues that elite theory and more recent neo-Marxist theory oversimplify how influence is exercised. He also recognizes the contribution of pluralist and managerial theorists. However, he argues that the result of politics at the local level is quite similar to that suggested by the elite theorists and neo-Marxists:

> Local government in the United States is nourished currently by political crumbs falling from the table of higher State levels. Its functions are defined by the interplay between systemic needs of the larger social structure and the actions of powerful interests that bind decision-making to specific social outcomes. Democratic participation in this process has very little to do with the way this system functions (Gottdiener, 1987:269).

An Illustration: The "Fiscal Crisis" and Its Aftermath

During the last half of the 1970s urban governments (especially large cities and those in older industrial areas of the North) experienced a "fiscal crisis." Local government expenditures were rising faster than tax revenue. Aid from the federal government (which had been increasing rapidly) leveled off. Consequently, budgets either slipped into deficit or threatened to do so. A few large cities appeared to face the prospect of bankruptcy (i.e., they would not be able to pay their current expenses and also meet their obligations to make payments on their indebtedness). One large city, Cleveland, actually did default by failing to meet its obligations to its creditors. The response was an attempt to reduce expenditures and find alternative sources of revenue. By the mid-1980s most local governments had weathered the crisis: their budgets were in balance and they were able to meet their long-term financial obligations to their creditors. A new round of fiscal crises began to appear in 1990 (Hinds and Eckholm, 1990). At the time of this writing, it is difficult to assess the extent or duration of the problem; thus, our discussion will center on the better-researched crisis of the 1970s. The recurrent nature of the problem, however, indicates that fiscal crises are not simply episodes of over-spending but are rooted in the very nature of our political structures.

Scholars of local government have regarded the fiscal crisis and its subsequent resolution as a good test case to evaluate the theories we have just examined. Hence, these analyses provide a vivid way to illustrate those theories. The nature of the response to the fiscal crisis also represents one source of some of the current problems of urban areas and deserves some discussion in its own right.

The Context of the Crisis

Certain long-term trends made the financial crisis of the 1970s likely. Some contributed to rapidly rising expenditures. Others limited possible revenue sources.

By the mid-1970s, city government expenditures had been rising rapidly for almost two decades. The big central cities in the North were confronted by the growing service needs of an increasingly poor population. Sunbelt cities were attempting to keep up with the needs of a rapidly growing population. Almost all cities were attempting to provide an increasing range and/or improved level of services. Older cities were faced with aging physical facilities which required replacement or repair. Rapidly growing cities had to build new facilities to service their growing populations. In some of the larger cities in the North, the growing power of municipal workers' unions led to unusually high wage increases for a municipal labor force which was growing rapidly. High levels of inflation further increased the costs of materials, equipment, fuel, purchased services, and interest rates paid on municipal bonds used to finance large-scale construction projects (Petersen, 1976; Bahl and Schroeder, 1978).

At the same time, cities experienced increasing difficulty financing these expenditure increases. As their populations declined, the old, industrial cities of the North had fewer people to tax. The population which remained was poorer and less able to pay taxes. Property taxes on real estate yielded less income as property values declined (or increased slowly) in poorer neighborhoods. There were more poor neighborhoods as the middle class left the cities and the poor arrived. Industrial and retail trade decline further reduced taxable property. As tax rates were increased to compensate for this decline in the *tax base* (the value of property available to tax) opposition to further increases grew. Ever higher rates threatened to encourage more affluent homeowners to move to the suburbs. They also encouraged business flight. In the growing cities of the Sunbelt, the tax base grew, but the political pressures to keep rates low were even stronger (to attract business investment). Finally, the limited authority of urban government to impose new taxes and the unwillingness of state governments to grant them new authority made it difficult to tap new tax sources (Petersen, 1976; Bahl and Schroeder, 1978).

For a while, city governments got around these revenue limitations by obtaining more and more federal aid. Many new services were provided through federally funded programs such as the anti-poverty programs introduced in the 1960s and urban renewal programs. After 1970 the federal government also provided funds through various revenue sharing programs, discussed previously. In the early 1970s a job training program (CETA) was targeted at cities with high unemployment and provided money to hire the unemployed to work for city governments (Reischauer, 1978). The result was that city governments increasingly relied on federal funding to augment their own revenues. In most large cities in the mid-1970s, federal aid had come to equal about half of all the money raised from local sources. The ability to increase city expenditures thus came to be more and more dependent on the availability of increased federal aid each year (Bahl and Schroeder, 1978; Reischauer, 1978).

The actual crisis occurred when economic recession in the mid-1970s created unanticipated shortfalls in local revenue and federal aid did not increase enough to compensate for that revenue loss. In fact, federal aid dipped slightly in the mid-1970s and then grew slowly until 1980. After that, the Reagan administration significantly reduced urban oriented anti-poverty programs, job training programs, and the various forms of revenue-sharing. Congressional opposition to these cuts meant they were not as large as the administration intended them to be (Bahl and Schroeder, 1978; Fainstein and Fainstein, 1989). Still, federal aid dropped from 23 percent of municipal revenue in 1980 to 15 percent in 1984 (Fainstein and Fainstein, 1989:45).

Causes of the Crisis: Contending Interpretations

The broad outlines we have just sketched are generally accepted by most observers. However, each of the approaches to urban politics we have examined put different emphases on the various factors leading to the crisis and provides sharply contrasting explanations for them.

Those working in the pluralist tradition (e.g., Shefter, 1977) argue the basic problem generating the crisis was the escalation of demands by various interest groups for a share of city resources and the inability of political leaders to resist those demands. In this view, elected leaders, seeking to assemble coalitions of interest groups to support them in elections, attempted to buy off the various groups by providing increased services or other special favors. Many who share this view single out public employees and the poor as particularly important in creating these escalating demands. These groups (service providers on the city payroll and those particularly dependent on services) had a strong interest in increasing expenditures (thereby obtaining increased wages or services) and little interest in limiting taxation. The growing number and political organization of unionized public employees (and their ability to disrupt city services) and the growing number of the poor supposedly made these groups an important source of electoral support. Managerial theorists add to this pluralist view that both elected officials and civil service bureaucrats also have a strong vested interest in increasing the size and activities of government. Hence, they made natural allies of those interest groups who stood to gain the most from increasing government expenditures (Buchanon, 1977).

Many theorists working in the elite and/or political-economy traditions now reject this pluralist argument. They argue instead that most cities which experienced severe fiscal crises (with the possible exception of New York) had not markedly increased their expenditures on services for the poor. Instead, most of the increased expenditures were the result of programs designed to subsidize corporate investment (Friedland, 1980; Rubin, 1985). For elite theorists these subsidies were the predictable result of the political influence of business interests on local government. Others argue that these subsidies reflected the increased need that large corporations had for subsidies under current conditions in capitalist economies (O'Connor, 1973). A slightly different neo-Marxist view, suggested earlier in the chapter, is that corporate subsidies may have simply reflected the attempts by city governments to compete for corporate investment under conditions in which capital had become highly mobile.

Responses to the Crisis

By the mid-1980s most of the cities which seemed to be approaching bankruptcy a decade before were financially healthy: they had balanced budgets and were considered good credit risks by lenders. How did they avert financial disaster?

The most important means employed were reductions in both the level and scope of services that these governments deliver. Social programs oriented toward the poor were particularly likely to be cut back. Where cities operated social programs with federal funds and the funding was cut in the 1980s, cities usually did not shift to their own funds to maintain the programs. Cities were more reluctant to cut "basic services" (e.g., police and fire protection), but many eventually did so. Expenditures on physical facilities were selectively reduced. Those viewed as contributing to encouraging business investment were maintained or, if possible, even increased. Others (e.g., neighborhood parks, school buildings) were allowed to deteriorate. Some services were *privatized*. In some cases that meant that the city simply stopped providing the service and allowed private businesses to deliver it for a fee. In other cases, cities contracted the service out to private business at a set price. Some cities even tried to give away some services (e.g., city-owned hospitals or colleges) to other levels of government, such as counties or states (Rubin, 1985; Ganz, 1985).

On the revenue side, cities made limited attempts to increase tax levels. Concern over the effect of increased taxation on business investment both limited the amount of the increase and tilted it toward taxes on citizens (e.g., sales taxes). A very common form of "revenue enhancement" was to institute users' fees for city services. It should be noted that in most cases, such fees impose the greatest burden on the poor, since they have the least ability to pay them.

Despite often quite draconian service reductions, most cities did not actually reduce their budgets very much. That is because they increased their efforts to encourage business investment. For example, major projects were undertaken to refurbish downtown business districts in order to make them more attractive for corporate offices. Direct subsidies or tax relief were provided for developers of downtown office centers and corporations willing to build factories. Government "development bonds" were issued to provide low interest loans for the same purposes (Rubin, 1985; Kantor, 1987). Those cities in the most financial trouble and/or with the highest unemployment rates were the ones that spent the most to encourage investment. Ironically, most research suggests that such programs have little or no impact on the actual investment decisions of corporations. What is offered is usually only of marginal economic significance to the corporations. Moreover, in a situation in which almost all localities now offer incentives, it is hard for any one locality to offer a significantly better deal (Rubin and Rubin, 1987; Kirby, 1985). Other scholars have argued that what benefits accrue from economic development are primarily concentrated in the hands of local developers and their allies, rather than being spread to the whole community (Logan and Molotch, 1983; Kirby, 1985).

Why This Response? Contending Interpretations

Thus, the resolution of the fiscal crisis involved reducing services to the general public and most especially the urban disadvantaged, while increasing subsidies to business. Meanwhile, more of the burden of local government was shifted to the less affluent by means of regressive taxes and users' fees. For those working in the pluralist tradition these changes represented a necessary adjustment of city expenditure and revenue-raising patterns. Urban governments were portrayed as having caved in to special interests in the 1960s and 1970s. Consequently, they were attempting to do too much for special groups and were delivering services inefficiently to the general community. Besides creating a fiscal crisis, this tendency had created an excessive burden of taxation which discouraged private investment. In this view, urban government needed to leave more services to the market. Private providers could deliver services more efficiently and citizens could pick and choose services based on their preferences and willingness to pay. In the long run, decreased tax burdens on business and a more favorable investment climate would pay dividends in the form of increased corporate investment and a healthier local economy (Savas, 1982).

For those working in the elite or neo-Marxist tradition these changes simply reflected the current realities of corporate power. The threat of capital flight forced city governments to increase their corporate subsidies and other incentives, while providing them with tax relief. These shifts provided no real benefit to the general community since they were ineffective in promoting real employment growth. Local business interests linked to such things as downtown development were the prime beneficiaries of the change in fiscal policy. In addition, large corporations are able to play one community off another to obtain the most favorable terms under which to invest capital. Predictably, the least advantaged citizens have ended up bearing the brunt of service cuts and have suffered from changes in the way cities raise revenues. They have the least political power, and city governments are confronted with the fundamental constraint posed by capital mobility (Kantor, 1987).

Long-Term Implications

Budget reductions have had a crippling effect on city services. As we will see in succeeding chapters, balanced budgets in the old central cities have been obtained at the price of dirtier streets, understaffed police departments, closed library branches, and further deterioration in already crisis ridden school systems. In the newer, growing urban areas, avoidance of financial crises and the maintenance of lower tax rates have meant continued low levels of service and an inability to respond to the problems of growth.

The cumulative effects of years of neglect are now becoming apparent. Central cities are failing to meet the challenge of educating a labor force with adequate skills to meet the needs of a changing economy. Crumbling public facilities threaten the ability of business to either expand or improve efficiency. Ancient bridges, poorly maintained highways and public transit systems, inadequate fire protection, an overwhelmed criminal justice system, and overburdened water and sewer systems all make for a poor business climate. Nor should we ignore the human costs of service reductions. For the least advantaged, basic needs are even more poorly provided than before. Cuts in city-provided medical facilities make access to low-cost medical care more difficult in many cities. Poor quality schools make it harder to escape poverty. Reduced fire and police protection threaten the poor the most because they are at the most risk of criminal victimization and fire. User fees exclude the poor from services and facilities previously accessible to them. For all of us, less reliable public services and deteriorated facilities adversely affect our quality of life.

Main Points

1. Urban government is limited in what it can do by four structural constraints: limited authority, fragmentation, high capital mobility, and the general requirements of a capitalist system.

2. Taken together, these constraints limit how effective urban governments can be in dealing with the problems of urban areas and being responsive to citizen demands.

3. Besides the effect of structural constraints, urban government actions are strongly shaped by pressures exerted by a number of groups with political influence: business leaders, organized interest groups, government officials themselves, public employees, and unorganized voting blocks.

4. Traditionally, there have been two theories of how much influence various groups have over local government: elite theory and pluralist theory.

5. Pluralists believe that influence is relatively widely distributed between the various groups, and, as a result, local decisions are relatively democratic in nature. The problem is that this may result in paralysis when the various groups refuse to compromise.

6. Elite theorists believe that business leaders have the ability to dominate local government, and the problem of local government is that it is undemocratic and not responsive to the needs of all groups in the community.

7. More recent theorizing about political influence at the local level has attempted to combine the two older theories.

8. State managerialist theorists emphasize the strong, independent role of government officials, pursuing their own interests, in shaping public policy. Some of these theorists argue that this "political elite" operates within the context of an essentially pluralist system of competing interest groups. Others argue that the most important group with whom state managers must contend are business interests.

9. Logan and Molotch argue that there is a coalition of interests whom they call the "urban growth machine" that consists of those who benefit the most from rapid economic growth and have a disproportionate influence on urban government. However, they acknowledge the role of other groups or factors in limiting the power of that coalition.

10. Gottdiener argues for a "two-tiered theory of the state." The first tier is constrained by the nature of capitalism itself to enforce the system of private property through the use of police powers and the courts. The second tier engages in activities which affect the distribution of wealth in society. Policies undertaken by this tier are determined by a complex struggle between government officials, capitalists, and workers. In this struggle, a number of factors operate to give capitalists the greatest advantage.

11. During the 1970s many cities experienced a financial crisis because of rising expenditures, an inability to raise local revenues, and a growing reliance on external aid. Those working in the pluralist tradition argue that the crisis was caused by city officials who surrendered to the growing demands of special interests, including the poor and public employees. Those working in the elite theory tradition blame increasing subsidies of business investment.

12. The response to the crisis were major cuts in public service expenditures (especially for the poor), privatization, and increased user fees and nonbusiness taxes. Growing emphasis was placed on policies to promote business investment. Pluralist-oriented observers viewed these changes as necessary and appropriate. Others considered these responses as evidence of the disproportionate role of business interests in influencing public policy.

Key Terms

Authority   The power conferred on a person or agency of government by laws, constitutions, charters, and other recognized legal means.

Capital Mobility   The ability of large corporations to shift their investments and business operations to different locations with relative ease.

Elite   As used by elite theorists of community power, the elite consists of that group of business leaders and the wealthy who dominate the informal structure of political influence in a community.

Fragmentation   The division of government authority in urban areas between a large number of local governments and agencies.

Influence   A kind of informal political power which exists outside of the official framework of authority created by laws.

Informal Structure   A system of political influence relationships.

Interest Group   A group of people (more or less formally organized) with some shared political goal which attempts to influence government policy.

Pluralist   As argued by pluralist theorists of community power, the view that political influence is fairly widely distributed between various segments of the community.

Structural Constraints   The relatively fixed set of conditions in which governments operate which limits what they can attempt to do.

Tax Base   The total assessed value of the property of a community on which taxes are levied.

Suggested Reading

Dahl, Robert. 1961. *Who Governs? Power and Democracy in an American City.* New Haven, CT: Yale University Press. The classic pluralist interpretation of community power.

Gottdiener, Mark. 1987. *The Decline of Urban Politics.* Newbury Park, CA: Sage. A recent re-examination of the nature of local politics and government, this book explains the "two-tiered" approach.

Hunter, Floyd. 1952. *Community Power Structure.* Chapel Hill, NC: University of North Carolina Press. The classic elite theory study of community power.

Logan, John and Harvey Molotch. 1987. *Urban Fortunes: The Political-Economy of Place.* Berkeley, CA: University of California. Probably the best-known of recent attempts to re-examine the issue of community power.

8

Urban Government
The Delivery of Services

Outline of Topics

C oncentration of large numbers of people under conditions of relatively high density is only possible and reasonably tolerable if at least some minimum level of governmental services is provided. Preindustrial cities were places in which the ability and concern of government to deliver safe water, remove wastes, maintain public order, and assist the helpless were limited. Consequently, they were places of disease, disorder, squalor, and frequent misfortune for a majority of their residents. Indeed, conditions were generally so bad that the death rate exceeded the birth rate, and population was only maintained by the continued addition of new residents from the countryside (Sjoberg, 1960). Conditions in contemporary urban areas are so much more tolerable and safe in large part because of a massive effort on the part of government to maintain a high level of basic services.

The range of services provided urban residents by government is immense. It would be impractical even to list them all here. However, it is possible to distinguish between two general categories: (1) physical services and (2) social services. Physical services consist of those activities which provide residents with a habitable environment and meet certain basic physical needs best provided collectively. They include such things as waste disposal, water supply, and disease control. Social services refer to a wide range of efforts to assist people in their day-to-day social activities and to make collective social life possible. They include such activities as assistance to the needy and helpless, maintenance of public order and safety, and education. Our concern in this chapter is to examine a few of the more critical of these physical and social services with an eye to evaluating their quality and some of the problems government faces in delivering them.

Physical Services

Most physical services have as their common goal the maintenance of an acceptable level of public health and safety. Here we will focus on four areas which are particularly fundamental to achieving this goal and which, in the past, most North Americans have taken for granted: air quality, water supply, waste disposal, and infrastructure maintenance. As we will see, we cannot take these services for granted any longer.

Air Quality

Until fairly recently, government played a relatively minor role in trying to control urban air quality. That was not because air pollution was not a severe problem. Coal burning (and before that, wood burning) created very foul and unhealthy air over our cities in the past. However, public resignation and a limited ability to do much about the problem meant that control measures were crude and indifferently enforced, when anything was done at all. It was only in the 1960s that increased public awareness of the problem and increasing research evidence on the effects of air pollution created political pressure for a nationwide effort to curb air pollution.

Current press coverage of environmental problems, particularly air pollution and acid rain, give the impression that these are coming under control. Widespread evidence to the contrary, however, suggests that efforts to combat air pollution since the early 1970s have had only limited success. At least 150 million Americans, according to the EPA (Environmental Protection Agency) breathe unhealthy air. Acid rain is ruining forests, lakes, crops, and buildings across great stretches of the United States and Canada (French, 1990:98).

Specific threats to health result from acid precipitation, whereby sulfur dioxide is changed into particles that in the long run do serious lung damage. One estimate suggests that 50,000 deaths occur annually from this source. Acid deposited can cause several dangerous metals, including aluminum and mercury as well as lead, to be more soluble. These metals can contaminate municipal and home water systems. Car pollutants contribute to the formation of ozone. Recent research emphasizes that the breathing of this substance causes more serious and short-term lung problems than was formerly believed to be the case. A 1987 EPA study concluded that air toxic emissions may result in at least 2,000 cancer deaths annually. Thomas Crocker of the University of Wyoming estimates that air pollution costs at least $40 billion annually in both health care and lost productivity expenses (French, 1990:101-104).

Air pollution results in great harm not only to health, but also to nature. Numerous studies have shown that acid deposition in water destroys fish and aquatic organisms. Much of the Great Lakes area, several states in the Southeast and Northeast, and much of the Mountain West are massively contaminated. The economic consequences for forests, forest industries, and tourism are very dire. Air pollution endangers crops as well. Total crop losses in 1987 were estimated at from 5 to 10 percent of total production (French, 1990:104-07).

In addition, many historical monuments (including Independence Hall, the Statue of Liberty, and the Washington Monument) are either actually being eroded or in danger from this process. Recent studies suggest that the nation may face an ultimate loss of billions of dollars in damage to its public buildings and monuments (French, 1990: 109-10).

There has been a great effort during the last several decades to deal with at least some of the causes of air pollution. For example, acidic particles (e.g., sulfates and nitrates) form outside the smokestacks of power plants, producing great harm to both people and environment. However, scrubbers, used in coal-burning power plants, can take out up to 95 percent of acidic emissions. Generally speaking, new power plants are built to higher, more stringent specifications. Little, though, is being done to remodel older plants to conform to recent legislation mandating air pollution control (French, 1990:110-11).

Serious problems remain. Auto manufacturers have been reluctant to meet standards set by the federal government. Authorities responsible have been reluctant to enforce these standards. The Environmental Protection Agency has not pressed the enforcement of the Clean Air Act provision which bans the use of federal funds for new highway and industrial construction in areas not complying with that act's mandates. All levels of government have been negligent in failing to act promptly to deal with air pollution. Tougher rules could be enacted. New cars could comply with stricter laws. No standards exist for older vehicles, even though they tend to pollute more than recent models. This slow response to auto emissions has been viewed by some observers as the result of government-business collusion. Auto manufacturers do not want to meet standards; government accedes to their wishes (Renner, 1989:108; 1988:41-42). Other special interest groups have also successfully lobbied to delay the implementation of pollution control standards. The energy crisis in the 1970s created pressures to loosen controls where those controls resulted in increased fuel consumption or increasing reliance on foreign oil. The increasing emphasis on coal as an energy source to replace oil is a particularly ominous trend given the cost and difficulty of burning coal cleanly. At the current state of technology, a number of difficulties remain to be solved. Moreover, all sources of pollution have not been identified and we do not know precisely the exact effects of all kinds of pollution and the levels at which these effects are triggered. Control technology is still not available for all kinds of pollution, and, very importantly, much currently available equipment is extraordinarily expensive.

The policy challenge now lies in focusing on pollution prevention as opposed to pollution control (French, 1990:118). After over a decade of inaction, the passage of the Clean Air Act of 1990 may be a first step in that direction. Though the bill by no means represented the desires of the strict environmentalists, neither did it represent a complete surrender to pollution control opponents. President Bush also favors moderate legislation to deal with air pollution (*U.S. News and World Report*, 4/16/1990:22-24). Hence, the question is no longer one of values or public concern. The environmentalists have won that battle. The problem now is that of policy implementation based on solid scientific evidence (Broder, 1990; Easterbrook, 1990).

Plans developed for the Los Angeles area provide some idea of the kinds of policies which appear likely to be adopted in the near future. Recently a twenty-year air quality plan was developed by California's South Coast Air Quality Management District (AQMD). The plan includes a heavy emphasis on car pooling. Methanol-fueled buses have already been adopted, while the use of rechargeable batteries is a growing possibility for cars and mass transit vehicles. There also are plans for a subway (Weisman, 1989).

Even these kinds of policies are only short-term solutions, which can themselves create environmental problems. How, for instance, can ash resulting from scrubbing be safely disposed of? No really viable technique has emerged (French, 1990:111). A far more appropriate policy approach is that of energy efficiency. For example, readily available measures could reduce electricity demand by 15 percent in the Midwest, the region producing one-third of sulfur dioxide emissions. The ACEEE (American Council for an Energy-Efficient Economy) has concluded that savings of from $4 to $8 billion would result if emission control and conservation were national policy. Increased recycling would not only save scarce landfill space, it also would eliminate some pollution by reducing the emissions from production facilities such as those producing aluminum and paper (French, 1990:111-112). Alternate fuels (e.g., methanol) may reduce ozone but produce much more formaldehyde as does gasoline. A more viable approach would be to produce automobiles both low in emissions and high in fuel economy. In summary, waste minimization and energy conservation are more hopeful and realistic strategies than is air pollution control alone. The U.S. Office of Technology Assessment (OTA) concludes that United States industry could lower waste and pollutant production by 50 percent in the near future (French 1990:113-114).

Water Supply

Clean, abundant, and cheap water has been something most urban residents in the United States have come to expect. And, indeed, the total national supply of water is not in doubt. The problem lies in getting enough water of adequate quality to where it is needed at a reasonable cost (Commission, 1972:61). Despite past successes in doing so, current trends suggest that many urban areas face a real possibility of a serious water supply crisis in the near future.

The problem is most severe in the West and Southwest. On the average, this is an area of light rainfall. Massive efforts have been required to create the current water-supply system. Most traditional sources of water have been tapped and are being used to near or even beyond their long-term capacity. The most important single source is the Colorado River. A complex system of reservoirs and diversion canals have now fully exploited this source. Other smaller rivers are also heavily utilized. Pumping of ground water out of wells is depleting this source faster than it is being replaced by nature.

Yet, demand for water is still increasing. Agriculture based on irrigation (the largest single user) is a major regional industry and a significant contributor to the national food supply. Rapid industrialization, urbanization, and population growth have also resulted in rapid increases in water use. Future growth will require major increases in water supply (Sibley, 1977:49-68). Thus, the West and Southwest are faced with the prospect of water demand outstripping existing supply systems in the near future (Commission, 1972:61; Postel, 1990).

Building dams and reservoirs has been the traditional response to growing water demand in the West. Reservoir capacity in the United States grew steadily, an average of 80 percent increase per decade, between the 1920s and the 1960s. The list of appropriate dam sites, however, has decreased, while at the same time their cost has risen sharply (Postel, 1985).

Hence, better management and more efficient use of existing supplies of water appear to be necessary. Water can be conserved in several ways. For example, present irrigation practices in the West are not sustainable—agricultural water users will have to become more efficient. Means to this end include raising water prices for irrigated water to a realistic level. Water is currently so cheap that few Western farmers attempt to improve their efficiency. They probably would do so, however, if prices were raised. Recycling irrigated water and using more efficient watering equipment (e.g., drip irrigation systems), will also aid the water management effort. In Texas these practices have already resulted in a decrease in water use of 28 percent between 1974 and 1987. Adoption of such measures by farmers frees water for use by urban communities. While there is a trend in this direction, a conflict over resources between agricultural interests and urban areas is increasing in intensity, particularly in California (Postel, 1990; Reisner, 1989).

In addition, a number of approaches which attempt to decrease industrial water demands have been enacted in recent years. Many industries recycle water several times. Recycling metals such as aluminum from scrap (rather than using ore) reduces the amount of water discharged by over 95 percent. Household fixtures, a traditional culprit in water waste, have been improved so that new toilets and shower heads can reduce consumption by at least 50 percent. New models of dishwashers and washing machines offer a savings of at least 30 percent. Tucson, Arizona recently attempted to combine increases in water prices with a public education program suggesting such approaches as the replacement of watered lawns with desert landscaping. Storing surplus runoff underground also offers a number of advantages. Competition for valuable land is decreased, and the great loss of water through evaporation that occurs with surface storage is prevented. Congress provided funds for this type of approach in 17 Western states in 1984. These recent efforts offer modest hope that conservation and better management can avoid disruptive water shortages (Postel, 1985:63-67).

The eastern half of the United States faces much different problems. On the whole, the total amount of water available from surface runoff is more than adequate. The problem is getting clean water to heavily populated areas. Part of the problem is that water sources near heavily urbanized areas tend to be polluted. As a result, urban water systems face the choice of cleaning up the local supply or moving clean water long distances. Both approaches are expensive. Past neglect has meant that rivers in urban areas received sewage that was only minimally treated. Nor would conventional treatment methods completely solve the problem. Industrial pollution dumps dangerous chemicals which are difficult or impossible to remove into water supplies. Hence, expensive controls at the plant site are required. Some urban areas face the additional problem of not being located near water sources adequate for their needs. They will have no choice but to construct expensive aqueduct systems (Commission, 1972:62).

Solid Waste Disposal

Urban areas face the immense task of removing huge amounts of residential trash and garbage as well as industrial wastes. In the past costs were kept low by careless dumping or burning. Open dumps created disease and pest hazards, allowed wastes to leak into the environment, and were public nuisances. Uncontrolled burning was a major source of air pollution. Hence, urban governments moved to create *sanitary landfills* where waste could be carefully buried.

However, this approach is encountering expensive problems. Land that can be used for landfills is being used up. Land costs are rising. As a result, solid wastes have to be transported further, and more expensive land has to be used (Council on Environment Quality, 1979:256). New York, Chicago, and Los Angeles were already having difficulty finding places to dump their solid wastes in the 1970s (Bukro, 1975); the solid waste crisis now confronts every urban area. In addition, there have been a number of accidents involving private dumps in which dangerously toxic chemicals were carelessly buried and resulted in environmental damage and illness. The current situation in Illinois illustrates the magnitude of the problem. That state will have all its land-fill areas closed by the year 2000. Though the state had more than 1000 dumps less than two decades ago, only 126 are currently operating.

In addition, recent findings suggest that refuse does not simply rot away, but rather lasts a long time. Landfill conditions tend to preserve rather than dispose of garbage (Bukro, 1989). There also has been growing concern recently at both state and federal levels of the threat of the pollution of groundwater supplies by municipal landfills. (Half the population depends on groundwater for its water supply.) A significant number of old landfills are currently listed among the more than one thousand worst waste dumps in the United States (Dishneau, 1989; Bukro, 1988).

Hence, major additional waste-disposal efforts are needed. Literally hundreds of old dumps may have to be cleaned up and the waste reburied (Council on Environment Quality, 1979:174-185). New waste-disposal techniques may have to be developed. Finally, the need to recycle increasingly scarce metals may require extensive changes in the way in which solid wastes are handled and processed. To do all these things, major new investments in solid waste disposal systems are probably needed (Council on Environment Quality, 1979:256-258).

However, there is considerable disagreement as to how the crisis should be handled. For example, burning trash to produce electricity and or simply to reduce waste volume has great appeal, but a number of problems arise from this approach. While air pollution from such incineration can be effectively controlled, the extremely toxic ash produced could leak after being placed in a landfill (Luoma, 1988; Church, 1988; Bukro, 1988).

As a consequence, heavy reliance on recycling to reduce waste volume may be less expensive over the long term. There is great potential for recycled products, although it will take time to develop markets for them. As the demand for these products increases, recycling will become more efficient and economical (Shea, 1988:12-18). One problem with recycling is that it sometimes meets considerable resistance. Many do not want to take the time and trouble to sort out their trash. People in our society have become used to a throwaway approach to waste disposal (Church, 1988). The Appalachian Regional Commission, including parts of 13 states, has experimented with a number of recycling approaches to overcome this resistance. A regional strategy designed by six southern New York State counties has attempted to get the people to see that recycling develops an outlook fostering responsible consumption and conservation (Gridley, 1989). The Los Angeles City Council has mandated trash separation and recycling in order to reduce the extent of garbage. Los Angeles thereby joined about 1000 other United States cities already engaged in recycling programs. In fact, Los Angeles, along with New York City and New Jersey, is among those jurisdictions having the most extensive programs of this type (Cook, 1989).

Infrastructure Decay

The condition of the basic physical service systems and facilities (infrastructure) in most urban areas has been steadily deteriorating. For example, the bridges, subways, highways, water, and sewer systems of New York City are currently in terrible shape. A glaring example is the Williamsburg Bridge, closed to traffic in the spring of 1988. The cost to repair New York's infrastructure will approach if not exceed $50 billion. This city's situation is paralleled by that of large cities across the nation (CBS, 2/19/1989; Szabo, 1989). Infrastructure decay means that urban areas now face the need to undertake expensive repairs to make up for past neglect. If they fail to do so, not only will urban residents face growing inconvenience from service breakdowns, but industries and businesses which rely on the physical services system will face growing operating costs.

Why did infrastructure decay occur? Quality infrastructure has been taken for granted by the public. It was assumed to work properly until a breakdown occurred. Hence, there was little political pressure to maintain infrastructure. This tendency toward complacency and neglect was powerfully reinforced by the growing financial problems of urban governments in the last two decades. In growing urban areas there has been, at the same time, increasing use of and even greater stress on these facilities (Giglio, 1988).

Besides increasing government expenditures on infrastructure, some observers suggest increased involvement of the private sector. For example, this approach has been proposed regarding toll roads. The

U.S. Chamber of Commerce has recommended the enactment of user fees in the financing of construction, maintenance, and rehabilitation of these roads (Szabo, 1989).

Evaluation

Providing clean water, removing solid wastes, assuring breathable air, and maintaining service systems and facilities are all activities which the public has a reasonable right to expect of government. However, governments are increasingly hard pressed to deliver such services. The problem is not primarily technical: technologies exist or are being developed which enable governments to pursue these activities. Rather, the problem is one of cost and the public's willingness to pay. To continue to enjoy the current high level of physical services and to clean up past environmental abuses is likely to require increasing expenditures by government and industry. That means diversion of capital badly needed for the industrial modernization required for continued economic growth. It means higher taxes, increased user charges for public services, and higher prices for consumer goods. In an already slowly growing economy, with rising costs for other government services, at least some economic sacrifice will be required.

The question is: who is going to sacrifice how much? Effectively dealing with the problems of physical services ultimately implies some "trade-off" between private consumption and collectively provided services. Allocating the burden of who will pay or be worse off will be no easy matter. However, failure to act will also impose major sacrifices in terms of filthy, unhealthy air; inadequate water supply, and the dangerous accumulation of improperly disposed solid waste. In that event, everyone will suffer, though the less affluent will suffer more because they lack the ability to buy alternative services or run away from the problem.

Some have proposed *privatization*, the transfer of public services into the hands of profit-oriented contractors. Phoenix has been touted as a model for such privatization. This city's administration has attempted to divide garbage collection into public and private sectors to decrease costs. John Donahue (1989) provides considerable insight as to the appropriateness and validity of privatization. Efficiency is the rationale usually given for such transfer. Yet, there are no data clearly demonstrating that private water or utilities are less expensive, and there is only limited evidence suggesting that private airline and rail systems are more cost effective. There is, however, significant research showing that private trash disposal is less expensive. Overall, the available research suggests that there is no guarantee that it is cheaper to contract out city services to the private sector. Donahue concludes that privatization has the most potential use for those service activities whose performance can be easily specified and monitored, such as garbage collection.

Social Welfare Services

During this century government has played an increasing role in providing assistance to people in need. Prior to 1930, the provision of these services was almost exclusively a state and local affair, and the range and extent of the services was quite limited. Private philanthropy augmented these efforts. The massive problems of the Depression in the 1930s overwhelmed these limited state and local efforts. In response to the problem, the federal government's "New Deal" intervened with a wide range of emergency assistance programs. In the process, the whole notion of government responsibility for helping citizens meet their social needs gradually changed. Increasingly, the government assumed the responsibility of assuring a minimum level of material well-being, helping people deal with their personal problems, and providing opportunities for economic and social advancement. The idea of the "welfare state" was born. Out of the welter of emergency programs designed to deal with the problems of the Depression emerged a permanent system of *social welfare* programs. This complex system of federal, state, and local programs (all of which were increasingly federally funded and mandated) attempted to assist the poor, the disabled and handicapped, the socially disadvantaged, the uneducated, and the emotionally disturbed (Wilensky and Lebeau, 1965).

Quite obviously, the provision of social welfare is not an exclusively urban problem or function. However, urban social welfare represents one of the major service efforts of government at all levels, and a significant minority of urban residents rely on those services. Central cities, as we saw in Chapter Four, bear an especially heavy burden because of the concentration of poor people with problems within their boundaries and the limited resources available locally for assisting them.

General Problems of the System

Given the complexity and range of social welfare services which exist, a review of individual programs is not possible here. However, despite their complexity and number, these programs constitute a system —

albeit a ramshackle one — with certain general characteristics and problems. Obviously, not all programs share these characteristics and problems to an equal degree. But enough commonality exists to make some limited generalizations about the system as a whole.

Unclear Goals

Social welfare remains a controversial program, and there is still no real public consensus on what the system should be trying to do. In addition, many existing programs (e.g., AFDC) evolved out of *temporary* New Deal programs. They are now being asked to do things they were not originally designed to do, such as providing long-term support and assistance. There is little notion of what the system as a whole is supposed to be accomplishing. Rather, individual programs have been added piecemeal to deal with specific problems either as they arose or as political pressure to do something mounted. Often, programs developed for one purpose end up being used for something else. For example, during the 1970s, the CETA program was officially designed to provide employment and training for the unemployed. It was instead used to subsidize the payrolls of financially distressed cities.

This lack of a clear set of central goals means that priorities are not clear. What things need doing first, which programs deserve the most support, and what efforts are most important are hard to determine. Effective, rational allocation of resources is therefore difficult. Program evaluation is rendered impossible if the intended results are not clear (Rein, 1970:249-68).

Weakness at the Local Level

Relatively little control or authority over the social welfare system resides in local government. Partly this reflects a lack of initiative or concern at the local level. This has been especially true in the Sunbelt (Heumann, 1979:242), but has also been true of other areas. When local governments do have some freedom over the use of federal money they tend to spend it on the nonpoor. For instance, one study of the Community Development Block Grants program found that only 5 percent of the funds (intended to prevent neighborhood deterioration) went to low-income neighborhoods in 1976 — with 26 percent going to moderate-income neighborhoods, 30 percent to middle-income neighborhoods, and 39 percent to high-income neighborhoods (Heumann, 1979:242). Some of this inertia and reluctance to provide help to the really disadvantaged also reflects the reality of the distribution of political influence at the local level. Those who need the help most have the least political power. However, weakness at the local level is also a reflection of the general lack of resources and authority at that level. Local governments have very limited authority to control the kinds of programs they undertake and to fund locally controlled services.

Thus, social welfare is primarily funded and controlled at the state and federal level. Combined with local inertia, this virtually guarantees a system which is not very sensitive to local needs. Decisions are made by distant bureaucrats who are unaware of local conditions, protected from public scrutiny, and insulated from the demands of both front-line case workers and their clients by multiple layers of bureaucracy.

In the 1980s the Reagan administration attempted to reduce the degree of detailed control which federal agencies have over some programs by granting states greater flexibility in meeting federal standards and reducing the proportion of the social welfare budget provided through categorical grants. However, this flexibility was accompanied by reduced federal funding. The federal budget from 1982 through 1984 included cuts of 10 percent each year for social programs. Food stamps, child nutrition, AFDC, and unemployment compensation, to name a few, were cut drastically. The basic strategy used was to increase eligibility requirements in order to decrease the number of those who could apply. This approach cut about a half million people off AFDC, and in the process also caused them to lose Medicare benefits. At least one million people were no longer able to receive Food Stamps (Johnson, 1987:167-168).

Poor Coordination

Social welfare services are delivered by a large number of different agencies. These agencies are under the control of a number of different government departments at the local, state, and federal levels. The result is a vast array of programs and service organizations all trying to deliver services more or less independently of one another. Despite the existence of local interagency planning councils and various attempts over the years at consolidation and reorganization, the result is still poor coordination of the social welfare system. Agencies often compete with one another for funds and find themselves in conflict with one another. Regulations and requirements in one program frequently contradict those of another program. Clients find themselves caught between the competing demands and rules of different agencies. Various programs work at cross-purposes or end up duplicating services (Rein, 1970:31-41).

Rising Costs

As the range and size of service programs have increased, the total cost of the social welfare system has grown immensely. For example, though federal and state government allocations were almost nothing in 1900, by 1929 they had risen to about $4 billion. This figure grew to $24 billion by 1950, accelerating to $770 billion by 1986. Cash allocations to poor people went from $2.5 billion in 1950 to $104 billion by 1986 (Bixby, 1988:27). The sum total of welfare expenses in America, both public and private, amounted to 13.5 percent of the Gross National Product in 1968, rising to 28 percent by 1985 (Kerns and Glanz, 1988:4). Recent federal administrations, reacting to public resentment against welfare, were able to slow the increase of many welfare programs, and to decrease others. This is, though, a temporary trend. Growth probably will go on, albeit at a less rapid rate than during the 1960s and 1970s. There has been no reversal of social trends resulting in the need for welfare. Increases in existing problems will continue (e.g., children born out of wedlock, illiteracy, drug abuse, and school dropouts). Unemployment and underemployment will continue to be high. In addition, new concerns, such as AIDS and spouse abuse will probably require welfare funding (Popple and Leighninger, 1990:54).

In the past, increased social spending was possible and politically acceptable because of rapid economic growth and increasing purchasing power. Government could spend more (and people were willing to be concerned about those in need) as long as the increase in taxes was less than the total increase in purchasing power. However, those conditions came to an end in the 1970s. Slow economic growth, stagnant purchasing power, and upward pressures on expenditures for other programs (e.g., military expenditures) created tremendous pressure to contain or reduce social welfare expenditures. Hard-pressed taxpayers became resentful of social welfare expenditures, and the result has been a growing financial squeeze (Dluhy, 1979:143-144).

As a result of lowered federal spending, median benefits for those receiving AFDC went down by about one-third in purchasing power during the period from 1972 to 1985. During the same period, the poor increased by over 33 percent (Nasar, 1986:74-80). The "safety net", the set of programs designed for poor who are not working, was weakened in the 1980s. The working poor suffered most from this weakening (Gottschalk, 1987; Center on Budget and Policy Priorities, 1984).

Disparities in Service Levels

The quality, range, and extent of social welfare services continue to vary widely on a regional basis. Where a person lives profoundly affects the amount of assistance she or he can expect in time of need. The major variation is between the old industrial states of the North Central and Northeast regions and the South. Traditionally, the South has had extremely low levels of social welfare services. These low levels appear to be attributable to a number of factors. In part, in the past, they reflected the relative poverty of the South, which severely limited government taxing power. However, these low levels were also a reflection of a greater degree of upper class elite domination of the political system at state and local levels. The "political culture" (the generally accepted political beliefs and values) was also one which tended to downplay the role and responsibilities of government (Lupsha and Siembieda, 1977:169-190).

In the recent past, this disparity between North and South has been reduced. Increased federal support and federally mandated service levels have played a major role. Increased prosperity has increased the taxing power of state and local governments in the South. At the same time, growing financial difficulties of state and local governments in the North have slowed the expansion of social welfare services there. However, considerable disparities continue to exist. Moreover, they may persist for a long time. The different political structure and political culture of the South may assure that the state and local governments of this region will remain reluctant to increase social welfare expenditures (Lupsha and Siembieda, 1977:169-190). Pressures to limit the federal role in equalizing service levels could have the same effect. Indeed, some observers have suggested that if service levels are to be equalized, it will be by service reductions in the North. These reductions may occur because state and local governments face severe financial difficulties, and these regions wish to limit their tax levels to stem the loss of industry to low-tax states.

Evaluation

It is relatively easy to enumerate the manifest problems of the social welfare system and criticize various specific aspects of its functioning. However, it is not so easy to evaluate the significance of these specific problems in trying to judge the system as a whole. One's overall evaluation of the system depends on the political perspective from which one views its specific problems. Hence, there are several ways to look at the system.

From a conventional liberal political perspective, it can be argued that for all its problems and failures the social welfare system functions as a real "safety net" of basic services which assure significant protection against personal disasters. It has brought about an unprecedented degree of basic security in the sense that the general population is assured that its most basic needs will be met and the neediest and weakest in society will not be totally neglected. Liberal observers acknowledge that, like any large bureaucratic system, the social welfare system has its share of problems, abuses, and waste. In any event, the real challenge is that there are still so many unmet human needs which will ultimately require an expansion and intensification of social welfare efforts (Rein, 1970).

Conservatives, on the other hand, argue that the whole notion of a welfare state is based on faulty premises, and the consequences of the system may be socially dangerous. For one thing, they say, it is simply wrong to assume that government can or should intervene in a major way in the lives of individuals. Government is not wise enough and large governmental bureaucracies are not manageable enough to achieve the intended results. The waste, disorganization, and growing body of wrong-headed bureaucratic regulations are the predictable results of the mistaken idea that government can successfully engage in effective social engineering. The unfortunate consequence is that we are paying dearly for the effort. In this view, the social welfare program has resulted in the weakening of individual initiative and moral responsibility, the restriction of individual rights, and the partial destruction of traditional family and community structures. The immense cost of the system has, at the same time, diverted resources from private consumption and investment, reducing the efficiency of the economy and long-term economic growth (Murray, 1984).

Leftist observers couch their evaluation of the social welfare system in a more general criticism of the social and economic system. They see the social welfare system as an attempt to deal with and contain the symptoms of more fundamental social failures which reflect economic and political inequalities in society. They argue that the social welfare system cannot possibly be expected to deal with the problems of individuals effectively because those problems are rooted in the basic organization of society itself. Hence the various programs, quite predictably, fail. However, from the point of view of the powerful in society, the system really is a success. Elite power and privileges are not fundamentally threatened by the system. In addition, the social welfare system provides just enough assistance to the underprivileged to prevent widespread political discontent and channels the aspirations and frustrations of the underprivileged in individualistic, nonpolitical directions. The system also deflects efforts for social reform away from fundamental social changes which would endanger elite interests. In this sense, the social welfare system is really quite effective, not at helping people, but as a system of political and social control (Piven and Cloward, 1971).

Education

Operating the public school system has traditionally been one of the most important roles of urban governments. Education budgets constitute a major portion of the total local government budget, and education has been the focus of much public concern and interest. Most families are directly affected by educational policies and programs, either as users of the system or as taxpayers. In addition, the public expects much of the educational system. The schools are expected to transmit the dominant values of society and teach social skills. Simultaneously, they are called on to make sure that the whole population acquires the basic knowledge, discipline, and literacy skills necessary for participation in the labor force and to prepare a minority of the population for more advanced training. People in this society have also put enormous faith in the ability of the school system to equalize occupational opportunities and provide a channel for upward mobility for talented children of the disadvantaged (Dentler, 1977:311-119).

Not surprisingly, these expectations have proven difficult to satisfy. The public school system has never really done the things expected of it very well. Probably no more than 40 to 60 percent of the students in the public school system have ever emerged psychologically more adjusted, acculturated, and competent in basic literacy and job skills as a result of their experiences in school (Dentler, 1977:314). And this modest rate of success has been even more modest for the children of the lower classes. Consequently, the ability of the public school system to provide a real channel for mobility and a means of equalizing opportunity has always been much less than the general public has believed (Jencks et al., 1972).

The reasons for these more general difficulties of the public school system are beyond the practical scope of the present discussion. We will focus instead on those problems which have further increased the already enormous difficulties faced by urban public school systems. These problems threaten to make an already problem-ridden and chaotic system even more problem-ridden and chaotic.

Educational Finances

The most visible and fundamental problem facing urban school districts is finances. Total national spending on public schools has increased enormously in the last few decades in response to rising costs. Earlier, part of this increase was due to increasing enrollments as a result of the baby boom. However, stabilizing or falling enrollments in the 1970s and 1980s provided little relief from this cost spiral. In 1988-89 expenses for elementary and high schools were about $200 billion. This represented an increase of 21 percent as compared to 1978-79. The overall cost of education at all levels has increased nearly 70 percent during the last decade. The rapid increases started in 1983, when the stress on school reform began (*Condition of Teaching*, 1988:51).

Fifty years ago education was primarily funded at the local level. Since that time, the states and federal government have become progressively more involved. In 1988 the states provided 50 percent of school revenues, with 44 percent coming from local governments. Overall, education for elementary and high school students came to 20 percent of state and local budgets (U.S. Bureau of the Census, Statistical Abstracts, 1989:268). While federal expenditures are only a small part of the total federal budget, they have a very specific place in elementary and secondary education. They cover research, programs for special education (such as the handicapped and the disadvantaged), and such special programs as fighting the school dropout rates.

Most of a school district's budget goes for salaries and benefits for teachers and administrators. The growth in per pupil expenditure during the last twenty years is largely due to a decrease in the student-staff ratio. However, teacher salaries as a portion of total school expenses stayed about the same as they were in 1980-81 (National Center for Education Statistics, 1989:Table 56). Higher costs are due also to the initiation of programs for those having particular needs, such as the handicapped. Some such programs are required by state and federal governments. Costs for services required for the handicapped are much greater — over twice as much per child in 1985-86 (National Center for Education Statistics, 1989:56, 113). In addition, the last two decades saw a major increase in the types of programs most school districts attempted to offer. Part of this was an attempt to upgrade the quality of programs being offered. In the central city school districts, another major factor was the rapid increase in the proportion of children from disadvantaged families who needed special educational programs. State governments (and, to a lesser extent, the federal government) also mandated program changes and special services which increased costs. Central city districts were additionally burdened by the costs of increasingly elaborate efforts to achieve racial integration in the 1970s. In central city districts, additional security needs and the costs of repairing the damage from vandalism increased significantly (Coleman and Kelly, 1976:258, 260; Griffith et al., 1989:3-15, 22-23).

The problem with these cost increases was that they occurred in the context of the growing financial crisis faced by urban governments. As we have seen (Chapter 7), urban governments simply lacked the ability to raise sufficient revenues from local tax sources. The problem in education was compounded in many areas by the fact that school districts obtain their tax revenues from separate tax levies (mostly on real estate). Increases in these separate school taxes often require direct voter approval, but voters have been increasingly reluctant to approve increased school taxes (Coleman and Kelly, 1976:259; Parkinson, 1979:168; Griffith, et al., 1989:17-19). In addition, the states did not increase their total aid levels to education enough to relieve the local funding crisis. Political opposition to increased state spending in general and spending for education in particular slowed the rate of increase in state aid for education. The already financially desperate central city districts felt the squeeze the most, but even suburban districts found the slowdown in state aid increases put more and more pressure on their budgets as suburban voters also began to resist tax increases (Parkinson, 1979:168-173, Griffith et al., 1989:27-30).

Consolidation has been one attempt to cope with school expenses. School districts in the United States declined in number from about 100,000 in 1945 to only around 16,000 in 1987 (Griffith et al., 1989:27). To meet the decline in federal monies allocated for schools in the period 1985-87, states have used sales taxes (producing about one-third of state funding) as well as income taxes (which bring in one-fourth). State lotteries are growing as another source of revenue. The portion of school funding from local property taxes has slowly declined (Ballantine, 1989:241; Ornstein and Levine, 1985).

Central city districts have had greater economic difficulties than suburban school districts. The formulas used to provide state aid to local districts have failed to compensate for the larger tax base of suburban districts and have resulted in continued disparities in expenditures per pupil between cities and suburbs (Griffith, et al., 1989:28-29). While attempts to shift school funding bases have often been rejected, some very recent court decisions have given new hope to those pressing for equity. In a 9-0 decision, the Texas Supreme Court said that the considerable gap between richest and poorest school districts violated the state constitution's requirement for an adequate education. The court in its decision mandated a change in the system. This decision is one of nearly a dozen overturning state school systems on the grounds they violate state constitutions. This effort to equalize educational spending within states may lead to equalization between states. The Texas decision came only a week after President Bush and the nation's governors gave support to massive restructuring of schools and the writing of national performance goals. This approach suggests possible increased federal control and funding (Tifft, 1989).

Given their financial difficulties, school districts have had very little choice but to undertake cutbacks. Where possible, they reduced the size of pay increases. This was not always possible, however, because of the resistance of increasingly militant teacher unions. Some layoffs (especially in the North) were possible simply because of declining enrollments, and some school closings were possible for the same reason. Special programs were reduced or eliminated. However, in the extremely distressed central cities in the North, these relatively modest cutbacks were not enough. Major teacher layoffs, drastic curriculum reductions, limited replacement of textbooks, tight controls on supplies, reduced maintenance, and the elimination of all but the most critical capital improvements were employed to hold down budget increases or actually reduce budgets. Even that was not enough for many big city districts. Many faced outright bankruptcy and closed temporarily because they could not meet their payrolls and pay their suppliers. Others barely managed to keep operating.

The short-term prospects appear to hold continued financial difficulty. Cost pressures are not likely to abate even with declining enrollments. Maintenance cannot be put off indefinitely and books do not last forever. Pressures to maintain or increase teachers' salaries will not disappear. Yet, political opposition to increased taxes means that revenues are not likely to increase very rapidly. More and more districts will have difficulty operating at all. Most districts will experience financial difficulties to some degree (Parkinson, 1979:173-175; Griffith et al., 1989:27-30).

Performance Levels

Much has been written about declining performance levels in public schools. The popular impression is that the schools are doing a much worse job teaching basic academic skills than before. The weight of the evidence appears to be in favor of the interpretation that some declines have occurred. However, it is not quite the kind of decline perceived by the public. Scores for the most basic kinds of skills acquired in the lower grades (through fourth grade) have actually risen. Basic reading, writing, and arithmetic do not seem to be the heart of the problem. Rather, it is the more sophisticated skills and knowledge taught in the upper grades which appear to have declined. These declines are probably significant and merit concern. (However, even these declines have to be put into historical context. Because skill levels rose until the late 1960s, the statistically average high-school graduate probably knows more than his or her counterpart in 1920.)

Explaining these declines is even more difficult than documenting them. According to Christopher Jencks, most theories which were advanced to explain performance decline in the 1970s do not hold up to close examination. Jencks argues that there is strong circumstantial evidence that these theories are wrong, and certainly no hard evidence exists to support them. Hence, the performance decline may not be the result of such things as changes in the kinds of students taking standardized tests, baby-boom enrollment growth, television, parental permissiveness, declining school expenditures, desegregation, curriculum changes, "grade inflation," or "watered-down" textbooks (Jencks, 1978:29-41).

In the 1980s the most influential report on performance levels was *A Nation at Risk* (1984). This report stressed that the relative decline in quality of American schools had contributed to the economic decline of the United States during the last decade or so. Moreover, the report expressed concern over the decline of an informed citizenry, due to less adequate education and training. Comparisons of student achievement tests showed United States students were considerably behind their counterparts in other industrialized nations. In addition, they were often badly in need of remedial work in math, spelling, reading, and writing. This resulted in great financial costs both to industry and to institutions of higher education. Significant declines in achievement scores were also noted for those entering college and those graduating.

A Nation at Risk caused much evaluation of the U.S. school system and prompted reform efforts. The solutions advocated included an ongoing commitment to educating minorities and the less fortunate, while simultaneously increasing for high school students the number of required years of math, science and foreign language. Teachers were to receive higher quality training, and pay scales were to be increased. A higher level of funding for educational needs was strongly urged (Congressional Record, 5/5/1983:S6097-6101). Another reform movement developed in the late 1980s concentrated on basic subjects which students needed to be taught more adequately: history, science, and math (*Education Week*, 5/17/1989:1,8,10).

What has been the impact of reform? The growth in number of academic courses has not been as rapid as suggested in *A Nation at Risk*. But increased graduation requirements and competency testing have not caused dropout rates to go up (Center for Policy Research in Education, 1989). There has been a tendency toward greater uniformity of standards among and within states. Strong measures have been taken by the states to force local districts to meet improved standards (Griffith et al., 1989:32).

Still, the nation's schools are not training students to qualify for more demanding jobs. Lack of appropriate education is one of the basic causes of the employment difficulties for youth and the problems business has finding qualified workers (Hatfield, 1989). School dropouts are three times as likely to be unemployed as are high school graduates. A number of attempts are being made to cope with this situation. In Chicago, corporations and higher education institutions are attempting to structure programs which train applicants both in basic skills and also in computer-related techniques. Two-year colleges are another crucial resource for training workers. Over 50 institutions around the country are involved in such efforts (Goozner, 1988).

The Loss of Legitimacy

Jencks (1978) feels that at least part of the problem in education stems from a change in the social atmosphere of the schools. This, in turn, is seen as the result of a change in the nature of the "social contract" between the schools, students, and the community.

To the extent that schools succeeded in the past, they did so because a form of "social contract" (mutual agreement and understanding) existed between parents, students, teachers, and administrators. All parties recognized the school as an extension and embodiment of community values and standards. (In fact, these were the values and standards of the community's dominant social and economic group.) It was assumed that the educational professionals who operated the system accepted and enforced these standards and that the procedures and requirements of the schools were those appropriate to achieving the agreed upon goals. Parents were expected to reinforce and support the demands and requirements of the school.

In return for compliance with the community-sanctioned norms of the schools, students could expect to receive annual promotion in grade level and to be "fairly" evaluated and sorted into appropriate career or job channels. In short, the demands and the authority of the school were viewed as *legitimate* — that is, considered morally right and consistent with the values of the community (Dentler, 1977:313-314). The fact that the underlying assumptions of this social contract were dubious did not matter as long as it did not occur to many people to question them.

In the 1960s and 1970s, however, increasing numbers of people did begin to question the nature of the contract. Educators became less certain of the appropriateness of what they were teaching and how they were teaching it. Racial and ethnic minorities became more sensitive to the cultural biases built into the system. The cultural and class differences in central city schools between predominately white, middle-class staffs and predominantly poor, black student bodies called into question the existence of value convergence between school and community. In poor neighborhoods, schools became viewed as alien outposts of an impersonal and uncaring governmental bureaucracy. Even in middle-class districts, the introduction of new teaching methods, courses, and texts was increasingly seen as evidence of a school system run by arrogant professionals with different values than those of the parents and community. For example, the endless debate about sex education and school prayer has pitted the courts and school professionals against parents. Students who were more cynical about the institutions of society and the utility of education were less likely to internalize the norms and goals of the school. The traditional social contract in the schools was, as a consequence, severely weakened, and the legitimacy of school authority badly undermined.

One result was that the ability of the schools to impose traditional academic standards on their bored and cynical charges was substantially reduced. Most teachers interviewed in a recent Carnegie Foundation study felt that disruptive behavior, absenteeism, student apathy, and lack of parental support were problems. Nearly 70 percent also noted theft and vandalism; nearly half, student violence; about one-third, racial discord; and more than one-fourth, violent behavior against teachers. Over 20 percent mentioned that more than one-fourth of their students were poor. Nearly all reported that child abuse and child neglect were problems (*Condition of Teaching*, 1988:26). As a consequence, uncertain themselves of what they should be doing and faced with resistance from their students, the school staffs reached an uneasy accommodation with their students: they would not ask too much of the students if the students would not disrupt things too much (Jencks, 1978:39-40).

High School Dropouts

Among the issues dominating the 1980s was the high school dropout rate, about 25 percent of total enrollment in some systems (Ogintz, 1989). Jobs open to dropouts will probably decline from around 18 percent of all new jobs to 13 percent by the year 2000. Fortunately, rates for dropping out have declined over the last two decades, especially for blacks. Black dropouts aged 16-24 who either don't attend or have not yet finished high school dropped from almost 30 percent in 1968 to 15 percent in 1988. Rates for whites dropped only 2 percent in the same period, from 15 percent to 13 percent. Hispanic rates continued to be high: 36 percent in 1988 (Frase, 1989). Dropout rates continue to be significant for inner city youths from low-income, single-parent families (Griffith, et al., 1989:22, 23). Nonetheless, for pupils with low test scores (in the bottom quartile), whites are more apt to drop out than blacks and Hispanics. Many dropouts come back to school, either to complete their course work or to obtain an equivalence certificate (Griffith et al., 1989:24).

A number of experiments have been tried to reduce the dropout rate. Colleges and universities have adopted approaches designed to motivate inner-city children for higher education. Assistance is given, in order to help those interested become eligible. New York State has passed legislation substantially increasing funding, both for dropout prevention and also for college aid (Ogintz, 1989; Hundley, 1988). Alternative schools are an attempt at a within-system answer to dropping out. Chicago city colleges began this program to help dropouts complete high school. Alternative schools offer smaller classrooms, personal instruction, and readjustment assistance. Dropouts are referred to this program by high school counselors, social work agencies, and the juvenile court. This approach offers a second chance to students who leave school because of family problems, gangs, and boredom (Robinson, 1987).

The Community-Control Movement

The problems of urban school districts have given rise to numerous efforts to reform them. In the recent past, probably the best known of these reform proposals was the community-control movement. During the 1970s, a few large-city school districts (most notably, New York City) actually experimented with this kind of reform. The details of these programs varied, but they shared a common general strategy: that of giving people in each area of the city a direct voice in the operation of the particular schools serving their community. Power would shift from the distant and impersonal central school bureaucracy into the hands of the people directly affected and knowledgeable about conditions in their local schools. It was hoped that this decentralization of power would make each school more accountable and responsive to the needs of the community it served. This in turn would increase involvement of local parents with the schools and create support for improved educational programs. A further intent was to make sure that each school tailored its programs to the needs and cultural backgrounds of its students.

More generally, community control was seen as an important democratic reform with implications for creating a more responsive system of urban government, increasing the legitimacy of governmental institutions, and training people in democratic participation (Orleans, 1976:7-17).

A review of the various attempts at community control in a number of different cities suggests that, despite their early bright promise, such programs have not lived up to the expectations of their supporters. The programs often emerged out of genuine grassroots movements and initially enjoyed widespread community support and involvement. However, the impact of community-control boards was quickly blunted and contained by a number of factors. Funding for their operations often came from external sources, usually the federal government. This meant that local boards were hemmed in by outside controls and requirements which limited their freedom of action. It also meant that local boards became involved in federally mandated "community-service" activities which required paid staffs of professionals. The boards tended to be deflected from their original missions by these service activities and increasingly controlled by "professional activists" more interested in providing services (and assuring their own organizational survival). Grassroots involvement withered away. At the same time, community-control programs ran into massive resistance from existing educational interest groups who felt their power and economic interests were being threatened. Central district boards were reluctant to surrender their decision-making authority. State educational agencies and the central district bureaucracy resisted community control for the same reason. Teachers' unions felt that the privileges and protections provided under their contracts might be lost. These various interest groups were usually successful in undercutting community control through political pressure and bureaucratic delaying tactics. The result was that real, democratic community control with effective decision-making power either was never achieved or did not last (Gittel, 1980).

A new effort at community control in Chicago offers modest hope for the future. More than 500 school districts have been created and allowed to elect their own councils, made up of a mix of parents and teachers. Principals, while denied tenure, have been given the right to hire, evaluate and terminate teachers. Why should this attempt succeed while that of New York City failed? The New York system had 32 city-wide school districts. These were too large to be effective, and, in addition, were dominated by the Democratic Party and the Teachers' Union. Parents and citizens had no input. The Chicago approach has many more districts for a much smaller population. Parents hold 6 of the 11 positions in each district, with 2 more slots for people in the community (MacNeil/Lehrer Report, 11/8/1989). Bakalis feels that decentralization of schools will not in itself solve the problems of educational systems. The context of poverty, crime, and family disorganization will not simply disappear. Nor will any amount of participation by citizens and teachers help if they are not prepared or capable. The decentralization approach can, however, lead to opening up the system to new ideas and to accountability (Bakalis, 1987).

Evaluation

The crisis in education is not new. Critics of the public schools have never lacked for evidence of various failures and problems in the system. That is because the schools have never fully lived up to their promises and the high expectations of the public. The past century is littered with the wreckage of various reforms, each of which promised some sort of "quick fix" for the long-term problems of the schools.

It should now be clear that the problems are more complex than the educational reformers have assumed. For one thing, we are asking more of the system than it can probably ever deliver. For instance, to ask educational programs to correct the deep-seated consequences of unequal opportunity and the inequalities of wealth and power in society is really to ask the impossible. Even if we knew how to design such programs, they would encounter the powerful opposition of the already privileged and those educational interest groups who benefit from the status quo. It can be argued that in many ways the schools function the way they do because it is beneficial to many powerful interests in society. For example, are the schools intended to teach democratic values or are they really designed to teach obedience and discipline to the future labor force? We should also remember that many of the schools' problems exist in the context of more general problems in the society: crime, drug abuse, poverty, racism, the declining legitimacy of major institutions, and economic and demographic trends.

None of this is meant to imply that we should be either complacent or despairing about the schools. Education has severe problems which simply must be confronted by public policy. Besides its more fundamental problems, we have just seen that a number of more recent trends threaten the ability of the system to continue to function at all. Past mistakes are not grounds for inaction, but only suggest the magnitude of the problems that will have to be faced.

Presently, reform issues center around control of instruction by teachers, reorganization of the school decision-making process, and affirming teaching as a profession (Kerr, 1989:19-20). Some observers argue that a new consensus has emerged around the goals of educational reform. This agreement is centered on the need to give quality training to all students. Parents tend to see education as a means of getting ahead, while business executives focus on education as a way of increasing corporate earnings, and government views it as training for citizenship. We have moved toward an understanding that a more inclusive, complex approach is needed if reform is to be effective. Inherent in such an agreement is the need to have both broad training enabling the student to grasp issues creatively and specific training to qualify for a career. Traditional curricula will be broadened to cover the classics while simultaneously drawing material from other cultures. "Back to basics" must not only include traditional skills, but art and music as well. Schooling must pursue personal as well as economic goals. This consensus has the virtue of combining training in skills valued in the workplace and human values needed at work and in the community. This new agreement thus takes into account both short-term and long-term approaches and the basic needs of the nation as well as global society. It provides the challenge of a mature and comprehensive approach to education (Futrell, 1989).

Criminal Justice

From the point of view of the general public, the most important urban problem is that of crime (especially that associated with drugs). Primarily, this is a reflection of the widespread fear of being victimized by street crime, having one's home burglarized, or being caught in the violence generated by illegal drugs. These fears are reinforced by the tendency of the news media to give dramatic coverage to such crimes as murder and kidnapping. These fears have some basis in fact. The kind of crime most of the public is concerned about does seem to have increased in the last few decades.We will also see, however, that public fears and perceptions of the crime problem are oversimplified. Such crimes as street crime, murder, and burglary are only one aspect of the urban crime problem. Other forms of crime, which the public has tended to be much less concerned about, are at least as serious in terms of the cost to society. In addition, we will see that an effective response to crime is much more difficult than most people think.

We also need to put the current problem of crime in better perspective. There seems to be a widespread belief that serious crime problems are a very recent development and that crime represents evidence of some sort of contemporary breakdown in society. In fact, United States cities have always confronted serious amounts of crime and violence, and the current high level of public concern is not the first time the nation has felt threatened by a breakdown in public order. At the turn of the century in New York City, some slum areas were so dangerous that police would only enter them armed and in pairs. Labor violence flared repeatedly in urban areas between the 1870s and 1930s. During the railway strike of 1877, many hundreds of people were killed in various places across the country, and about two miles of railroad cars and buildings were burned in Pittsburgh as the result of violent clashes between strikers, railroad police, and the militia (President's Commission on Law Enforcement, 1967:22-23).

Officially Reported Crime

Traditionally, the focus of most governmental efforts to measure crime (as well as control it) has centered on a particular set of offenses which correspond to public perceptions of and concern about criminal activity. This represents a very biased and incomplete view of the total extent and nature of such activity. However, the crimes included in the "official crime rate" are serious ones which involve real public suffering, and therefore merit our careful consideration.

The Official Reporting System

The most important and best-known government effort to measure the extent of crime has been the Uniform Crime Report (UCR). For almost half a century, this report has been issued annually by the Federal Bureau of Investigation. It contains the official crime rates, which are calculated on the basis of reports sent the FBI by local police departments. The UCR does, however, have a number of problems and limitations. It is based on only a few kinds of crimes (rape, robbery, murder, aggravated assault, burglary, larceny-theft, and auto theft, for example). In addition, people don't always report these crimes. The UCR thus both understates the amount of crime, and gives a distorted image of the crime problem.

Trends in Official Crime Rates

Official crime rates for rape suggest almost 70 of every 100,000 women in the United States are victims of this crime (Federal Bureau of Investigation, 1988:14). Most experts feel that the true rate may be much higher, from two to ten times this figure (Barlow, 1990:190). Recent official rates suggest a rise in aggravated assault rates, continuing the trend and pattern of the 1970s. (Barlow, 1990:154-155; Bureau of Justice Statistics, 1988). Official statistics currently show a rise in serious assaults, while there has been a leveling off for homicides (Federal Bureau of Investigation, 1988:12). For 1987, official reports show a decline for robbery rates. This dropoff may be due partially at least to a decline in the percent of youth in the population, as well as the reduction in robbery attempts not successful (Federal Bureau of Investigation, 1988:17; Bureau of Justice Statistics, 1987:1).

Victimization Studies

A number of criminologists hold that a more realistic and extensive picture of crime is provided by victimization surveys (Barlow, 1990: 134-135; Spates and Macionis, 1987:384). In 1986, for instance, the Uniform Crime Reports reported 91,460 forcible rapes, as compared to 129,940 such crimes noted by victimization surveys. In this same year such surveys recorded nearly twice as many aggravated assaults (1,542,870) as the UCR (834,320). Much less contrast was found for auto theft — about 1.2 million for the UCR, compared to about 1.4 million for victimization surveys. Victimization studies are certainly not without flaws. Their findings are based on recall and memory, which may be somewhat selective. Fear of being found out to have told about a crime may cause the respondent to lie or distort replies to questions (Barlow, 1990:135-138).

Variations by Size of Community

Popular conceptions of the crime problem tend to associate living in large central cities with a high risk of being victimized by crime. Crime

Table 8.1 **The Official Rate of Crime 1979-88**

Year	Total Crime Rate*	Violent Crime Rate*	Property Crime Rate*
1979	5566	549	5017
1980	5950	597	5353
1981	5858	594	5264
1982	5604	571	5033
1983	5175	538	4673
1984	5031	539	4492
1985	5207	557	4651
1986	5480	618	4863
1987	5550	610	4940
1988	5664	637	5027
Percent Change 1979-88	+1.8%	+16.1%	+0.2%

*Number of reported crimes per 100,000 inhabitants

SOURCE: U.S. Federal Bureau of Investigation, *Crime in the United States,* (various years).

is viewed as one of the major disadvantages of city life compared to smaller, safer communities. There is considerable truth to this view. It does nonetheless oversimplify a complex situation.

There is a general relationship between city size and the official crime rate. In the recent past, the overall crime rate has tended to be higher in larger communities than smaller ones (see Table 8.2). Both property crimes and violent crimes are, on the average, highest in metropolitan areas, and consistently decline with city size (Spates and Macionis, 1987:384).

These findings in regard to crime and city size must be qualified. A great number of crimes are not known, not reported to police, and carelessly recorded. Official data thus has very real limitations. National surveys show slightly over one-third of all serious crimes go unreported (Spates and Macionis, 1987:384). Hence, comparisons between cities based on official statistics must be approached cautiously.

There is no clear explanation for the relation of crime extent and city size. We do know, however, that urban crime is concentrated in a few areas of cities. These districts are characterized by a great extent of ongoing poverty, unemployment, inadequate housing, teen pregnancy, and drug use (Flanagan, 1990:268). Most homicide victims and offenders are black, relatively poor, males and between 20 and 30 years of age. Most victims and offenders in rape cases are from relatively low socio-economic areas in the largest cities. In the case of robbery, blacks are victimized at three times the frequency of whites, though offenders tend to be black (Barlow, 1990:155-156, 194, 221). Generally speaking, a disproportionate percent of urban poor show up in national crime data, both as accused and victims.

Table 8.2 **Rate of Crime by Size of Place in 1987**

Size of Place	Total Crime Rate*	Violent Crime Rate*	Property Crime Rate*
250,000+	8951	1344	7606
100,000-249,000	7804	802	7002
50,000-99,999	6035	536	5499
25,000-49,999	5550	420	5130
10,000-24,999	4554	307	4247
under 10,000	4218	272	3946
All Cities	6484	700	5764
Rural Areas	1921	177	1744

*Number of reported crimes per 100,000 inhabitants

SOURCE: U.S. Federal Bureau of Investigation, *Crime in the United States,* (various years).

James Q. Wilson has argued that crime committed by those living in poor neighborhoods has increased because of the breakdown of inner control, and the adoption of crime as a way of life (Wilson, 1983:16-33). Many have taken issue with Wilson. It has been suggested by his opponents that the level of wages available to poor, inner-city youth offer little incentive to work, since illegal activities offer much more in the way of financial rewards (McGahey, 1986:249). Others argue that inner-city residents are much more apt to see unemployment as permanent, making them more open to crime as an alternative way of life (Duster, 1987:306-309). Rates for violent crime by youth thus reflect their limited choices in legitimate job markets. To survive in many neighborhoods, a person may have to become part of a gang. Gangs give personal protection as well as access into criminal income. Finally, procedures of arrest, sentencing, and pretrial and court arrangements show prejudice against blacks and Hispanics (Flanagan, 1990:272-274). Police and the court system, particularly during the last decade, deal with the breaking of the law, not the context of the offender (Flanagan, 1990:275).

White-Collar Crime

The public perception of crime as a problem of the urban poor is based on the failure to recognize the significance and prevalence of an entire class of criminal activity which is not primarily a lower-class phenomenon: *white collar crime*. This somewhat heterogeneous group of crimes has been variously defined. However, Herbert Edelhertz, former head of the Fraud Section in the Criminal Division of the U.S. Department of Justice, has suggested one definition. He defines white-collar crime as "...an illegal act or series of illegal acts committed by nonphysical means and by concealment or guile to obtain property, to avoid the payment or loss of money or property, or to obtain business or personal advantage" (cited in Demaris, 1974:15). Edwin Sutherland, who originally focused sociological attention on the problem, suggested a simpler, but narrower, definition which emphasized the class background of the offender. He defined white-collar crime as an act "...committed by a person of respectability and high social status in the course of his occupation" (Sutherland, 1949:9).

Sutherland was among the first to document the frequency and variety of illegal business practices. Based on research on the 70 largest nonfinancial corporations extending up to 1944, he found that the corporations had a total of 980 legal decisions rendered against them by a variety of enforcement agencies (about half by courts and the rest by other agencies). The violations involved such things as price-fixing among competitors, false advertising, unfair labor practices, trademark and patent violations, financial fraud, and violations of wartime regulations. Almost all the corporations had more than one violation. Sutherland likened the behavior of many of the corporations to that of habitual criminals (Sutherland, 1949:9).

The problem of white-collar crime is not just a matter of corporate misbehavior. There is a whole range of "respectable crimes" committed by individuals for individual gain. While some of these crimes are included in the official statistics (e.g., arson), it is generally believed that the official statistics grossly underestimate the extent of these crimes (Barlow, 1990: 284). Moreover, these crimes are not used in calculating the official crime rate. The majority of white-collar crimes involve some sort of fraud or nonviolent deception. They range from illegal tax evasion and embezzlement to phony insurance claims and charges for unnecessary medical procedures. There are no reliable statistics on the total cost of this kind of crime, but it is estimated to be very high indeed. Arson for profit (by building owners) reached epidemic proportions in urban areas and played a major role in increasing fire insurance premiums during the 1970s (Steglich and Snooks, 1980:438).

Some more recent forms of white collar crime include insider trading, the savings and loan scandal, the corruption at HUD (Department of Housing and Urban Development) during the 1980s, and computer crime. Insider trading can be defined as the obtaining of inside information in advance of stock transactions. It is in effect the same as fixing a horse race or athletic game (Francis, 11/7/1988). The Mafia has had a key part in the manipulation of low-price as well as conventional stocks, involving extensive use of insider trading practices (Stern and Poole, 1989).

The recent scandal in the Department of Housing and Urban Development involved allowing agency officials to use housing programs to provide loans for upper- and middle-class housing as well as for business developments. Members of Congress got grants and loans for themselves as well as their constituents (Waldman, et al., 1989; Cohn, 1989). The effects of those actions were both to deny housing loan assistance to the poor, as well as to disrupt real estate markets and thereby collapse prices.

The recent savings and loan (S&L) scandal is another instance of white collar crime. Three factors in particular contributed to the corrupting of S&Ls: the increase in deposit insurance to $100,000; power given (in 1982) to S&Ls enabling them to move from home mortgage loans to virtually any kind of higher-risk venture; and the weak legal constraints at both federal and state levels. The resulting financial collapse of hundreds of S&Ls will require a federal expenditure of hundreds of billions of dollars. This S&L "bailout" will primarily benefit the Sunbelt (the region where most S&Ls failed). The rest of the country, however, pays for the bailout at a cost of about $2,000 per person. Tightened mortgage markets resulting from the S&L collapse has further eroded home ownership among the less affluent (Adams, 1989; Pilzer, 1989).

Finally, computer crime, the stealing of information from computers, or damaging a computer, continues to be a major form of white-collar crime. This type of crime can take several forms: the changing of data to be entered or that's already in the computer, instructing the computer to perform unauthorized tasks, removing financial assets, modifying computer contents, and taking information from the computer, among other things. Losses from such crimes may run as high as $40 billion (Reid, 1988:310-311, 314, 318; Stoll, 1989).

Despite the fragmentary evidence, it is possible to make a few limited generalizations about the role of white-collar crime. First, it seems clear that white-collar crime is at least as serious a problem as the crimes used to calculate official crime rates. The total damage caused by white-collar crime certainly exceeds that caused by more conventional crimes. And it is certainly as common as other forms of criminal activity. The fact that white-collar crimes are committed by leading corporations and seemingly respectable people also contributes in a major, if unmeasurable way, to the diffusion of "criminal" attitudes and expectations in the population (Barlow, 1990:290).

Second, despite its seriousness, white-collar crime has failed to provoke the public concern and official control responses which other kinds of crimes have provoked. The general public does not conceive of the "urban crime problem" as a problem of rapacious corporations and greedy, dishonest, middle-class citizens. Reflecting these attitudes, the criminal justice system has made less of a sustained effort to detect and punish white-collar crime. As a consequence, most of the available evidence suggests that white-collar crime is fairly safe to commit. The risks of detection are probably fairly low, and the punishments for those crimes which are detected are often mild (Barlow, 1990:323-325).

Third, as its name implies, white-collar crime is committed primarily by middle- and upper-class people. This fact probably does much to explain both public and official apathy. Somehow, the criminal acts of a well-educated, articulate, white business person seem less serious than the crimes of a poor person. White-collar crime seems more an extension of "normal" (i.e., middle-class) behavior and is less likely to involve direct interpersonal, physical violence (though it may still kill people, as in the case of dumping dangerous chemicals). And, it should be remembered, white-collar crime is committed by people who have more political power and are better able to defend themselves in court than lower-class people.

Organized Crime

A major portion of the criminal activity in the United States consists of *organized crime*. This kind of criminal activity consists of more or less formally organized groups which operate "business" organizations which either provide illegal "services" or use illegal methods to provide legitimate services. Despite the sporadic investigations by law enforcement agencies and investigatory commissions, our knowledge of organized crime is very incomplete, and there remains considerable uncertainty about its precise nature, extent, and structure. There can be no doubt, however, that organized crime represents a serious problem, and most observers feel that the problem is most serious in major metropolitan areas.

Organized crime appears to dominate a number of areas of illegal activity. Very important is its role in the control of illegal gambling activities. "Loan sharks" (people who make loans to financially desperate people at extraordinarily high interest rates) also appear to be based in criminal organizations. Organized crime is also believed to be deeply involved in the production and distribution of pornography, the sale of stolen goods, prostitution, and narcotics. The sale of narcotics is especially important because a large number of street crimes are committed by narcotics addicts to support their habits. In addition, individuals connected with organized crime have used bribery, threats, and violence to infiltrate a number of labor unions where they attempt both to extort money from employers and to cheat the members by signing (for a price) weak contracts with employers. These criminals are also believed to have taken over a number of legitimate businesses which serve as covers for their illegal activities. Once involved in legitimate businesses, members of organized crime apparently use extortion and strong-arm tactics to eliminate their competitors. In many cities organized crime appears to have gained control of such activities as the vending-machine and jukebox industries, and to have major investments in bars, hotels, trucking companies, food companies, linen-supply houses, commercial garbage collection, and some factories (Cressey, 1969:xi). More recently, according to many press reports, organized crime has been linked with stock-fraud schemes and real estate speculation in the Sunbelt (Stern and Poole, 1989:42-44).

Of growing importance in the recent past has been the appearance of large-scale drug smuggling and drug gangs. The recent President's Organized Crime Commission concluded that drug trafficking was the most serious activity of organized crime. Billions of dollars are made in these transactions, which are often interregional and worldwide in scope. Countless individuals, their families, communities, and not the least, governments, are severely hurt through the sale and use of drugs (Reid, 1988:345-347). Commerce in illegal drugs is the world's most rapidly growing business. The United States is the world's biggest market. Producers range from Thailand and Lebanon to Mexico and Colombia, to name a few. Though immense quantities of drugs have been seized by U.S. authorities, the supply is so great that the flow into this country is virtually unaffected. Entire nations have been disrupted through bribery and intimidation by drug bosses. Colombia is perhaps the most flagrant example. A coalition of criminal families there has transformed the cocaine trade into an international industry. This worldwide surge of illegal drugs makes traditional law enforcement virtually impossible. Latin American-U.S. relations have been severely tested by the tendency of the United States to use military action to suppress the drug trade (Kraar, 1988:27-38).

Ethnic gangs are also an important element in the changing face of organized crime in the United States. The newer ethnic groups, especially those from Central America, Asia, and the Caribbean, started by living off those of their own nationality. Once they became stronger financially, they expanded into the larger society. Crime syndicates from Hong Kong have moved to the United States anticipating more stringent control when Hong Kong reverts to China in 1997. There is also a group of Taiwanese gangs with units in America (*U.S. News and World Report*, 1/18/ 1988:29-31). Jamaican gangs have come to light recently on the East Coast and in Texas, penetrating even into small cities such as Martinsburg, West Virginia. Inner-city gangs now have the chance to grow in power, due to sales of "crack" cocaine, as well as to the breakdown of the old organized crime groups. Contemporary gangs are much more violent than Mafia groups. Gang disputes and wars are no longer over neighborhood control, but rather over control of drug sales. Most such gang members are in their teens or early and mid-20s (*Newsweek*, 3/28/1988:20-24).

The total economic impact of organized crime is not known, and estimates vary widely. One early estimate stated that the total activity of organized crime amounts to more than twice the losses resulting from street crime (President's Commission, 1967). The problem of organized crime goes beyond the simple fact that it represents a violation of laws, leads to violence against citizens, and costs society tremendous sums of money. Organized crime subverts the basic institutions of society. Otherwise honest businesses are forced to make illegal arrangements to survive. Workers are forced to accept working arrangements which violate their supposedly legally guaranteed rights to be represented by organizations of their own choosing. Perhaps most importantly, organized crime corrupts government at a number of levels. Organized crime survives in part by the routine and widespread bribery and corruption of the police and the courts. Every few years, evidence of the bribery of elected officials and the role of organized crime in financing political campaigns comes to light and gets a lot of media attention. Quite literally, government has been heavily infiltrated by organized crime (Barlow, 1990:353-354).

This brings us to the most disturbing aspect of organized crime—it has proven to be almost impervious to efforts by law enforcement agencies to control or stop its activities. Indeed, organized crime has even defied efforts to discover the full nature and extent of its organization and operation. There is considerable debate, for example, about the extent to which various organized crime syndicates coordinate their activities and participate in regional or national central organizations. Numerous reasons have been given for this failure of law enforcement to effectively control organized crime. Certainly, corruption of the police and public officials has played a role. In addition, organized crime has been very effective in intimidating potential witnesses and maintaining discipline among its members. Moreover, the operations of organized crime are both complex and sophisticated. Proving court cases against alleged leaders has proven very difficult and generally has exceeded the resources and ability of local law enforcement agencies. Finally, because organized crime provides services which a substantial number of people want or believe they need (gambling, prostitution, and illegal drugs), there is a germ of truth to the frequent justification used by these criminals for their activities: they really can exist only because there is a market for their services (Barlow, 1990:359).

Responding to Crime: The Dilemma

Crime is clearly a serious problem, and the public expectation that government should do something about it is understandable. The question is: what should be done? The fact is that public policy makers are faced with a number of problems dealing with crime which severely limit the available policy options.

A Limited Understanding of the Causes of Crime

There are a number of general theories about the nature and causes of crime. Each of these theories has its intellectual supporters, sources of empirical support, and some utility in explaining crime. However, these theories are frequently contradictory, many are fairly crude and incomplete, and none can claim overwhelming evidence which supports its claims (Gibbons, 1972:262-278). Hence, we lack a full and precise model of criminal behavior on which to base public policy. Indeed, as we have seen, there are major gaps in our knowledge about the nature and extent of specific forms of criminal activity (e.g., organized crime). As a result, it is very hard to predict what kinds of policy responses will work in dealing with crime.

The Difficulty in Eliminating the Causes of Crime

Despite our limited understanding of the causes of crime, past efforts at attempting to understand and/or control crime have made one thing fairly clear: seeking to deal with crime by eliminating its causes is extraordinarily difficult. While sociologists may differ in regard to their specific theories of crime, there does seem to be some agreement on the general nature of those causes. Apparently, those causes are deeply embedded in the basic culture and social structure of United States society. Hence, "simple" solutions (no matter how desirable on other grounds or how hard to achieve) are not likely to substantially reduce the causes of crime.

The Harris thesis, for example, suggests that there is a connection between unemployment, AFDC, traditional male (macho) behavior, and the cultural acceptance of crime. Implied here is the larger context of a positive correlation between increasing inequality and crime. How can these relationships be explained? The rate of violent crime in the United States is disproportionately high because this country has a permanent, distinct underclass. The impoverished ghetto conditions where millions of blacks and Hispanics live fosters both motive and opportunity for violent criminal behavior. The crucial explanation is not one of race or ethnicity, but rather long-term poverty and unemployment, with extremely high rates for black youth. Blacks are unemployed because available work does not provide enough money to exist. The employment situation of black males is compounded by their high dropout rate. Any policy seriously attempting to decrease black ghetto unemployment will have to provide appropriate training and equal opportunities for ghetto blacks and Hispanics (Harris, 1981:122-125, 127-140).

It seems likely, then, that reducing the motivation or the pressure to commit crime would involve very fundamental changes in the nature of United States society. For example, some suggested changes include major reductions in the degree of income inequality and wealth, changes in the opportunities available for mobility, changes in the economic environment in which corporations operate, changes in the control of corporate behavior, and changes in cultural values (Flanagan, 1990:272-274). These would be very major changes indeed. In the near future, they also are probably very unlikely. At the very least, this means that short-term policy options will be limited to efforts to control criminal activity and minimize the damage done by crime rather than eliminating the causes of criminal behavior.

The Dilemmas of Crime Control

As in the study of the causes of crime, efforts to determine what forms of crime control will work have met with limited success. In recent years, cities and states have increased the penalties or instituted mandatory sentencing for many crimes. The result has been a dramatic increase in the prison and jail population without a corresponding decrease in the crime rate. Although public opinion may favor long sentences, there is no evidence that longer sentences — or the ultimate, capital punishment — effectively deters crime. On the contrary, the experience of being incarcerated can reduce the chances of an offender returning to a non-criminal life (Irwin, 1983). State and local governments are spending an increasing proportion of their revenues on corrections and police, but we have little evidence that this spending is effective in preventing crime.

Main Points

1. Urban social life remains reasonably safe and tolerable only because government delivers a wide range of physical and social services.
2. Air pollution creates serious health problems and physical damage. The efforts of the last several decades to control air pollution have met with only limited success; serious problems remain.
3. The western half of the United States faces a growing shortage of water which could hamper continued urban growth. The basic problems in the rest of the country are the pollution of potential water supplies, and the need to move clean water to areas of population concentration.
4. Safe, environmentally acceptable disposal of solid waste is likely to involve increasing costs, the development of new procedures, and the clean-up of dangerous old waste dumps.
5. The primary problem urban government faces in dealing with these physical services and problems are high costs in a time when economic resources are limited.
6. The last half century has seen the creation of a substantial social welfare system in the United States. This system faces the problems of unclear goals, weakness at the local level, bureaucratic inertia, poor coordination, program design and evaluation, rising costs, and disparities in service levels.

7. The public school system has always had difficulty in meeting the demands of the public. There are serious problems of declining performance levels, financial difficulties, and increasing demands for services. A number of reform efforts are under way that attempt to correct these problems.

8. The official crime rate is based on police reports of crimes against property and crimes against the person.

9. The official statistics underreport the true rate of most crimes; these can be corrected somewhat by use of data from victimization studies.

10. White-collar crime, committed by both corporations and individuals, is at least as common as traditional crime (and exacts an equal if not greater cost to both individuals and society. This type of crime is receiving more attention than formerly.

11. Organized crime is that perpetuated by organizations that provide illicit services and are involved in subverting legitimate businesses and unions. It is especially pernicious because of the ability of such a system to conceal operations and to corrupt public officials.

12. The recent spending on state and local criminal corrections may be a response more to public opinion than to actual indications of its effectiveness in reducing crime.

Key Terms

Community Control   In reference to school systems the attempt to decentralize control of large school systems into the hands of local groups representing the community being served by a particular school or schools.

Organized Crime   Crimes committed by criminal organizations, usually involving either the provision of illegal services or the use of illegal means to provide legitimate services.

Physical Services   Those services which provide for the physical needs of the population and are intended to maintain the general level of physical health and safety of the community.

Privatization The transfer of public services into the hands of private contractors.

Social Welfare Services   Services designed to help members of the community meet their social needs in areas such as education, protection against crime, economic well-being, and assistance in time of illness or need.

Uniform Crime Reports   The annual report issued by the Federal Bureau of Investigation, which contains the official crime rates.

Urban Infrastructures   The physical systems delivering urban services, such as water, sewer, and transit systems, as well as streets and sidewalks.

Victimization Studies   The effort made to obtain a more realistic set of data on actual rates of crimes, by use of large representative sample, in which people are asked if the have been the victim of a crime.

White Collar Crime   Crimes by individuals or corporations involving illegal acts committed by nonphysical means and by concealment and guile to obtain property, avoid payment or loss of property, or to obtain business or professional advantage.

Suggested Reading

Bell, Terrel. 1983. National Commission on Excellence in Education, April 1983 report, *A Nation at Risk*. Washington, DC: U.S. Government Printing Office. This report caused a terrific reaction and impetus for educational reform in the United States. Contains a set of proposals for improving the quality of education by raising standards for teachers, students and curricula.

The Common Good: Social Welfare and the American Future. 1989. New York: Ford Foundation. A recent, readable report providing a basic analysis of the nature of and problems of the welfare system, with proposals for reform. It seeks to present the welfare problem and proposed solutions in the larger context of national, society-wide problems and proposals for change.

Griffith, Jeanne, Mary Frase, and John Ralph. 1989. "American Education: The Challenge of Change". *Population Bulletin* 44, 4. An interesting and comprehensive outline of recent developments in United States education, set in historical context, with relevant tables.

Wilson, James. 1975. *Thinking About Crime*. New York: Basic Books. A reasoned, if somewhat conservative, introduction to the urban crime problem which considers some of the dilemmas facing the criminal justice system.

9

Urban Problems in Other Societies

As Compared to the United States

Outline of Topics

245

S o far, the focus of this book has been exclusively upon urban conditions in the United States. However, before we attempt an overall evaluation of conditions in this country, we need to briefly examine urban conditions in other societies. In a single, brief chapter it is not possible to provide a comprehensive treatment of those conditions. The discussion, of necessity, will have to be quite general, and many of the generalizations made will not fit all countries equally well. Moreover, not all the topics addressed in relation to the United States in the previous chapters can be examined here. However, even such a general and selective overview should provide a sufficient basis to allow a useful comparison with the United States.

Such a comparative overview will serve several important purposes. First, it will allow a consideration of the extent to which urban trends in the United States are unique or are the result of more general tendencies common to other societies. Second, comparison of our problems to those in other countries will provide a basis for evaluating their relative seriousness. Granted that we have serious problems, are we better or worse off than other countries? Third, such a comparison will make it possible to see the effects of different government policies on urban conditions. What policies in other countries have (or have not) worked to deal with urban problems? Finally, in an increasingly interdependent world, in which events in other countries are more and more likely to affect the United States, some familiarity with conditions in those countries seems advisable.

The discussion will begin with urban areas in Western Europe. Because of the general similarities of these countries to the United States, their urban development has been the most similar to it. What differences do exist mostly can be explained by the impact of different government policies. We will then examine countries whose general social, economic, and political circumstances are more dissimilar to those of the United States: Japan, Eastern Europe, and the Third World.

Western Europe

Until a few decades ago the Western European countries were, along with North America, the primary location in which advanced industrial production was concentrated. They participated (with some difference in timing) in the Industrial Revolution of the 19th and early 20th centuries. They remain among the wealthiest and most technologically advanced countries in the world. Average income levels range from about half as high as the United States in Great Britain, to slightly higher in Switzerland (World Bank, 1987:203). Their economies are essentially capitalist (private ownership and reliance on markets), and their governments are relatively stable, electoral democracies. However, most have a strong tradition of working-class based political parties which have forced their governments into a much wider range of social welfare services and other forms of government regulation and intervention in the economy than has been true of the United States. Both these fundamental similarities and this important political difference are reflected in their urban development and handling of urban problems.

Similarities

Like the United States, urbanization in Western Europe occurred in response to industrialization, and the overwhelming majority of the population now resides in urban areas. In the 19th and early 20th centuries, European cities were even more compact and densely settled than their United States counterparts of the period. However, during this century they have also experienced rapid suburbanization of population and industry. The result has been the kind of sprawling metropolitan areas surrounding the older "industrial cities" quite similar in their general patterns of land use to those in the United States.

Western European urban ecological structure primarily reflects the operation of market forces. The result has been relatively homogeneous areas in which particular economic activities occur (e.g., industrial districts) and the different social classes reside. Central downtowns remain the location of corporate headquarters, large financial institutions, and the like, and white-collar workers commute to them from the suburbs. Central cities have experienced industrial decline, both as a result of suburbanization and the contraction of older industries (e.g., steel and textiles) in response to foreign competition. Older working-class areas in the central cities have increasingly become the residences of the poor, including immigrants either from the Third World (e.g., Turkey, Algeria) or poorer regions in Europe (e.g., Greece, Yugoslavia). Gentrification of some central city neighborhoods has also occurred. (In fact, the term was first used to refer to developments in London in the 1960s and early 1970s.) Suburban areas include districts with large-scale industrial activity and working class housing; as well as affluent, middle-class residential communities. In a few countries, especially West Germany and Great Britain, some metropolitan areas have experienced severe industrial decline, resulting in high chronic unemployment and population stagnation in the 1970s and 1980s. In the last three decades, automobile ownership has become very widespread, and the proportion of commuting trips by mass transit has declined. Like cities in the United States, European cities have had to struggle to accommodate the resulting traffic congestion (Hall, 1988; Light, 1983:222-231).

Thus, much of what has been discussed in regard to urban trends in the United States is at least partially applicable to Western Europe. The same social, economic, and political factors which have shaped and reshaped our urban areas have also influenced Western Europe's urbanization. Many of the problems they have had to face are quite similar to those in this country.

Differences

Despite their overall similarity to United States urban areas, those in Western Europe also display some significant differences. To the foreign visitor the most obvious one is that many (though not all) of the industrial cities of Europe were built around a historic core consisting of a pre-industrial city. In the case of a few of these cities (e.g., London, Paris, Vienna), this historic core is quite large. In the 19th century the central parts of these areas were often substantially modernized, especially for governmental purposes and the construction of cultural centers. Since that time, at least in part because these areas are important tourist attractions, considerable efforts have been made to assure their preservation. Central business districts were consequently deflected slightly to the edge of the historic centers (often near central railroad stations). However, despite the preservation of some historic areas, the centers of Western European cities function similarly to those in the United States. In the recent past, residential neighborhoods near the historic centers (those that escaped commercial development) have become prime locations for gentrification (Light, 1983:222).

Western European governments have made more aggressive attempts to control and plan urban development than in the United States. Besides preservation of their historic centers, after 1945 they also attempted to restrict and/or control the process of suburbanization. A number of the largest cities (e.g., London) established *green belts*. Usually located at the outer edge of the area of early suburban development, these green belts were rings of land several miles wide surrounding the central urban area in which most development was prohibited.

These governments also tried to reduce suburban sprawl outside the green belts by creating relatively high density suburban towns (often located on mass transit lines) in which most housing was multi-family. In the hope of reducing central city congestion, they also encouraged industry and retail centers to locate in these suburban satellites. In some countries (e.g., Great Britain, Sweden) these communities were completely government planned and primarily government constructed *new towns*. In Great Britain the hope was that these new towns would become relatively self-sufficient industrial and retail centers that would divert development from London. In Sweden the new towns were intended essentially as residential centers with good transportation links for commuting to the central city. In other cases (e.g., France, West Germany) greater reliance was placed on employing land-use regulation to direct private development, although several massive suburban centers were constructed in the 1970s by the French government. In Holland, severe restrictions on the conversion of rural land to urban purposes has forced the more intense use (e.g., high-rise apartment buildings) of existing urban land (Palen, 1987:290-298; 305-309; Hall, 1977:23-149).

Most Western European governments also tried to restrict urban sprawl by encouraging economic development away from their largest urban centers. They did so primarily by providing subsidies to corporations to locate their facilities in smaller, more slowly developing urban centers and by providing other forms of assistance to local governments in those centers (Palen, 1987:294).

These interventions in the process of urban development achieved mixed results. At best, attempts to redirect the geographical location of urban development may have somewhat slowed the development of the largest urban centers, such as London and Paris. Several new towns were constructed around London and Stockholm, and they were reasonably successful in providing adequate housing and services (though sometimes criticized for their drabness and architectural monotony). However, the attempts to control suburbanization in London and Paris were overwhelmed by the sheer magnitude of the process. Private suburbanization of residence, industry, and retail centers occurred more rapidly than expected in those countries and created the familiar pattern of suburban sprawl and automobile congestion that their governments sought to avoid. Government ownership of much of the land around Stockholm made possible a higher degree of control of the suburbanization process in Sweden. The Dutch (faced by a very large population relative to the very small size of their country) have avoided the worst aspects of suburban sprawl by mandating high-density urban land use (Jones, 1988; Palen, 1987:290-298;305-309; Light, 1983:223-229).

Housing is another area in which most Western European governments have played a much greater direct role than in the United States.
Many Western European countries faced a severe housing shortage after
World War II as a result of wartime devastation. In all of them, slow
housing construction during the 1920s and 1930s and rapid economic
growth and modest population growth after 1945 further contributed
to the need to provide additional housing units and replace worn-out,
outmoded ones. In the face of this crisis, Western European governments embarked on a large-scale program to construct apartment
buildings (or semi-detached row houses in Great Britain) and demolish
the most deteriorated older housing units. These new housing units were
government-owned, and rents were heavily subsidized. More recently,
greater emphasis has been placed on renovating older units (by
government or through subsidies to individuals or nonprofit housing
cooperatives), subsidizing private new construction, and providing
housing subsidies to families. Sweden provides housing allowances to
encourage larger families, Germany pays housing allowances to families
based on income, and France provides general subsidies to families
based on the number of children. Germany and the Netherlands give
loans to nonprofit housing cooperatives. Great Britain provides rent
rebates based on family income. Many provide mortgage subsidies of
various kinds, even to middle-class households, to purchase privately-
constructed housing. Overall, the direction of policy in the last twenty
years has been toward less government construction of large-scale
housing projects and more reliance on the private housing market.
However, government regulation and subsidization remain much greater
than in the United States (Palen, 1987:291-292; 295-298; Marcuse,
1982; Light, 1983:402-409).

In part as a result of this government involvement, housing patterns
and conditions are significantly different in Western Europe than in the
United States. Overall, Western Europeans are very well-housed in
comparison to residents of most other countries, but their housing is
less luxurious than that of the North American middle classes. Government subsidies keep the average cost of housing to between 15 and
20 percent of household income. That is higher than in the past (as is
the quality of the units), but substantially less than in the United States.
On the other hand, the actual cost of housing (per unit of space) born
by the combination of households and government is much higher. This
is in part due to more limited availability of land (and restrictions on
its use for housing) and relatively limited housing supply.

These cost pressures mean that housing units are much smaller than
in the United States and occupy much more limited land area. This
creates higher average urban population densities in Western Europe

(even in the suburbs) than in the United States. Except in Great Britain, even much of the middle-class is likely to live in multi-family apartment units. In Great Britain the middle-class ideal is the semi-detached row-house with a tiny front yard and enclosed back garden. Government involvement in large-scale housing construction in the postwar period also means that a much larger percentage of the population lives in government-provided housing. For example, around one-third of the housing stock in Great Britain and Germany is government owned. Public housing in Western Europe is not just for the poor, but for much of the working class (Palen, 1987:291-192; 295-298; Light, 1983:402-406; Marcuse, 1982, Hall, 1977).

Overall, Western European countries have managed to increase substantially their housing supply, and the quality of housing has generally improved. However, housing remains a problem. Construction has never quite kept up both with the demand for new units, the need to replace old units, and the desires of an increasingly affluent population for improved housing amenities. Long waiting lists characterize public housing. High costs for private housing confront middle-class households and limit the size, degree of privacy, and amenities available in the housing that they occupy. Substandard, slum housing exists to varying degrees in these countries and is occupied by the poor. Homelessness is a visible problem in France and Great Britain. Doubling up by families and postponement of marriage because of the lack of housing is widely reported (though hardly common in most countries). The percentage of income devoted to housing has been rising (Palen, 1987:291-192; 295-298; Light, 1983:402-406; Marcuse, 1982; Hall, 1977).

Transportation patterns also differ from those in the United States. While car use has skyrocketed in the last thirty years, mass transit (especially for commuting) remains much more important in Western Europe. In London, for example, 71 percent of those commuting into central London rely on mass transit (Jones, 1988:105), and in Stockholm 60 percent do (Palen, 1987:292). On the other hand, suburban use of automobiles is much more similar to that of the United States. What explains this difference? Car ownership (and two-car families) is still less common in Western Europe than in the United States, but that difference is not enough to account for the difference in transit use. One factor is simple traffic congestion. In older parts of the cities the streets are very narrow and both driving and parking are thereby made more difficult. In addition, as part of government policy, there has been a reluctance to expand the automobile infrastructure rapidly in order to discourage commuting by car. Both highways and parking facilities have been intentionally kept inadequate. At the same time, more emphasis has been put on building and maintaining mass transit systems. The rationale behind this policy is that it is cheaper for government, reduces the use of mostly imported petroleum, and discourages suburban sprawl. Heavy taxation of gasoline (again to reduce imports) also increases the cost of commuting by car. Of course, the result is intense urban traffic congestion. Public pressure to reduce that congestion and preference for the automobile created heavy pressures to build urban expressways in the 1960s, and most governments relented somewhat. However, the energy shortages of the 1970s and concern for the cost of highway construction in the 1980s slowed down the construction of urban expressways, and urban traffic congestion as the result of increasing car use continues to be a problem (Light, 1983:226-229).

An increasing concern in Western Europe has been the effect of rising pollution levels. In general, Western Europe has been slower to react to pollution than the United States. In addition, higher population density means higher densities of air and water pollution sources. The result has been very severe air, water, and soil pollution. For example, about one-third of the forests of Germany are dead or dying from the effects of air pollution. Despite some belated controls, the Rhine River basin is severely contaminated. Major damage to the lakes of Sweden has been reported as the result of acid rain (Brown and Flavin, 1988:6).

Finally, at a more general level, there is a greater commitment in Western Europe (though France clearly lags in this regard and Great Britain has been changing) to provide certain services and pursue certain policies which reduce the kinds of inequality and poverty which were discussed in Chapter 4. Especially after 1945, Western European countries created relatively elaborate "welfare states." Such things as more or less free medical care, subsidized housing, free university education (to those who qualified), extensive unemployment payments, income support for the poor, a wide range of social services, and generous pensions represented an ambitious attempt to guarantee a relatively high minimum level of living for the whole population and eliminate extreme poverty. Compared to the United States, this system of welfare benefits and services to the whole population was much more extensive. Moreover, it did reduce some of the extreme disparities in living conditions which otherwise would have existed and which continue to characterize United States urban areas. However, the increasing cost of the welfare state, middle-class resistance to high tax levels, and concern with international economic competition in the 1980s have led most Western European governments to attempt to reduce some of the benefits and social services previously provided.

Japan

Japan rose rapidly to the first rank of the advanced capitalist countries after 1945. Currently it has per capita income and urbanization levels typical of the richest and most technologically advanced capitalist countries. Besides being among the largest and most economically important countries, Japan is of interest here because it achieved high levels of urbanization and industrialization later, but much faster, and under different circumstances than North America or Western Europe. Unlike most of those countries, small, mountainous Japan had very limited agricultural land, virtually no natural resources, and a high population density relative to its arable land. Hence, its strategy was one which emphasized rapid technological development and productive efficiency to make its manufactured goods competitive in the world market. Government (continuously controlled by the same conservative, business-oriented political party) and the large, export-oriented corporations worked together closely to achieve economic development objectives. Policies not directly related to this goal were given low priority and allocated only limited resources:

> . . . the Liberal Democratic Party (LDP), [is] an 'unabashed spokesman' for big business; in the interest of free enterprise; the LDP has resisted government intervention to protect the urban environment and has received in return generous subventions from big corporations (Light, 1983:166).

The result was urbanization which has many similarities to that in other advanced capitalist countries but displays a number of unique characteristics and problems.

Our discussion here will focus on the greater Tokyo metropolitan area. Japanese urbanization has tended to concentrate in a few very large urban areas, and Tokyo is the largest one. The Tokyo conurbation (including the cities of Yokohama, Kawasaki, and Chiba) alone accounts for almost 25 million people (Yeung, 1988:159). The problems of the other large metropolitan areas are less severe but the basic patterns of development are quite similar to Tokyo.

Similarities

The general ecological structure of the Tokyo region is similar to large metropolitan areas in the United States. The central area of the city of Tokyo has progressively been given over to corporate headquarters, financial institutions, and business services, with mass retailing still important but losing out to satellite subcenters. Central Tokyo now specializes in administration and services, and most of the white-collar labor force commutes in from the suburbs. Subcenters have developed at points where suburban rail lines meet a loop railroad and commuters transfer from rail lines to other forms of mass transit for the trip downtown. They are primarily retail centers, but have developed as secondary office centers. (These subcenters are roughly similar to those which have been developing at the intersections of urban expressways in places like Los Angles). Overall, the central "wards" of the city of Tokyo have been losing population and industry. Industry has been suburbanizing to the northeast (smaller manufacturing plants), south (large manufacturing), and to the southwest (small high-technology installations). The wards immediately east of the downtown are the older industrial districts (built on swampland next to the bay). They contain many small industrial enterprises and many of the older, declining industries.

Working class housing has expanded outward in the same sectors. The western and northwestern sectors of the suburbs are the primary location for higher status residential housing, although they contain some major industrial subcenters. Overall, in the last few decades most of Tokyo's (very substantial) economic development and population growth has occurred in the steadily expanding suburban ring (Nakamura and White, 1988). Thus, Tokyo land-use patterns are quite similar to those in the United States and reflect the predominance of market-based mechanisms and corporate interests in land allocation. Government intervention has been attempted, and relatively elaborate general plans have been drawn up, but with limited real impact. For example, in the 1950s a plan very similar to that for London was proposed. A large green belt was established at what was then the fringe of Tokyo, and new towns were planned beyond it. However, intense pressures for suburban development resulted in abandoning the green belt to residential development. The attempt to create new towns also had very limited impact on the pattern of suburbanization. Some existing towns were designated as new towns, and their development encouraged. One very large new town (Tama) was built by government, and an "academic garden city", containing a national university and some research institutes, was established. However, these towns were quickly swallowed up in the tide of unplanned suburbanization. Tama became essentially a residential suburb with the majority of its workers commuting to central Tokyo. Similarly, programs have been announced repeatedly to encourage economic development of smaller urban areas in regions away from Tokyo, but their impact has been extremely limited (Light, 1983:165; Nakamura and White, 1988:143-144).

Tokyo suffers from extreme traffic congestion and has very limited street space. Only 12 percent of the land area of central Tokyo is devoted to streets, compared to 23 percent in London and 35 percent in New York (Hall, 1977:231). Nonetheless, car ownership and use in Tokyo has been steadily increasing. As elsewhere, the response on the part of government was at least a half-hearted attempt to create an urban expressway system, including elevated expressways in central Tokyo.

Differences

While the pattern of urban land use is similar to the United States, the intensity of its use in Japan is different. Only about 15 percent of Japanese land area is level and arable (in a country the size of California). Urban areas must compete with agriculture for this limited land area to accommodate an urban population of more than 80 million. In addition, government policy has had the effect of making the land available for urban uses even more scarce and expensive. A number of laws made it difficult to convert agricultural land adjacent to urban areas to nonagricultural purposes. For example, farmers are protected from paying taxes which would reflect the (very high) market value of their land and are paid large subsidies for their products. This makes it possible for them to farm profitably near urban areas and hold on to their land until the price for it becomes very high. The official justification for this policy is the desire to maintain self-sufficiency in rice production and near sufficiency in other products. It also results in extremely high food prices for urban consumers. The policy also probably reflects the disproportionate political importance of the "farm bloc" because of its importance in giving the ruling political party the margin necessary to win each national election since the 1940s (Fallows, 1986; 1989). Other, often well-intended, zoning and land development restrictions further increased the cost developers had to charge to make a profit. In addition, prohibitive taxes on land sales (designed to discourage short-term land speculation) have encouraged landowners to hold on to undeveloped land. Land owners wait for the price to rise on their land until the transaction tax is offset by the higher price (Nakamura and White, 1988:146-147).

Concern over earthquakes (a real and serious threat in Tokyo) and the effect of high-rise buildings on their neighbors (e.g., blocking out sunlight) also led to restrictions on the height of buildings. While some of these restrictions were eased for office buildings in the 1970s (because of the development of more earthquake-resistant building techniques), most areas of Tokyo still restrict height. Average building heights remain little over two stories. Hence, the number of workers or residents which can be accommodated on a given parcel of land cannot be increased by building higher buildings (Nakamura and White, 1988:145).

The limited supply of urban land, restrictions on building height, and the tremendous demand for land as Tokyo grew had a predictable result. The price of urban land has grown astronomically over the last three decades. If 1955 is taken as the base year in which the index price of residential land in Tokyo was 100, by 1983 the index price stood at 3,100. Primarily as a result of these high land prices, in 1983 the price of a condominium-type residence in central Tokyo was estimated as being twice as high per square meter of space as a comparable unit in London and slightly less than three times as high for such a unit in New York (Nakamura and White, 1988:140). The rate of price increases accelerated in the 1980s (Fallows, 1989).

The effect of these prices on housing conditions in Tokyo has been profound. The high price of land severely limits both the size and quality of the housing Tokyo residents can afford. In the city of Tokyo itself, lot size for a house is 100 square meters or less, and (as of 1980) average living space per person was about 10 square meters. While the percentage of housing units with full bathrooms has increased markedly, about 35 percent of Tokyo units still lacked them in 1980. Almost one-third of Tokyo's housing units were judged poorly constructed and highly flammable in 1980. More generally, the high cost of land leaves little money to invest in the house or apartment building itself, and consequently, even new housing tends to be flimsy and poorly constructed (Fallows, 1986). The high cost and crowded conditions of housing closer to central Tokyo has also forced increasing percentages of middle-class workers to seek cheaper housing further and further away from their places of work. By commuting 60 to 90 minutes (one way) workers can find housing built on land which costs "only" half as much as in the city of Tokyo. These still astronomical (by U. S. standards) land costs mean that even distant suburban housing is likely to be on lots of little more than 100 square meters, and houses are likely to be built right up to the property line, with little or no open space between structures. A house similar to the typical new suburban house in the United States (but on a smaller lot) is financially out of reach of all but the rich in Tokyo. While about 40 percent of households in Tokyo own their residences, that percentage has not increased very much in the last 20 years, despite the fact that income levels have risen markedly. However, general measures of housing quality (e.g., indoor plumbing, amount of space) indicate slow but steady improvement over conditions in the past (Nakamura and White, 1988: 140-141).

Most housing in Japan is provided privately. Public housing is quite limited and not necessarily even targeted toward the poor. One government agency does construct apartments (very small and often without such amenities as private bathrooms) for low-income households. Despite their unattractiveness, they are cheap to rent and demand for them greatly exceeds supply. Other agencies have constructed larger, better quality apartments in such areas as the new town of Tama. However, these agencies are required to break even financially and must charge rents which only more affluent households can afford (Hall, 1977:226; Palen, 1987:375).

The search for affordable housing has been an important impetus in Tokyo suburbanization. In turn, that suburbanization has meant steadily increasing time spent commuting and massive increased demands placed on the transportation system. Half of all commuters to central Tokyo in 1983 spent one hour (one way) to get to work, and one-fifth spent more than an hour and a half (Nakamura and White, 1988:141). As of 1984, the average total commuting distance for Tokyo workers was 50 kilometers (Yeung, 1988:161). While some workers commute by car, the grossly inadequate expressway system, narrow city streets, and the lack of parking make car use by most commuters out of the question. Traffic congestion has reached monumental proportions, and movement by street or highway is extremely slow, despite constant efforts to expand the expressway system. Most commuters rely on the mass transit system. The suburbs are served by commuter railroads which terminate at several stations on a rail loop around the western edge of central Tokyo. Commuters then transfer to the city mass transit system. At one time this system primarily consisted of streetcars and buses, but due to traffic congestion they were mostly replaced by a fast, efficient subway system in the 1960s and 1970s. More subways are under construction. The entire mass transit system is well-engineered, fast, and provides easy access to all of central Tokyo. However, the number of commuters has consistently increased faster than the system has expanded. The result is a massively over-crowded system. Over the last two decades, the system has never carried less than 200 percent of its planned capacity (Nakamura and White, 1988:132-134).

Construction of basic physical infrastructure in Tokyo has been slow, and that city's basic systems are still not adequate. In the 1980s about a fourth of the dwellings in Tokyo still lacked sewer connections, and the percentage of dwellings without sewer connections was even higher in many suburban areas. Complete provision of an adequate municipal water supply also has yet to be achieved. Public open space such as parks and recreational facilities are almost totally lacking (Hall, 1977:228; Nakamura and White: 1988:140).

Air, water, chemical, and noise pollution in the Tokyo area are arguably the worst of any urban area in an advanced capitalist country. Deaths directly attributable to pollution have been documented, and an estimated 76,000 to 200,000 people have been crippled as a result of exposure to pollutants in their communities or at work. Air pollution is the cause of a high level of respiratory disease. Sewage treatment is primitive, at best, and industrial pollution of rivers, bays, and ground water is severe. Until the late 1960s pollution was treated by government as simply the unavoidable consequence of economic growth, and virtually nothing was done about it. Public protest since then has led to some efforts to control pollution, and the levels of some air pollutants have fallen. However, the control effort has been only partially successful, and the problem remains serious (Yeung, 1988:165; Light, 1983:165).

Most social services and welfare programs in Japan remain undeveloped relative to the United States and Western Europe. The government-funded retirement system is very limited, and most Japanese attempt to save a major portion of their incomes to provide for retirement. On the other hand, because of its importance for labor productivity, Japan places great emphasis on the educational system, and its elementary and secondary school systems obtain high performance levels from students (Fallows, 1989).

A relatively unique feature of Japanese urban life is the role of neighborhood associations. These associations are highly organized and cooperate with municipal government in the provision of services. For example, they take responsibility for keeping the streets clean in their neighborhoods. They also report fires and criminal activity to the authorities. Their activities may help to account for the low crime rate and the relative safety of the streets in Japanese cities (Nakamura and White, 1988:139-40).

Finally, Tokyo faces the severe threat of a devastating earthquake. The last (very disastrous) quake was in 1923, and one of equivalent magnitude is overdue. Its downtown modern high-rise buildings are theoretically designed to withstand an earthquake, and emergency plans are in place. Nonetheless, other characteristics of Tokyo point to potential disaster: a high proportion of flammable wooden buildings, industrial and working-class residential zones constructed on unstable landfill, elevated expressways, huge numbers of commuters in subways during the rush hour, potentially explosive petrochemical complexes, and a woeful lack of accessible open space to which it would be possible to evacuate the population (Nakamura and White, 1988:143).

Eastern Europe

Since a brutal revolution and civil war at the end of World War I, the Soviet Union has been governed by a centralized "Marxist-Leninist" political party. The rest of Eastern Europe was ruled by similar regimes, forcibly established and maintained by the Soviet Union, from the 1940s until the late 1980s. These states were characterized by a high degree of centralization of power in state and party apparatus and systematic repression of their populations. Government ownership of most productive enterprises (except for small peasant farms in some of the Eastern European countries outside of the Soviet Union) and centralized state planning of economic activity prevailed in all these countries. With the partial exceptions of East Germany and parts of Czechoslovakia, these were only partially industrialized and urbanized societies in 1950. All attempted rapid industrialization (or reconstruction of industry in the case of East Germany) in the last four decades. Overall levels of industrialization and urbanization did rise rapidly between 1950 and 1980. Still, levels of output per worker, total industrial output, and the level of technological sophistication remained significantly below that of the advanced capitalist countries. In pursuit of rapid industrialization, centralized control of the economy was used to maintain a high level of capital investment in new manufacturing facilities at the expense of private consumption and many public services. Especially in the case of the Soviet Union, a very high level of military expenditures was a further economic drain. On the other hand, economic inequality was much less than in the advanced capitalist societies, and the population enjoyed relative employment security and (except for top government officials) shared equally in a wide range of free or heavily subsidized services (Chirot, 1986:263-275).

By the 1980s these countries were experiencing growing economic difficulties and political unrest. Their huge centralized state bureaucracies were inefficient, inept, and frequently riddled with corruption. Inadequate work incentives, overstaffing, and backward technology kept worker productivity low. The standard of living stagnated or declined as their economies began to flounder. Attempts at economic and political reform, begun in the Soviet Union, set off a series of dramatic political changes which eliminated one-party rule in Eastern Europe. Attempts began to reform their economies by relying more on privately owned enterprises and market mechanisms in place of centralized state planning. At this writing, it is impossible to predict where these changes will take Eastern Europe in the 1990s. However, what will happen in part depends on the legacy of a half-century (more in the Soviet Union) of state socialism. That legacy conditions both the resources these countries will have to deal with their problems and defines the nature of many of those problems. Hence, our concern here will be with the state socialist legacy in regard to urban conditions.

Similarities

Despite fundamental differences in the basic system of political economy between the United States and Eastern Europe, there have been some general similarities in their urban development. As in Western Europe, the United States, and Japan, the driving force behind Eastern European urbanization has been industrialization. Jurgen Friedrichs (1988) points out:

> . . . there are no specific socialist types of land use, distribution of new housing, internal organization of residential blocks, or location of companies. Even the principal goal of socialist city planning — to locate new residential areas close to working areas — has been pursued in Western planning too, and failed, since most residents did not have jobs in the adjacent working areas (128).

Faced with relatively rapid urbanization and industrialization, limited resources, and the overriding obligation to facilitate industrialization, state planners found themselves approving land use patterns with many similarities to those in the West.

In the last two decades central areas of Eastern European cities became more and more specialized as centers of administration and, secondarily, cultural and retail centers. At the same time, inner districts lost population while outer districts, suburbs, and more distant satellite cities grew rapidly. A growing separation between places of residence and work increased commuting distances and time. Central cities gained employment in the service sector, and manufacturing employment became a smaller percentage of total city employment. New manufacturing enterprises were constructed in suburban locations.

Residential patterns changed as these urban areas grew. Initially, luxury housing for the political leadership (often upper-class housing left over from prerevolutionary or prewar days) was located conveniently near government administrative offices. Hence, the existing good housing was nearer the center of the city, and the least privileged workers were relegated to peripheral (often self-built) slums on the outskirts. That pattern was reinforced in those cities in which workers needed government permits to live inside the city limits. New migrants, often with the lowest status jobs, could not get such permits and so had to live outside city limits. These "peripheral slums" are still much in evidence in most cities. However, beginning in the 1960s, most of the newer and better housing was built on the outskirts of the cities. The reason is simple — such a location provided the open land which made possible the inexpensive construction of large-scale housing projects. Exclusive housing compounds or weekend retreats also were constructed in exurban areas for the political elite, while they retained their exclusive, centrally located apartments. Older buildings outside of the exclusive residential district (often drastically subdivided into tiny apartments with communal kitchens and bathrooms) became the least desirable housing. Consequently, a pattern of better quality housing in the suburbs emerged which is roughly analogous to that in advanced capitalist countries (Friedrichs, 1988; Palen, 1987:301-302).

Differences

One fundamental difference in urban conditions between Eastern Europe and the United States is based on the simple fact that these are substantially poorer countries. In the late 1980s overall economic production per person still remained in a range of from less than one-fifth to not quite four-tenths as high as that in the United States (World Bank, 1987). Such a huge difference meant not just comparatively low living standards in relation to the United States, but also much more limited resources available to government to deliver services.

In principle, Eastern European urban development occurred according to centrally controlled government plans which were to assure coordinated and rational land use, adequate provision of services, and geographically balanced urbanization. State control of industrial investment decisions, ownership of most urban land, and control of urban housing construction, gave it the ability to implement the central plan.

However, in practice the planning process did not yield many of its expected benefits. In general, the concerns of the economic planners for rapid industrial development took precedence and the lion's share of the available resources. This emphasis almost guaranteed that the efforts of urban planning authorities frequently would be frustrated. Factories came first; housing, services, and concerns about geographical balance came in a distant second. Economic and urban planning were also poorly coordinated. For example, until 1976 in the Soviet Union each industrial department developed its plans independently of each other and of urban governmental agencies. One problem this created was that the location of new housing and industry was often poorly coordinated, creating unanticipated demands for transportation. Urban planning agencies were equally uncoordinated. The construction of huge apartment complexes on the outskirts of the cities was often undertaken without adequate preparation to provide services and consideration of transportation needs. Around Moscow these new complexes were often occupied for years before basic retail outlets, medical facilities, and transportation links were put into place. Inflexible national guidelines often were inappropriate to local conditions. For instance, new complexes were provided with hospital accommodations of a certain capacity relative to the size of the complex, without any consideration of the age distribution of the residents.

At the local level, urban government officials often had very limited authority to make decisions and respond to citizen complaints. Especially in smaller cities, the major industrial enterprises actually had more control over local conditions and services than did local officials. Soviet factories often built their own housing complexes and provided their own services (e.g., water, power, medical care, and retail stores). The managers of the factories consequently had more control over local urban conditions than did municipal government. Failure to anticipate changing conditions also meant that plans were out-of-date before they were fully implemented. Soviet planners consistently underestimated the rate of growth around Moscow, for example. More generally, the attempt to control regional urbanization had only a limited impact. It did have some impact and led to urban development in some undeveloped regions (e.g., Soviet Siberia). Nonetheless, it never created the sort of balance that the urban planning authorities sought to achieve (Friedrichs, 1988; Palen, 1987:298-301; Hall, 1977).

In the 1980s housing remained perhaps the greatest problem for Eastern European urban areas. There was a severe absolute shortage of housing units, the units were extremely small, and their quality was low. Several factors contributed to the housing crisis: (1) the poor quality and deteriorating condition of the pre-1940 housing stock, (2) the devastation of urban areas during World War II, (3) extremely rapid urbanization requiring new housing units, and (4) inadequate resources available to construct housing. The latter factor in part reflected the policy of initial neglect of urban housing needs to concentrate investment resources on industry. However, in the last three decades more resources were released for housing, and the overall rate of construction was quite high. Beginning in the late 1950s, construction of housing in the Soviet Union averaged over two million units annually, although the economic crisis of the last few years probably has reduced that rate. The problem was that even such a relatively high construction rate (the Soviet rate was comparable to that of the United States) was insufficient to make up for past deficiencies and meet the needs of a rapidly growing urban population. The result of the continuing shortage of units was that there were long waiting lists for apartments, adult children (even if they married) often had to double-up with parents in already cramped apartments for years, and people had to accept grossly inadequate accommodations (e.g., single rooms with communal bathrooms and kitchens) because nothing else was available (Friedrichs, 1988; Palen, 1987:299-300; Light, 1983:409-412).

In the Soviet Union almost all urban housing has been state-owned by a housing authority or an industrial enterprise. In the rest of Eastern Europe there has been a mixture of state-owned buildings, independent housing cooperatives (tenant or factory controlled, but with construction money borrowed from the state), and private ownership. In the past, private housing was often the worst. It was constructed by low-status workers who had been unable to obtain state-provided housing. It was often located on the periphery of urban areas in places poorly provided with physical infrastructure and transportation. More recently, private construction by the more affluent (especially outside of the Soviet Union) created better-than-average quality private housing.

By Western standards, even new state-owned housing is incredibly cramped: in the Soviet Union 97 square feet of living area per person has been the goal of urban planners, and in the 1980s about half the population still lived in units which did not meet that standard. In older buildings shared kitchens and bathrooms remain common. In the Soviet Union, most new housing consists of large, high-rise apartment buildings built from standardized components made in factories and assembled on the site. The buildings are drab, utilitarian, poorly constructed, and prone to deterioration. As already mentioned, the new complexes are often built prior to completion of planned service facilities (e.g., schools, medical centers), transportation links, and even such basic physical infrastructure as road paving. This makes living in them difficult, involving long trips on inadequate public transportation to work, shop, go to school, or seek medical attention. On the other hand, as bad as they are, and despite continuing shortages, housing conditions have improved relative to those in the grim decade following World War II. Moreover, housing is heavily state-subsidized. Apartments rent for very low rents, and the average family pays only a small fraction of its income for housing (Friedrichs, 1988; Palen, 1987:299-300; Light, 1983:409-410; Hall, 1977:158-163).

Eastern European planners have consistently favored public transportation over accommodating the automobile. Until recently, automobiles were in extremely limited supply and priced at intentionally prohibitive prices. Little attention was given to providing automotive services, and limited numbers of automobiles meant that urban expressways did not need to be built. Only in the last decade did street congestion from private automobiles become noticeable in most Eastern European cities. Hence, the bulk of the urban population had no choice but to rely on public transit facilities. The reason for this policy was simple: mass transit provided the cheapest way to provide urban transportation.

Considerable resources were devoted to expanding and improving the urban transit system, and heavy state subsidies kept fares low. In many cities (e.g., Moscow) a rapid and efficient transit system (including subways) provided high quality service to central city areas. However, expansion of these systems did not keep up with demand due to rapid urbanization and the decentralization of housing and industry. Also, more workers ended up needing to commute from the urban outskirts to the central city than was anticipated. Hence, residents in outlying residential areas faced limited, crowded, and inconvenient transportation facilities (usually buses) and long commuting times (Friedrichs, 1988; Hall, 1977:168).

Consistent with their socialist ideology, these countries attempted to provide a wide range of basic health, educational, and recreational facilities to urban residents, available to all at little or no cost. (Until recently, these governments also attempted to guarantee employment to all citizens.) Given the economic limitations imposed by their relatively backward economies, the range of basic services accessible to average citizens was impressive. On the other hand, the quality of those services was generally low and inadequate facilities led to "rationing by waiting in line." For example, medical facilities were crowded, ill-equipped, and often poorly supplied with even basic medicines. Hence, general living conditions were more equal, but at a uniformly low level by Western standards. At the same time, government and party leaders had access to a wide range of specially reserved service facilities, housing, and consumer goods stores, which allowed them a much better living standard than that of the general population.

Government emphasis on increasing production above all else led to another serious problem. Pollution reached levels much worse than in the advanced capitalist countries. Air pollution from industry, toxic dumping, careless deforestation, unsafe work environments, and the like received little or no attention from the authorities. Air pollution-related respiratory illness became a major health problem in many cities. Toxic chemicals or bacterial contaminants were found in the water supplies of many Polish cities. Forest death due to industrial pollution and acid rain was widespread in East Germany, Poland, and Czechoslovakia. Contamination of agricultural areas and fisheries were widely reported in the 1980s. Only limited and belated remedial action was taken in the last decade (Brown and Flavin, 1988:7; *Roanoke Times*, January 28, 1990:F1).

The Third World

The most extraordinary urban trend of the last half century has been the historically unprecedented rate of urbanization in the *Third World* (sometimes called the "periphery" in relation to the "core" of North America and Western Europe). These are the relatively poor and less industrialized countries of South America, Africa, the Middle East, and Asia. Because of the increasing diversity of conditions in these countries, it is now common to distinguish between those in the *periphery* proper and those in the *semi-periphery*. The poorest countries are those in the periphery. They include most of sub-Saharan Africa and South and East Asia (including India and China.) They are extremely poor: average income per person (GDP per capita in 1987) ranged from less than $200 to about $1000 per year (compared to around $18,000 per year in the United States). Their economies are still primarily agricultural and over two-thirds of their populations are rural. However, compared to the past, many of these countries (most importantly, China and India) now have significant industrial facilities. The countries of the semi-periphery include most of the countries of Latin America, North Africa, the Middle East, and a few smaller countries in Southeast Asia. They are more affluent than the periphery: average income per person ranged from about $1000 to $4000 per year in 1987. These countries are "partially industrialized," with about one-half to two-thirds of their populations living in urban areas. A few of these countries (e.g., South Korea, Taiwan, Singapore) achieved such rapid rates of industrialization in the last two decades that they have been called the "Newly Industrialized Countries" or NICs (Shannon, 1989:82-106; World Bank, 1989:218-219).

Despite immense diversity, it is possible to identify one general common problem of these countries: their rapid rate of population growth. Beginning about four decades ago, their mortality rates (the probability of dying at a given age) fell dramatically. This drop was primarily in response to improvements in such public health measures as vaccination, pest control, and antibiotic use. Until recently (when it began to decline slowly) the fertility rate (the number of children a woman has on average) remained high. The result was explosive population growth. Total population almost doubled from 1960 to 1990 (to 4 billion). The most rapidly growing countries have been doubling their populations in less than 20 years. Most countries are actively seeking to encourage smaller families. China has the most successful fertility control program (but also the most coercive one). It has already cut fertility down to about two children per woman. Most observers are now hopeful that fertility will decline to the point at which population will actually stop growing in about a century. However, that means that massive population growth will continue (especially for the next half century), and even the most optimistic projections are for there to be at least 8 billion people in the Third World by the middle of the next century (Weeks, 1989).

All of the countries of the Third World have been attempting to modernize: they are seeking to raise their average standard of living through industrialization and agricultural improvements and create "modern" social institutions such as educational systems. Most have achieved some modest degree of success. Average levels of production per person, life expectancy, literacy, industrial output, and the like have risen at least slowly in most of these countries (except sub-Saharan Africa, where declines occurred in the 1980s) and rapidly in a few. However, most remain dismally poor by United States standards. The World Bank estimated that over one-fourth of the population of the Third World (about one billion people) was living in "absolute poverty" in 1980; that is, they lack the economic means to sustain a healthy life (World Bank, 1981:18). More recent estimates, while very crude, suggest that the number of absolute poor has not declined, and may have increased slightly, although the percentage of Third World population which is absolutely poor may be slightly less (Durning, 1990:136). In addition, the majority of the rest of the population lives under conditions which would qualify as abject poverty in the United States. At current rates of improvement, only a few countries can hope to achieve living conditions for most of their people even remotely comparable to those now enjoyed in the advanced capitalist countries within the lifetime of anyone reading this book. Indeed, because incomes in the advanced capitalist countries have also been increasing, the absolute gap between the average incomes in the Third World countries and those of the advanced capitalist countries has been increasing since 1950 (World Bank, 1984:6; Durning, 1990:137).

The reasons for this disappointing rate of improvement are complex and a matter of some controversy. Most observers agree that the rapid increases in population have had and will continue to have major negative effects on these countries' efforts to modernize, and even threaten the most crowded of them with the inability to feed themselves (Weeks, 1989). On the other hand, few sociologists would argue that population growth by itself explains the continued poverty of most of the Third World. Some sociologists (called *modernization theorists*) have emphasized the problems caused by the continued social and cultural "traditionalism" of these societies, which has made them slow to adopt necessary social, political, and economic reforms. Other sociologists (called *world-system theorists*) argue that Third World countries have been relegated to a disadvantaged position in the international economy. World trading and investment patterns benefit the advanced capitalist countries at the expense of those in the Third World. Only those countries which have been able to achieve a high degree of political autonomy from the advanced capitalist countries (e.g., Japan) have been able to avoid or break out of this disadvantageous position in the world economy and achieve rapid modernization (Shannon, 1989).

It is in this context of extreme poverty, rapid population growth, and frustratingly slow attempts to modernize that Third World urbanization has been occurring. The overall rates vary, and there are major differences in the overall levels of urbanization that they have achieved. However, what is striking for most of these countries is the very rapid rate at which they are urbanizing. The rate of urbanization in the Third World has been much higher than that which has occurred elsewhere. Moreover, when combined with population growth, the total numbers of people being added to urban areas in the Third World is immense. In 1950 about 280 million people lived in urban areas out of a total Third World population of 1.6 billion. By 2000 there will be about 2.2 billion urban dwellers out of a population of about 5 billion (Light, 1983:134). In the recent past the rate of urbanization has been slowing somewhat. Nonetheless, even this slower growth will still result in a huge increase in the number of large cities in the Third World. In 1950 there were only 31 metropolitan areas in the Third World with more than a million population, but by 2000 there will be 297, and by 2025 there will be 486. By 2025, current projections call for there to be 135 giant metropolitan areas in the world with populations exceeding 4 million. Of these giant urban centers, 114 (with 1.1 billion people) will be in the Third World, and almost 20 of them will have populations over 10 million (Dogan and Kasarda, 1988:13-18).

Causes of Rapid Urbanization

Part of the growth of urban areas in the Third World is simply due to the high fertility and low mortality rates of the people living in them, causing a high rate of natural increase in their populations. However, the extreme rapidity of the recent growth reflects massive migration

Table 9.1 **Third World Urbanization: Percent Urban Population**

	1960	1980	2000*	2025*
All Countries	21	29	43	56
Selected Countries				
China	19	26	39	46
India	18	22	36	53
Brazil	46	65	83	89
Mexico	51	67	77	85
Pakistan	22	28	38	57
Indonesia	15	20	38	56
Thailand	13	14	23	43
Nigeria	13	20	33	53
Egypt	38	45	55	70
Zaire	16	34	56	72
Kenya	7	14	26	46

*Projected

SOURCE: United Nations. Department of International Economic and Social Affairs. 1985. *Estimates and projections of Urban, Rural, and City Populations. 1950-2025: The 1982 Assessment.* New York: United Nations.

of rural residents to urban areas. This large-scale migration will not continue indefinitely. Eventually, the populations will be predominantly urban, and (like the United States) migration will cease to be a major cause of growth. Completion of the "urban transition" (having 70-80 percent of the population in urban areas) is one reason (besides slowing overall population growth) that rates of urban growth are expected to begin to decline significantly in the most urbanized countries of the Third World in the next century (Kelley and Williamson, 1984:179). Yet, for the time being, migration is expected to continue. What accounts for this massive shift?

In part, the answer is (as it was for the United States in the nineteenth century) that workers have been attracted by the development of large-scale industry, corporate and government offices, large retail establishments, and the like (the *formal sector* of the urban economy). However, the number of workers being added to the labor force in Third World cities greatly exceeds that needed to work in the formal sector. Hence, the cause of rural-to-urban migration has not been simply conventional industrialization by itself. Indeed, early observers of Third World urbanization argued that those workers not in the formal sector constituted "excess urbanization," and as a result, Third World countries were experiencing "over-urbanization." This nonfunctional urbanization was occurring simply because of rapid population growth in general and excess population in the countryside in particular (Gibbs and Schnore, 1960). However, more recent research and theorizing calls this view into question.

It is true the rural conditions are generally appalling and provide a strong motivation to look for better opportunity in the cities. Income levels are extraordinarily low, and the growth in opportunities for employment have not been keeping pace with population growth. In some cases rural population densities (especially in Asia) are such that peasant landholdings are an acre or less, and consequently, can neither support a household adequately nor be further subdivided for the next generation. In many countries the situation is made worse by the fact the much of the land is held by large landowners (the native aristocracy or foreign corporations), leaving large numbers of peasants impoverished tenant farmers or landless day laborers. The development of commercial agriculture (often for export) using modern mechanized methods has also reduced the demand for rural labor in some countries. In addition, many Third World governments have favored urban areas at the expense of people in the countryside. Price controls on agricultural products have kept rural incomes low to assure cheap food for the cities. Government investment in infrastructure, industrial facilities, education, and other services have tended to favor the cities — especially capital cities (Firebaugh, 1979; Geisse and Sabatini, 1988; Rondinelli, 1988; Sachs, 1988, Dogan and Kasarda, 1988).

Nonetheless, most recent research indicates that it is the relative attractiveness of the cities, not the problems of the countryside, which primarily accounts for rural-to-urban migration. While the formal sector of the urban economy has been unable to absorb the growing urban labor force, a larger (and more rapidly growing) *informal sector* of the urban economy has provided most of the employment opportunities. The informal sector consists of small enterprises and self-employed workers who produce a wide range of services and small-scale production of goods. Women who sew garments in their homes, scavengers, shopkeepers of tiny stores, water carriers, manual day-laborers, pedicab pullers, and self-employed carpenters are all members of the informal sector. Incomes of most workers in this sector are as low or lower than those in the formal sector, and usually several members of the family must work even to assure the minimum subsistence needs of the household.

Early observers of the informal sector argued that it represented a form of "under-employment" in which workers engaged in relatively unproductive labor simply as a means of survival because of inadequate employment opportunities in the formal sector and the countryside.

More recently, the informal sector has come to be viewed as an integral part of the urban economy in the Third World:

> [The informal sector]...subsidizes export manufacturing by providing the factories with production inputs at low prices and cheap goods and services to poorly paid workers. . . . [It] helps make possible wages below that necessary for the subsistence of manufacturing workers' households. Workers in manufacturing industries supplement their inadequate wages by 'moonlighting' in the informal sector or by having other family members work in that sector (Shannon, 1989:90).

In societies where capital for modern, large-scale production is inadequate, the informal sector thus represents a means of employing labor and obtaining necessary goods and services with minimal capital investment. It is "labor-intensive" production, but it is as productive as labor-intensive rural agriculture (or even more productive where agriculture is especially backward or land is scarce). It is part of a larger economic system which is based on the exploitation of extremely cheap labor to produce inexpensive goods and agricultural commodities for the national and world market. Such production has been the traditional role of peripheral and semi-peripheral countries in the world economic system. The informal structure simply represents, therefore, a new urban form of the kind of economic activity which has characterized these countries for a long time. As such, it is a reflection of the disappointing progress these countries have made toward full economic modernization (Shannon, 1989:89-90; Geisse and Sabatini, 1988:323-324).

Low income levels in both the formal and informal sector mean massive urban poverty and squalid living conditions. As we will see, general conditions in these cities are extremely unpleasant. Why then do workers come from the countryside? Wage levels may be higher in the cities, but it is likely that higher living costs wipe out any benefit. Hence, part of the reason people continue to come is simply that the lack of any opportunity for many in the countryside makes even the limited opportunities in the cities look attractive. In addition, even if the probability of real economic success is low, urban areas are also attractive because they provide at least the possibility of success:

> Third World cities . . . act like a giant Las Vegas in the sense that the bulk of their populations are gamblers, though the games are different. . . . The rewards [of city life] may look insignificant when compared to the excessively high price . . . in terms of daily life difficulties. . . [but] [t]he important thing is that there are rewards for some. The large cities are places of hope, while the drudgery of rural life looks hopeless (Sachs, 1988:337-339).

Special Characteristics and Problems

Not only has urbanization proceeded with extraordinary rapidity in the Third World, it has tended to concentrate in a limited number of very large cities. Small and medium-sized cities are fewer and have grown more slowly than one would expect (based on the United States experience) given overall levels of urbanization. Instead, one very large city (or a few large cities in the bigger countries) has been the primary focus of urbanization. The resulting giant cities are called *primate cities*. For example, Mexico City was projected to contain about 20 million people in 1990 (up from 14 million in 1980), representing 20 percent of the total population of the country. Some projections are for it to reach 35 million in 2025, making it the largest single metropolitan area in the world. It also dominates the Mexican economy. It accounts for over half of national non-agricultural economic activity, 35 percent of government employees, and almost 70 percent of national financial assets (Schteingart, 1988:270-289).

In part, primate cities are a legacy of the colonial past. During the colonial period each colony developed a single administrative center that also functioned as the center from which to collect production from the countryside for export and to import manufactured goods. Modern infrastructure was concentrated in the colonial capital to serve the needs of the import-export enterprises, colonial administrators, and the consumption needs of European colonists and native elites. The export facilities and internal transportation and communication systems were all oriented toward this city.

Once one city had this overwhelming advantage, it continued to be the most attractive location for new activities. It had the best infrastructure, the largest market for manufactured goods, the best living amenities for foreign business executives and native elites, a large pool of available labor, the best transportation and communication links, and the most developed business services. The primate city simply became the best location into which to introduce manufacturing activities and other business enterprises. In many cases, the primate city is the seat of national government, and the concerns of government officials for good conditions for themselves and to maintain urban civil peace lead them to further focus expenditures for services on the capital city (Palen, 1987:344-345).

There has been a debate about the effect of primate cities on economic development in Third World countries. On the one hand, many critics argue that concentration of economic activities in one city occurs at the expense of the rest of the country. The development of agriculture, the provision of services, and the creation of nonagricultural employment opportunities in outlying areas are retarded (Rondinelli, 1988:307-309). On the other hand, others have argued that primate cities represent the most efficient location for modern industrial activity, and hence, investment in those cities will provide the highest rate of return and the most rapid growth of the economy (Stark, 1980).

However, the effect of concentrating most urban growth in a limited number of large cities on the overall living conditions and quality of life in those cities is unambiguous. Growth has been so rapid, the population is so overwhelmingly poor, and the ultimate size of the populations is so huge that Third World cities are confronted with seemingly insurmountable problems (Palen, 1987:333-431; Yeung, 1988; Nagpaul, 1988; Rondinelli, 1988; Geisse and Sabatini, 1988; Sachs, 1988; Teune, 1988).

Housing supply has not even approximately kept up with demand. That has meant escalating land and rental housing costs. For more affluent segments of the population, the tight, expensive housing situation severely limits the size and quality of housing. For the great bulk of the population with extremely low incomes, it has meant being housed in squalid, crowded slums and even worse squatters' shanty towns. Government attempts to build even the most basic, low-income housing have not even made a dent in the need for such housing. These governments are themselves very poor, and the size of the population in need and its rate of growth greatly exceed the ability to commit government resources. The more fortunate find accommodations in tiny, rundown apartments or subdivided houses, often one family per room, without indoor water or sanitary facilities. The rest of the population (one-third or more in most cities) reside in flimsy shacks on tiny parcels of land for which they may pay rent to an owner or on which they *squat* (illegally occupy the site). In turn, they may own the shack (often built out of scavenged materials, sheets of tin, cardboard, and lumber scrap) or rent it from a slightly better-off "landlord" who owns several structures or rents out part of his own residence. Structures are crowded closely together along narrow dirt pathways with a limited number of narrow streets.

Slum areas usually lack even the most basic physical services: paved streets, piped water, sewers, garbage collection, and electricity. In squatters' settlements infrastructure (except, perhaps, electricity and a limited number of central water faucets) is almost totally lacking. As illegal squatters, residents are in no position to demand physical infrastructure or police, fire, or educational services (even if the government could afford to provide them). Open latrines and sewage ditches, lack of weather-tight and insect-proof housing, accumulating garbage, rat and insect infestations, contaminated and inadequate water supplies, and virtually no public health facilities make the slums and squatters' settlements squalid, fetid, unhealthy places to live.

Rapid urbanization has also contributed to grossly inadequate and over-utilized public physical and social services. Most of these cities have public service systems that would be minimally adequate (by even the most generous criteria) for populations only a fraction of their current size. Water, sewage, and garbage collection facilities are available for only the more affluent part of the population. Public transportation systems carry two and three times their engineered capacities and still do not meet the need for transportation. Streets and main thoroughfares are hopelessly congested. Construction of schools and the provision of teachers rarely have kept up with the growing population. Public medical facilities are of poor quality, massively over-crowded, and limited in number.

Pollution problems are also severe, getting rapidly worse, and represent immediate threats to urban health and general environmental quality. Third World cities have the worst pollution problems in the world. Industrial air and water pollution, smoke from cooking fires, growing automobile use, toxic waste dumping, lack of adequate sewage treatment and garbage disposal, and unsafe industrial practices all contribute to massive urban pollution problems. Many Third World cities already have pollution problems which harm the health of their populations. For example, pollution-caused respiratory disease and exposure to air and water-borne carcinogens and other toxins are common. Desperate to attract foreign investment, Third World governments have been hesitant to impose any pollution restrictions on foreign corporations. Indeed, some countries have been accepting waste from the advanced capitalist countries to earn desperately needed foreign exchange. Anxious to encourage domestic industry, lacking much capital for industrialization (let alone pollution control equipment), and faced with the need to increase production as fast as possible, Third World governments have emphasized industrialization at the expense of environmental damage.

Faced with these problems created by the rapid growth of giant cities, many governments in the Third World have made some attempts to encourage more decentralized urbanization and/or development of nonagricultural employment opportunities in rural areas. For the most part, these efforts have been limited in scope and have not had much effect on the pattern of urbanization. Perhaps the most ambitious efforts have been those in China. Observing the problems accompanying urbanization in the rest of the Third World, the Chinese government has made decentralized urbanization a cornerstone of its economic modernization program (Goldstein, 1988; Yueng, 1988; Chen, 1988).

In the 1950s, 1960s and early 1970s implementation of this approach involved relatively crude and coercive policies. Migration to the cities was regulated by permit. Peasants were organized into collective farms that they could not leave. Rural collectives were encouraged to start small-scale industrial enterprises. Little was invested in urban housing and infrastructure. These policies appear to have slowed the rate of urbanization. However, the overall strategy of modernization, of which they were part, yielded only mixed results. For example, small-scale industrial production on collective farms resulted in low quality goods produced at high prices, and collective agriculture raised agricultural output and peasant income only slowly. Subsequently, Chinese policy changed to one of directing investment to provincial cities and smaller market towns. At the same time, an increasingly strict system of population control sought to bring population growth to a rapid halt (and thereby, as a side benefit, slow urban growth). By the early 1980s a system of incentives and punishments was introduced to restrict couples to one child. The "responsibility" system in agriculture replaced most collective farms. Peasant families leased land from the collective and were free to farm as they pleased and sell most of their production on the open market. The hope was that this would increase rural incomes and encourage production of consumer goods for the farmers in towns and smaller cities. At the same time, private enterprise, foreign investment in manufacturing facilities, and increased reliance on markets to control prices and production decisions were introduced. Initially, agricultural production soared and the rate of industrialization increased. However, by the end of the 1980s China experienced growing economic difficulties and political unrest.

The change in policy also had mixed consequences for Chinese urbanization. With peasants now free to try to maximize their incomes by maximizing production, the labor of children has become more valuable. Consequently, there has been increasing resistance to family size limitation that will postpone population stabilization. Moreover, allowing free movement of peasants, the creation of private enterprises providing unrestricted urban employment, and the elimination of other economic controls meant fewer restrictions on the growth of China's large cities. The explosion of small enterprises in Chinese cities closely resembles the growth of the informal sector in other Third World cities. The fact that the state no longer guarantees employment has left increasing numbers of young workers looking for a means to support themselves. Foreign investment also tended to be concentrated in a few large cities, especially the special "free zones" around cities on the coast. Consequently, in the 1980s there were indications that large-scale industrialization was going to remain concentrated in a small number of large cities. The most extreme example of this tendency was Shanghai. Already China's largest port and biggest industrial center, it continued to grow very rapidly. By the late 1980s conditions and problems in Shanghai were similar in many respects to those in the largest of the primate cities in the rest of the Third World (Murphey, 1988).

In short, Third World governments have simply been overwhelmed by the rapid pace of urbanization and their very limited financial resources with which to deal with the problem. Continued rapid urbanization and even more austere government budgets as the result of economic difficulties and a huge foreign debt burden in the 1980s have meant that service levels continued to deteriorate. The short-term prospects for general improvements appear to be poor. Long-term improvements would depend upon much more rapid economic development, stabilizing overall population growth, and the end of massive rural-to-urban migration. Under those circumstances, urban governments in these countries might begin to marshall the resources to deal with their accumulating problems.

Main Points

1. Western European countries are economically advanced capitalist societies which experienced processes of industrialization and urbanization relatively similar to those in the United States. Currently, their urban areas continue to display significant similarities to those in the United States: suburbanization of population and industry, some decline of traditional industries, the continued success of central downtown districts as administrative centers, and growing reliance on the automobile.

2. Besides often having developed around a "historic core" of a pre-industrial city, Western European urban areas display differences from those in the United States which primarily reflect the greater intervention of government into the urban development process: green belts; new towns; tighter control on urban land use; attempts to decentralize urban development geographically; more government subsidized, multi-family housing; high levels of public services; and greater reliance on mass transit. Housing, traffic congestion, and pollution continue to be serious problems in these urban areas.

3. Tokyo shares with other advanced capitalist cities certain basic features: an administratively oriented downtown, growing suburbanization of population and industry, decline of older industries in the central city, and growing automobile use.

4. The land available for urban use is severely limited in Japan by topography and government policy. High-rise construction has been limited until

recently because of the threat of earthquake. The result is intense competition for the available land and very high prices. In turn, these high land costs have severely limited the size and quality of urban housing (almost all privately provided) and forced workers to look for housing far from their places of work.

5. Limited street capacity and government policy has meant extremely heavy reliance on public transportation in Japan, which is of good quality, but has not expanded rapidly enough to accommodate the growing population and increasing amount of commuting. Japan has been slow to invest in urban infrastructure and services, which are inadequate and of low quality (except for education). Until recently, extremely high levels of pollution had not prompted any effective control measures by government.

6. Eastern European urbanization has taken place in the context of state ownership of the economy, centralized economic planning, and the attempt to achieve maximum investment in industry by limiting consumption. Overall levels of production and national wealth are still much lower than in the advanced capitalist countries. The result has been cities where the requirements of industry have taken precedence over other considerations, and the resources available to meet the needs of the urban population have been limited.

7. In principle, urbanization in Eastern Europe was centrally planned. In practice the planning mechanisms worked poorly and the pressures to minimize costs resulted in an emerging urban ecology roughly analogous to that in capitalist countries. Despite efforts to increase the housing stock, housing remains cramped, of low quality, and in extremely short supply. Limited purchasing power and state policy means people have to rely on an extensive system of mass transit, which however, has not expanded fast enough to meet growing populations and increasing suburbanization. Many urban services, food, housing, transportation, medical care and the like are state-subsidized at nearly uniform low prices or provided free. That guarantees less inequality in living standards for the population, but state-provided goods and services are of low quality and in chronic short supply. Pollution problems are severe and there has been almost total neglect of pollution control.

8. The most rapid urbanization in the recent past has been in the Third World. Populations there are growing rapidly and also migrating from rural to urban areas. Migration is the result of a combination of the lack of real opportunity in the countryside and at least some prospects for employment in the cities. Most workers in the cities work in the very low-wage informal sector of the urban economy, which helps to subsidize the operation of the modern industrial sector. The resulting rapid urbanization has tended to concentrate in a limited number of cities which are quickly achieving gigantic size. These urban populations are extremely impoverished. The majority live in cramped, squalid slums or squatters' shanties. Modern urban services reach only a minority of the urban population, and water,

garbage, sewage, electrical, and communications systems are hopelessly overloaded and inadequate. Pollution levels are dangerously high and rising.

Key Terms

Formal Sector   The most "modernized" sectors of the economy in Third World countries, including such activities as large industrial plants, corporate and government offices, and large retail establishments.

Green belts   Areas adjoining cities in which urban development is prohibited.

Informal Sector   The sector of the economy in urban areas of the Third World which consists of small enterprises or self-employed workers producing a wide range of services and simple, often handicraft, goods.

Modernization   The process by which Third World countries are attempting to develop more productive and technologically sophisticated economies and the social and political institutions appropriate to such an economy.

New Towns   Planned satellite communities in suburban or exurban areas, often designed to provide places of residence, employment, shopping, and services.

Periphery   The poorest and least industrialized countries in the world, with per capita incomes of under $200 up to $1000 in 1987. They include China, India, sub-Saharan Africa, and a few of the poorest countries in Latin America.

Primate Cities   The "giant" cities that are the result of the concentration of Third World urbanization in a limited number of very large cities.

Semi-periphery   Those countries which have achieved partial industrialization, but continue to have substantial rural populations and relatively low per capita incomes of from $1000 to $4000 in 1987. They include most of the countries of Latin America, the Middle East, and a few of the smaller countries of Southeast and East Asia.

Suggested Reading

Dogan, Mattei and John Kasarda (eds). 1988. *The Metropolis Era*, vols. 1 & 2. Beverly Hills, CA: Sage. A collection of articles which summarize urban trends and problems in areas of the world and also examine conditions in a number of specific giant cities.

10

Urban Problems in Perspective

Outline of Topics

T he previous chapters have painted a fairly dismal picture of urban woe. That is because the urban problems of the United States really are quite serious. However, we need to put these problems into better perspective. Otherwise, we run the risk of falling into a common intellectual trap: there is a persistent tendency for observers of the American urban scene to see urban problems in a parochial and historically unconnected fashion. Each problem is viewed independently of the others and its seriousness is evaluated by a set of contemporary expectations or standards (which usually change even faster than the conditions being described). The result of this kind of thinking is a "crisis" mentality in which alarms are raised and dire predictions are made, only to have the problem forgotten when attention is drawn to yet another "crisis."

If we are to avoid this "Chicken Little" approach to urban problems, we need to put the problems discussed in previous chapters into both a comparitive and historical perspective. We have to examine how urban conditions in the United States differ from those of other societies. Comparing the United States to other countries will help highlight the extent to which our problems are the result of unique national circumstances or reflect tendencies common to many societies. We also need to consider the problems of the present in relation to the past. By doing so, we should be in a better position to evaluate current problems. Such an attempt should also help us better understand the broader structural and institutional context in which urban problems occur and from which most urban problems arise. In this final chapter, therefore, we will attempt to draw together a number of issues which have been raised and evaluate them both in an international and historical context.

Once we have established some sort of perspective on the urban problems we have discussed, we will be in a position to address a final important issue: the urban future. At the present "state of the art" in the social sciences it would be presumptuous to claim to be able to predict the urban future. However, we can at least attempt to think about it systematically.

Urban Conditions in a Global Context

The problems faced by United States urban areas clearly are not unique. The process of using industrial technology to concentrate millions of people together poses a set of basic challenges to every society that has urbanized. For example, all modern cities need to find a better way to deal with the wastes generated by industrial processes. However, the specific conditions under which urbanization has occurred has shaped both the ability of societies to confront those challenges and the specific methods which they have employed.

Not surprisingly, urban conditions in the United States are most similar to those in countries which share our basic level of wealth and system of political economy. The wealthy, capitalist, electoral democracies of Western Europe and Japan experienced an urbanization process roughly similar to our own. Resource allocation and land-use patterns basically reflect the operation of the market, in the context of economies dominated by large private corporations with considerable political power. All these countries now enjoy a level of wealth which allows a high standard of living and provides the resources for a high level of public services. They also confront many of the same problems that we do: what to do with automobile congestion, how to reduce pollution levels, how to assist those whom the private economy does not adequately support, how to meet the demand for affordable, good quality housing, and what to do about the decline of traditional manufacturing industries.

The key difference between the advanced capitalist countries in the last few decades has been the extent to which government has actively intervened to deal with urban problems and control the urbanization process. In general, Western European countries have relied the most on government action and Japan the least. The approach of the United States has been somewhere in between those of Western Europe and Japan. However, in the last decade, the role of the federal government in dealing with urban problems in the United States has been reduced. Similarly, concerned for their competitiveness in the international economy and facing slower economic growth, many Western European countries also have scaled back some of their more generous social programs.

Other than variations in average income (now narrowing) and the relative scarcity of urban land, these differences in government involvement go a long way toward explaining differences in urban conditions among the advanced capitalist countries. Western European cities have done the best in regard to those things which government can provide most effectively: social services, mass transit, and subsidized housing for the poor. The cost, of course, has been a greater diversion of private income to public purposes. In contrast, while the middle classes in the United States also enjoy very good conditions and even enjoy relatively good public amenities where those are provided by local government (in the affluent suburbs), many publicly provided urban services are more limited and the conditions faced by the economically disadvantaged are much worse. In other words, living conditions vary more in the United States, depending upon a family's private income. Moreover, progressive neglect and deterioration of the publicly provided physical infrastructure threatens even the suburban middle classes. Japan has been extremely slow in providing services not directly related to the success of its giant corporations. As a consequence, Japanese urban dwellers face the least desirable general living conditions among the advanced capitalist countries.

Overall, people in the formerly "state socialist" countries of Eastern Europe endure substantial hardship in comparison to urban residents in the advanced capitalist countries. The most important reason for this difference is economic. These are simply much poorer countries. However, the lack of economic resources was compounded by authoritarian governments that sought national power through a single-minded pursuit of rapid industrialization. Centrally planned economies based on state-owned enterprises gave these governments almost complete control over the allocation of economic resources. Both private consumption and public services were limited so that investment could be concentrated in heavy industry. For example, limited funds devoted to housing meant that urban housing was of poor quality and in chronic short supply. On the other hand, there was a commitment to provide universal employment security, subsidized housing and basic necessities, and universal access to a wide range of (often low quality) services. After initial success, the industrialization drive foundered, and these countries entered a period of economic stagnation and political unrest. Improvements in basic urban conditions will have to await the resolution of that crisis.

Urban problems are most daunting of all in the Third World. A number of factors make this urbanization different from that which occurred in the advanced industrial countries: (1) the extreme poverty of these countries, (2) unprecedented rates of population growth, (3) very high rates of urbanization (4) inadequate supplies of capital to invest in modern industrial production, (5) economies based on the exploitation of low-wage labor and (6) the tendency to develop primate cities. The resulting giant cities, teeming with desperately poor people, have simply been overwhelmed with problems. In comparison, urban problems in the United States look benign indeed.

Urban Problems in an Historical Context

American urban areas have always faced serious problems. As we saw in Chapter 1, many of the problems these areas now face are either

continuations of problems which arose in the past or are the consequences of trends which developed over a long period of time. In other
words, there is a significant degree of historical continuity to American
urban problems. However, that is not true in all cases. Some problems
are either new or significantly different from those of the past. So there
are historical discontinuities as well as continuities in urban problems.

Continuities

One persistent historical theme in American urban conditions and
problems has been their connection to various kinds of socio-economic
inequality. Throughout this book we have referred repeatedly to various
kinds of inequality in terms of income, education, opportunities for
employment, housing, treatment by government, access to transportation, and political influence. There is nothing new about this pervasive
inequality. Inequality has been a persistent fact of life in American
society from the very beginning. To be sure, in some ways and to some
degree (there is considerable debate on just how much), inequality has
been reduced over time. Such things as changing opportunities for
employment, the extension of legal rights and guarantees, and government "transfer payments" (taxation of the affluent to help the less
affluent) probably have had some moderating influence on the extent
of inequality in American society when examined over the long-term.

However, as we have seen, very significant inequality continues to
exist in American society. Moreover, in the last couple of decades, there
have been indications that certain kinds of inequalities are increasing.
For example, poverty increased in the 1980s relative to the 1970s,
homelessness became a serious urban problem, budgetary cutbacks
at all levels of government disproportionately affected the poor, and
the overall degree of income and wealth inequality increased.

The problem this inequality creates is not "merely" the problem that
some people are deprived relative to others in society. There are very
few problems which we have discussed which are not at least intensified
by continued inequality. For instance, many of these problems can be
directly linked to the continued existence of large numbers of the poor
and near poor in our urban areas. Some kinds of crime, the difficulties
faced by urban school systems, the persistence of slums and urban
decay, the financial crisis of the central cities, the heavy burdens on
the social-welfare system, the movement of the more affluent from the
central cities, and more generally, the continued debate over the
appropriate allocation of limited governmental resources can all be
linked to the persistence of large pockets of low-income people in urban
areas.

A second recurrent theme in American urban history has been that of how we, as a culture, perceive cities and urban life. As was pointed out in Chapter 3, Americans have a long tradition of being uneasy about urban life and longing for a mythological rural past of simplicity and close community ties. This "anti-urban bias" and romantic quest for community has repeatedly colored the American response to urban conditions and contributed directly and indirectly to the problems we have examined.

One consequence of the negative perception of urban life is that Americans have spent considerable effort trying to run away from or ignore cities. At least in part, the various waves of suburbanization which have characterized this century (and the more recent nonmetropolitan growth) may be seen as a manifestation of this tendency. Of course, only the more affluent segments of the population have been able to indulge in the luxury of this sort of escapism. And part of the basis for dislike of cities is that they have always been seen as centers of lower-class residence. Once established in our suburban enclaves, we have tried to insulate ourselves from the "evils" and problems of the cities by erecting zoning barriers, supporting discriminatory real estate practices, resisting annexation and regional government, and opposing those policies and programs which would help the cities deal with their problems.

More generally, rural nostalgia and resentment of things urban have repeatedly provided an ideological basis and justification for socio-political movements seeking to reverse social or cultural trends of which they disapprove. The evils of modern society are contrasted with the "simple virtues" of the rural past, and these movements call for the reestablishment of cultural or social patterns presumed to have existed in rural America. Again, the first targets (or victims) of these movements often have been efforts to deal with the problems of the cities and the needs of urban population groups (such as foreign immigrants or the poor).

On a more sophisticated level, this distrust or ambivalence felt toward cities has often extended even to intellectual observers of American cities. For instance, we saw that what has been called the "classical view" of urban society among American social scientists (and some of their European predecessors) primarily focused on the negative aspects of urban life. At the very least, these theories have reinforced popular biases against the cities. In some cases, they may also have led to an incorrect identification of the problems and needs of urban communities (e.g., the view that the real problem of the urban poor was their "social disorganization") and hence to the misdirection of public policy and resources.

Of course, this anti-urban bias has not meant a total refusal to collectively address urban problems. There have been several waves of urban reform. Programs adopted during the Great Society period (1960s), the New Deal (1930s), and the Progressive Era (1900s) all included major elements intended to ameliorate urban conditions. More recently, public opinion polls in the 1980s showed high levels of public concern for such problems as pollution and homelessness. Although some of the reforms proposed were biased by anti-urbanism (e.g., attempts to weaken the power of immigrant-based political machines in the early part of this century), others represented sincere attempts to deal with urban problems. Private, volunteer efforts to deal with such things as urban poverty or homelessness also have been a recurrent feature of the urban scene. Some of these efforts had a real impact on improving urban conditions. Still, one cannot help but be struck by the limited nature of these efforts and the fact that the impulse toward reform was quickly dissipated.

The constraints imposed by our particular system of "political economy" is a third historical continuity. Despite an immense increase in the size and scope of governmental activities, the United States political system has continued to operate within a particular institutional context. That framework consists of a capitalist economic system and a social-class system in which there is considerable economic inequality and a system of political influence which favors the affluent.

Within a capitalist society, there is, almost by definition, considerable tension between the demands that government solve problems and the desire of private interests to make decisions in their own self-interest, dispose of property as they please, and allocate resources as they choose. Moreover, not all groups have equal political power. While there is considerable room for debate on how centralized political power is, it seems clear that some groups are disproportionately influential in the political system. They may not get their way all the time, but they have more say than others. Generally speaking, these more influential groups consist of the more affluent and the large corporations which dominate the private economy. As a result, the tension between the private sector and the government has always been most acute when government has attempted to tax or regulate the activities of the more affluent and (especially in the last century) the large corporations. Conversely, these powerful groups have also been in a better position to make demands on government for services and resources which benefit them.

We have observed the consequences of this situation repeatedly in our examination of urban problems and trends. The basic direction of urban development has depended on corporations' decisions regarding the nature and location of their investments. We have seen that this power to direct the location of investment severely constrains the actions of local governments. They feel that they must please corporate interests to maintain the local economy. We have also seen that the role of government has frequently been limited to a "reactive" role concerning corporate investment decisions. When these decisions have created problems for various groups or localities or generated the need for government services, government has then stepped in to provide additional services and repair the social or physical damage. Hence, much of the focus of government effort has been on responding to, rather than controlling or preventing, the problems created by private economic decisions.

Even when the government has taken a more "activist" role in attempts to deal with urban problems, it has remained especially sensitive to the interests and concerns of the more affluent and the large corporations. We saw this, for example, in the apparently greater tolerance of the criminal justice system in dealing with white-collar crime, as well as the way in which urban renewal turned into displacement of the poor from areas adjacent to business districts. Similarly, we saw that when the government intervened in the urban housing market, the bulk of the available resources was employed to provide subsidies for more affluent home buyers, protect the interests of the banks, and expand the market for private building contractors.

This bias in government policy does not mean that various programs have not benefited the less affluent and less powerful. Nor should we conclude that corporations and the wealthy always have received everything that they have wanted. However, government policy has displayed a clear tendency to consider the interests and respond to the demands of some groups more than others.

Discontinuities

It should also be obvious that not all the problems urban areas face today are the same as those of the past. In some very important ways, both the specific problems urban areas now face and the circumstances under which they are occurring are different from the past.

One clear difference is simply that many urban areas now face the problems of age rather than the problems of newness and growth. (The obvious exceptions to this pattern are the newer urban growth areas.) For the first time in our history, we have a significant number of large, old cities. These cities' problems are not those of the past: rapid population growth, the construction of service and physical infrastructures, and rapid land-use conversions. Instead, they now face the problems of maturity: economic bases consisting of old factories and stagnant industries, a rapidly aging housing stock, population losses or stagnation, limited ability to increase tax revenues, and worn-out, antiquated physical infrastructures.

The large concentration of blacks in many central cities represents another new problem. It would be a mistake to assume that the problems blacks now face are the same as the problems that foreign immigrants faced in the past. Granted, there are obvious similarities. There are also fundamental differences. The immigrants came to the central cities when employment opportunities for unskilled, uneducated workers were growing rapidly. Educational requirements for occupational advancement were less, and changes in the nature of employment opportunities favored upward social mobility. Blacks in the cities now face a decline in the absolute numbers of jobs, even more rapid declines in unskilled jobs, greater educational barriers to employment, and increasing competition for jobs in middle-class occupations. At the same time, the nature of the racial prejudice and discrimination that blacks have faced has been more pervasive, deeply held, and harder to avoid (because of skin color) than the ethnic prejudice and discrimination faced by immigrant ethnic groups. On balance, it thus appears likely that blacks have faced more obstacles and problems than the urban migrants who preceded them.

Public awareness of and tolerance for certain conditions and problems has also changed. As a consequence, what people consider an "urban problem" in which government should become involved has changed. We are much less tolerant of abusive or corrupt behavior on the part of the police and public officials. Awareness of the potential seriousness of environmental pollution has increased immensely in the last two decades. Despite continued manifestations of prejudice and discrimination, tolerance for racism and its consequences certainly is much less than before. In general, our ideas of "acceptable" conditions of life have undergone considerable upgrading, and our expectations about the responsibility of government in guaranteeing certain minimum conditions have increased immensely. The huge increase in public concern about crime reflects both changing perceptions of its threat and real increases in the commission of some kinds of crime.

American urban areas face both these new problems and the problems inherited from the past under rapidly changing conditions which influence both the nature of the problems and our response to them. Despite the apparent prosperity of the 1980s and relief from the high inflation and rising energy prices of the late 1970s, some long-term economic trends remain ominous. Whole industries that were once the basis of much of our economic success and the primary support of our older industrial regions are either stagnant or in decline. Even many of the industries which relocated to the South in the 1970s have begun to experience difficulty dealing with foreign competition. This has only been partially balanced by the growth of the newer high technology industries. In addition, as we have seen, the economic bene-fits of this new industrial growth have not been distributed equally between the regions or among categories of workers. The overall nation-al loss of better-paying industrial work and the rapid growth of lower-paying service employment has been an especially disturbing trend.

One consequence of these difficulties is that our ability to deal with urban problems has been greatly reduced. Much of the past improvement in urban conditions was simply a reflection of the growing affluence of the urban population. Moreover, the improvements in conditions brought about by government actions were possible because economic growth provided the resources to expand government activities. With slower economic growth, government activity must compete with private investment and consumption for resources. Hence, expansion of government activities, much more than in the past, can be purchased only at the cost of withdrawing an increasing proportion of the resources from the private economy. This reduces the potential of the private economy for growth based on private investment.

That dilemma was amply demonstrated in the 1980s. Total federal expenditures as a percentage of the GNP remained the same and budgetary growth was limited as a matter of public policy. Commitment to a military build-up therefore occurred at the expense of other programs. Disproportionately, social programs (many urban-oriented) were the ones that suffered. At the same time, tax cuts passed in the hope of stimulating private investment reduced federal income as a percent of GNP. Unfortunately, that also meant growing deficits which had the effect of absorbing private capital, consuming more of the federal budget to pay interest on the debt, and driving up interest rates, making long-term productive investment unattractive relative to high yield, short-term financial speculation. The overall effect was to create a budgetary crisis (at the federal, state, and local level) as federal domestic expenditures were tightened. Investments in government infrastructure, education, and various social needs were limited. We now face accumulating problems, many of which may call for new government initiatives as the result of low expenditure levels in the 1980s.

Long-term structural changes in the economy have increasingly created another limitation on local, state, and even federal efforts to deal with urban problems. Large, often multinational, corporations have come to dominate more and more of the economy. One thing this means is that industry is more than ever before both willing and able to transfer operations to those places it regards as most favorable to profitable operations. If government in a particular locality, region, or country attempts to increase taxes, impose regulations, or protect efforts at unionization, it runs the risk of having its economic base undermined by industrial flight. Such flight carries with it the prospect both of increasing the problems faced by government because of economic decline and reducing the ability to raise revenues to deal with the problems. This is already a major problem in the older industrial regions.

Over the longer term, we may well face additional economic problems associated with increasing cost and declining availability of energy and other resources. Ample petroleum supplies in the 1980s should not blind us to the long-term limited supply of that resource. (Domestic petroleum supplies will be depleted even sooner.) While domestic coal and (to lesser degree) natural gas supplies are much more ample, and alternative technologies may offer longer-term solutions, conversion to new sources will be costly. In addition the need to deal with increasingly complex and dangerous problems of environmental deterioration caused by fossil fuel burning are becoming very pressing. The need to do something about these environmental problems will further complicate our energy problems and certainly will entail higher costs. These increasing costs will directly affect such things as transportation and industrial production and also limit the resources available to deal with other urban problems.

Of course, the story of the last two decades has not been simply one of industrial decline. Business and financial services have flourished in the last two decades. The United States economy has shifted in the direction of functioning as a "command center" for the management of enterprises and the provision of capital and technological expertise for an increasingly integrated world market. This trend has had highly visible consequences for a few of our large cities. Their central business districts have continued to function as centers of administration, finance, and communication activities. Central business districts have retained their economic importance despite the loss of some white-collar office operations and the frequent failure of attempts to maintain these districts as centers of mass-market retailing. This resilience seems to be especially marked in a few large central cities, and may portend a new economic role for these cities.

Certain recent social trends also represent relatively new developments with at least a potential effect on future urban conditions. For example, the nature of the households which make up the urban population have changed markedly since the 1950s. The number of children per family is down to around two. The proportion of married women (including those with young children) who work has risen substantially. The majority of married-couple households now have two wage earners. The marriage rate has fallen slightly, and the number of people who never marry has increased. The number of single-parent households has risen substantially. As the baby-boom generation ages in the next two decades, there will be a bulge in the population of middle-aged couples who have completed their child-rearing years. When this group retires (after 2015), a very rapidly growing proportion of households will consist of the elderly.

Associated with these family composition trends have been trends in the economic circumstances of households over the last two decades. Perhaps the most important of those trends have been the declining availability of good-paying industrial jobs (which has meant declines in real wages for less educated workers) and virtually stagnant purchasing power of all workers except those at the top of the occupational structure. These trends account for the pressure on even middle-class households to have two wage earners. In turn, women's participation in the labor force has been a major motivation to have few or no children. Only married-couple, dual-income households have seen significant increases in income (per family member), and those who have remained childless have fared best of all. Conversely, single-earner families have lost ground, and single-earner families (especially those headed by women) with children have fared very badly indeed. As we have seen, the growth of the latter type of household contributed to the growth of poverty in the 1980s (Albeda and Tilly, 1990).

As we have already seen, these household composition and income trends also have had, and probably will continue to have, other major impacts on urban conditions. For example, better educated, childless households provided the major market for housing in gentrified neighborhoods. A smaller proportion of the population seems likely to be attracted to traditional suburban single-family homes. The large number of households with few or no children means that there is less need for the space of the conventional suburban house. Such households are also less concerned with child-oriented services such as schools and recreation facilities. Working couples are less willing to devote time to commuting and house upkeep and prefer to spend time on adult-oriented leisure activities. On the other hand, single-earner households with children are those who are most at risk from rising housing costs and make up a growing proportion of those who are homeless. (See Chapter 5.)

Another fundamental change which we now confront in regard to our urban problems has to do with the extent of the role of government. Compared to the earlier part of the century, we depend much more on the services government provides. Large numbers of people in our urban areas depend on government for income as employees, pensioners, and recipients of various transfer payments (e.g., welfare, food stamps, Medicare). Government absorbs a major portion of our total national income and is a major purchaser in our economy. Tax policies, economic policies, and regulations have a major impact on business operations. We have seen repeatedly what this means in terms of urban developments and problems. Much of what occurs in urban areas is either caused by or strongly influenced by government policies. Indeed, what we have seen is that government is not only an agency for solving urban problems, it also has been a source of them.

However, the economic trends of the last two decades have contributed to a resistance to government involvement. Some groups and individuals have been increasingly unwilling to pay the taxes necessary to support existing levels of public services or to provide the resources for additional government initiatives. At the same time, there has been growing distrust of government and increased skepticism about the ability and effectiveness of government to deal with problems. The more affluent have become more concerned with holding on to their existing standard of living and less sympathetic toward the problems of the less fortunate.

Evaluation: Urban Problems Past and Present

Where do all these considerations leave us? How do our present problems stack up against those of the past?

On the positive side, there clearly are good reasons to have a sense of urban progress. Judged by a set of absolute standards based on conditions in the past, many of the "old" problems of the urban past are now less severe. This is especially true of those which were linked to economic conditions and the standard of living. Certainly, general living conditions are immensely better than they were in our early industrial cities. We are much safer, healthier, and more comfortable than were our urban forbearers. In addition, many of the other problems of the urban past are at least not much worse today (e.g., relative inequality and deprivation). Some are probably less severe (e.g., racism, ease of transportation). Many of our "new" problems are simply the result of rapidly rising expectations (e.g., housing) or higher standards and better knowledge (e.g., pollution). In the light of the past then, these problems are not nearly as severe as they appear to us. Finally, some of the things which observers in the past considered as fundamental problems of urban areas now appear to be less severe than they feared (e.g., "social disorganization"). On balance, general conditions in our urban areas are much better than they were at the end of the 19th century.

On the negative side however, urban problems remain serious. Even a partial list of some of the issues which have been addressed in previous chapters is sobering. While we have made progress in improving general living conditions, many urban dwellers live under conditions which, given our general affluence, are offensive, demeaning, demoralizing, and debilitating. Relative deprivation is real deprivation. Urban poverty not only has not gone away in the recent past, it has increased. That we were ignorant of the effects of pollution a century ago does not make it any less of a threat now. Moreover, we are now facing the effects of world-wide environmental disruption with potential consequences that we are only now beginning to grasp. The threat of service retrenchment or breakdown and governmental insolvency in the central cities is a problem which affects millions of urban residents. Our failure to maintain the basic physical infrastructure of our metropolitan areas threatens not only to affect the quality of life but also the efficiency and competitiveness of our industry. The unmet social and physical needs of the disadvantaged even in our growing urban areas is a time bomb ticking behind the glittering facades of those cities. The energy inefficiency of our transportation system represents a potential "Achilles heel" of our sprawling, low-density urban complexes. Water supply, pollution, and waste removal represent problems which will require very expensive solutions during a time of limited governmental resources. Economic trends may create new problems and limit our ability to respond to them. Under conditions in which the total economic "pie" is not growing very much, there may be increased political conflict over how to divide it up between various groups and problems.

Thus, there are valid historical grounds to be concerned about both current urban conditions and future trends. The next generation of urban dwellers is not likely to be sympathetic to our complacent argument that things are better now than they were in the past if we allow our problems to accumulate and conditions to deteriorate in the future.

The Urban Future: Emerging City Types

It is not possible to predict the precise nature of urban development in the next quarter century. There are simply too many unpredictable factors. Nonetheless, it is possible to examine what would happen if current trends were to continue. This "projection" cannot hope to be more than a crude approximation of what will, in fact, happen. It is a useful exercise primarily because it addresses the possible implications of current trends and is, thereby, another way of evaluating those trends.

There has always been considerable variation in United States urban areas in terms not only of size, but also economic activities. John Logan and Harvey Molotch (1987) argue that, as a result, the trends we have discussed will have different impacts on each urban area. They contend that five general types of cities will emerge, reflecting an emphasis on a particular kind of economic activity. Of course, most urban areas will combine some or all of these activities. Indeed, one of the reasons for the unusually rapid growth of the Los Angles basin has been that it has combined most of these activities. However, in most cases, Logan and Molotch argue each area will become more specialized in one of them. Our discussion here will generally follow Logan and Molotch, but will expand on their argument to deal specifically with some of the issues addressed in the previous chapters.

International Headquarters Cities

A few of our largest cities have traditionally been the location for the headquarters of a large percentage of our national corporations and have also functioned as national or regional financial centers. Certain trends in the national and world economy suggest that these cities will continue to experience similar growth, along with the growth of the business services necessary to those operations (e.g., corporate law firms, investment houses, marketing firms, engineering consultants, and accountants). Corporate consolidation (through mergers and acquisitions) is further concentrating the administration of corporations in the hands of a few giant companies. Expansion of overseas operations, given modern transportation and communication, allow even multinational companies to administer their operations from one main administrative center. As we saw in Chapter 2, there is less and less connection between the location of productive facilities and corporate headquarters. The growing integration of the world economy into a single world market (or at least a few giant regional ones) and electronic communications and computing capabilities have also created a single vast financial system. This system has a small number of central financial markets operated by relatively a select group of increasingly large financial institutions located in a few large cities (e.g., Zurich, London, New York, and Tokyo). The result is that these cities are becoming headquarters for the administration and finance of corporations whose scope of operations is global. In addition, these same centers are the logical locations for branch offices of foreign corporations doing business in a particular country.

In these cities, central business districts have continued to experience rapid expansion. The concentration of high status managers and professionals there also provides markets for luxury retail goods, restaurants, hotels, and cultural activities. It is in these cities that centrally located residential districts have experienced the most gentrification. Not surprisingly, the cost of housing has skyrocketed, and the market for luxury housing experienced a boom in the 1980s. (Like most booms in the housing market, the result was overbuilding and overpricing which led to a slowdown in many of these housing markets in the early 1990s.) In most of these cities, government, anxious to encourage the boom, poured resources into these central office districts and gentrifying neighborhoods to fund such things as cultural facilities, convention centers, and slum removal. The result of these trends has been cities with glittering cores of prosperous business districts, affluent neighborhoods, restored parks, and upgraded recreational and leisure activities. Journalistic observers of these developments have proclaimed that an "urban renaissance" is underway.

Such a judgment may be premature. In most such cities, economic development has been uneven. The cores may glitter, but slums continue to fester. Headquarters cities do provide employment for large numbers of high status managers and professionals. Other employment trends in most of them are less hopeful. The largest percentage of new jobs created by headquarters operations and financial institutions are low-paid clerical positions. The other growth area is in retail trade and services, again dominated by low-paid workers. At the same time, in most of these cities the better paid manufacturing jobs, that less educated and skilled workers used to do, continue to disappear. Unemployment (especially among black males) remains high. "Booming" New York and Los Angles both had almost one-fourth of their households below the poverty line in the mid-1980s. It is hardly coincidental that homelessness became a visible and serious problem in our largest cities in the last decade. What appears to be emerging in these cities is a bipolar class system composed of an affluent managerial and professional class at one end and an impoverished class of working poor and unemployed at the other. One observer of New York City even argues that what is emerging in the poor neighborhoods of that city resembles conditions in the Third World, in that there has been a rapid growth of the informal sector of the economy (Sassen-Koob, 1987).

Hence, even in these cities, economic revival does not appear to be enough to provide the tax base necessary to reverse the decline in city services. (New York started the 1990s with another financial crisis.) City governments have concentrated on providing high quality services to prosperous areas. It appears likely that they will be forced to allow continued deterioration of such things as the streets, schools, police protection, transportation, and fire protection outside those areas. Continued poverty, low service levels, and the displacement of the poor from central areas of the city will result in spreading urban decay. Eventually, this urban decay will spill over in a major way (some already has) into the inner ring of suburbs. Many of the problems discussed in earlier chapters therefore will continue in these cities, although their location will have shifted away from city centers.

The suburban areas (except for the older working class and industrial suburbs) of these cities continued to prosper in the 1980s. To the extent that their prosperity is not tied to traditional manufacturing industry, that trend seems likely to continue. More suburban office complexes, often adjacent to malls, are creating mini-downtowns. Routine, clerical operations involving large numbers of workers are less costly in the suburbs (because of lower rental costs and an ample supply of trained workers). Some kinds of corporate headquarters operations, such as trucking firms and wholesale distributors, do not require a downtown location and have been moving to the suburbs. In some cities (e.g., Boston, Los Angeles) various kinds of high-tech manufacturing are concentrated in suburban locations. The trend in the growing suburban areas is thus one in which there will be even more "city" activities (e.g., offices, factories, and central shopping areas). The central city consequently will be even more irrelevant to most suburban workers, except in the bedroom communities of high status managers and professionals who mostly will continue their downtown employment). Increasing numbers of clerical workers, rising land costs, and the economic and social trends discussed above may also lead to further increases in the amount of multi-family housing in the suburban areas of larger cities.

Innovation Centers

The American economy has become increasingly dependent on research and development activity to maintain its competitiveness. Most of our newer industry has been spawned by that activity. In addition, a major source of technical innovation in the last few decades has been military research. Certain types of research and development, carried on by a combination of government agencies, private firms, and nonprofit institutions, do not need to be near either production facilities or corporate headquarters. Rather, they are most dependent upon the ability to attract and/or interact with highly trained technical professionals. Consequently, research and development facilities have tended to concentrate together to take advantage of existing labor pools of needed professionals. Often they have been consciously planned and subsidized by government and have tended to be located near major research universities. Examples of innovation centers include Austin, Texas; Cambridge, Massachusetts; the Silicon Valley in Northern California; and the Research Triangle area of North Carolina.

These innovation centers tend to dominate the smaller cities where they are usually located. The professionals who work in them expect high quality services (e.g., education) and numerous cultural and recreational facilities. Housing costs (due to rapid growth and an affluent population) and taxes (to pay for services) usually are relatively high. That often causes difficulties for the large number of lower-paid service workers employed in most universities and in the research facilities. High-tech firms that are the spin off of research activities provide some industrial employment. However, once a production process becomes large-scale and routine, the search for lower wages and land costs is likely to mean relocation of the production facilities. (That has already happened in the computer industry in Silicon Valley.)

Module Production Places

As we have seen, traditional forms of industrial production have become increasingly flexible in terms of where they are located. They need not be near corporate headquarters, or even in the same country. They are located where overall costs are lowest and the degree of labor control is greatest. For most industries, there is a large number of places which will meet their basic production requirements. Hence, these locations are expendable. If the relative advantage of a place declines, corporations have little long-term commitment to remaining and will seek newer, more attractive locations. That means that cities (and their workers) are in competition with one another for large-scale industrial investment. With increasing global competition among corporations, the competition for industrial investment has also become global. United States steel workers not only compete with those in Japan and Europe but also those in South Korea and Brazil.

Those cities which cannot offer what is required to specialize in nonindustrial activities appear to be relegated to function as "production modules:" more or less interchangeable components of industrial production processes. To attract investment they will have to offer a mix of cheap land, low taxes, trained workers, docile labor forces (i.e., weak unions), low wages, minimal regulation, and good transportation links. That does not necessarily mean that each place has to have the lowest wages or taxes compared to its competitors. Rather, it has to have the most attractive combination of factors relative to the needs of particular industries. For some industries (e.g., garment making) where the primary concern is labor costs, cities in the Third World appear to be winning. Producers of toxic chemicals have been fleeing the United States across the border to Northern Mexico, where environmental regulation is virtually nonexistent. In other cases, locations in the United States remain the most attractive. Witness, for example, the substantial investment of Japanese auto manufacturers in final assembly plants in the United States, though not in the big cities.

Even those metropolitan areas which are relatively successful in this competition for corporate investment face an uncertain future. Success will always be contingent upon maintaining attractiveness in a rapidly changing world economy. For example, attracting enough investment to achieve full employment will tend to drive up labor costs and decrease competitiveness. Many communities in the South, which attracted industry with low wages, now find themselves losing out to low-wage areas in the Third World. Hence, industrially-oriented metropolitan areas will be locked into a permanently dependent relationship with corporate investors. Whether that will allow them to raise taxes, provide services, or control development in order to benefit their areas seems doubtful. Consequently, most of the urban problems we have discussed here, especially those relating to poverty and low service levels, seem likely to persist even in industrial growth centers. The experience of the Sunbelt cities during the 1970s seems to be instructive. Even though they enjoyed rapid growth, relatively high levels of poverty persisted and service levels remained low. In similar areas, attempts to revive the city center will enjoy only limited success, since their ability to function as corporate headquarters will be limited. The experience of Akron-Canton, Ohio is suggestive. All but one of the giant tire companies centered there is now owned by foreign corporations with headquarters elsewhere, although a number of tire plants still remain.

In addition, not all metropolitan areas are likely to be winners. Some of our older industrial cities have been only marginally successful in attracting new industry. For example, David Perry (1987) argues that the Buffalo, New York region is a good example of a declining, old industrial center. Buffalo's experience suggests an ominous future for such metropolitan areas. These cities persist as regional marketing and financial centers and attempt to market themselves as places with a large pool of unemployed or low-wage workers. As industrial jobs have declined, most job creation has been in the low-wage service sector. Out-migration is high, and those who remain are the old and least-skilled. An increasing percentage of the population is dependent on welfare (if they are young) or social security (if they are old). Long-term unemployment means expansion of the informal economy among discouraged workers. Declining income levels and growing poverty imply increasing decay of the oldest part of the housing stock. Central business districts are increasingly moribund and more dependent on such things as government office buildings. Central city governments have been especially hard hit. Rapid declines in their tax bases have had devastating impacts on their ability to deliver services and repair infrastructure. Their declining populations are increasingly poor. These cities are coming to function as reservations of the unemployed or subemployed poor. In short, what appears to be emerging are a number of chronically depressed metropolitan areas in which urban conditions appear likely to continue to deteriorate.

Third World Entrepot Cities

Another kind of emerging city is also tied to global economic trends: the "entrepot city" or intermediary city. Examples include Miami, El Paso, Brownsville, and San Diego. They have large numbers of legal and illegal immigrants (mostly Hispanic). These "new immigrants" have tended to concentrate disproportionately in a few areas. Limited skills and/or their illegal status make these workers willing to accept very low wages and unpleasant working conditions. Hence, urban economies in these areas are increasingly based on the exploitation of low-wage labor. These workers are employed in service work (e.g., the tourist industry in Miami), illegal sweatshops (e.g., garment making), and even high-tech industries which require low-wage, semi-skilled workers. What appears to be emerging in the United States are areas in some cities which function economically much like cities in the Third World. Their basic economic activities are those based on the exploitation of low-wage labor. Hence, some industries, instead of relocating their plants in the Third World, are taking advantage of the emerging "internal periphery" of entrepot cities.

These border cities are also trade and financial centers for importing, marketing, and distributing imports (including illegal drugs) and exports, especially to Latin America. Miami has become a city essentially tied to Latin America. Cities along the border with Mexico are increasingly integrated into a "Rio Grande valley" economy operating on both sides of the border (see Bloomberg and Martinez-Sandoval, 1982).

Retirement Centers

In another three decades, more than one-fifth of the United States population will be elderly. In addition, more workers are retiring early. Increasingly, more of this growing elderly population is migrating to cities whose climate and other amenities make them attractive places to retire.

Some of these retirement centers contain relatively high-income residents. They are in a position to offer the high levels of services and support for the elderly because they have local tax resources similar to affluent suburbs. However, more typically, while most are not officially poor, residents of retirement communities are lower income. Their income is heavily dependent on Social Security payments. At the same time, especially among those of more advanced age, their service needs are relatively great. Hence, what will happen in these communities depends on future developments in the federal provision of services for the elderly. If the federal government leaves service provision to the elderly primarily in the hands of the private sector or local government, these retirement centers will be faced with service demands which will outstrip local tax resources. The result could be "retirement slums" in which the local support networks are inadequate. Since women live longer and tend to have much lower retirement incomes if they are divorced or widowed than do married couples or men, it may mean that we can anticipate the development of ". . . old people's slum cities, disproportionately female, dependent, and empty of resources" (Logan and Molotch, 1987:277).

Main Points

1. Urban conditions must be evaluated in relation to those of other countries and in the past.
2. United States urban conditions are similar to those of other advanced capitalist countries. However, the extent of government intervention varies and has some effect on urban conditions in those countries. Urban conditions in the rest of the world are substantially worse than those in the United States.
3. Some problems urban areas face arose in the past or are the consequence of trends which developed over time. Some of the continuities with the urban past include: continued inequality and the problems associated with inequality, the quest for community, and the relative success of powerful economic interests to either limit government actions or use government for their own benefit.

4. Other urban problems or the context in which our problems develop differ from those in the past: the aging of older cities, the problems faced by blacks, public awareness of and tolerance for certain urban problems, the growing importance of relative rather than absolute deprivation, the effects of a changing economy, our changing ability and/or willingness to deal with urban problems, the dilemmas raised by continued reliance on fossil fuels, the effects of changing family composition and income levels, and the extent urban conditions are shaped by government actions.

5. If current trends continue, five major kinds of urban areas seem likely to emerge: international headquarters cities, research centers, module production places, entrepot cities, and retirement centers. While the central economic activities and relative economic prosperity of these cities is likely to vary substantially, most of them will continue to be likely to encounter most of the problems currently being faced by various urban areas in the United States.

Suggested Reading

Allman, T.C. 1978. "The Urban Crisis Leaves Town." *Harpers Magazine*, December, 1978. An argument for the notion that urban revitalization will be limited and will not eliminate many of the fundamental problems of the older metropolitan areas. In the light of the events of the 1980s this article retains its relevance.

Logan, John and Harvey Molotch. 1987. "The Dependent Future." Chapter Seven in *Urban Fortunes*. Berkeley, CA: University of California. This discussion will amplify the urban scenarios addressed in this chapter.

References

Achtenberg, Emily and Peter Marcuse. 1986. "Toward the Decommodification of Housing." In *Critical Perspectives on Housing*, edited by R. Bratt, C. Hartman, and A. Meyerson. Philadelphia: Temple University Press.

Adams, Bert. 1968. *Kinship in an Urban Setting*. Chicago: Markham.

Adams, James. 1989. *The Big Fix: Inside the S&L Scandal*. New York: Wiley.

Albelda, Randy and Chris Tilly. 1990. "What's Work Got to Do With It?" *Dollars and Sense* 154:16-18.

Alford, Robert and Roger Friedland. 1975. "Political Participation and Public Power." In *Annual Review of Sociology*, edited by A. Inkles. Palo Alto, CA: Annual Reviews.

Anderson, Charles H. 1974. "The Poor." In *Toward a New Sociology*, 2nd ed. Homewood, IL: Dorsey Press.

Apgar, William and H. James Brown. 1988. *The State of the Nation's Housing, 1988*. Cambridge, MA: Harvard University Joint Center for Housing Studies.

Armour, David. 1972. "The Evidence on Busing." *The Public Interest* 28:90-126.

Bahl, Roy. 1984. *Financing State and Local Government in the 1980's*. New York: Oxford University Press.

Bahl, Roy and Larry Schroeder. 1978. "The Outlook for City Fiscal Performance in Declining Regions." In *The Fiscal Outlook for Cities*, edited by R. Bahl. Syracuse, NY: Syracuse University.

Bakalis, Michael. 1987. "City's Schools Need Emergency Surgery: Decentralization Urged as a First Step." *Chicago Sun Times* 6/17/87:33.

Baldassare, Mark. 1989. "Public Support for Regional Government in New Suburbia." *Urban Affairs Quarterly* 24:460-469.

_____. 1978. *Crowding in Urban America* Berkeley, CA: University of California.

Ballantine, Jeanne. 1989. *Sociology of Education*. Englewood Cliffs: Prentice-Hall.

Banfield, Edward and James Wilson. 1966. *City Politics*. New York: Vintage.

Barber, Bernard. 1957. *Social Stratification*. New York: Harcourt Brace.

Barlow, Hugh. 1990. *Introduction to Criminology*. Glenview, IL: Scott, Foresman.

Barry, Patrick. 1989. "Downtown Transit: Lessons From Other Cities." *Transit Brief*. Chicago: Metropolitan Planning Council.

Beeghley, Leonard. 1988. "Individual and Structural Explanations of Poverty." *Population Research and Policy Review* 7:201-232.

_____. 1983. *Living Poorly in America*. New York: Praeger Publishers.

Bell, Wendell. 1958. "Social Choice, Life Styles and Suburban Residence." In *The Suburban Community*, edited by W. Dobriner. New York: Putnam.

Bendick, Marc and David Rasmussen. 1986. "Enterprise Zones and Inner-City Economic Revitalization." In *Reagan and the Cities*, edited by G. Peterson and C. Lewis. Washington, DC: The Urban Institute.

Bendix, Reinhard. 1960. *Max Weber: An Intellectual Portrait*. Garden City, NY: Doubleday.

Berry, Brian. 1973. *The Human Consequences of Urbanization*. New York: St. Martin's Press.

Berry, Brian and Donald Dahlman. 1978. "Population Redistribution in the United States." *Population and Development Review* 3:468.

Berry, Brian and Phillip Rees. 1969. "The Factorial Ecology of Calcutta." *American Journal of Sociology* 74:445-491.

Beyond Gridlock: The Future of Mobility as the Public Sees It. 1988. Washington, DC: Advisory Committee on Highway Policy, 2020 Transportation Program.

"Big City Metro." 1990. Series presented by KETC-TV, St. Louis.

Bingham, Richard, Roy Green, and Sammis White, eds. 1987. *The Homeless in Contemporary Society.* Beverly Hills: Sage.

Bish, Robert and Elinor Ostrom. 1973. *Understanding Urban Government.* Washington, DC: American Enterprise Institute.

Bixby, Ann. 1988. "Overview of Public Social Welfare Expenditures Fiscal Year 1986." *Social Security Bulletin* 51:27.

Blauner, Robert. 1964. *Alienation and Freedom: The Factory Worker and His Industry.* Chicago: University of Chicago Press.

Block, Fred. 1980. "Beyond Relative Autonomy: State Managers as Historical Subjects." *Socialist Register, 1980:*227-242.

Bloomberg, Warner and Rodrigo Martinez-Sandoval. 1982. "The Hispanic-American Urban Order: A Border Perspective." In *Cities in the 21st Century,* edited by G. Gappert and R. Knight. Beverly Hills, CA: Sage.

Bluestone, Barry and Bennett Harrison. 1988. *The Great U-Turn.* New York: Basic Books.

_____. 1982. *The Deindustrialization of America.* New York: Basic Books.

Bolton, Dan. 1989. *Interview.* (Director of Transportation in Danville, Illinois.)

Bradbury, Katherine L. 1986. "The Shrinking Middle Class." *New England Economic Review* 9/10/86: 41-55.

Bradford, Calvin and D. Marino. 1977. "Redlining and Disinvestment as a Discriminatory Practice in Residential Mortgage Loans." Washington, DC: U.S. Department of Housing and Urban Development.

Bratt, Rachel. 1986. "Public Housing: The Controversy and Contribution." In *Critical Perspectives on Housing,* edited by R. Bratt, C. Hartman and A. Meyerson. Philadelphia: Temple University Press.

Broder, David. 1990. "Pure Hearts and Gimmickry Aren't Enough." *Chicago Tribune* 4/22/90: 5,11.

_____. 1990. "Skinner's 'Moving America': A Cop-out." *Chicago Tribune* 3/11/90: 5,15.

Brown, Deborah. 1979. "Off the Track." *The Progressive* (July): 17.

Brown, James. 1972. "A Look at the 1970 Census." In *Appalachia in the Sixties,* edited by D.S. Wells and J.B. Stevenson. Lexington, KY: University of Kentucky.

Brown, Lester and Christopher Flavin. 1988. "The Earth's Vital Signs." In *State of the World 1988,* edited by L. Brown. New York: W.W. Norton.

Browne, Lynne. 1989. "Shifting Regional Fortunes: The Wheel Turns." *New England Economic Review* May/June:27-40.

Buchanon, James. 1977. "Why Does Government Grow?" In *Budgets and Bureaucrats,* edited by T. Borcherding. Durham, NC: Duke University.

Bukro, Casey. 1989. "To 'Garbologists', Study of Landfills Isn't All Rot." *Chicago Tribune* 10/15/89:1,1.

_____. 1988. "Incinerating Trash Gains Popularity, but Pollution Concerns Persist." *Chicago Tribune* 8/14/88:1,6.

_____. 1975. "Garbage Dumps Fill Up at a Crisis Rate." *Chicago Tribune* 12/18/75:1,4.

Bureau of Justice Statistics. 1988. *B/S Data Report, 1987.* Washington, DC: U.S. Department of Justice.

_____. 1987. *Special Report: Robbery Victims.* Washington, DC: U.S. Department of Justice.

Burgess, Ernest. 1924. "The Growth of the American City: An Introduction to a Research Project." *Publications of the American Sociological Society*. 18:88-97.

Butler, Edgar. 1977. *The Urban Crisis: Problems and Prospects in America*. Santa Monica, CA: Goodyear.

Calhoun, John B. 1960. "Population Density and Social Pathology." *Scientific American* 206:139-148.

Caplovitz, David. 1967. *The Poor Pay More*. New York: The Free Press.

Case, Karl and Leah Cook. 1989. "The Distributional Effects of Housing Price Booms: Winners and Losers in Boston, 1980-88." *New England Economic Review* May/June:3-12.

CBS. 1989. "New York is Falling Apart." *60 Minutes* 2/19/89.

Center for Policy Research in Education. 1989. "Graduation from High School: New Standards in the States." *CPRE Policy Briefs*, RB-02-04-89. New Brunswick, NJ: Eagleton Institute of Politics.

Center on Budget and Policy Priorities. 1984. *End Results: The Impact of Federal Policies Since 1980 on Low-Income Americans*. Washington, DC: Interfaith Action for Economic Affairs.

Chen, Xiangming. 1988. "Giant Cities and the Urban Hierarchy in China." In *The Metropolis Era*, vol. 1, edited by M. Dogan and J. Kasarda. Beverly Hills, CA: Sage.

Chicago Tribune. 8/14/89. "Taking the Bus to Opportunity":1,10.

Chicago Tribune. 5/24/89. "Personalize Schools, Black Panel Urges":1, 5.

Chicago Tribune. 3/22/89. "Keeping Pace with Transportation":1,12.

Chicago Tribune. 2/27/89. "Metra's Promising Track to the Future":1,10.

Chirot, Daniel. 1986. *Social Change in the Modern Era*. New York: Harcourt Brace Jovanovich.

Choldin, Harvey. 1985. *Cities and Suburbs: An Introduction to Urban Sociology*. New York: McGraw-Hill.

Church, George. 1988. "Garbage, Garbage, Everywhere." *Time* 9/5/88:81-82.

Clark, Terry. 1968. "Community Structure, Decision-Making, Budget Expenditure and Urban Renewal in 51 American Communities." *American Sociological Review* 33:576-593.

Cohn, Bob. 1989. "Looking Beyond the HUD Scandal." *Newsweek* 8/21/89:19.

Coleman, James. 1966. *Equality of Educational Opportunity*. Washington, DC: U.S. Government Printing Office.

Coleman, James and Sara Kelly. 1976. "Education." In *The Urban Predicament*, edited by W. Gorham and N. Glazer. Washington, DC: The Urban Institute.

Collins, Sharon M. 1983. "The Making of the Black Middle Class." *Social Problems* 30:369-382.

Commission on Population Growth and the American Future. 1972. *Population and the American Future*. New York: Signet.

The Condition of Teaching: A State-by-State Analysis. 1988. Princeton, NJ: The Carnegie Foundation for the Advancement of Teaching.

Congressional Quarterly. 1978. "Mass Transit Legislation." In *Urban America: Policies and Programs*. Washington, DC: Congressional Quarterly, Inc.

The Congressional Record. 1983. S6097-6101, 5/5/83.

Cook, William. 1989. "A Lot of Rubbish." *U.S. News and World Report* 12/25/89.

Cooley, Charles. 1930. "The Theory of Transportation." In Sociological Theory and Research, edited by C.H. Cooley. New York: Henry Holt.

Council on Environment Quality. 1979. *Environment Quality: 1979*. Washington, DC: U.S. Government Printing Office.

Cressey, Donald. 1969. *Theft of the Nation*. New York: Harper and Row.

Currie, Elliot and Jerome Skolnick. 1984. *America's Problems*. Boston: Little, Brown.

Dahl, Robert. 1961. *Who Governs? Power and Democracy in an American City*. New Haven, CT: Yale University.

Danziger, Sheldon and Daniel Weinberg, eds. 1986. *Fighting Poverty: What Works, What Doesn't*. Cambridge, MA: Harvard University Press.

Darden, Joe T. 1987. "Choosing Neighbors and Neighborhoods." In *Divided Neighborhoods*, edited by G. Tobin. Newbury Park, CA: Sage.

_____. 1986. "Accessibility to Housing: Differential Residential Segregation for Blacks, Hispanics, American Indians, and Asians. In *Race, Ethnicity and Minority Housing in the U.S.*, edited by J. Momeni. New York: Greenwood Press.

Darden, Joe, Richard Hill, June Thomas and Richard Thomas. 1987. *Detroit: Race, Class and Uneven Development*. Philadelphia, PA: Temple University Press.

Davis, Kingsley. 1975. "The American Family in Relation to Demographic Change." In *U.S. Commission on Population Growth and the American Future*. Volume I, Demographic Aspects of Population Growth, edited by C. Westhopp and R. Parker. Washington, DC: U.S. Government Printing Office.

DeLeeuw, Frank, Ann Schnare, and Raymond Struyk. 1976. "Housing." In *The Urban Predicament*, edited by W. Gorham and N. Glazer. Washington, DC: The Urban Institute.

Demaris, Ovid. 1974. *Dirty Business*. New York: Avon Books.

Dennis, Elissa. 1989. "Shared Housing: An Innovative Approach." *Shelterforce* July/Aug:12-15.

Dentler, Robert. 1977. *Urban Problems: Perspectives and Solutions*. Chicago: Rand McNally.

Dishneau, David. 1989. "Illinois' Land Fills Could Be Full in Less Than 10 Years." *Jacksonville Journal Courier* 12/11/89:14.

Dluhy, Milan. 1979. "Design and Delivery of Social Welfare Services: Politics and Issues at the Local Level." In *The Changing Structure of the City*, edited by G. Tobin, Beverly Hills, CA: Sage.

Dogan, Mattei and John Kasarda. 1988. "Introduction: How Giant Cities Will Multiply and Grow." In *The Metropolis Era*, vol. 1, edited by M. Dogan and J. Kasarda. Beverly Hills, CA: Sage.

Dolbeare, Cushing. 1986. "How the Income Tax System Subsidizes Housing for the Affluent." In *Critical Perspectives on Housing*, edited by R. Bratt, C. Hartman and A. Meyerson. Philadelphia: Temple University Press.

_____. 1983. "The Low-Income Housing Crisis." In *America's Housing Crisis*, edited by C. Hartman. Boston: Routledge & Kegan Paul.

Dollars and Sense. 1988. "Corporate Executives Go to the Trough." 138:10-11.

Dollars and Sense. 1985. "Displaced Workers: Bearing the Costs of a Changing Ecomony." 110:12-13.

Dollars and Sense. 1980. "The Energy Crisis." July/August:5-7.

Donahue, John. 1989. *The Privatization Decision: Public Ends, Private Means*. New York: Basic Books.

Downie, Leonard. 1974. *Mortgage on America*. New York: Praeger.

Downs, Anthony. 1973. *Opening Up the Suburbs: An Urban Strategy for America*. New Haven: Yale University.

Dreier, Peter. 1989. "Affordable Housing Without Profit or Scandal." *Shelterforce* May/June:12-15.

Duncan, Greg. 1984. *Years of Poverty, Years of Plenty*. Ann Arbor, MI: University of Michigan Institute for Survey Research.

Durkheim, Emile. 1951. *Suicide*. Translated by J. Spaulding and G. Simpson. Glencoe, IL: Free Press.

Durkheim, Emile. 1947. *Division of Labor in Society*. Translated by G. Simpson. Glencoe, IL: Free Press.

Durning, Alan. 1990. "Ending Poverty." In *State of the World 1990*, edited by L. Brown. New York: Norton.

Duster, Troy. 1987. "Crime, Youth Unemployment, and the Black Urban Underclass." *Crime and Delinquency* 33:300-316.

Easterbrook, Gregg. 1990. "Everything You Know About the Environment is Wrong." *New Republic* 4/30/90:14-27.

Education Week. Various dates.

Eitzen, D. Stanley. 1978. *In Conflict and Order*. Boston: Allyn and Bacon.

Ellwood, David. 1988. *Poor Support: Poverty in the American Family*. New York: Basic Books.

Espenshade, Thomas J. 1990. "A Short History of U.S. Policy Toward Illegal Immigration." *Population Today* 18, 2:6-9.

Fainstein, Susan and Norman Fainstein. 1989. "The Ambivalent State: Economic Development Policy Under the Reagan Administration." *Urban Affairs Quarterly* 25:41-62.

Fallows, James. 1989. "Tokyo: The Hard Life." *Atlantic Monthly* 263, 3:16-19.

_____. 1986. "East Asia: Letter from Tokyo." *Atlantic Monthly* 258, 2:14-19.

Farley, John. 1987. "Segregation in 1980: How Segregated are America's Metropolitan Areas?" In *Divided Neighborhoods*, edited by G. Tobin. Newbury Park, CA: Sage.

Farley, Reynolds. 1984. *Blacks and Whites: Narrowing the Gap?* Cambridge, MA: Harvard University Press.

_____. 1975. "The Economic Status of Blacks: Have the Gains of the 1960s Disappeared in the 1970s?" Ann Arbor, MI: Population Studies Center.

_____. 1964. "Suburban Persistence." *American Sociological Review* 29:38-47.

Farley, Reynolds, Howard Schuman, Suzanne Bianchi, Diane Colasanto, and Shirley Hatchett. 1978. "Chocolate City, Vanilla Suburbs." *Social Science Research* 7:319-344.

Fava, Sylvia. 1975. "Beyond Suburbia." *Annals of the American Society of Political and Social Science* 422:10-24.

Feagin, Joe. 1988. *Free Enterprise City: Houston in Political and Economic Perspective*. New Brunswick: Rutgers University Press.

_____. 1968. "The Kinship Ties of Negro Urbanites." *Social Science Quarterly* 49:660-665.

Federal Bureau of Investigation. 1988a. *Population At-Risk Rates and Selected Crime Indicators*. Washington, DC: U.S. Department of Justice.

_____. 1988b. *Crime in the United States, 1987*. Washington, DC: U.S. Department of Justice.

Firebaugh, Glenn. 1979. "Structural Determinants of Urbanization in Asia and Africa." *American Sociological Review* 44: 199-215.

Fischer, Claude. 1982. *To Dwell Among Friends*. Chicago: University of Chicago.

_____. 1981. "The Public and Private Worlds of City Life." *American Sociological Review* 46: 306-316.

_____. 1976. *The Urban Experience*. New York: Harcourt Brace Jovanovich.

Fischer, Claude, Mark Baldassare, and Richard Ofshe. 1975. "Crowding Studies and Urban Life: A Critical Review." *Journal of the American Institute of Planners* 41:406-418.

Flanagan, William. 1990. *Urban Sociology: Images and Structures*. Needham Heights, MA: Allyn and Bacon.

Francis, Diana. 1988. "Business as Usual in the Greed Game." *Maclean's* 11/7/88.

Frase, Mary. 1989. "Dropout Rates in the United States: 1988." *National Center for Education Statistics: Analysis Report*. Washington, DC: U.S. Department of Education.

Fremon, Charlotte. 1970. "The Occupational Pattern in Urban Employment Change, 1945-67." In Paper 114-31:11. Washington, DC: Urban Institute.

French, Hilary. 1990. "Clearing the Air." In *State of the World: 1990*, edited by L. Brown. Washington, DC: Worldwatch Institute.

Frey, William H. 1979. "Central City White Flight: Racial and Non-Racial Causes." *American Sociological Review* 44:425-448.

Fried, Marc. 1973. *The World of the Urban Working Class.* Cambridge, MA: Harvard University.

_____. 1969. "Grieving for a Lost Home." In *The Urban Condition*, edited by Leonard Duhl. New York: Simon and Schuster.

Friedland, Roger. 1980. "Corporate Power and Urban Growth." *Politics and Society* 10:203-224.

Friedman, F.G. 1953. "The World of 'La Miseria'." *Partisan Review* 20: 218-231.

Friedrichs, Jurgen. 1988. "Large Cities in Eastern Europe." In *The Metropolis Era*, vol. 1, edited by M. Dugan and J. Kasarda. Beverly Hills, CA: Sage.

Futrell, Mary. 1989. "Mission Not Accomplished: Education Reform in Retrospect." *Phi Delta Kappa* September:9-14.

Galle, Omer and Walter Gove. 1978. "Overcrowding, Isolation and Human Behavior: The Extremes in the Population Distribution." In *Social Demography*, edited by K. Tauber and F. Sweet. New York: Academic Press.

Gallup, George. 1976-77. "Human Needs and Satisfaction: A Global Survey." *Public Opinion Quarterly* 40:465-467.

Gallup Poll. 1978. *Gallup Opinion Index*, November. Princeton, NJ: American Institute of Public Opinion. Cited in Kain, 1987.

Gans, Herbert J. 1968. "Culture and Class in the Study of Poverty: An Approach to Anti-Poverty Research." In *On Understanding Poverty*, edited by D.P. Moynihan. New York: Basic Books.

_____. 1962. *The Urban Villagers.* New York: Free Press.

Ganz, Alexander. 1985. "Where Has the Urban Crisis Gone?" *Urban Affairs Quarterly* 20:449-468.

Geisse, Guillermo and Francisco Sabatini. 1988. "Latin American Cities." In *The Metropolis Era*, vol. 1, edited by M. Dogan and J. Kasarda. Beverly Hills, CA: Sage.

Gibbons, Don. 1972. "Observations on the Study of Crime Causation." *American Journal of Sociology* 72:262-278.

Gibbs, Jack and Leo Schnore. 1960. "Metropolitan Growth: An International Study." *American Journal of Sociology* 66:160-170.

Giglio, Joseph. 1988. "The Challenge of Keeping America in Good Repair." *Chicago Tribune* 12/28/88:1,13.

Gilderbloom, John and Richard Appelbaum. 1988. *Rethinking Rental Housing.* Philadelphia: Temple University Press.

Gist, Noel and Sylvia Fava. 1974. *Urban Society.* New York: Crowell.

Gittel, Marilyn. 1980. "The Impact of Community Organization on Urban School Systems." Address at the Sixth Annual Conference on the Urban South. Norfolk, VA.

Glasgow, Douglas. 1980. *The Black Underclass.* New York: Jossey-Bass, Inc.

Gluck, Peter and Richard Meister. 1979. *Cities in Transition.* New York: Vintage.

Goldsmith, William. 1982. "Enterprise Zones: If They Work, We're in Trouble." *International Journal of Urban and Regional Research* 6:435-442.

Goldstein, Sidney. 1988. "Levels of Urbanization in China." In *The Metropolis Era*, vol. 1, edited by M. Dogan and J. Kasarda. Beverly Hills, CA: Sage.

Goode, William. 1963. *World Revolution and Family Patterns.* New York: Free Press.

Goodman, Robert. 1981. *The Last Entrepreneurs.* Boston: South End Press.

Goodwin, Leonard. 1983. *Causes and Cures of Welfare*. Lexington, MA: D.C. Heath & Company.

Goozner, Merrill. 1988. "Industrial Assignment for Colleges." *Chicago Tribune* 9/11/88:4,1.

Gordon, David M. 1977. "Class Struggle and the Stages of American Urban Development." In *The Rise of the Sunbelt Cities*, edited by D. Perry and A. Watkins. Beverly Hills, CA: Sage.

Gorham, William and Nathan Glazer, editors. 1976. *The Urban Predicament*. Washington, DC: The Urban Institute.

Gottdiener, Mark. 1987. *The Decline of Urban Politics*. Newbury Park, CA: Sage.

_____. 1977. *Planned Sprawl: Public and Private Interests in Suburbia*. Beverly Hills, CA: Sage.

Gottman, Jean. 1964. *Megalopolis*. Cambridge, MA: Massachusetts Institute of Technology.

Gottschalk, Peter. 1987. "Retrenchment in Antipoverty Programs in the U.S.: Lessons for the Future." Author's research. Cited in Levine, 1988.

Gove, Walter, Michael Hughes, and Omer Galle. 1979. "Overcrowding the Home: An Empirical Investigation of Its Possible Consequences." *American Sociological Review* 44:59-80.

Green, Mark. 1972. *The Closed Enterprise System*. New York: Bantam.

Greenwald, Gerald. 1990. "This Week with David Brinkley." *WAND-TV* 3/4/90: Decatur, IL.

Greer, Scott. 1962. *Governing the Metropolis*. New York: John Wiley.

Gridley, Clark. 1989. "Solid Waste Problems Pile Up." *Appalachia* 22:28-33.

Griffith, Jeanne, Mary Frase, and John Ralph. 1989. "American Education: The Challenge of Change." *Population Bulletin* 44:1-4.

Guest, Avery. 1978. "Suburban Social Status: Persistence or Evolution?" *American Sociological Review* 43:251-264.

Guest, Avery and James Zuiches. 1971. "Another Look at Residential Turnover in Urban Neighborhoods." *American Journal of Sociology* 77:457-467.

Habermas, Jurgen. 1975. *Legitimation Crisis*. Boston: Beacon.

Haggerty, Lee. 1971. "Another Look at the Burgess Hypothesis: Time as an Important Variable." *American Journal of Sociology* 76:1084-1093.

Hall, Peter. 1988. "Urban Growth and Decline in Western Europe" In *The Metropolis Era*, vol. 1, edited by M. Dogan and J. Kasarda. Beverly Hills, CA: Sage.

_____. 1977. *World Cities*, 2nd ed. New York: McGraw-Hill.

Hannerz, Ulf. 1980. *Exploring the City: Inquiries Toward an Urban Anthropology*. New York: Columbia University.

Harris, Chauncey and Edward Ullman. 1945. "The Nature of Cities." *Annals of the American Academy of Political and Social Science* 242:7-17.

Harris, Marvin. 1981. *America Now*. New York: Simon and Schuster.

Harrison, Bennett. 1984. "Regional Restructuring and 'Good Business Climates': The Economic Transformation of New England since World War II." In *Sunbelt, Snowbelt*, edited by L. Sawers and W. Tabb. New York: Oxford University Press.

Hartley, Shirley. 1972. *Population Quantity vs. Quality*. Englewood Cliffs, NJ: Prentice-Hall.

Hartman, Chester. 1975. *Housing and Social Policy*. Englewood Cliffs, NJ: Prentice-Hall.

Harvey, David. 1973. *Social Justice and the City*. Baltimore: Johns Hopkins University Press.

Hatfield, Larry. 1989. "Nation's Youth Ill-Prepared for Employment: Job Skills Scarce as Competition Rises." *San Francisco Examiner* 8/6/89:A1.

Hawley, Amos. 1971. *Urban Society*. New York: Ronald Press.

_____. 1950. *Human Ecology*. New York: Ronald Press.

Heumann, Leonard. 1979. "Housing Needs and Housing Solutions: Changes in Perspectives from 1968 to 1978." In *The Changing Structure of the City*, edited by G. Tobin. Beverly Hills, CA: Sage.

Hill, Richard C. 1984. "Economic Crisis and Political Response in the Motor City." In *Sunbelt, Snowbelt*, edited by L. Sawers and W. Tabb. New York: Oxford University Press.

Hinds, Michael and Erik Eckholm. 1990. "80's Leave States and Cities in Need" *New York Times* 12/30/90:1, 16

Hoff, Jeffrey. 1988. "Homing in on the Problem that Won't Go Away." *Planning* September:11-12.

Houston, Jack. 1989. "It's All Aboard for Disabled as Metra OKs Lifts for Its Trains." *Chicago Tribune* 9/16/89:1,5.

Hoyt, Homer. 1939. *The Structure and Growth of Residential Neighborhoods in American Cities*. Washington, DC: U.S. Government Printing Office.

Hughes, James. 1974. *Suburban Dynamics and the Future of the City*. New Brunswick, NJ: Center for Urban Policy Research.

Hundley, Tom. 1988. "Colleges Going to High Schools to Help Minorities Get Prepared." *Chicago Tribune* 12/4/88:1,5.

Hunter, Floyd. 1952. *Community Power Structure*. Chapel Hill, NC: University of North Carolina.

Hyman, Herbert. 1971. "Trends in Voluntary Association Memberships of American Adults: A Replication Based on Secondary Analysis of National Sample Surveys." *American Sociological Review* 36:191-206.

Ibata, David and Blair Kamin. 1990. "Mass Transit Mostly Runs on Empty." *Chicago Tribune* 2/21/90:1, 1.

Irwin, John. 1983. *The Jail*. Berkeley: University of California.

Jackman, Mary and Robert Jackman. 1986. "Racial Inequalities in Home Ownership." In *Race, Ethnicity and Minority Housing in the United States*, edited by J. Momeni. New York: Greenwood Press.

Jackson, Kenneth. 1985. *Crabgrass Frontier: The Suburbanization of the United States*. New York: Oxford University.

Jencks, Christopher. 1978. "What's Behind the Drop in Test Scores." *Working Papers for a New Society* July/August:29-41.

Jencks, Christopher, M. Smith, H. Acland, M. J. Bane, D. Cohen, H. Gintis, B. Heyns, and S. Michelson. 1972. *Inequality*. New York: Basic Books.

Johnson, Leonard, D.M. Rote, J.R. Hull, H.T. Coffey, J.G. Daley, and R.F. Geise. 1989. *Maglev Vehicles and Superconductor Technology: Integration of High-Speed Ground Transportation Into the Air Travel System*. LeMont, IL: Center for Transportation Research, Argonne National Laboratory.

Johnson, Norman. 1987. *The Welfare State in Transition*. Amherst, MA: University of Massachusetts.

Jones, Emrys. 1988. "London." In *The Metropolis Era*, vol. 2, edited by M. Dogan and J. Kasarda. Beverly Hills, CA: Sage.

Kain, John. 1987. "Housing Market Discrimination and Black Suburbanization in the 1980's." In *Divided Neighborhoods*, edited by G. Tobin. Newbury Park, CA: Sage.

Kain, John F. and John R. Myer. 1970. "Transportation and Urban Poverty." *The Public Interest* 18:75-87.

Kantor, Paul. 1987. "The Dependent City: The Changing Political Economy of Urban Development in the United States." *Urban Affairs Quarterly* 22:493-520.

Kapinos, Thomas. 1989. "Attitudes Toward Mass Transit." *Mass Transit* April:10-15.

Kasarda, John. 1989. "Urban Industrial Transition and the Underclass." *Annals of the American Academy of Political and Social Sciences* 501:26-47.

_____. 1983. "Entry Level Jobs, Mobility and Minority Unemployment." *Urban Affairs Quarterly* 19: 21-40.

Kasarda, John and Morris Janowitz. 1974. "Community Attachment in Mass Society." *American Sociological Review* 39:328-339.

Kelley, Allen and Jeffrey Williamson. 1984. *What Drives Third World City Growth?* Princeton, NJ: Princeton University.

Kemp, Michael and Melvyn Cheslow. 1976. "Transportation." In *The Urban Predicament*, edited by W. Gorham, and N. Glazer. Washington, DC: Urban Institute.

Kerns, Wilmer and Milton Glanz. 1988. "Private Social Welfare Expenditures, 1972-1985." *Social Security Bulletin* 51:4.

Kerr, Stephen. 1989. "Reform in Soviet and American Education: Parallels and Contrasts." *Phi Delta Kappan* 29:19-20.

Kim, Illsoo, 1981. *The New Urban Immigrants: The Korean Community in New York*. Princeton, NJ: Princeton University.

Kirby, Andrew. 1985. "Nine Fallacies of Local Economic Change." *Urban Affairs Quarterly* 21:207-220.

Kleniewski, Nancy. 1984. From Industrial to Corporate City: The Role of Urban Renewal. In *Marxism and the Metropolis* edited by W. Tabb and L. Sawers. New York: Oxford University.

Koepp, Stephen. 1988. "Gridlock!" *Time* 9/12/88: 52-60.

Kotler, Milton. 1969. *Neighborhood Government: The Local Foundations of Political Life*. Indianapolis, IN: Bobbs-Merrill.

Kozol, Jonathan. 1988. *Rachel and Her Children*. New York: Fawcett.

Kraar, Louis. 1988. "The Drug Trade." *Fortune* 6/20/88:27-38.

Larsen, Calvin and Stan Nikkel. 1979. *Urban Problems*. Boston: Allyn and Bacon.

Laurenti, Luigi. 1960. *Property Values and Race*. Berkeley: University of California Press.

Lave, Charles A. 1979. "The Mass Transit Panacea." *The Atlantic Monthly* October:39-52.

LeGates, Richard and Chester Hartman. 1986. "The Anatomy of Displacement in the U.S." In *Gentrification of the City*, edited by N. Smith and P. Williams. Boston: Allen Unwin.

Lemonick, Michael. 1989. "The Heat Is On." *Time* 10/19/89:58-64, 67.

Leven, Charles. 1979. "Economic Maturity and the Metropolis's Evolving Physical Form." In *The Changing Structure of the City*, edited by G.A. Tobin. Beverly Hills, CA: Sage.

Levitan, Sar and Isaac Shapiro. 1987. *Working But Poor*. Baltimore: Johns Hopkins University Press.

Lewis, Oscar. 1966. "The Culture of Poverty." *Scientific American* 215:3-9.

Lieberman, Joseph. 1989. "America's Belching Tailpipes." *Christian Science Monitor* 8/25/89:19.

Light, Ivan. 1983. *Cities in World Perspective*. New York: Macmillan.

——. 1972. *Ethnic Enterprise in America*. Berkeley: University of California Press.

Lineberry, Robert. 1970. "Reforming Metropolitan Governance: Requiem or Reality?" *Georgetown Law Journal* (March/May):675-718.

Lipsky, Michael. 1976. "Toward a Theory of Street-Level Bureaucracy." In *Theoretical Perspectives on Urban Politics*, edited by W. Hawley, et al. Englewood Cliffs, NJ: Prentice-Hall.

Litwak, Eugene. 1965. "Extended Kin Relations in an Industrial Democratic Society." In *Social Structure and the Family*, edited by E. Shanas and G. Streib. Englewood Cliffs, NJ: Prentice-Hall.

Logan, John. 1988. "Fiscal and Developmental Crises in Black Suburbs." In *Business Elites and Urban Development*, edited by S. Cummings. Albany: SUNY Press.

Logan, John and Harvey Molotch. 1987. *Urban Fortunes: The Political Economy of Place*. Berkeley, CA: University of California.

Logan, John and Mark Schneider. 1984. "Racial Segregation and Racial Change in American Suburbs, 1970-1980." *American Journal of Sociology* 89:874-888.

Logan, John and Mark Schneider. 1981. "The Stratification of Metropolitan Suburbs, 1960-1970." *American Sociological Review* 46:175-186.

Luoma, Jon. 1988. "Using New Incinerators, Cities Convert Garbage into Energy." *New York Times* 8/2/88:C4.

Lupsha, Peter and William Siembieda. 1977. "The Poverty of Public Services in a Land of Plenty." In *The Rise of the Sunbelt Cities*, edited by D. Perry and A. Watkins. Beverly Hills, CA: Sage.

Lyon, Larry. 1987. *The Community in Urban Society*. Homewood, IL: Dorsey Press.

Macionis, John. 1989. *Sociology*. Englewood Cliffs, NJ: Prentice-Hall.

MacLeod, Jay. 1987. *Ain't No Makin' It*. Boulder, CO: Westview Press.

MacNeil-Lehrer Report. 1989. *KETC-TV* 11/8/89. St. Louis.

Mallach, Alan. 1988. "Opening the Suburbs: New Jersey's Mt. Laurel Experience." *Shelterforce* August/Sept:12-15.

Marcuse, Peter. 1982. "Determinants of State Housing Policies: West Germany and the United States." In *Urban Policy Under Capitalism*, edited by N. Fainstein and S. Fainstein. Beverly Hills, CA: Sage.

Marger, Martin. 1987. *Elites and Masses: An Introduction to Political Sociology*. Belmont, CA: Wadsworth.

Marsden, Peter. 1987. "Core Discussion Networks of Americans." *American Sociological Review* 52:122-131.

Marshall, Harvey. 1979. "White Movement to the Suburbs." *American Sociological Review* 44:975-994.

Mateja, Jim. 1990. "Car-Owning Cost Up Sharply; Year's Tab Can Hit $4,400, Study Estimates." *Chicago Tribune* 3/5/90:4,9.

Mayer, Harold and Richard Wade. 1969. *Chicago: Growth of a Metropolis*. Chicago: University of Chicago.

Mayer, Susan and Christopher Jencks. 1989. "Growing Up in Poor Neighborhoods: How Much Does It Matter?" *Science* 243:1441-1445.

McGahey, Richard. 1986. "Economic Conditions, Neighborhood Organization, and Urban Crime." In *Communities and Crime*, edited by A.J. Reiss and M. Tonry. Chicago: University of Chicago.

McKelvey, Blake. 1973. *American Urbanization*. Glenview, IL: Scott, Foresman.

McLanahan, Sara, Irwin Garfinkel and Dorothy Watson. 1988. "Family Structure, Poverty and the Underclass." In *Urban Change and Poverty*, edited by M. McGreary and L. Lynn. Washington, DC: National Academy Press.

Meyer, John R. 1970. "Urban Transportation." In *The Metropolitan Enigma*, edited by J. Q. Wilson. Garden City, NY: Doubleday.

Milgram, Stanley. 1970. "The Experience of Living in Cities." *Science* 167:1461-1468.

Mishel, Lawrence and Jacqueline Simon. 1988. *The State of Working America*. Washington, DC: Economic Policy Institute.

Molotch, Harvey. 1988. "Strategies and Constraints on Growth Elites." In *Business Elites and Urban Development*, edited by S. Cummings. Albany, NY: State University of New York.

_____. 1972. *Managed Integration: Dilemmas of Doing Good in the City*. Berkeley: University of California Press.

Morrissy, Patrick. 1987. "Receivership: A Step Toward Community Control." *Shelterforce* Jan/Feb:8-10.

Moscovitch, Edward. 1990. "The Downtown in the New England Economy: What Lies Behind It?" *New England Economic Review* July/August:53-65.

Muller, Peter. 1981. *Contemporary Suburban America*. Englewood Cliffs, NJ: Prentice-Hall.

Murphey, Rhoads. 1988. "Shanghai." In *The Metropolis Era*, vol. 2, edited by M. Dogan and J. Kasarda. Beverly Hills, CA: Sage.

Murray, Charles. 1984. *Losing Ground: American Social Policy 1950-1980*. New York: Basic Books.

Nagpaul, Hans. 1988. "India's Great Cities." In *The Metropolis Era*, vol. 2, edited by M. Dogan and J. Kasarda. Beverly Hills, CA: Sage.

Nakamura, Hachiro and James White. 1988. "Tokyo." In *The Metropolis Era*, vol. 2, edited by M. Dogan and J. Kasarda. Beverly Hills, CA: Sage.

Nasar, Sylvia. 1986. "America's Poor: How Big a Problem?" *Fortune* 5/26/86:74-80.

A Nation at Risk: The Full Account. 1984. The National Commission on Excellence in Education. Cambridge, MA: USA Research.

National Center for Education Statistics. 1989. *Digest of Education Statistics*. Washington, DC: U.S. Department of Education.

National Commission on Urban Problems. 1968. *Building the American City*. Washington, DC: U.S. Government Printing Office.

National Housing Task Force. 1988. *A Decent Place to Live*. Washington, DC: National Housing Task Force.

New York Times. 9/27/88.

Newsweek. 3/28/1988. "The Drug Gangs":20-24.

Newsweek. 1/14/1980. "A City's Growing Pains":45.

Newton, Kenneth. 1978. "Conflict Avoidance and Conflict Suppression: The Case of the United States." In *Urbanization and Conflict Market Societies*, edited by K. Cox. Chicago, IL: Maaroufa.

———. 1976. "Feeble Governments and Private Power: Urban Politics and Policies in the United States." In *The New Urban Politics*, edited by L. Masotti and R. Lineberry. Cambridge, MA: Ballinger.

Numbers News. Published by American Demographics, Inc. Ithaca, N.Y. Various dates.

O'Connor, James. 1973. *The Fiscal Crisis of the State*. New York: St. Martin's Press.

Ogintz, Eileen. 1989. "Education Inc.: Business and Community Leaders Merge So Inner-city Kids Can Profit." *Chicago Tribune* 12/4/89:1,5.

———. 1989. "'Adopting' the Future. Millionaire Shares a Dream So Kids Can Make College Come True." *Chicago Tribune* 11/2/89:2,2.

Olsen, Marvin. 1970. "Social and Political Participation of Blacks." *American Sociological Review* 35:682-697.

Orfield, Gary. 1986. "Minorities and Suburbanization." In *Critical Perspectives on Housing*, edited by R. Bratt, C. Hartman, and A. Meyerson. Philadelphia: Temple University.

Orleans, Peter, and Miriam Orleans. 1976. *Urban Life: Diversity and Inequality*. Dubuque, IA: Brown.

Ornstein, Allan and Daniel Levine. 1985. *Introduction to the Foundations of Education*. Boston: Houghton Mifflin.

Ostrom, Elinor. 1983. "The Social Stratification-Government Inequality Thesis Explored." *Urban Affairs Quarterly* 19:91-112.

Our Nation's Highways: Selected Facts and Figures. 1987. Washington, DC: U.S. Department of Transportation.

Pahl, Raymond. 1977. "Managers, Technical Experts and the State." In *Captive Cities*, edited by M. Harloe. New York: John Wiley.

Palen, John. 1987, 1975. *The Urban World*. New York: McGraw-Hill.

Parkinson, Michael. 1979. "Dilemmas for the City Schools: Racial Isolation and Fiscal Stress." In *The Changing Structure of the City*, edited by G. Tobin. Beverly Hills, CA: Sage.

Parks, Roger and Ronald Oakerson. 1989. "Metropolitan Organization and Governance: A Local Public Economy Approach." *Urban Affairs Quarterly* 25:18-29.

Parsons, Talcott. 1969. *Societies in Evolutionary and Comparative Perspective.* Englewood Cliffs, NJ: Prentice-Hall.

Pearce, Diana. 1978. "Gatekeepers and Homeseekers: Institutional Patterns in Racial Steering." *Social Problems* 26:325-342.

_____. 1990. "Women and Housing." Washington, DC: Wider Opportunities for Women (mimeo).

Perrin, Constance. 1978. *Everything in Its Place.* Princeton, NJ: Princeton University.

Perry, David. 1987. "The Politics of Dependency in Deindustrializing America: The Case of Buffalo, New York." In *The Capitalist City,* edited by M. Smith and J. Feagin. New York: Basil Blackwell.

Persell, Caroline. 1987. *Understanding Society,* 2nd ed. New York: Harper & Row.

Personal Travel in the U.S. 1986. 1983-1984 Nationwide Personal Transportation Study. Washington, DC: U.S. Department of Transportation.

Petersen, George. 1976. "Finance." In *The Urban Predicament,* edited by W. Gorham and N. Glazer. Washington, DC: The Urban Institute.

Peterson, William. 1961. *Population.* New York: Macmillan.

Pilzer, Paul. 1989. *Other People's Money: The Inside Story of the S & L Mess.* New York: Simon and Schuster.

Piven, Frances and Richard Cloward. 1971. *Regulating the Poor: The Functions of Public Welfare.* New York: Vintage.

Polsby, Nelson. 1963. *Community Power and Political Theory.* New Haven, CT: Yale University.

Popenoe, David. 1985. *Private Pleasure, Public Plight: American Metropolitan Community Life in Comparative Perspective.* New Brunswick, NJ: Transaction Books.

Poplin, Dennis. 1979. *Communities: A Survey of Theories and Methods of Research.* New York: Macmillan.

Popple, Philip and Leslie Leighninger. 1990. *Social Work, Social Welfare, and American Society.* Needham Heights, MA: Allyn and Bacon.

Population Today. Various dates.

Postel, Sandra. 1990. "Saving Water for Agriculture." In *State of the World: 1990,* edited by L. Brown. Washington, DC: Worldwatch Institute.

_____. 1985. "Managing Fresh Water Supplies." In *State of the World: 1985,* edited by L. Brown. Washington, DC: Worldwatch Institute.

Postel, Sandra and Lester Brown. 1987. "Life, The Great Chemistry Experiment." *Natural History* April:41-48.

Pred, Allen. 1971. "The Intrametropolitan Location of American Manufacturing." In *The Internal Structure of the City,* edited by L. Bourne. New York: Oxford.

President's Commission on Law Enforcement and the Administration of Justice. 1967. *Task Force Report: Organized Crime.* Washington, DC: U.S. Government Printing Office.

President's Commission for a National Agenda for the Eighties. 1981. *A National Agenda for the Eighties.* New York: Mentor.

Prewda, Bob. 1989. "Effectively Marketing Community Transportation." *Community Transportation Reporter* 7:8-9.

Rainwater, Lee. 1970. *Behind Ghetto Walls.* Chicago: Aldine.

Reconnecting Rural America: Report on Rural Intercity Passenger Transportation. 1989. Washington, DC: U.S. Department of Agriculture, Office of Transportation.

Redfield, Robert. 1947. "The Folk Society." *American Journal of Sociology* 52:293-308.

Reich, Robert. 1989. "As the World Turns." *The New Republic* 5/1/89:23-28.

Reid, Sue. 1988. *Crime and Criminology*. New York: Holt, Rinehart and Winston.

Rein, Martin. 1970. *Social Policy: Issues of Choice and Change*. New York: Random House.

Reischauer, Robert. 1978. "The Economy, the Federal Budget and Urban Aid." In *The Fiscal Outlook for Cities*, edited by R. Bahl. Syracuse, NY: Syracuse University.

Reisner, Marc. 1989. "The Emerald Desert." *Greenpeace* July/August:6-10.

Renner, Michael. 1989. "Rethinking Transportation." In *State of the World 1989*. Washington, DC: Worldwatch Institute.

———. 1988. *Rethinking the Role of the Automobile*. Worldwatch Paper 84. Washington, DC: Worldwatch Institute.

Roanoke Times and World News 1/28/1990: "Pollution in the Wake of Stalinism":A6.

Robinson, Tracey. 1987. "Dropouts Get New Chances at School, Success." *Chicago Sun-Times* 6/15/87: 3.

Roethlisberger, Fritz and William Dickson. 1939. *Management and the Worker*. Cambridge, MA: Harvard University.

Rondinelli, Dennis. 1988. "Giant City Growth in Africa." In *The Metropolis Era*, vol. 1, edited by M. Dogan and J. Kasarda. Beverly Hills, CA: Sage.

Rubin, Irene. 1985. "Structural Theories and Urban Fiscal Stress." *Urban Affairs Quarterly* 20:469-486.

Rubin, Irene and Herbert Rubin. 1987. "Economic Development Incentives." *Urban Affairs Quarterly* 23:37-62.

Ryan, William. 1981. *Equality*. New York: Random House.

Sachs, Ignacy. 1988. "Vulnerability of Giant Cities and the Life Lottery." In *The Metropolis Era*, vol. 1, edited by M. Dogan and J. Kasarda. Beverly Hills, CA: Sage.

Sale, Kirkpatrick. 1976. "Six Pillars of the Southern Rim." In *The Fiscal Crisis of American Cities*, edited by R. Alcaly and D. Mermelstein. New York: Vintage Books.

———. 1975. *Power Shift*. New York: Random House.

Salholz, E., M. Reese and L. Buckley. 1988. "California's Slow Growth Spurt." *Newsweek* 9/26/88:26.

Saltman, Juliet. 1989. *A Fragile Movement: The Struggle for Neighborhood Stabilization*. Westport, CT: Greenwood Press.

Sassen-Koob, Sakia. 1987. "Growth and Informalization at the Core." In *The Capitalist City*, edited by J. Feagin and M. P. Smith. New York: Basil Blackwell.

———. 1984. "The New Labor Demand in Global Cities." In *Cities in Transformation*, edited by M.P. Smith. Beverly Hills, CA: Sage.

Savas, Emanuel S. 1982. *Privatizing the Public Sector: How to Shrink Government*. Chatham, NJ: Chatham House.

Saxenian, Anna Lee. 1983. "The Urban Contradictions of Silicon Valley: Regional Growth and the Restructuring of the Semiconductor Industry." *International Journal of Urban and Regional Research* 7: 237-257.

Schnaiberg, Allan 1980. *The Environment: 'From Surplus to Scarcity'*. New York: Oxford University.

Schneider, Mark and John R. Logan. 1982. "Suburban Racial Segregation and Black Access to Local Public Resources." *Social Science Quarterly* 63:762-770.

Schnore, Leo. 1972. *Class and Race in Cities*. Chicago: Markham.

Schteingart, Martha. 1988. "Mexico Citry." In *The Metropolis Era*, vol. 2, edited by M. Dogan and J. Kasarda. Beverly Hills, CA: Sage.

Schuman, Howard, Charlotte Steeh and Lawrence Bobo. 1985. *Racial Attitudes in America: Trends and Interpretations*. Cambridge, MA: Harvard University Press.

Schur, Edwin. 1969. *Our Criminal Society*. Englewood Cliffs, NJ: Prentice-Hall.

Schwartz, David, Richard Ferlauto and Daniel Hoffman. 1988. *A New Housing Policy for America: Recapturing the American Dream*. Philadelphia: Temple University.

314   References

Scott, Richard. 1983. "Blacks in Segregated and Desegregated Neighborhoods." *Urban Affairs Quarterly* 18:327-346.

Seeman, Melvin. 1958. "On the Meaning of Alienation." *American Sociological Review* 24:783-791.

Shannon, Thomas R. 1989. *An Introduction to the World System Perspective.* Boulder, CO: Westview.

_____. 1980. "Traditional Mass Transit in Southern Cities: A Mistaken Priority." *The Sixth Annual Conference on the Urban South.* Norfolk, VA: Norfolk State University.

Sharff, Jagna. 1987. "The Underground Economy of a Poor Neighborhood." In *Cities of the United States,* edited by L. Mullings. New York: Columbia University.

Shea, Cynthia. 1988. "Building a Market for Recyclables." *Worldwatch Magazine* 1:12-18.

Shefter, Martin. 1977. "New York's Fiscal Crisis: The Politics of Inflation and Retrenchment." *The Public Interest* 48:98-127.

Shevsky, Eshrev and Wendell Bell. 1955. *Social Area Analysis.* Stanford, CA: Stanford University.

Shorter, Edward. 1975. *The Making of the Modern Family.* New York: Basic Books.

Sibley, George. 1977. "The Desert Empire." *Harper's* 255: 49-56.

Sidel, Ruth. 1986. *Women and Children Last.* New York: Penguin.

"Sixty Minutes." 1980. *CBS* 9/28/80.

Sjoberg, Gideon. 1960. *The Pre-Industrial City: Past and Present.* New York: Free Press.

Smelser, Neil. 1967. "Process of Social Change." In *Sociology: An Introduction,* edited by N. Smelser. New York: John Wiley.

Smith, Joel. 1970. "Another Look at Socioeconomic Status Distributions in Urbanized Areas." *Urban Affairs Quarterly* 5:423-453.

Smith, Neil. 1986. "Gentrification, the Frontier, and the Restructuring of Urban Space." In *Gentrification of the City,* edited by N. Smith and P. Williams. London: Allen & Unwin.

_____. 1984. *Uneven Development.* New York: Basil Blackwell.

Spates, James and John Macionis. 1987. *Sociology of Cities.* Belmont, CA: Wadsworth.

Stack, Carol. 1974. *All Our Kin: Strategies for Survival in a Black Community.* New York: Harper & Row.

Stahura, John. 1979. "Suburban Status Evolution and Persistence." *American Sociological Review* 44:937-947.

Stark, Oded. 1980. "On Slowing Metropolitan City Growth." *Population and Development Review* 6:95-102.

Steglich, W.G. and Margaret Snooks. 1980. *American Social Problems.* Santa Monica, CA: Goodyear.

Stein, Robert. 1989. "Market Maximization of Individual Preferences and Metropolitan Service Responsibility." *Urban Affairs Quarterly* 25:86-116.

Stern, Richard and Claire Poole. 1989. "Like a Slaughter-house for Hogs." *Forbes* 12/25/89: 42-44.

Sternlieb, George and James Hughes. 1986. "Demographics and Housing in America." *Population Bulletin* 41:1-34.

Stoll, Clifford. 1989. *The Cuckoo's Egg: Tracking a Spy Through the Maze of Computer Espionage.* New York: Doubleday.

Stone, Michael. 1986. "Housing and the Dynamics of U.S. Capitalism." In *Critical Perspectives on Housing,* edited by R. Bratt, C. Hartman and A. Meyerson. Philadelphia: Temple University.

Summary of Travel Trends. 1985. *1983-1984 Nationwide Personal Transportation Study.* Washington, DC: U.S. Department of Transportation.

Sussman, Marvin and Lee Burchinal. 1962. "Kin Family Network: Unheralded Structure in Current Conceptualization of Family Functioning." *Marriage and Family Living* 24:231-240.

Sutherland, Edwin. 1949. *White Collar Crime.* New York: Holt, Rinehart and Winston.

Suttles, Gerald. 1968. *The Social Order of the Slum.* Chicago: University of Chicago.

Swanstrom, Todd. 1989. "No Room at the Inn: Housing Policy and the Homeless." *Journal of Urban and Contemporary Law* 35:81-105.

Szabo, Joan. 1989. "Our Crumbling Infrastructure." *Nation's Business* August: 16-17, 22-24.

Taeuber, Karl. 1983. "Racial Residential Segregation in 28 Cities, 1970-1980." Working paper, University of Wisconsin Center for Demography, cited in J. Farley, 1987.

Taeuber, Karl and Alma Taeuber. 1965. *Negroes in Cites.* New York: Atheneum.

Taub, Richard, D. Garth Taylor and Jan Dunham. 1984. *Paths of Neighborhood Change.* Chicago: University of Chicago.

Teune, Henry. 1988. "Growth and Pathologies of Giant Cities." In *The Metropolis Era*, vol. 1, edited by M. Dogan and J. Kasarda. Beverly Hills, CA: Sage.

Thompson, Roger. 1987. "A Father of Innovation." *Nation's Business* April:61-62.

Tifft, Susan. 1989. "The Big Shift in School Finance: A Texas Case Reignites a National Debate Over Funding Inequities." *Time* 10/16/89: 48.

Time. 1988. "Gridlock!" 9/12/88:54.

Tönnies, Ferdinand. 1957. *Community and Society.* East Lansing: Michigan State University.

Transit in Toronto. 1987. Toronto: Toronto Transit Commission.

U.S. Bureau of the Census. 1989a. *Statistical Abstract of the United States.* Washington, DC: U.S. Government Printing Office.

_____. 1989b. *Spells of Job Search and Layoff . . . and Their Outcomes.* Current Population Reports Series P-70, No. 16-RD-2. Washington, DC: U.S. Government Printing Office.

_____. 1988a. *Poverty in the United States, 1986.* Current Population Reports Series P-60, No. 160. Washington, DC: U.S. Government Printing Office.

_____. 1988b. *Education Attainment in the United States.* Current Population Reports, Series P-20, No. 426.

_____. 1988c. *School Enrollment-Social and Economic Characteristics of Students: October 1986.* Current Population Reports, Series P-20, No. 429.

_____. 1979. *The Journey to Work.* Washington, DC: U.S. Government Printing Office.

_____. 1973. *Census of the Population 1970.* Volume 1. *Characteristics of the Population*, Part I. Washington, DC: U.S. Government Printing Office.

U.S. Department of Labor. 1978. *Handbook of Labor Statistics.* Washington, DC: U.S. Government Printing Office.

U.S. Department of Transportation. 1972. *1972 National Transportation Report.* Washington, DC: U.S. Government Printing Office.

U.S. House of Representatives. 1985. *Children in Poverty.* Hearing before the Subcommittee on Public Assistance and Unemployment Compensation of the Committee on Ways and Means, House of Representatives. Washington, DC: U.S. Government Printing Office.

U.S. News and World Report. "The Clean Air Sweepstakes." 4/16/90:22-24.

U.S. News and World Report. 1/18/88. "Ethnic Gangs and Organized Crime":29-31.

Van Valey, Thomas, W.C. Roof,and J.E. Wilcox. 1977. "Trends in Residential Segregation: 1960-70." *American Journal of Sociology* 28:826-844.

Wacquant, Loic and William J. Wilson. 1989. "The Cost of Racial and Class Exclusion in the Inner City." *Annals of the American Academy of Political and Social Science* 501:8-25.

Walberer, Julie. 1989. "Metra, Disabled Must Keep Harmony." *Chicago Tribune* 10/14/89: 1,10.

Waldman, Steve. 1989. "The HUD Ripoff." *Newsweek* 8/7/89: 16-22.

Walker, Richard A. 1978. "Two Sources of Uneven Development Under Advanced Capitalism: Spatial Differentiation and Capital Mobility." *Review of Radical Political Economics* 10:28-37.

Wall Street Journal. 11/20/89. "Busing in Higher Costs":A-14.

Wallace, Samuel E. 1980. *The Urban Environment.* Homewood, IL: Dorsey.

Walton, John. 1966. "Discipline, Method, and Community Power." *American Sociological Review* 33:576-593.

Ward, David. 1989. "The Private Path to New Highways." *Nation's Business* August: 19.

Warner, Sam Bass, Jr. 1962. *Streetcar Suburbs.* Cambridge, MA: Harvard and Massachusetts Institute of Technology.

Warren, Roland. 1956. "Toward a Typology of Extra-Community Controls Limiting Local Community Autonomy." *Social Forces* 34:338-341.

Washburn, Gary. 1989. "CTA Riders Face New Challenge." *Chicago Tribune* 10/29/89:1,20.

Washington Post. 1975. 6/15/75.

Watkins, Alfred J. and David C. Perry. 1977. "Regional Change and the Impact of Uneven Urban Development." In *The Rise of the Sunbelt Cities*, edited by D. Perry and A. Watkins. Beverly Hills, CA: Sage.

Weeks, John. 1989. *Population*, 4th ed. Belmont, CA: Wadsworth.

Weiner, Edward. 1988. *Urban Transportation Planning in the United States: An Historical Overview.* Washington, DC: U.S. Department of Transportation.

Weisman, Alan. 1989. "L.A. Fights for Breath." *This World* 8/6/89: 19.

Wellman, Barry and S.D. Berkowitz. 1988. *Social Structures: A Network Approach.* Cambridge, MA: Cambridge University.

White, Morton and Lucia White. 1962. *The Intellectual Versus the City.* Cambridge, MA: Harvard and Massachusetts Institute Technology.

Whyte, William. 1956. *The Organization Man.* Garden City, NY: Doubleday Anchor.

Widrow, Woody. 1987. "Dispelling the Myths of Housing Vouchers." *Shelterforce* Sept/Oct: 15.

Wilensky, Harold and Charles LeBeau. 1965. *Industrial Society and Social Welfare.* New York: Free Press.

Wilson, James. 1983, 1975. *Thinking About Crime.* New York: Vintage.

Wilson, Robert and David Schulz. 1978. *Urban Sociology.* Englewood Cliffs, NJ: Prentice-Hall.

Wilson, William J. 1987. *The Truly Disadvantaged.* Chicago: University of Chicago.

Wilson, William J. and Robert Aponte. 1985. "Urban Poverty." *Annual Review of Sociology* 11:231-258.

Wirth, Louis. 1938. "Urbanism as a Way of Life." *American Journal of Sociology* 44:1-24.

Wolff, Kurt. 1950. *The Sociology of Georg Simmel.* New York: Free Press.

Wong, Bernard. 1982. *Chinatown.* New York: Holt, Rinehart and Winston.

Wood, Robert. 1964. *1400 Governments: The Political Economy of the New York Metropolitan Region.* Garden City, NY: Doubleday.

Woolbright, Louie and David Hartmann. 1987. "The New Segregation: Asians and Hispanics." In *Divided Neighborhoods*, edited by G. Tobin. Newbury Park, CA: Sage.

Work, Clemens. 1987. "Jam Sessions." *U.S. News and World Report* 9/7/87:20-26.

Working Group on Housing. 1989. *The Right to Housing: A Blueprint for Housing the Nation.* Washington, DC: Institute for Policy Studies.

World Bank. 1987; 1989. *World Development Report.* New York: Oxford University.

Yates, Larry. 1988. "A National Priority: Rescuing At-Risk Housing." *Shelterforce* Oct/Nov:12-14.

Yeung, Yue-Man. 1988. "Great Cities in Eastern Asia." In *The Metropolis Era*, vol. 1, edited by M. Dogan and J. Kasarda. Beverly Hills, CA: Sage.

Yinger, John. 1987. "The Racial Dimension of Urban Housing Markets in the 1980's." In *Divided Neighborhoods*, edited by G.Tobin. Newbury Park, CA: Sage.

_____. 1979. "Prejudice and Discrimination in the Urban Housing Market." In *Current Issues in Urban Economics*, edited by P. Mieszkowski and M. Straszheim. Baltimore: Johns Hopkins University.

Zito, Jacqueline. 1974. "Anonymity and Neighboring in an Urban High-Rise Complex." *Urban Life and Culture* 3:243-263.

Zorbaugh, Harvey. 1929. *The Gold Coast and the Slum*. Chicago: University of Chicago.

Zukin, Sharon. 1982. *Loft Living: Culture and Capital in Urban Change*. Baltimore: Johns Hopkins University Press.

Index